# ACTION IN ORGANIZATIONS

SECOND EDITION
# ACTION IN ORGANIZATIONS

**DONALD D. WHITE**
**University of Arkansas**

**H. WILLIAM VROMAN**
**Towson State University**

**ALLYN AND BACON, INC.**
**Boston, London, Sydney, Toronto**

Managing Editor: Michael E. Meehan

**Library of Congress Cataloging in Publication Data**

White, Donald D.
    Action in organizations.

    Bibliography: p.
    Includes index.
    1. Organizational behavior.  2. Organizational behavior—Case studies.  I. Vroman, H. William.
II. Title.
HD58.7.W48    1981    658.4    81–2024
ISBN 0–205–07353–0        AACR2

Printed in the United States of America.

10 9 8 7 6 5 4 3 2    85 84 83 82

# CONTENTS

Experiential Exercises

# FOREWORD

Once again I appreciate the opportunity to make a few introductory comments for this new edition of *Action in Organizations: Cases and Experiences in Organizational Behavior*. Like the cigarette commercial says, "we've come a long way" in the field of organizational behavior since this book first came out in 1977. I am amazed and encouraged by the way things have progressed in our understanding of human behavior in organizations. The development and refinement of theoretical frameworks, as well as the increasing number and sophistication of empirical research studies, has greatly contributed to this understanding.

The conceptual framework for this book reflects these latest developments, in particular by first examining individual behavior from the perspective of personality, learning, and motivation; then moving to an analysis of the nature of organizations from the perspective of function and structure and organizational climate; then moving to the dynamics of organizations in terms of communication, groups, and conflict and stress; and ending with the applied aspects of career development and organizational development. This makes for a very logical and comprehensive way to study and understand organizational behavior.

Despite substantial progress being made in our *understanding* of organizational behavior, our linkage to the more effective *practice* of human resource management remains a major challenge for the future. To date, the efforts of scholars in organizational behavior has been almost entirely devoted to developing a sound theoretical and research base. Like any scientific pursuit, this, of course, is how it should be. The earlier human relations approach, for example, made the mistake of jumping right to application without first developing a theoretical framework substantiated by empirical research. However, the field of organizational behavior is unlike most of the classic academic fields such as philosophy or even psychology in that there is more of a direct link to actual practice. Organizational behavior is positioned more toward the applied end of the academic continuum. Whereas many academic disciplines can be pursued for knowledge's sake, organizational behavior is more directly linked to the actual practice of human resource management. Therefore, the development and application of pedagogical techniques for relating theory and research findings to actual practice becomes especially important to the field of organizational behavior.

The case method has been used as a teaching approach in management education for the past couple of decades. Particularly in the area of adminıstrative policy, students are given realistic cases to analyze and discuss. This pedagogical technique has served effectively to involve students in the decision-making process of management. This book uses the proven case method to involve students in actual problems facing human resource management. Professors White and Vroman have developed and selected realistic problems and situations from a wide variety of organizational settings. These cases do not necessarily have right or wrong answers. Instead, the student has the opportunity to translate the theories and research findings into pıactice. The *process* of problem identification, organizational behavior analysis and solution is stressed throughout.

In addition to cases, this book also contains experiential exercises. Many students have little formal organization experience as an employee. ᴿven if they do (and, of course, students often fail to realize that they have a great deal of organizational experience as a member of a family, church group, athletic team, or housing unit), no attempt is made systematically to analyze or process what went on during the experience. The experiential exercises featured in this book permit the student to experience the actual dynamics of organizations first hand. The analysis and processing of this experience has arrived as an extremely important pedagogical technique in the educational process for organizational behavior. Besides being fun and generally revealing of the participant's concept and how he or she relates to others, the exercises serve as an effective supplement to the cases in building that important bridge between organizational behavior theory and research and the actual practice of human resource management. This latest edition has many new, excellent cases and exercises and should prove to be an even better learning experience for today's organizational behavior students than was the highly successful first edition.

Fred Luthans
Professor of Management
University of Nebraska

# PREFACE

*Action in Organizations* was first published in 1977. In the few short years since then, the field of organizational behavior has progressed significantly. This progress can be traced to a rapidly expanding research base along with the growing acceptance and application of evolving behavioralistic theory. The field, itself, is more exciting today than ever before and promises to continue to challenge both student and practitioners, alike.

The second edition of *Action in Organizations* represents a major revision of the orginal text. This revision was prompted by the authors' desires to provide students in organizational behavior with timely and practical insights into the world of contemporary organizational systems. In addition to significantly expanded text material, new sections on "Learning and Applied Behavior Analysis," "Effective Leader Behavior," "Communications and Organizational Systems," and special sections on stress and career development have been added. A large number of new and original cases and exercises also have been added to the book.

Our purpose has not been to provide students with answers, alone. As Henry Thelen observed, "findings are sciences's short-range benefits, but the method of inquiry is its long-range value." This book is intended to help students learn what questions to ask and which analytical processes may be used to obtain the answers they seek. The case and experiential exercise approach to learning represents perhaps the most meaningful way for students of organizational behavior to bridge the gap between the theory and practice. To this end, we have committed the labor that has gone into *Action in Organizations.*

*Action in Organizations* could not have been written without the support and assistance of many people. A special debt of gratitude goes to the many contributors of cases and exercises as well as to Professors Fred Luthans of The University of Nebraska and E. Mark Langemo, The University of North Dakota whose encouragement and early guidance helped make this volume possible. We also wish to express our appreciation to Mrs. Wanda Dixon and Mrs. Vickie Eubanks who aided in the typing of the manuscript, and to Dennis Henderson, Mary Coulter, Janet Adams, and Anita Williams who provided research assistance. The administrative support of Professor Dale A. Level, Head, Management Department, and Dean John P. Owen, both of the College of Business Administration at the University of Arkansas, also is acknowledged.

Finally, we would like to thank our wives Joyce and Janet who endured with us the traumas that all authors must face and our children, Gregory and Christopher and David and Mark, for the number of times they heard the phrase, "As soon as I finish this page."

This book, along with a companion volume entitled *Contemporary Perspectives in Organizational Behavior*, will provide teachers and students of organizational behavior with an up-to-date, exciting learning package intended to stimulate individual as well as organizational growth.

Legend:
C = Case
E = Experiential exercise

## A TOPICAL CROSS REFERENCING GUIDE FOR CASES

| Section | Type | Attitudes | Communication | Conflict | Decision Making | Formal Organization | Inter-Group Behavior | Intra-Group Behavior | Job Design | Learning | Leadership | Management and Career Development | Motivation | Org. Change and Development | Organization Climate | Perception | Personality | Role | Stress Management | Women and Minorities |
|---|---|---|---|---|---|---|---|---|---|---|---|---|---|---|---|---|---|---|---|---|
| II.1 Personality and Development | C | | 1,2 | 4 | | | | | | | 1,2 | 3 | 2 | 1 | 1 | 5 | 1,2 | | | 1 |
| | E | | | | | | | | | | 1,2 | | | | | 1,5 / 1,2 / 3,4 | 1,2 | | 1,4 | |
| II.2 Learning and Applied Behavior Analysis | C | | | 6 | | | | | | 5,6 / 7 | | | 5,6 | 7 | | | | 11 | | |
| | E | | | | | | | | | 3 | | | | | | | | | | |
| II.3 The Motivation to Work | C | 14 | | | 12 | 12 | 13 | | 8,9 | | 10 | | 4,5 / 8,9 / 10,11 | 10 | 10 | | | | | |
| | E | | | | | | | | | | | | | | | | | | | |
| III.1 Formal Organization: Function and Structure | C | | | 15 | 12 | 12,13 / 14,15 | 13 | | | | 13 | | | 13 | 12,13 | | | | | |
| | E | | | | | | | | | | | | 17,18 | | 7 | | | | | |
| III.2 Organizational Climate | C | | | 16 | | 6 | | | | | 17,19 | | 17,18 | | 16,17 / 18,19 | | | | | 16 |
| | E | | | | | | | | | | | | | | | | | | | |
| III.3 Effective Leader Behavior | C | | | | | | | 9 | | | 20,21 / 22,23 / 8,9 | | | | 20 / 7 | | | | | |
| | E | | | | | | | | | | | | | | | | | | | |
| IV.1 Communications in Organizational Systems | C | | | 25,26 / 27 | | 24 | | | | | 24,26 | | | | 25 | 10 | | | | 27 |
| | E | | 10,11 | | | | | | | | | | | | | | | | | |
| IV.2 Group Behavior and Impact | C | | 24,25 / 26,27 | 29,31 | 36 | 35 | 30 | 28,29,31 / 12 | | | 29 | | | 30 | | | | | | |
| | E | | | | | 31 | | | | | | | | | | | | | | |
| IV.3 Organizational Conflict and Stress | C | 35 | | 32,33 / 34,35,36 | 36 | 35 | | | | | 36 | 37,38 / 39,40 | | | | | 33,36 | 33,34 | 36 | 35 |
| | E | | | 14,15 | | | | 14,15 | | | | | | | | | 40 | 13 | 39 | |
| V.1 Management and Career Development | C | | 17 | | 40 | 42 | | | | | 38 | | | 16,17 | 42 | | 40 | | 40 | 37 |
| | E | | | | 44 | 42 | | 43,44 | | | 41 | | | 41,42 / 43,44 | | | 16 | | | |
| V.2 Organizational Development and Change | C | | | | 19 | | | | | | | | | 18,19 | | | | | | |
| | E | | | | | | | 18 | | | | | | 18,19 | | | | | | |

# ACTION IN
# ORGANIZATIONS

# PART I

# INTRODUCTION TO ORGANIZATIONAL BEHAVIOR ANALYSIS: A SYSTEMS PERSPECTIVE

Human behavior may be studied in a number of different ways. One student may prefer to read psychological or sociological theories about behavior. Another may prefer to observe and analyze the behaviors of others. Still others may wish to experience, for themselves, different actions and reactions and reflect upon their experiences after they have taken place. A combination of these approaches would provide a well-rounded study of human behavior.

Understanding human behavior is a complex but challenging task. It becomes even more complicated when that behavior is an integral part of organizational activity. Organizations are social systems. They consist of persons who interact with one another. Each individual member seeks to attain some level of personal satisfaction in the process of contributing to the achievement of the organization's objectives. The resulting behaviors may have positive as well as negative consequences for individuals and for the organization.

A good manager commits much energy to understanding human behavior within his or her organization. Essentially, a manager must be able to predict or anticipate the behavior of subordinates and others in order to successfully accomplish the organizational unit's objectives. Unfortunately, the complex nature of human behavior has not permitted us to develop a foolproof means of predicting a person's future actions.

## Human Relations and Organizational Behavior

At least one outgrowth of this managerial quest for understanding and predicting behavior is the growth of the study of human relations and organizational behavior. Throughout history, managers, administrators, and others in leadership positions have practiced their own style of dealing with human problems. Some approaches to managing human resources were rigid and forceful, while others incorporated a much "softer" line. The management style adopted was largely one that evolved within an organization or was one determined by an individual to be the "best approach for him." Only in this century have men and women seriously studied the true nature of human behavior in organizations and how it can best be understood.

*The human relations approach.* Many managers, researchers, and authors have contributed to the study of human behavior in organizations. However, the major thrust was provided through the work of Elton Mayo, a Harvard University sociologist. Mayo's research and subsequent writings laid the foundation for the human relations approach to management. This movement emphasized the individual as a contributor to the final product or service of an enterprise. Mayo's research at the Hawthorne Western Electric Plant provided the impetus for an outpouring of literature about human beings in their work environments. It also was largely responsible for influencing managers to adopt the "human relations" philosophy of management.

Unfortunately, many managers drew erroneous conclusions from the human relations movement's literature. For example, many concluded that a well-managed organization was one where all workers were happy. It was all too often assumed that high morale would automatically result in high productivity. This interpretation of the human relations philosophy had numerous positive effects on worker-manager relations. However, too many managers discovered at the expense of their organizations' goals that the high morale = high productivity formula did not always balance.

During the last two decades, astute managers and tireless researchers have focused their attention on obtaining objective answers to questions about human behavior in organizations. Their efforts have resulted in a field of study which we refer to as Organizational Behavior.

*The organizational behavior field.* Organizational behavior differs from human relations in that it focuses on organizational effectiveness as well as the satisfaction of individual needs. In addition, the field concentrates less on factors that maintain or improve employee morale and more on factors that truly satisfy their individual needs.

Contributors to the organizational behavior field recognize that the study of human behavior in organizations can be limited neither to a single perspective nor to a single method. The field is truly eclectic in nature. It draws heavily on contributions from the behavioral sciences and management. Recent major contributions have come from applied psychology and sociology, and significant contributions have been forthcoming from anthropologists and practicing managers. In some instances, those to whom the field owes a debt gathered their information in order to expand the frontiers of their own behavioral sciences (*pure research*); it was not their intent to apply their findings in an organizational system. Other more recent contributors have sought answers to questions posed in existing organizational environments in an attempt to solve specific organizational behavior problems (*applied research*). In either case, the wise student of organizational behavior needs open eyes and an open mind to all sources of information that may help us better understand human behavior in organizations.

### Information and Method

Theories and specific findings from writers in the field are important. They help us understand the basic elements of human behavior in organizations. Yet holding the pieces of a puzzle in our hands does not always enable us to assemble the final picture correctly. Arriving at the best solution requires an acceptable method of analysis. No two individuals will see or analyze a situation in exactly the same way. Furthermore, no single approach to analyzing organizational behavior situations will work best for everyone all of the time.

It is important that you develop a means, through study and practice, by which you can successfully identify the factors that contribute to organizational behavior situations as well as arrive at an acceptable solution to the problems at hand. The rest of this chapter examines a number of analytical approaches that may be applied to the understanding of human behavior in organizations. These methods and models can be used to help you understand and solve a variety of human behavior problems that you will one day encounter.

## Models of Analysis

The analysis of behavior in organizational systems provides the basic foundation for managerial actions concerning the human factor. Although not synonymous with problem solving, such analysis is a necessary prerequisite to problem identification and solution. Problem solving itself is not unique either to the study of management or to the study of human behavior in organizations. A number of problem solving techniques have been developed in science and industry. Some approaches appear on the surface to be more complete than others; they may emphasize steps which may be taken in order to ensure thorough analysis of any problem. Other approaches concentrate less on sequential steps and more on the elements or inputs affecting the situation. Such is the case with most models of organizational behavior analysis.

Any student of human behavior would be well advised to examine many analytical schemes and to adopt for subsequent use one of the approaches or a combination thereof that best suits one's own abilities and the immediate situation. The methods and models of analysis that we will examine will provide you with alternative approaches to understanding and solving human and organizational behavior problems.

First we will consider the scientific method. Although not normally considered a behavioral analysis model per se, the scientific method does help us understand the appropriate ways problems in general may be defined and systematically analyzed.

Next we will examine certain intrapersonal models of analysis. Our purpose, here, will be to reflect briefly upon approaches which concentrate on the individual rather than on the operating environment. It is in this context that the id–ego–super ego and parent–adult–child models will be introduced.

Contemporary approaches to organizational behavior analysis emphasize not only the contribution of the individual but also that of the environment within which the individual is found. Norman Maier's SOBA analytical model provides an excellent illustration of how an individual interacts with the environment to produce various behaviors. Finally, systems concepts are explored through Seiler's sociotechnical systems model. Seiler's model illustrates major variables within the organizational setting that should be examined during organizational behavior analysis. The model is not discussed in its entirety. However, principal elements affecting behavior in an organizational setting and the interaction of those elements are examined.

### The Scientific Method

The scientific method is characterized by a systematic endeavor to establish facts. Attention is focused on precise definitions and objective information collection in an effort to achieve greater understanding of a general principle or specific situation. The ultimate purposes of the approach are explanation, understanding, and prediction.[1] The scientific method itself consists of a number of steps which are intended to be executed systematically. Problem solvers and researchers sometimes differ on the exact number and names of the steps. However, the following six stages of problem investigation are generally accepted.

1. Define the problem;
2. Search the literature;
3. Develop alternative hypotheses;
4. Systematically obtain information;
5. Analyze and draw conclusions;
6. Test and follow up.

Problems in human behavior may be considerably more complex than those in the physical sciences. It is difficult to know what goes on inside people's minds. At best, we can attempt to acquire as much information as possible in order to better understand an individual's unique behavior pattern in a given situation.

*Define the problem.*   Definition of the problem is the first and—according to many researchers—the most important step in the scientific method.

An inability to define the problem adequately has caused many a student to labor unnecessarily over volumes of information which may not be germane to the research topic. Likewise, managers who are unable to "pin down" the underlying problem or cause of a situation waste much time and effort and arrive at poor or counterproductive solutions. Whenever possible, it is necessary to identify clearly the nature of the problem at hand.

Unfortunately, problem definition is easier said than done in organizational behavior situations. In some cases, the true nature of the problem may be so deeply rooted within an individual's past experience that the manager or problem solver is unable to identify it clearly. Moreover, while the cause of a particular undesirable behavior may be known, it also may be beyond the capability and resources of the manager to deal with the cause directly. For this reason, increasing interest is being developed in solutions that emphasize the treatment of symptoms rather than of underlying causes. Applications of instrumental learning theory in the form of organizational behavior modification (OB Mod)[2] would be one such example of this approach.

*Search the literature.*   The second step of the scientific method is to examine available information sources related to the problem. While any human behavior problem deserves first-hand attention, there is no need for a manager to "re-invent the wheel." Managerial and supervisory personnel confront human behavior problems daily. As these men and women broaden their own understanding of human behavior problems, they often share their findings with others through academic and professional publications. Such publications provide an excellent source of groundwork for one's own investigation, or, in some rare instances, they may actually provide relatively complete solutions to a problem at hand.

The search of existing literature may reduce the economic and human expense of solving organizational behavior problems. On the other hand, the time frame of the problem may not permit the problem solver to go to the library. He or she may need to make a decision and act immediately. In this case, an ongoing program of reading centered on organizational behavior may be beneficial.

*Develop alternative hypotheses.*   An hypothesis may be defined as a tentative explanation or solution to a problem. This third phase of the scientific approach calls for the formulation of one or more possible explanations as the cause of the problem. The function of the hypothesis is to provide some direction in our search for the answer; therefore, the hypothesis is an important step. Yet students and managers should not regard hypotheses as preconceived ideas which themselves unduly influence the inquiry. Arthur J. Bachrach in his book, *Psychological Research,* refers to this phenomenon as "hypothesis myopia."[3] He defines hypothesis myopia as "a disorder of vision, a research nearsightedness in which the sufferer has the facts clearly in view, and because of preconceived notions, either refuses to accept them or attempts to explain them away." Such would be the case with relying too heavily on commonsense solutions to problems.

*Systematically obtain information.* By the fourth step, the problem solver should have some idea of the nature of the problem, know what information already published may help solve it, and should have one or more tentative explanations as to the cause of the problem. At this point, it is time to systematically identify the facts of the situation. In human behavior problems, this sometimes means looking carefully at the overt behavior pattern of various individuals involved in a situation and at underlying influences on behavior, such as personal background, past experiences, related behavior patterns, and conditions that constitute the immediate environment of the problem.

The nature and consequences of most human behavior problems tend to limit the amount of time available to discover their solutions. This is not to say that solutions should be arrived at haphazardly—on the contrary. However, it is not always possible to submit employees for extensive psychological testing, to call in outside consultants, or to set up long-range, time-consuming experiments within the organization.

Students using cases in this book will analyze situations based on the information presented and the assumptions agreed upon by members of the class. Nevertheless, the facts as they are interpreted, along with the information and logic which support them, are of critical importance in the solution of any organizational behavior problem.

*Analyze information; draw and test conclusions.* The final steps of the scientific approach include the drawing of conclusions and the actual testing of their validity. Conclusions must be drawn. Coming to a final solution often is a complicated process. "Facts" are sometimes interpreted differently by different observers and assumptions themselves may not always be held in common. Yet the critical function is to make the final decision when faced with a problem. A manager must become committed to a course of action—at least in the short run. The manager is also obligated to note carefully the actions of persons involved after the decision has been implemented. From these post-implementation observations, one is in a position to assess the effectiveness and correctness of the solution. Note that the decision maker is not called upon to enforce the decision under "any and all" circumstances: rather, one must observe objectively the results of an action and take further corrective action if and when it becomes necessary.

The scientific approach provides the problem solver with a systematic process for analyzing a problem situation. The process requires the problem solver to be specific, thorough, and open to a variety of explanations, conclusions, and solutions to a problem. Certain situations may prohibit a step-by-step analysis completely consistent with the scientific method.

However, this approach can contribute to the thoroughness and depth with which organizational behavior problems are analyzed.

## Intrapersonal Models

Professors Secord and Backman[4] note that two extreme views exist of the factors which determine how an individual behaves. "One view is that behavior springs fully from structured dispositions within the individual; the other is that a person's behavior is determined by the situation he is in." Some students of behavior suggest that the individual is a self-contained unit which carries around a structured disposition responsible for the individual's interests, nervous maladjustments, and moral strengths and weaknesses. This view of individual behavior "assumes that the behavior patterns which characterize a person reflect intra-individual structures or mechanisms such as habit, need, cognitive structures or most frequently, personality traits. The Freudian psychoanalytic model is one such model."[5]

Freud concluded that the interactions of three major systems within the personality (id, ego, super-ego) were responsible for most, if not all, overt behavior. He saw the three systems working together cooperatively and thereby enabling the individual to carry on efficient and satisfying transactions with his environment. He believed that the purpose of these transactions was to fulfill basic human needs and desires.[6]

Closely related to the Freudian psychoanalytic model, but in a more contemporary vein, is another intrapersonal model known as transactional analysis (TA or PAC). According to this second model, the personality consists of three states produced by the playback of recorded data of events in the individual's past. The three states are referred to as the parent, adult, and child. They represent information sources which when cued serve as the basis for an individual's immediate behavior.

The parent recordings are believed to be information taken in by a small person without the benefit of any editing by that person. The parent recordings are admonitions, rules, and laws learned at a very early age. Child recordings, on the other hand, represent internal events and emotional responses to things an infant sees and hears. While the child state is dominated by emotional responses, it also is responsible for creativity, curiosity, and the desire to explore and experience new ideas and environments. Adult recordings are the accumulation of information which is acquired and tested logically by the individual.

Transactional analysis suggests that the personality develops in relation to the intensity with which different recordings are received and the extent to which they are reinforced by the individual or by others with whom he or she has daily transactions. Behavior patterns are attributed to the dominant recording or combination of recordings and to the exclusion or contamination of one set of recordings by another.[7]

The intrapersonal models such as those just discussed serve as reminders that individual behavior is influenced by internal (in some cases unconscious) activities of the human mind. In a practical sense, the relationship between overt behavior and the underlying intrapersonal activities may be difficult to understand. However, we cannot afford to overlook possible contributions to and explanations of behavior emanating from within an individual. In fact, certain theories of learning and motivation that will be discussed later in the book may be traced in part to intrapersonal theories of behavior.

### Environmental Influences on Behavior

Most students of human behavior are familiar with Kurt Lewin's postulate that behavior is a function of the person and his or her environment. This statement suggests simply that a complete and proper analysis of human behavior may only take place when both the individual and the environment in which the individual functions are considered together. Everything from learned culture to the stimuli of the immediate situation will influence a person's behavior. The influence on human behavior of the environment and of the particular individual is demonstrated through Norman Maier's S↔O→B→A (SOBA) analytical model.[8] S includes the stimulus situation such as light, sounds, job routines, other people, and other aspects of the environment to which an individual is sensitive; O includes heredity, maturation, physical and psychological needs, and values; B refers to the behavior of an individual; and A refers to the accomplishments or outcomes of the behavior.

The organism (the individual) does not operate exclusive of its environment; it interacts with various environmental stimuli through its senses and perception, and behavior results. Borrowing from the work of Homans,[9] we may add that the individual-environment interaction may be either direct (actual) or indirect (symbolic). It may take the form of activities, ideas or expressed attitudes, and social interaction.

The interaction between the organism and situational stimuli is not a simple process. The interaction is as complex as the stimuli themselves may be numerous, varied, and changing. A single stimulus may be interpreted differently by an organism depending upon the state of the organism at a given point in time and that of any additional stimuli which may be being received. In addition, different individuals will place different values and different interpretations on the same stimulus. Nevertheless, the importance of the model is that the individual's behavior—and eventually his or her accomplishment—depends on what environmental stimuli exist, what meaning the individual attaches to those stimuli, and the state of the individual at the time.

The significance of the SOBA model is increased further when considered in terms of behavioristic (learning theory) interpretations of human behavior. Recent attempts to explain behavior in terms of instrumental or operant learning theory have focused heavily on the importance of the stim-

**Figure 1. The Causal Sequence. In order to explain behavior, one must include a description of the S as well as of the O. The interaction between them must precede the behavior which results from the interaction. The behavior (B) causes changes which alter the relationship between the organism (O) and its world. The change produced by behavior is an accomplishment, (A), which may be desirable or undesirable. In either case it may alter the stimulus-situation for the organism or it may serve as the stimulus for other organisms. Thus the behavior of one person may influence that person's world and it may also influence other people. In this way the accomplishment of one bit of behavior may become the stimulation for further behavior.**

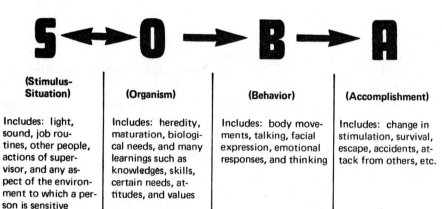

| (Stimulus-Situation) | (Organism) | (Behavior) | (Accomplishment) |
|---|---|---|---|
| Includes: light, sound, job routines, other people, actions of supervisor, and any aspect of the environment to which a person is sensitive | Includes: heredity, maturation, biological needs, and many learnings such as knowledges, skills, certain needs, attitudes, and values | Includes: body movements, talking, facial expression, emotional responses, and thinking | Includes: change in stimulation, survival, escape, accidents, attack from others, etc. |

uli or reinforcements available in the environment.[10] The organization is seen as a potential source of numerous positive and negative reinforcements (consequences of behavior) which, if carefully designed into the organization's internal environment, will be sought out by individual participants. The result is a behavior pattern related directly to the stimuli or the consequence of behavior in the individual's working environment. Thus, Maier's model can be modified behavioristically by replacing the element of accomplishment (A) with that of consequence (C).[11] These relationships will be explored further in the section on learning and applied behavioral analysis.

## Systems Theory and Organizational Behavior

Systems theory has been applied in the biological and physical sciences for almost half a century. Some have even traced its roots as far back as the mid-nineteenth century.[12] However, the application of systems theory in organizational behavior is a relatively recent phenomenon. Although Chester Barnard [13] spoke of organizations as cooperative systems as early as 1938, and operations researchers adopted systems logic to develop quantitative decision models in the 1940s and 50s, it has only been during the last two decades that the impact of systems theory has been felt in organizational behavior.

A system may be defined as a group of interrelated and interdependent elements that can be viewed as a single entity. It may be identified by the configuration of its elements or by its boundaries. Inputs to the system are altered or otherwise transformed, resulting in system outputs. Thus, we may say that system inputs (e.g., raw materials) are transformed through the interplay of system elements (manufacturing techniques) and produce output (goods) that reflect the purposes of the system. As another example, a refinery (system) is dependent on crude oil (input) which goes through a complex distilling and separation process (transformation) producing gasoline, fuel oil, petrochemicals, and other products (output).

Let us look more closely at organizational systems. An enterprise requires inputs in the form of manpower and material. The qualities and forms of such resources may be determined by the nature of the output desired (intended purpose) and the transformation processes available. Elements of the organizational system are arranged according to the decisions of administrative personnel. For example, a marketing organization may choose to perform its marketing research at the national level or to form separate research groups in various regions of the country. Another organization might be subdivided along product lines. The necessary personnel (resources) and organizational groupings (departments) are intended to meet the organization's transformation needs.

As we have already seen, the application of systems theory can help us understand the activities that take place in and about an organization. Systems theory encompasses many concepts (one author has identified 165 testable hypotheses[14]); however, we will address only a few of the more useful concepts that can add to our understanding of organizational behavior.

*Subsystems.* Systems are composed of interrelated parts. Some of those parts may themselves be smaller systems. For example, each department (marketing, production, finance, and the like) is itself a system and is therefore a subsystem of the enterprise (system).

*Suprasystem.* A system exists within an environment. To the extent that the environment may itself be identified as a system, it becomes a suprasystem to the enterprise. For example, a College of Business Administration operates within the framework of a larger system, the university (suprasystem).

*Open versus closed systems.* Open systems exchange information and energy (interact) with their environments. Closed systems, on the other hand, are self-contained; they are neither dependent upon the environment as a source of inputs or as a receptacle for outputs. Technically, it is difficult to defend the existence of closed systems: "we prefer to think of open-closed as a dimension; that is, systems are relatively open or relatively closed."[15] In organizational behavior we recognize the importance of occurrences in the environment and their subsequent impact on behavior in the system. At the same time, however, solutions to organizational problems may be confined within the boundaries of the system and may not attempt to alter the environment.

*Equifinality.* Equifinality suggests that open systems may achieve their purposes using diverse sets of inputs and different configurations of system components. There is not a single set of resources, methods, or management styles that will produce a desired output. Rather, outputs may be attained by transforming different inputs in different ways. For example, the Director of Personnel Training knows that not all newly employed persons have the same background and education. Therefore, training programs may be tailored to meet individual needs in order to reach organizational objectives.

*Feedback.* An organizational system must receive information concerning activities that lead to outputs or information about those outputs. Returning information to a system (or subsystem) for evaluation is referred to as feedback. Feedback may take the form of formal reports, employee grievances, customer complaints, or informal conversations. In some cases, important feedback takes the form of nonverbal expressions or gestures.

Many other concepts associated with systems theory may increase our awareness of and our ability to manage organizational systems. The preceding list is meant only to acquaint you with a few key concepts that may contribute to organizational behavior analysis. In the following section, we will apply systems theory in organizational behavior analysis through the sociotechnical systems model.

## Sociotechnical Systems

So far we have explored a variety of approaches for examining and explaining human behavior. In the scientific approach, certain systematic steps should be followed in identifying specific problems, acquiring information on which problem-related decisions will be made, and developing a solution.

The intrapersonal models, on the other hand, tend to emphasize the importance of the individual as a relatively closed system affecting his or her own behavior. Maier's SOBA model contributed to our understanding of human behavior in organizations by focusing attention not only on the organism but on the various stimuli with which the organism is involved.

At least one additional model for behavioral analysis also is worth examining. John A. Seiler, in his book, *Systems Analysis in Organizational Behavior,* attempts to examine "the complex interdependence of forces which culminate in organizational behavior." [16] Interestingly, the structure of the sociotechnical systems model parallels that of SOBA. However, its application is more comprehensive than Maier's model in that it focuses upon behavior in organizational systems, while SOBA focuses on individual behavior analysis alone.

The sociotechnical approach views forces in the system's external environment as coming from three kinds of sources: human, technological, and organizational. These forces interact with the internal environment of the organizational system. Within this internal environment are four major inputs that interact with one another:

1. Human inputs (i.e., the personal qualities which people bring with them to an organizational setting);
2. Technological inputs, such as the type of industry, the division of labor, or the nature of the task to be performed;
3. Organizational inputs, including an enterprise's goals, structure, policies, and administrative systems;
4. Social structure and norms (group patterns) within the organization.

With regard to the fourth category, Seiler states, "Social structure and norms, then, are products of the human, technical and organizational inputs of the system, but out of this convergence emerges a force which operates in its own right as an important input and determinant of behavior in the system."[17]

Interaction of these inputs results in actual behavior which in turn leads to organizational outputs such as productivity and satisfaction. The model is shown in its entirety in Figure 2.

The sociotechnical systems model provides a framework that identifies the crucial inputs into organizational behavior problems. It expands upon Maier's model by identifying the major areas from which situational stimuli may evolve. The model focuses on elements that constitute the internal environment of the organizational system as well as on areas outside the organization's (and therefore, the individual's) immediate control.

Figure 3 illustrates more clearly the parallel structure of the SOBA and sociotechnical systems models. An in-depth examination of these two models of analysis is beyond the scope of this book. However, their similar structures suggest the recognition of the need for problem solving models that examine system inputs and their relationship to environmental forces. These two patterns of interaction in turn result in system behavior and ultimately system outputs.

### Organizational Behavior Models in Perspective

Situations involving problems in human behavior demand the attention of managers in all types of organizations. Moreover, every individual deals with these problems in a unique way. Unfortunately, an individual's approaches are too often ill conceived and the findings erroneously applied.

Means for conceptualizing organizational behavior situations may be enhanced when the decision maker is familiar with alternative approaches

**Figure 2. An elementary framework for diagnosing human behavior in organizations. From John A. Seiler, Systems Analysis in Organizational Behavior, Homewood: Richard D. Irwin, Inc., and the Dorsey Press, 1967, p. 33.**

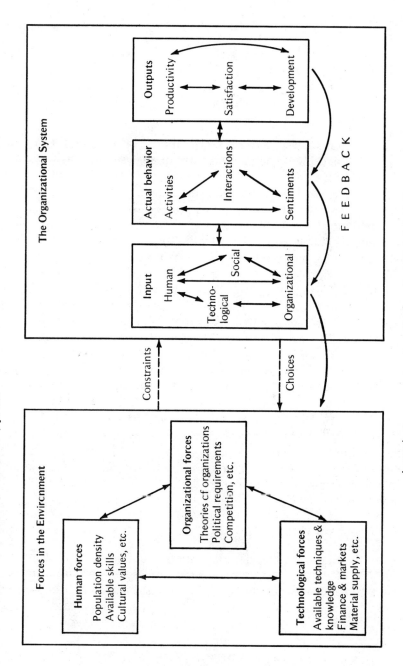

**Figure 3. Comparison of the SOBA and sociotechnical systems analytical models.**

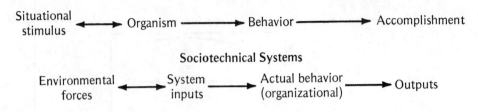

to behavioral analysis. Among the methods and models already explored are those focusing on sequential steps of analysis, such as the scientific method, and models that emphasize more directly the substantive elements contributing to an imbalanced situation. In the latter category, analytical models tend to fall into two groups. The first group includes intrapersonal models of behavior such as the Freudian analytic models and transactional analysis models, and the second group includes models that emphasize the importance of situational or environmental stimuli on individual behavior. Maier's SOBA model is a situational model, for instance. A third dimension brought to the organizational behavior model is a systems approach to human behavior situations. Seiler's sociotechnical systems approach to behavioral analysis introduces as important inputs in any organizational behavior model the human, technological, organizational, and social inputs as they relate to one another in an open system.

No single model or approach to behavioral analysis can be guaranteed to provide the best solution in a difficult situation. You, as an individual, must develop your own means for understanding and coping with human behavior problems based on what you have learned and experienced. However, as a student of individual behavior, you should keep in mind the contributions of other model builders to understanding and solving organizational behavior problems, and try to approach all human behavior situations in a systemic manner.

## A Case Approach to Learning

A case is a narrative that describes some situation that has taken place. The purpose of a case is to transcend the process of learning from the classroom to real-life experiences. This may best be accomplished for you if you allow yourself to become immersed in each of the cases you read and analyze. Remember, case study is meant to *actively involve* you in the processes of learning, developing, and decision making.

The cases in this book were written and assembled to provide the basis for a productive analysis of behavior. Many facets of organizational behavior are depicted. Each case is authentic and catches a glimpse of some incident or chain of events that actually took place. You have been involved in various organizations throughout your life, so some of the situations may seem familiar to you. In fact, your past experiences are important to your future learning. Remember, though, that each new situation requires its own systematic analysis.

You can learn about behavior in any organizational setting. What can we learn from a classroom, a ship, a business, a survival school? The answer is a great deal. Cases were selected for this book because they exhibited behaviors worth discussing—not because they took place in a certain setting or are told in an interesting way.

Regardless of the context in which you study this text, what you learn will affect your interrelations with others in the future. Your next job or interpersonal experience may take place in a setting unrelated to those presented in these cases. However, a common denominator that will affect your success is your developed ability to understand the situation and interact accordingly with people around you.

These cases are intended to be inputs to your imagination and knowledge about human behavior situations. Not all of the detail is in the cases. You may have to provide explanations when the case does not. As you acquire skill for understanding human behavior problems, you will find yourself increasingly able to grasp details in a situation based on a very sketchy description. This ability is important to managing. The manager must know what the problem is and be able to initiate corrective action even without having personally seen or experienced the situation. In addition, she or he must be able to sort out irrelevant information and make sound assumptions when certain facts are not available.

A few guidelines may help you. First, read the case thoroughly. Then read it again. It is not possible to develop a thorough understanding of an organizational behavior situation without examining it closely. Second, try to establish in your own mind the nature of the problem and its underlying causes. You may wish to use an approach or a combination of approaches similar to those models discussed in the previous section. We suggest you adapt your own problem solving techniques to the situation at hand. In some cases it may not be possible to determine the cause of a problem, or it may be unrealistic for you to deal directly with the cause. However, it is necessary that you look beneath the surface of the case to arrive at a meaningful solution.

Once the elements of the case are understood, try to generate as many alternative solutions as possible. Do not be satisfied with the first answer that comes to your mind. Your fourth or fifth solution, or a combination of solutions, may provide the best answer. Explore the consequences of solutions you have developed, including the value of the possible outcomes and the risks that are involved.

Finally, take a stand. State your position and tell how you would implement your solution in the setting in question. Always be prepared to support the reasons for your position and be able to show how you would put that decision into effect. Too often, the benefits of organizational behavior analysis are lost when we are unable to develop specific ways to implement a chosen solution.

Not all cases contained in this book describe *problems* encountered by managers or employees. Some cases illustrate conditions that exist in organizations or behavioral patterns you may encounter on the job. Thus, you will not always be asked to provide a solution or select a managerial alternative to the present situation. In fact, your earliest use of cases no doubt will focus on developing analytical skills in order to increase your understanding of behavior in organizational systems.

Let us turn to a case. Below you will find a case entitled *Airman Bannister's Letter to Home.* You will discover that it is merely a letter written by Airman Dick Bannister to his mother and father in which he describes his first experiences living on an Air Force base. An initial reading of the letter may leave you with little more than an opinion as to whether or not you yourself would like the life style Dick describes. However, a closer look at the content of the letter reveals interesting insights about the behavior that takes place within this organizational system (Calhoun Air Force Base).

Read the case and mark passages that you believe describe some meaningful facet of organization life within the system. Following the case is a brief analysis of its content by the authors. When you have completed writing down your own observations, compare them with those of the authors.

## Airman Bannister's Letter to Home

Dick Bannister was 19 years old. He had lived in a small farming community. Now, he has for the first time found himself away from home. Dick had joined the Air Force and had just been assigned to his first permanent station, Calhoun Air Base. The following is a copy of one of Dick's first letters to home since arriving at the Base.

Dear Mom and Dad,

I thought I'd write this letter and tell you what it's like living here at Calhoun Air Force Base. It's sure a lot different than when I lived at home. Everything we do here has been planned out by somebody else first. We're told what to do and when to do it. My job is pretty specialized but it hasn't seemed to cause me many problems. Any time a difficult situation arises, I simply go to one of the manuals and find out exactly what to do. Each person in my work crew has his own required job. Guidelines exist for everybody's job and they must be followed closely in order to get things done and have them be OK. Everything here is standardized. I've received instructions about everything from the length of my hair to the way to write this letter.

At home I was used to going to whoever I wanted to get information or help. It's different here at Calhoun. We all have to follow the chain of command. That means they tell us who we report to and who we shouldn't talk to. It also helps us know who is responsible for different jobs and other things on the Base.

The Air Force takes care of most of our social and recreational needs as well. The center of most off-the-job activities are the Officer and NCO clubs on base. There are also some other recreation facilities for us on the Base. The Base plans all kinds of activities, including competition between some of the units and more individual sports like jogging for anyone who wants to participate. It seems like the Air Force has thought and planned for just about anything a guy could want to do here. It might drive him crazy, but I guess a guy could live on this base for four years and never have to leave.

Although all of the activities I mentioned are available to anyone on the base, just about everybody stays in his own group. There seem to be two completely separate groups of guys here on the Base. One group is the "lifers." These guys joined the Air Force by their own choice and have decided to make a career out of the military. Everything they do is completely committed toward the military way of life. You talk about some hard-nosed authoritarian types—but I'll tell you one thing, Dad, they do stick together and they really get the job done. I think *they* could live on the Base for four years and never think a thing about it!

The other group of guys are just like me. A lot of us joined the Air Force because we didn't want to go into the Army. Most of us feel like this was the lesser of two evils, and none of us are too happy about it. I don't feel too strongly one way or the other right now, but I can tell you for sure that not many of these guys care much for doing it by the book. In fact, I've noticed that a lot of them get satisfaction from beating the system. They do as little as they can and break the rules whenever possible. Some guys do a pretty good job, but I think it's only because they're afraid that someone will jump on them with both feet. Most of them get their kicks off the job.

Well, I just thought you'd like to hear about life on the Base. What do you think?

Dick

### Analysis

Let's take a close look at what Airman Bannister's letter tells us about Calhoun Air Force Base as an organizational system. A systematic approach to understanding the content of the case would be to adopt some model of analysis. We have based our analysis on the "organizational system" elements of the sociotechnical systems approach described earlier in this chapter. This model suggests that organizational systems may be viewed according to a broad framework in which critical elements referred to as system inputs may be grouped into four major areas: (1) human inputs, (2) task (or technological) inputs, (3) organizational inputs, and (4) social structure or group inputs.

Airman Bannister begins his letter by stating that the environment in which he now finds himself is different from that to which he was accustomed in the past. As you no doubt have discovered, moving from one environment (for example your home) to another (such as college) heightens your awareness of differences in the two organizational settings. Initially, Dick described to his parents what he saw as outstanding *organizational* characteristics. For example, the Air Base provides a highly structured work environment. The content and schedule of Dick's activities are governed by formal rules and regulations. His job is narrow (specialized) and leaves little discretion as to how it is to be performed. In other words, Dick's task is highly structured.

The system's organizational inputs (its structure, policies, and channels of communications) are clearly reflected. Relationships with persons on the Base are influenced by rules governing communications between individuals. The strict chain of command along with a clearly delineated ranking system within the organization hierarchy structures interpersonal relationships both on and off the job.

The environment on the Base is further controlled in that off-the-job recreational activities also are planned and provided for by the organizational system. In fact, this organization has been so comprehensively designed that it is virtually a self-contained unit in which the members can exist in relative isolation from the outside world. As Dick pointed out, some organization members are comfortable in this environment. However, others feel the need for greater flexibility than the system affords them. The organizational characteristics described by Dick reflect a bureaucratic organization structure designed to enhance clearcut responsibility and efficient operation.

The informal social structure of the base according to Dick depends upon the personal goal orientation of system members. Those who have chosen to make a career of the Air Force tend to associate with one another and set themselves apart from those not having a career orientation. Centers of activity, for example, and common behaviors of groups of individuals on the Base tend to be influenced by the social group of which each person is a part. Goal orientations and organizational life styles also seem to be related to group affiliations. Both the "lifers" and airmen like Dick appear to be able to cope with life in the system. However, their approaches are significantly different. One group (lifers) adheres closely to Base rules and regulations (system structure). The other group (enlisted men) attempts to subvert the system or seek satisfaction outside of it. The ability to survive in the organizational system also depends on individual characteristics of the members, some of whom are motivated by conditions on the job while others seek their motivation away from their work.

Our brief analysis of the organization system described by Dick Bannister was neither extensive nor comprehensive. Moreover, the information provided in the case did not require that either a solution or a managerial alternative be recommended. If Dick's letter had suggested difficulty adjusting to the organization, we might have borrowed from other models of analysis such as the SOBA model or an intrapersonal approach in order to provide additional information. Recommendations directed at Dick or possibly his immediate superior might then have been made, based upon this more extensive analysis.

Each case you study will require an assessment of the proper model or models of analysis that you believe should be employed. Your level of analysis may concentrate on individual behavior, the behavior that takes place within organizational units (e.g., departments), or the organizational behavior of the enterprise as a whole. Whatever level of analysis you choose, you will be examining the behavior of a system.

It will be necessary for you to identify the elements that make up the system and to understand how those elements interact with one another. Furthermore, you must recognize the way people, organizations, and other factors outside the system affect its behavior as well as the impact of the system behavior on those in its external environment. Your understanding of these complex and interdependent relationships is essential if your analysis of the behavior situation in question is to be complete.

The content of this book allows you to develop your problem solving skills in major areas of organizational behavior. While all of these areas are interrelated, each merits the individual attention given it in the book. These major areas include: formal organizations, individual behavior (with specific emphasis placed on personality and development, learning and applied behavioral analysis, employee motivation, leadership style, and behavior in conflict situations); group influences on organization action; organizational climate and power, and organizational change and development. Each case is preceded by a brief discussion of the theoretical highlights of the area and their significance to the study of organizational systems.

## References

1. Bernard Berelson and Gary Steiner, *Human Behavior: An Inventory of Scientific Findings,* (New York: Harcourt, Brace & World, 1964), p. 17.
2. Fred Luthans and Robert Otteman, "Motivation versus Learning Approaches to Organizational Behavior," *Business Horizons,* December 1973.
3. Arthur J. Bachrach, *Psychological Research,* (New York: Random House, 1962), pp. 21–22.
4. Paul F. Secord and Carl W. Backman, *Social Psychology,* (New York: McGraw-Hill Book Co., 1964), p. 576.
5. Ibid., p. 577.
6. Calvin S. Hall, *A Primer of Freudian Psychology,* (New York: The American Library, 1954), p. 22.
7. For a more complete discussion of transactional analysis, see Claude Steiner, *Scripts People Live,* (New York: Grove Press, 1974); also Thomas A. Harris, *The Book of Choice,* (London: Jonathan Cape, 1970).
8. Norman R. F. Maier, *Psychology in Industry,* (Boston: Houghton Mifflin, 1965), pp. 26–29.
9. George C. Homans, *The Human Group,* (New York: Harcourt, Brace and Co., 1950), pp. 34–40.
10. Craig Eric Schnier, "Behavior Modification in Management: A Review and Critique," *Academy of Management Journal,* September 1974, pp. 528–548.

11. Fred Luthans, *Organizational Behavior*, 2nd ed. (New York: McGraw-Hill Book Co., 1977), pp. 103–111.

12. Fremont E. Kast and James E. Rosenzweig, "General Systems Theory: Applications for Organization and Management," *Academy of Management Journal*, vol. 15, December 1972, p. 448.

13. Chester I. Bernard, *Functions of the Executive*, (Cambridge: Harvard University Press, 1938), pp. 3–113.

14. James G. Miller, "Living Systems: Basic Concepts," *Behavioral Science*, July, 1965, p. 193–297.

15. Kast and Rosenzweig, op. cit., p. 450.

16. John A. Seiler, *Systems Analysis in Organizational Behavior* (Homewood: Richard D. Irwin, 1967), p. 23.

17. Ibid., p. 28.

## Recommended Readings

Readings marked with an asterisk are included in *Contemporary Perspectives in Organizational Behavior,* edited by Donald D. White (Boston: Allyn and Bacon, 1982).

R. Bolt, "Organizations That Serve Several Values," in *Management of Change and Conflict,* edited by John M. Thomas and Warren A. Bennis (Baltimore: Penguin Books, 1972).

*L. L. Cummings, "Toward Organizational Behavior," *Academy of Management Review,* vol. 3, January 1978, pp. 90–98.

Tim R. V. Davis and Fred Luthans, "A Social Learning Approach to Organizational Behavior," *Academy of Management Review,* vol. 5, April 1980, pp. 281–290.

Fremont E. Kast and James E. Rosenzweig, "General Systems Theory Application for Organization and Management," *Academy of Management Journal,* vol. 15, no. 4, December 1972, pp. 447–465.

Frederick G. Lippert, "Toward Flexibility in Application of Behavioral Science Research," *Academy of Management Journal,* vol. 14, no. 2, March 1971, pp. 195–203.

*Raymond E. Miles, Charles C. Snow, and Jeffrey Pfeffer, "Organization-Environment: Concepts and Issues," *Industrial Relations,* vol. 13, October 1974, pp. 244–266.

# PART II

# INDIVIDUAL BEHAVIOR

Many factors affect an individual's behavior. As we will see later in this book, organization structures and processes, reward systems technologies, and group forces all influence people to behave in different ways. However, it is the individual that is examined in Part II. Behavior, whether consciously or not, is significantly related to our growth and development, past learning, and motivational processes.

## Analyzing Individual Behavior

The SOBA model discussed in Part I provides a useful approach for analyzing individual behavior. Organization policies, interpersonal relationships, inanimate objects (e.g., large desk, computer) or nonverbal gestures represent stimuli (S) in the individual's environment. In addition, there are many other, subtle sources of stimulation (e.g., colors, noises, textures). Sometimes a stimulus like the sound of a voice or a raised eyebrow is the most important factor affecting a person's behavior. At other times, it has no effect at all.

The organism (O) stands between the stimulus and behavior. Some theorists believe that the contribution of the O is too complex to understand and control. They contend that if managers plan and control the environment (and thus the source of stimuli) the ultimate behavior (B) can be predicted. Such an approach to understanding behavior is closely related to stimulus–response (S–R) behavior theory or a variation of the approach known as instrumental conditioning. In other words, S determines B and the contribution of the O is minimized. Those who support this theory of individual behavior are often referred to as learning theorists or Skinnerians (after B. F. Skinner). They represent a behavioral school known as "behaviorism."

Others believe the organism is most important. The O, between the stimulus and the behavior, consists in learned values and attitudes, traits, and motives. Since the personal backgrounds of individuals are not identical, their personalities and responses to situations will not be identical. Two people have learned to see the same stimuli differently. One person sees running a business as a great opportunity to "get ahead." Another person, instead, fears losing everything he or she has. Interpreting stimuli in the environment in different ways is due largely to different perceptions by individuals.

Perception relates to how a person pictures an event. The primary emphasis is on the organism and on what the organism's cognition (thinking) does to the stimuli before a response or behavior is formulated. The connection between how a person responds to a stimulus and why two people respond differently to the same stimulus lies in interpretation, or perception.

The way we perceive a situation and our response have been determined by many experiences we have had in the past. Chapter One highlights several of the forces or processes that play a role in developing our personalities and that underlie our perspectives and behaviors. The way we learn from these forces, together with motives that influence behavior, are addressed in Chapter Two, "Learning and Applied Behavior Analysis," and Chapter Three, "The Motivation to Work," respectively.

# CHAPTER ONE

# Personality and Development

What is meant by *personality?* Why should we examine personality as an element in organizational behavior? Some theorists believe a person's personality is largely formed by the age of six. If this is true, why should we spend our time trying to understand the formative process itself? These and other similar questions will be explored in this chapter.

First, let us agree on what personality is *not.* You may one day be asked to fill out a rating form on another person. In such evaluations you may be asked to rate "personality" on a scale from "very undesirable" to "very desirable." Such use of the term is misleading and inappropriate. Morgan, King, and Robinson define personality as "the various enduring and distinctive patterns of behavior and thought that are characteristic of a particular person."[1] Personality, therefore, refers to specific (measurable) qualities. Such traits as intelligence, aggressiveness, docility, and the like may be said to be characteristic of an individual's behavior. However, "grading" someone's overall personality as "good" or "bad" reflects a subjective assessment on the part of the evaluator, not a measurable trait of the person being evaluated.

We need to understand what impact personality characteristics might have on an individual's functioning within an enterprise. Might persons possessing certain personality characteristics be more effective in one type of job than another? What qualities affect decision making? Finally, we are interested in the impact the organization itself has on a member's personality.

## Influences on Personality

Personality characteristics are not the function of a single stimulus, nor may they be traced to a purely genetic source. Personality is the result of a complex interaction of genetic and environmental inputs.

Kluckhohn and Murray, in their classic treatise on personality, concluded that every person is in certain respects:[2]

a. like all other persons,
b. like some other persons,
c. like no other person.

In other words, we have some attributes in common with all other human beings, some that are similar to the characteristics of those around us, and other qualities that are totally unique. The logic that underlies these observations hinges on factors that influence personality development.

There seem to be four major influences on personality development. First, we are human beings. As a result of our biological makeup, and the birth process we all experienced, we share certain characteristics with all other human beings. Moreover, certain physical traits limit the ways we can adapt to our environment.

A second important factor in personality development is the culture of which we are a part. Much behavior is learned from those around us. Significant contributors to this developmental process are family influences and, later, peer groups—our associates and friends. In both cases, certain norms (accepted ways of behaving) influence our daily actions and our habitual behaviors.

The third and fourth influences on our personalities are those which add individuality. Kluckhohn and Murray conclude, "the ultimate uniqueness of each personality is the product of countless and successive interactions between the maturing constitution and the different environing situations from birth onward." [3] In other words, every individual from birth until death experiences events and sensations which, due to that person's unique physical and psychological makeup, are unlike those experienced by anyone else. These experiences, coupled with different interpretations of different situations, establish the uniqueness which leads to the conclusion that every person is like no other person.

Of course, it is the interaction of all of these influences and their effect on personality development which is responsible for those overt behaviors which we tend to classify as personality.

## Personality Structure

Personality may be viewed in terms of its structure. Structural approaches to understanding personality include Freud's id–ego–superego model and the transactional analysis model (parent–adult–child).

### Id–Ego–Superego

In Part I of this book, Freud's three-part personality structure was discussed. Briefly, Freud saw the human personality as having three separate and distinct parts, called the id, the ego, and the superego. The function of the id, or unrestrained drive, is to provide an immediate outlet for tension. The super-ego was seen as the moral part of the personality—your conscience. The superego represents standards and ideals that have been inculturated into the individual over time. The ego functions as the "real-world mediator" between the id and the superego. In other words, Freudian personality theorists believe the ego determines outlets for tension that are consistent with standards set forth by the superego and which can be realistically pursued in the individual's immediate environment. It is the subconscious interaction of these three parts of the personality that ultimately results in some form of behavior.

The id–ego–superego structure helps us in understanding the importance of unconscious influences on behavior. However, while the model has been used in clinical settings to explain unusual behaviors, it fails to provide us with an operational approach to analyzing personality inputs in organizational behavior settings. The parent–adult–child (PAC)[4] approach to personality structure provides one such means for placing these inputs in perspective.

### Parent–Adult–Child

A person sees and reacts to various stimuli by "reliving" or playing back recordings of past events and feelings, according to Thomas Harris.[5] These recordings are categorized as either parent, adult, or child states and domi-nate both intrapersonal and interpersonal behavior.

The parent ego state relies on information provided to a child during the early formative years. Some of this information is good, loving, and life-saving. Other messages are of a scolding or of a "bad" nature. Parent information is characterized by phrases like, "Do as I say," or, "Children are to be seen not heard," or automatic responses such as, "You poor dear."

The adult ego state is in control of behavior. It reflects what it sees and not what it wants to see or has been told it will see (prejudice emanating from the parent). Statements like, "I hear you saying . . . ," "As I see it," or "It is only my opinion, but . . ." are common to the adult. The adult state, then, represents a mature, rational approach to dealing with environmental stimuli.

The child ego state must have everything *now*. When the child is con-trolling behavior, it may express a full range of emotions from sadness to hilarity. However, expressions in the child state demand immediate satis-faction.

All three ego states are believed to be active whether the person is five or sixty-five years old. Physical size or age has nothing to do with the ego state in control of behavior at any given moment. In addition, all three ego states play an important role in individual expression. For example, the child ego state may be important in releasing pent-up frustrations. The parent, on the other hand, can act as a time-saver. Parent information that is not prejudicial but which provides us with time-tested guidelines to behavior allows us to function more efficiently in our environment (e.g., "Always look both ways before crossing the street!") One's time need not be spent analyzing every situation before acting.

A healthy balance between the parent, adult, and child is necessary for an individual to function effectively on or off the job. The adult ego state, however, is particularly important for the manager. When in this ego state, the manager is capable of making rational decisions based upon an objective analysis of the information and conditions at hand. In the adult state one is not misled by emotional overtures (child) or constrained by "what worked best for someone else" (parent).

The knowledge that any of the three ego states can control behavior at various times helps a manager put his or her own behavior and the behavior of others in perspective. Momentary lapses into the child ego state can be understood and/or ignored by managers. Recognizing that one is in a parent state may enable us to step back and take a second, more objective look at a situation. For example, a manager confronted by a hostile subordinate might say, "If you don't come over here immediately, I will fire you." Here the manager's behavior is controlled by the parent ego state. If able to recognize this fact, the manager may be able to stop the interaction temporarily and take a more rational (adult) approach to the problem at hand.

The three ego states increase our knowledge of individual behavior and personality. In terms of the SOBA model, environmental stimuli (*S*) have "hooked" or encouraged one of the ego states (*O*) to emerge and control our behavior (*B*). The net result is an accomplishment which may be satisfactory or unsatisfactory depending on whether it is consistent with our intent or the desires of those with whom we are interacting.

## Critical Stages in Development

Many different situations may influence personality development. A small child who is disciplined repeatedly for violating a household rule (like "no eating before dinner") may be permanently influenced by the experience. On one hand, he or she may "learn the lesson" and cease eating before meals—perhaps even become nervous when others eat snacks. On the other hand, she or he may develop a "reaction formation" to the parent and attempt to violate that rule and other parental rules whenever possible.

Particular situations, as just described, may have a significant impact on personality development. However, some personality theorists suggest that certain stages of development are more critical than others. For example, Freud suggested that the ease with which a child adjusts to certain psychosexual stages (e.g., thumb sucking, toilet training) are largely responsible for later personality. While Freud[6] and other "developmentalists" emphasized early stages of development (generally up to the age of five or six), Erik Erikson expanded the number of critical stages and included in his theories of personality development crisis periods such as early adulthood, young and middle adulthood, and mature adulthood.[7] Figure 1 shows the relationship of the developmental stages set forth by Erikson to those described by Freud.

Identifying developmental stages by chronological age patterns is not done merely as a matter of convenience. Early researchers, supported by the more recent work of Levinson and his colleagues, strongly support the idea of "age-linkages"[8] in personality development.

The relevance of personality development in organizational behavior (and vice versa) under a scheme like that of Erikson is clear. Adjustments to crises not related to the job may affect job-related activities. Moreover, studies indicate that the job may have a substantially greater impact on one's psychological adjustments than the reverse.[9] This will be dealt with more extensively later. For now, however, the important point is that a person's personality does develop throughout life. And critical stages throughout life must be confronted and dealt with successfully in order for the personality to develop in a healthy manner.

## Personality: Life Changes and the Meaning of Work

To this point, our discussion has focused on factors that influence personality, personality structure, and the fact that personality evolves and changes as we pass through critical stages in our lives. But of what significance is personality to organizational behavior?

As we have seen from Erikson, personality continues to develop through critical stages of one's life. Sarnoff observes, "as the adult lives out his existence, his behavior will reflect (a) old elements of personality—derivatives of childhood and adolescence; and (b) new elements—new motives, additives, interests—that he acquires in the course of his adult years."[10] Thus, we may conclude that our personalities are shaped in our early years, but they continue to be altered as we age and encounter new life experiences.

**Figure 1. A chronology of developmental stages: Freud versus Erikson.**

| *Freud's Stages* | *Ages* | *Erikson's Stages* |
|---|---|---|
| Oral | 0 to 1 year | Oral-sensory |
| Anal | 1 to 3 years | Muscular-anal |
| Phallic | 4 to 5 years | Locomotor-genital |
| Latency | 6 to 12 years | Latency |
| Genital | 13 to 18 years | Puberty and adolescence |
|  | 19 to 25 years | Young adulthood |
|  | 26 to 40 years | Adulthood |
|  | 41 and beyond | Maturity |

*Levinson's Theory of Adult Development*

Daniel J. Levinson has studied male development during early and middle adulthood.[11] His findings and subsequent theory of "individual life structure" have direct implications for the relationship of adult development and organizational behavior. Life structure—the pattern of a person's life at a given point in time—is the result of the interaction of three components: (1) one's sociocultural environment, (2) one's participation in the environment through relationships and multiple roles, and (3) aspects of the self which are either lived out or inhibited within the structure. The life structure evolves through intermittent stable and transitional periods. These periods are defined by the major tasks and processes of building and shaping the life structure rather than in terms of specific events or inner states.

Perspectives and commitments to work play an important role in each of the periods from early adulthood on. The first period is referred to by Levinson as "Getting into the Adult World" (GIAW). The period lasts from the early twenties through to the late twenties. It is during this time in our lives that critical events such as establishing an occupation become important. GIAW also is a period of exploration. The young adult begins to evolve a more serious interpretation of his or her role, memberships, and longterm goals. According to Levinson, GIAW involves "exploratory searching, making provisional choices, assessing choices and alternatives, and increasing commitments to certain choices as a more stable life structure is sought."

GIAW culminates with a relatively mild re-examination of oneself known as the "Age Thirty Transition." Falling between ages twenty-eight and thirty-two, this period is when initial occupational choices are reevaluated. The central question one faces is whether one's life structure should be stabilized around one's selected occupation; i.e., should a deeper commitment be made, or should a change be made? Since the investment in the young adult's work is not yet great, the decision does not normally exact a high emotional toll. However, the transition is more difficult for some than others.

During the next period, "Settling Down" (SD), the individual deepens commitments and invests more of himself or herself into the life structure that has evolved out of the Age Thirty Transition. Stability, security, and control become more important during this phase of life. The job becomes a means to an end. It offers a vehicle for "settling in." SD also may be accompanied by the desire to move forward, to set and obtain major goals. In a sense, an individual has selected an occupation (the means for achieving personal security and self worth), and now throws himself or herself into work in order to achieve both goals.

Settling down involves a second phase known as "Becoming One's Own Man" (BOOM). The phase, occurring in the late thirties, is characterized by feeling that no matter what one has accomplished, one still has yet to become one's own person. In the work setting, she or he may feel constrained by those in authority or others whose influence is significant.

**Figure 2. Developmental periods, early through late adulthood. Adapted from Daniel J. Levinson, et al., The Seasons of a Man's Life, New York: Alfred A. Knopf, 1978.**

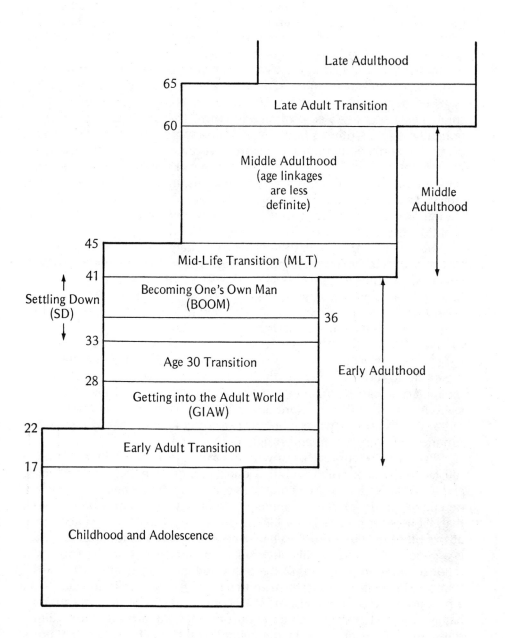

There is a feeling that superiors "control too much and delegate too little." Moreover, "there is a feeling that while those around him may have helped him to grow and progress, there now is a need to 'make it on his own.' "

Much of this growth may have been aided by a friend or colleague referred to as a *mentor*. The mentor provides a model after which an individual may pattern behavior and acts as a coach. So important to the Settling Down period is the mentor that Epstein has concluded that the lack of such a model has been a major obstacle in the professional development of women.[12] This could explain why women often must take on highly assertive postures to attain the same ends as their male counterparts.

Becoming One's Own Man, then, culminates with the desire to attain some life- or work-related goal on one's own. That goal may be a promotion, a new job, writing a book, or attaining some elected office. A period of waiting and working for the goal to be realized ensues. Perhaps due to our lack of experience in attaining such goals or because we still retain some of youth's idealism, not all of our goals, much less our means, are viewed as satisfactory. Personal and occupational barriers and their resulting frustrations lead us into yet another period known as the Mid-Life Transition (MLT).

Neugarten[13] alleges that the forties are characterized by the realization that neither our commitment nor our hard work has sufficiently satisfied our need to achieve. Further, she states, "those who fail to achieve recognition have failed not to achieve the extraordinary but merely the ordinary." Levinson, on the other hand, has concluded that the major concern during MLT is not whether or not goals have been attained but rather whether the life structure that has been formed over the last ten years is really the life structure that one wishes to live with. Repressed and latent feelings and the desire to reconcile them with the present life structure become paramount. Some pass through this stage with little difficulty. They either do not question their life structure or are able to "manage" the transition without a major crisis. However, the great majority (approximately 80 percent) experience inner turmoil and struggle.

Behaviors often associated with the Mid-Life Transition include dissatisfaction with (possibly quitting) one's job, divorce, leaving the family, and the like. For the less adventuresome, a "change of scenery," alone, may be enough to find a new beginning. One person's crisis may be so severe that, "if he stays put, he faces a living death . . . yet to make a major change at this point may be hurtful to his loved ones as well as to himself." MLT is a period when individuals question many aspects of their lives and when rational and staid processes of the past often give way to seeming irrationality. Perhaps it is only through this lack of structure (irrationality) that a person can become free from his or her existing life structure. Unfortunately, for most people such a period can not be approached in a calm, self-controlled manner but involves emotional turmoil and personal upheaval. As a result, a person "breaking out" may find herself or himself alone, abandoned by, or at least not understood by, colleagues, acquaintances and "the broader occupational system in which he works."

Finally, Mid-Life Transition not only results in a reexamination of the central issues in our lives, but it also provides us with a glimpse of things to come. For example, the aging process with its sagging chins and expanding waistlines causes us to recognize that we do have certain animal limitations. Noting the physical as well as the career declines of those around us results in a closer monitoring of our bodies, our occupational progress, and our very existence. Thus, MLT, like all transitions, involves breaking out of one life structure and breaking in another.

*Middle and late adulthood.* Levinson's studies of adult development focused primarily on age-related life structures through early adulthood. However, age-linkages and life cycles become less definite as we approach old age. This may be due to the different rates of physical degeneration experienced by individuals, to unique work and social environments, and to a divergence of post-work alternatives available to different members of society and different cultures.

Those who have examined middle and old age generally have observed a "restabilization" of the life structure. Neugarten[14] points out that middle-aged adults become more self-aware and selective. They experience an increasing desire to regain control over their environment and to exercise a wide array of cognitive strategies. As Robert Peck has observed, of importance is not only how people adjust to those attributions which decline, but how they transcend the decline—how they develop new, different, uniquely human powers, to the fullest extent—that marks the truly developmental aspects of the second half of life.[15] Specifically, Peck identifies the following as important adjustment patterns during this time: (1) valuing wisdom versus valuing physical powers, (2) socializing versus sexualizing human relationships, (3) cathetic (emotional) flexibility versus cathetic impoverishment (the capacity and necessity to shift emotional investments from one person or activity to another), and (4) mental flexibility versus mental rigidity.[16] In other words, later stages of middle adulthood are characterized by cognitive, social, and emotional maturation.

Finally, the Late Adulthood Transition and Old Age address yet another set of salient issues that will affect the life structure. In some cases, the older worker may become apprehensive about the future. Aware of his physical limitations relative to job performance, he or she is also confronted by concerns over maintaining status in the organization and over future financial security. Ironically, while work once again is viewed as a means to an end, the older worker also focuses on the intrinsic value of work.

Peck identifies certain critical pattern transitions associated with Old Age. First, the older adult experiences an ego differentiation rather than a work role preoccupation; that is, she or he addresses a broader range of role activities from which to derive satisfaction and with which to identify and define self-worth than simply the lifelong work role alone. As Peck points out, "thus someone who has been in a position of authority and dependence may have to readjust his understanding of self and environment." Second in Peck's critical transitions is the pattern of body transcendence versus body preoccupation; and third is ego transcendence versus ego preoccupation (the recognition of and dealing with our own mortality).[17]

## Preparing to Meet Life Crises

Our ability to make healthy transitions from one stage of life to another relies on the way we have confronted and managed earlier life crises, the tolerance and support of our immediate environments, and our preparedness for the imminent crises. For example, an inability to identify an occupational goal during the GIAW period may further complicate the Settling Down period, since the individual has failed to identify what he or she is settling into. Likewise, nuclear families (parents and siblings) have traditionally provided a transitional link or buffer to aid an individual through life's crises in our culture. However, our population's geographic mobility has caused the nuclear family to separate more often, thereby interfering with needed mutual support. Finally, society focuses on and rewards achievement, not failure; growth, not decline.

In order to deal more successfully with life structure crises, we must learn to accept risks and failure. Learning to change or adapt goals and expectations can help us avoid feelings of failure. Adolescents recognize that failure is a part of learning, but adults often find it difficult to accept failures. Placing failure and change in proper perspective can help us manage transitions through life's many developmental periods.[18]

In some cases, a direct commitment of organizational resources may ease such transitions. These resources may take the form of departments or jobs—such as organizational psychologist—or special programs designed to meet specific employee adjustment needs. An example of one such program is the pre-retirement counseling provided by Lockheed–California. Lockheed's efforts have successfully contributed to the retirement transition and well-being of many of the firm's employees. Those involved in the program have found that such preparation must take place over an extended period of time due to the many and complex elements involved in career decline and transition.[19] Whatever the life cycle stage, awareness and preparation can ease the transition for all those it touches.

## Summary

The personalities of organizational members are important elements in understanding the behavior of any organizational system. Each organizational participant has a pattern of behaviors and thoughts which is unique. Four major influences on these patterns include biological and physiological makeup, the cultural environment, unique personal experiences, and situational inputs.

Personality is dynamic. It changes and evolves throughout one's life. While some theorists have focused on early stages of personality development through adolescence, recent studies show that developmental periods exist throughout our lives. Levinson, through his research on adult development, has concluded that personality changes occur in relationship to age-linked periods in our lives. These time frames result in the life structure passing through intermittent periods of stability and transition. Not only may periodic personality adjustments affect on-the-job behaviors, but work-related activities may significantly influence changes in our personalities.

Individual models of analysis like the SOBA model focus attention on the personality. Understanding the structure and "activities" of the personality provides one means for viewing personality inputs in organizational settings. Freud's id–ego–superego model and the transactional analysis parent–adult–child model permit analysis via an individual's personality structure.

A combination of two or more models might benefit your analysis of the cases in this chapter. For example, it might be helpful to look at ego states that are apparently influencing an individual's behavior in a situation. Is she or he reacting to a specific stimulus, a situation, or because of some anticipated reward? Are thought patterns and behaviors the result of an emotional interpretation of situational stimuli, or are they linked in some way to developmental periods in life? Placing behavioral patterns into chronological and situational perspective may help you understand the important contribution that personality makes to organizational system behavior.

*References*

1. Clifford T. Morgan, R. A. King, and Nancy M. Robinson, *Introduction to Psychology* (New York: McGraw-Hill Book Co., 1979), p. 652.
2. Clyde K. Kluckhohn and Henry A Murray, *Personality in Nature, Society and Culture* (New York: Alfred A. Knopf, 1953) p. 53.
3. Ibid., p. 55.
4. Eric Berne, *Games People Play* (New York: Grove Press, 1964); also see Jut Meininger, *Success Through Transactional Analysis* (New York: Grossett and Dunlap, 1973).
5. Thomas Harris, *I'm OK, You're OK* (New York: Harper and Row, 1969).
6. Leon Rappoport, *Personality Development* (Glenview, Ill.. Scott Foresman, 1972) pp. 70–76.
7. Ibid., pp. 84–92; also see Erik H. Erikson, *Childhood and Society* (New York: W. W. Norton, 1963) pp. 225–274.
8. Daniel J. Levinson et al., "Periods in the Adult Development of Men: Ages 18 to 45," *The Counseling Psychologist*, vol o, (January 1976), pp. 21–25.
9. Melvin L. Kohn, and Cormi, "Occupational Experience and Psychological Functioning: An Assessment of Reciprocal Effects," *American Sociological Review*, vol. 38, 1973, pp. 116–117.

10. Irving Sarnoff, *Personality Dynamics in Development* (New York: John Wiley, 1962) pp. 402–403.

11. Except where specifically indicated otherwise, the subsequent discussion of Levinson's Theory of Adult Development is taken from Daniel J. Levinson, "The Mid-Life Transition: A Period in Adult Psychological Development," *Psychiatry*, vol. 40, May 1970, pp. 99–112; and D. J. Levinson et al., "Periods in the Adult Development of Men," *The Counseling Psychologist*, vol. 6, January 1976, pp. 21–25.

12. C. F. Epstein, "Encountering the Male Establishment: Sex-Status Limits on Women's Careers in the Professions," *American Journal of Sociology*, vol. 75, 1970, pp. 965–1982; also see Gerard R. Roche, "Much Ado about Mentors," *Harvard Business Review*, January–February 1979, pp. 14–28.

13. Bernice L. Neugarten, "Adult Personality: Toward a Psychology of the Life Cycle," in William C. Sze, *Human Life Cycles* (New York: Jason Aronson, 1975), p. 383.

14. Ibid.

15. Robert Peck, "Psychological Developments in the Second Half of Life," in W. C. Sze, *Human Life Cycles*, pp. 610–618.

16. Ibid.

17. Ibid.

18. Gary Albrecht and Helen C. Gift, "Adult Socialization: Ambiguity and Adult Life Crises," in Nancy Daton and Leon H. Ginzberg. *Life-Span Developmental Psychology: Normative Life Crises* (New York: Academic Press, 1975) p. 242.

19. Wayne R. Davidson and Karl R. Kunze, "Psychological, Social and Economic Meanings of Work in Modern Society: Their Effects on the Workers Facing Retirement," in W. C. Sze, *Human Life Cycles*, pp. 691–700.

## Recommended Readings

Readings marked with an asterisk are included in *Contemporary Perspectives in Organizational Behavior*, edited by Donald D. White (Boston: Allyn and Bacon, 1982).

*Chris Argyris, "Personality versus Organization," *Organizational Dynamics*, vol. 3, Fall 1974, pp. 3–6.

Daniel J. Levinson, "The Mid-Life Transition: A Period in Adult Development," *Psychiatry*, vol. 40, May 1977, pp. 99–112.

Harry Levinson, "What Killed Bob Lyons?" *Stress, Success . . . and Survival* (Harvard Business Review, Special Reprint Series, 1976), pp. 19–35.

*Clifford T. Morgan, Richard A. King, and Nancy M. Robinson, "Personality as the Self," *Introduction to Psychology*, Sixth ed. (New York: McGraw-Hill Book Co., 1979), pp. 531–534.

*John Senger, "Seeing Eye to Eye: Practical Problems of Perception," *Personnel Journal*, vol. 53, October 1974, pp. 744–751.

Gail Sheehy, "Introducing the Postponing Generations: The Truth about Today's Young Men," *Esquire*, vol. 92, no. 4, October 1979, pp. 25–33.

# CASE 1
# Happiness Is Success!?

Roseland Florist opened for business sixteen years ago as a one-room, privately owned business specializing in occasion floral arrangements. The shop was opened by Mrs. Ann Conrad because, "I wanted to have something to keep me occupied and bring in a few extra dollars." Palos, the town in which the shop was located, had a population of 25,000. However, it, and many of the towns in the area, were growing rapidly. Two larger florists already were operating in Palos when Roseland was opened.

At first, Ann had only one employee, Ellen Holland. Ellen was a neighbor and long-time friend of Ann. Ellen also was interested in "occupying her time" while her children were at school. Although business was slow at first, their friends in the community constituted a large enough patronage to allow the women to maintain an adequate level of business. Soon, Roseland's reputation for quality service and low prices began to expand its list of customers. By the end of the first year of operation, Ann had added a combination secretary-bookkeeper and another part-time floral arranger.

## "Up" the Ladder of Success

One day, a close friend of Ann's mentioned that he had just heard about a new hospital which was to be built close to an existing medical center. Ann immediately saw the opportunity for which she had been waiting. That night, she sat down with her husband, Paul, and talked over the potential for opening a new shop closer to the hospital site. "Is this what you want?" asked Paul. Ann thought for a moment and then replied, "I've always wanted to see the shop be successful. And I think that this is the way to do it." The two discussed the matter further, and Ann decided at least to look into the matter.

Ann spent the next week talking with the various merchants and a banker about her plan. She told them that her work force had climbed to as high as twelve or fifteen persons on holidays and special occasions and that she needed more room for the people to work. In addition she explained, "I think this may be the opportunity that every business person wants . . . a chance to grow and be successful. You know, I've never really had any experience in business before, and neither Paul nor I graduated from high school. So you see, we really do need some advice about this move." The advice Ann received was mixed. But when she heard later that week a shop in the medical center soon would be vacant she made the decision to move Roseland Florist.

Roseland's success continued for several years. Sales grew and profits became larger, but Roseland was plagued by one continuous problem. The turn-

Prepared by Donald D. White, University of Arkansas.

over among the shop's employees was high. Three to four months were required to adequately train flower arrangers. And employees often left within five to six months after they were hired. Some took positions in other florist shops while others sought other types of employment. Since Ann had built the reputation of Roseland on the high quality of its work, she was faced with a serious problem. The volume of business was increasing rapidly; however, the lack of trained personnel had caused the quality of work to fall off badly.

## New Problems

A climax was reached when Ellen, Ann's first employee, quit her job at Roseland and took employment with a rival florist. Ellen explained her reasons for leaving to a fellow employee.

This used to be a pleasant atmosphere to work in, but Ann has changed. All she cares about now is money. Roseland is her whole life. She is so involved in making money that she forgets that people have to work with her. It's making me a nervous wreck; I just couldn't take it any longer. And frankly, Paul is just as bad. We have been friends and neighbors for years. But he hangs around the shop, gets in the way, criticizes your work, and well, just sticks his nose in where it doesn't belong.

The profit margin at Roseland has not been good for the last two years. Ann explains her money problems in the following way:

Costs have really gone up over the years. It's harder to get certain types of flowers and wholesale prices are much higher. In fact, transportation costs for my shipment of flowers have gone up as much as 600 percent in the last five years. This energy crisis has hurt us too. You know, artificial flowers are made of plastic and they are in short supply. Plus, it costs more to operate by delivery truck. I have tried to raise my prices as little as possible and they are lower than my competitors, so I try to increase my volume. It used to be that I would turn down some funeral pieces and cut off orders early on special occasions because I could not handle them all, but since my profits are lower I take as much as I can get.

Recently, Roseland workers have been complaining about having to remain on the job after regular working hours in order to get all orders out. One employee confided in a friend,

The thing that bothers me is that either Mr. or Mrs. Conrad always seem to be watching you to be sure you don't waste anything. Even if we drop a small piece of wire that we use to make arrangements, they tell us to pick it up and use it. Mr. Conrad is like a watchdog. One of Mrs. Conrad's favorite practices is, when we do flowers for a wedding, she waits until after the ceremony and tries to get the flowers and candles so that she can use them again.

Before leaving Roseland Florist, Ellen and Ann talked about Ellen's reasons for leaving. After listening to what Ellen had to say, Ann replied, "Hard work is the secret to success, and since I opened this business, I have worked hard seven days a week with only a couple of vacations. That is the only way that I know how to run the business."

# CASE 2
# Dave Melton

## Part A

Dave Melton sat in his office pondering the series of events that had led to his contemplating resigning from his position at National Paper, Inc., where he had been employed for over eleven years. The incident that had forced him to make a decision on whether or not to resign was his recent removal as head of the black recruitment effort at National Paper, Inc. and the subsequent installing of a white counterpart in his former position. Dave mused at how quickly the word had spread that he was upset with National. A few days after the change, he had received job offers from two large corporations to head up their black recruitment effort. The salaries in both offers were somewhat higher than he was making at National.

### Early Life

Dave Melton was born and raised in the small town of Summer Falls, Illinois. When he was born in 1930, the town had only three black families, one of which was very self-contained and did not associate with the other two. The other two families, including Melton's family, had a great deal of interaction, partly because both had migrated from the same section of North Carolina, where, in addition to knowing each other, they had provided the black leadership for their area. Dave described his early life as follows:

I had two brothers, one older and one younger. But the younger one died in infancy and I don't remember him at all. My mother and father were separated when I was three years old, for reasons which were standard for black families at that time; my father was unable to find work, but my mother could—so a matriarchy developed. However, my father would not accept the position of being supported by his wife, nor the role he was forced to play by her, so they separated. We went to live with my father's parents. My grandfather died when I was young—nine or ten—and grandmother became head of the household. She continued to manage the matriarchy and, even today at eighty-eight years of age, she feels she runs the household. She and my father still live together.

My relationship with my grandmother has always been strong. She taught me her moral values which were strict black Southern Baptist—no drinking, no smoking, no running around with women. However, today I do all three to some extent and she understands that I do. But I still do not drink in her presence.

Unlike many blacks at that time, Melton felt that his education in the Summer Falls school system was quite adequate. He attributes this to the over-

Prepared by Cyrus F. Gibson and Dyctis Moses of Harvard University. © 1968 by the President and Fellows of Harvard College. Reproduced by permission.

whelming interest that the town's large Jewish population had in the quality of their children's education. One of the attitudes held by the townspeople was their expectation that blacks participate in high school athletics. Both Dave and his older brother participated in athletics during their high school years. However, Dave never rivaled the skill of his brother in sports.

The casewriter asked Dave about his attitude toward whites during his high school years:

*Melton:* In my freshman and sophomore years of high school, I viewed whites as friends and competitors since most of my social interaction was in athletics. In my junior and senior years, I recognized the social difference, but it did not bother me since the discrimination was not overt. My first exposure to blatant discrimination came later in my life, during the war, when a large military base was established nearby. Southern soldiers there were extremely cruel verbally, and at one point, I was assaulted by one. I was just eleven years old at that time. However, I did not regard the soldiers as townspeople; hence there was no conflict in my mind about whites.

*Casewriter:* What did you do after high school?

*Melton:* I had to drop out of high school when I was sixteen to help support the family. The job situation at that time was very bad, but since I had spent the previous summers refinishing floors for people in the community, I decided to start my own floor refinishing business. I had developed a very good reputation during the summers for dependability, so I soon found myself with more work than I could handle. In order to keep the contracts, I hired two older men as helpers. Strange as it may seem, my hiring helpers was the cause of all my problems because then I had to meet a weekly payroll and I soon ran into cash flow problems. The problem was mainly caused by my large customers, often contractors, who would not pay me for my work until they had completed the entire contract.

Being young and inexperienced, I could not force my customers to pay me on time, nor could I secure short-term loans from the local bank. In order to keep my business afloat I would have to work eight hours during the day on big jobs with my helpers and then work an additional eight hours at night on smaller, individual jobs from which I demanded cash upon the completion of the job. After seven months the constant physical strain was really getting me down, but by that time the family's financial situation had improved so I gave up my business to go back to high school and complete my education.

About a year after I graduated from high school, I married a girl who was attending a college near Summer Falls. She came from a southern family that was considered well off by black standards, while my family was poor. As a result, I was less concerned with socializing than she was and more concerned with work. Our married life could be characterized as a long period of acquiring things—houses, cars, etc., and wondering what to purchase next to appear as good as our neighbors and our social peers. I considered it nonsense and made it obvious that I did so. In retrospect, I believe our marriage was destroyed because of my unwillingness to fall into a matriarchal situation, along with my unwillingness to make adjustments that would prevent me from pursuing goals I thought would make my life successful. The long separation during military service destroyed the marriage for all practical purposes and after that it was only a matter of time before the formal separation and divorce.

## The Army

In 1951, at the age of twenty-one, Dave was drafted by the army. Unlike many young men, Dave found the army to be a tremendous learning experience, but he also felt that his experience was a little different from that of others.

The first thing that I recall is that both the army and I considered Dave Melton to be a misfit right from the start. In addition to the normal problems of adjustment, the army was the first time in my life that I came face to face with American racism. During the time I was a private, this racism was articulated in the form of an abnormal amount of menial assignments being shoved my way, and many degrading comments by the noncommissioned officers who, for the most part, were crude and not very bright. In an effort to get out from under the hammer, I decided to become an officer and applied for OCS. I passed the necessary exams and was accepted at OCS at Ft. Sill. It was tough and I wanted to quit on many occasions, but I remembered how much tougher it was being a private, so I stayed with it and graduated at the top of the class.

I had to *fight* to do it, but all the people I've known that have succeeded were fighters. I was able to compete successfully in athletics because I was tough-minded as well as physically tough. I was successful at OCS and in Korea for the same reasons.

After graduation from OCS, I was sent to Korea as one of the first black artillery officers assigned to the First Cavalry Division. As an example of what my tour of duty was to hold for me, when I arrived Korea, my commanding officer became so flustered at seeing a black man as one of his new officers that he introduced himself to me as Dave Melton.

During my entire tour of duty I was ostracized by all but the most junior officers. Since the officer corps was like a college faculty, the junior officers had to stick together in order to survive and there weren't enough of us to allow my white counterparts the luxury of discrimination. However, the senior officers never had anything to do with me socially. I was never invited to any of the parties given by a senior officer even though the white junior officers were invited. On the other hand, when it came to technical ability, they were surprised that, unlike most junior officers, I was an expert at gunnery. Eventually, I was recognized as having the best battery in the entire command and we were always assigned to shoot the more important missions.

After leaving Korea, Dave chose to stay in the army because of the "competition and the challenges." However, his feelings toward the service were gradually reversed after he served as trial counsel at "many court-martials and witnessed first-hand the workings of the army's archaic legal system." He was also bothered by his inability to defend himself against an unwarranted, derogatory, verbal attack by a white senior officer. By 1956 Dave had decided to give up his commission and leave the service. He described his decision as follows:

I was disturbed by the attitudes I could see developing in the senior officers. The officer's club became the social center and "happy hour" was the most important part of the day. I began to suspect that I liked the army because of the security and the easy job. That worried me. Besides, the social activity, which included catering to wives of generals and colonels, was just not my cup of tea. Many of the officers I talked with who had ten to fifteen years of service, regarded the military service not as on occupation but as a total way of life. I felt that they had little knowledge or concern for what was going on outside, so I decided it wasn't the life I wanted and got out.

*National Paper, Inc.*

In 1956, Dave obtained a job in the personnel department with National Paper, Inc. Even though there were very few blacks working for National at that time, Dave did not experience any difficulty in obtaining his job. He attributes this to the fact that his older brother had been working for National for four years and had a good record with the company. He was also fortunate enough to be interviewed by a member of his old army unit.

After initially working in Trenton, New Jersey, Dave arranged a transfer to Philadelphia to work toward a college degree in the evening division of Temple University. At that time, his job assignment was in personnel recruitment advertising. After attending Temple for one year, Dave became bored with school and quit. His disappointment over school, however, was offset by a new job assignment which dealt with personnel planning, an aspect that Dave indicated started him looking beyond strictly personnel issues and achieving a managerial perspective. Still feeling that he needed a college education, Dave enrolled in LaSalle University's night division one year later, but once again dropped out after another year, this time because he seemed to find himself working for a "union card" instead of knowledge. His discussions with faculty members at LaSalle developed this idea. One faculty member refused to grade him because he said "he would not grade talent." After that time, however, Dave continued to enroll in courses offered in night school that he felt were interesting or related in some way to his job. When asked if his lack of a college degree had hurt his career at National, Dave responded by saying:

No. Initially it did, but not anymore. Anybody who challenges me on my lack of a degree is only taking a cheap shot that can be easily handled. If I am at a meeting and a guy tries to show me up by quoting from a college textbook or something, I have enough book knowledge to refute his point by quoting several academic references on the issue. Education and a college degree are not synonymous. As a matter of fact, one of my career goals is to become a corporate vice-president. That should show that I am not at all worried about not having a college degree.

You know, it was after I made an analysis of my ability to learn in this company that I decided I could probably be a vice-president. I also felt that the times would someday be on my side. This may not come to pass, and I will not see it as a sharp disappointment if it does not. However, if the opportunity is there, I want it and I am going to do what I can to make it.

The next five years saw Dave continue in his position in personnel planning with steady advancement but without any really significant promotions. Dave said of this period:

Along with gaining experience in my area, I also started to see how the corporate game is played. I began making a habit of listening to my white counterparts when they would discuss their career goals, their personal problems, hang-ups, and other topics with me, and I made mental notes of these conversations for my future use. You know, I never invited these little chitchats, but I guess they just didn't see me as being smart enough to be an opponent, so they didn't care what they told me. However, some of that "uninvited" information has been very useful to me during my years at National.

### Black Recruitment

In 1963, National initiated an extensive recruiting effort at black colleges throughout the country in an attempt to significantly increase the number of blacks working for the company. Dave Melton was chosen to head up this effort and was also given "carte blanche" authority to select his team from anywhere in the company.

*Melton:* Actually, I was picked to be the project leader over the administrative assistant to the corporate director of personnel, who was also black, because management felt that the other black was too aggressive, too hard to get along with, and too hard to control. However, interestingly enough, I later found out that a senior manager in the company had made a comment to the effect that "six months ago, you would not have even known that Dave Melton was around, but now you can't keep his mouth shut."

The first problem that I faced was the actual selection of my project team. I wanted to get a team of blacks who held relatively high positions in the company so that when we talked to black applicants about the potential for growth and advancement in National, the jobs being held by my recruiting team would serve to give that statement credibility. I was very pleased with the team I got. For example, one member was the manager of the Scientific Lab in Chester, Pennsylvania, another was a product manager of the International Services Division, and another was the administrative assistant to the director of personnel. I would say that my team was probably the best recruitment team ever assembled at National. The statistics just tell part of the story. We always surpassed our numerical objectives for each year and the number of blacks that we recruited into the company increased by over 100 percent in each of the five years that we were in operation. While the company-wide acceptance rate from people being offered jobs was around 50 percent, our acceptance rate was never below 80 percent, and one year got to 95 percent.

*Casewriter:* How did your team members relate to you as the head of the project?

*Melton:* Well, our record speaks for itself; however, I was working with some
pretty high-powered people and naturally there had to be some conflict.

Some of the conflict revolved around a policy that I initiated that gave
me the final say on whether or not an applicant should be considered and
if he was considered, where he could be assigned. Many of the conflicts were
caused by resistance to my theory that the company-wide screening test
must be given to all black applicants and a *B* or better grade be attained by
these applicants on the exam. (*A, B* or better score was the cutoff point for
all white applicants.) Many of the blacks on my team felt that the test should
not be used in the case of black applicants because 1) black people have historically been underachievers on IQ tests, and 2) the tests were oriented
toward white middle-class applicants and therefore were irrelevant and incorrect when it came to judging the ability of black applicants.

I prevailed because I felt we were underestimating the black talent and
we could not afford to reinforce the stereotype. My position was that I had
to maximize the possibility of success of blacks hired in the training program
in order to forestall the development of an I-told-you-so attitude by whites
in the company, and having the base data from the tests was the only way
that I could do this. I now feel that my position on the test score was correct,
because during my team's existence, the washout rate for the blacks that
we recruited into the company was very low (comparable to whites).

Additional conflicts arose when other members of the team, upon finding a very promising applicant, would try to get that applicant to work for
them. Many times, I would overrule my team members and reassign those
applicants to jobs or locations where I felt they would be better suited or
where the manpower need was greater.

*Casewriter:* Why was your team so successful in recruiting black college graduates?

*Melton:* I think that you could safely say that our entire approach was different
than that exhibited by most corporation recruiters. For one thing, we looked
upon ourselves as being the interface between the colleges and National, so
therefore we gave ourselves the title of College Relations Specialists. Also,
unlike most corporation recruiters who are usually just starting with a company and therefore "wet behind the ears," no member of my team had less
than five years experience with the company. This experience level was a
big help when my guys would sit down and tell an applicant what National
was all about and what he could expect as a black working for a big corporation.

Furthermore, they told the truth—they talked about discrimination in
the company, the forms that it usually took and the way it had affected their
careers. They also told the good side of the story, the potential for growth
in National, the pay, the advancement, and the other good points. As a matter of fact, I had to can one of my recruiters because he was going around
telling these college kids that National was heaven and that there was no
discrimination in the company. This kind of recruiting is unfair to both the
company and the applicant because it can only lead to disillusionment on the
part of both parties.

*Casewriter:* Did you have any other problems with your recruiters?

*Melton:* Yes. Right at the start of our effort, two of the guys took to renting
Cadillacs, throwing $300 cocktail parties for faculty members at the schools,

and getting involved in the coed scene. Now, I knew that it was going to be hard for any guy to stay away from the coed scene, but I also felt that since we were new faces on these campuses that we couldn't afford that kind of image, so I dropped those two guys from the team.

*Casewriter:* How was your team received by the colleges involved?

*Melton:* As I stated before, our approach was unique. Many times our first trip to the campus would be a nonrecruiting effort. If a recruiter was a chemist, let's say, he would often visit the chemistry department first and just talk shop with some of the professors. Many times this tactic would lead to our guys holding special seminars on their field for a certain department in the school. By talking shop, we would also get requests for lab equipment, literature, and things like that. If National had a surplus of the needed items, my guys would shop around the company until they found the items and then send them to the school. Eventually, the schools looked upon us not just as recruiters, but as a valuable resource. We also made no attempts to sell the schools our products and services, even though there was often a need at these schools. However, I must admit that we did try to plant a seed in the minds of the college administrators so that the request for our salesmen to call on them would come from the colleges and not from us.

*Casewriter:* Why was this approach to the faculty at the colleges necessary?

*Melton:* We realized right from the start if we went into these schools offering students more money than the large majority of the faculty was making without somehow smoothing the way, that we would pretty soon meet a lot of opposition from the faculty. You must also realize that the only concerns recruiting at black colleges in those days were the government and school boards, so we also had to give everyone at the colleges a chance to find out what we were all about and what we had to offer. In line with that policy, I was the only member of the team who dealt with the administrators and senior deans at schools. We did this to create an illusion of a hierarchy. In other words, the top man at National in charge of black recruitment would talk to the top people at the colleges. The fact that I was black enhanced the company's image and helped us to establish rapport with the administrator and senior deans in a very short period of time.

*Casewriter:* Did your team employ any special techniques with the students?

*Melton:* We realized that we were also a new animal to the students. For one thing, the student applicants were scared. They knew very little about the business world. So when we talked to them we had to do a good job in explaining National and the industry to them. This is where the experience level of my men and their telling the truth helped.

Another method we used was that when we made an offer to an applicant, the guy on my team who had talked to the student would be notified by my office. My guy would then call the student and explain the position being offered, the career paths that he could follow if he accepted, and any other details that the applicant was interested in learning. This tactic boosted our acceptance rate because it showed that my guys were really interested in the individual applicants, which they were.

We also initiated a summer program where my guys would pick one or two promising sophomores or juniors and offer them jobs at locations for the summer. This helped to orient the students to working in industry. In addition, when these students went back to their campuses in the fall, they became our messengers and would spread the word around voluntarily that ours was a good company to work for. Because of the success of the student summer programs, the company set up a similar program for the faculty members at these schools. However, my guys were not in charge of the selection process and whoever was in charge selected the "bottom of the barrel" from these schools so the program naturally failed.

Before we change the subject, I think I should talk about the fantastic cooperation that I received from my guys. Even though there was some conflict, overall the team pulled very hard for the success of the project because they felt a deep personal involvement and did not want to see their effort fail. This commitment was absolutely necessary because I was not given a clerical staff and without the support of my team members and the efficiency of my secretary, I would not have been able to carry out my duties. Even with my teammates' help, I still had to work many sixteen-hour days and seven-day weeks in order to complete the processing of applicants immediately after they had been submitted by team members.

### Replacement Head of Team

Dave was quite proud of his record in black recruitment and was disappointed with National's decision to replace him as head of the minority recruitment. However, Dave seemed very calm to the casewriter as he talked about his removal.

*Casewriter:* Given the success of your efforts in black recruitment, Dave, why was the job taken from you?

*Melton:* I believe that the corporate intent at the time was to include the recruitment of blacks into the regular recruitment program and to phase out our operation. I think they thought they could give the effort to personnel people and have them multiply our efforts and really make hay in getting at this source of talent.

*Casewriter:* Well, what happened to change that plan?

*Melton:* I can only give you my perception of the events that took place, so keep that in mind. About the time that the people in corporate headquarters were thinking about phasing us out, a white personnel officer by the name of Dick Pringle became the volunteer to the Plans for Progress Youth Motivation and Advisory Group in Washington, D.C. Since the Plan for Progress Group deals with black employment, Pringle became informed about our operation. I think that Pringle saw equal opportunity employment as his road to to the top of the corporate heap, and was just waiting for a chance to take over our operation.

*Casewriter:* How did Pringle finally pull off the coup?

*Melton:* It so happened that a few month's earlier we had interviewed the son of a wealthy black businessman for a job. However, the son had already accepted another job before he interviewed with us. As it turned out, this kid really wanted to work for us but he was in a quandary about his previous job commitment and telephoned me for advice. Naturally, I told him that the decision was his to make and I did not try to pressure him one way or the other. He subsequently made the decision, and I think it was the right one, to stick to his previous commitment. Several weeks later the father was a guest speaker at a National seminar in Washington, D.C. which was also attended by Dick Pringle. After his speech, he happened to tell Dick Pringle that his son had really wanted to work for National but that we hadn't offered him a position.

      Pringle then went into our files and pulled out this kid's application which was naturally very impressive. However, what Pringle did not have were the notes that I had taken on all my phone conversations with this young man. Without consulting me, Pringle took the file and the father's story to my boss as an example of how my team was failing to recruit highly qualified blacks. Again without consulting me, Pringle and my manager took his story straight up the corporate ladder.

*Casewriter:* What was the reaction to Pringle's story upstairs?

*Melton:* Well, before they got a chance to hear my side of the story, they had already bought Pringle's and I suppose they had made a commitment to him concerning his heading up the black recruitment effort. The announcement was made last week; he's the new head and I'm to be under him. He's given me my first assignment, to lay out objectives for the number of recruits the office should get next year.

*Casewriter:* Did they ever hear your side of the story?

*Melton:* Well, yes, but by that time, so many higher-ups had become involved I guess it was impossible for them to admit that they had all been wrong. They took the attitude of "how could Melton's team possibly be doing better than we could do?"

*Casewriter:* Is that when you decided to resign?

*Melton:* I haven't decided to resign yet. I'm not sure if Pringle will be able to handle the job. He doesn't understand that recruiting black kids from black colleges is a hell of a lot different than recruiting at Princeton or Penn. I don't think there are many anywhere in the company who do, although they are committed to black recruitment because they've seen how it pays off. If I could pull through this and regain my job, I would gain a lot of respect throughout the company for my ability to meet the problem head on.

      Another one of my alternatives would be to stay and go along with the company's decision. However, I really feel wronged in this matter and to simply acquiesce would be a bitter pill to swallow. Finally, I still have two job offers pending, but I really have to study them to see that the potential those companies are offering in terms of advancement. Until now, they have only talked to me about setting up their minority recruiting programs and nothing beyond that, as far as my future career, has been discussed.

Dave then went on to explain that he felt the need to make a decision very soon because the two companies that had made him job offers wanted his answer within five days.

## Dave Melton B

Dave Melton Part B has not been included for your analysis in this book. Briefly, Dave decided not to leave National. He remained and worked under Dick Pringle, his replacement. A combination of incidents along with

Pringle's failure to effectively administer the black recruitment program resulted in Pringle losing his job. Ironically, he was replaced by Dave Melton. Asked why he remained with National, Dave stated "it was just too good a fight to run away from."

The black recruitment program ultimately was integrated into the firm's regular recruitment program and Dave's job was eliminated. He then took a corporate staff position with his company's Urban Coordination Staff. Dave's goals seemed to be well established. He wished to become a corporate vice-president. He believed that this would probably require that he take on a management job in one of the company's larger plants. In addition, he planned to broaden himself (beyond social action programs) in order to enhance his opportunities to move in an upward direction.

## Dave Melton C

In September 1973, the casewriter talked to Dave Melton to find out what had happened in his career and in his thinking toward his work since the (A) and (B) cases were written.

Melton has had two promotions since 1970. In June of 1971 he was made personnel manager for the headquarters, sales, and plant facilities of a geographical region of National Paper's operations involving some 2,000 employees. In November, 1972, he was made personnel manager of the United States's part of National's international subsidiary. In addition to personnel responsibilities for 1500 employees in the headquarters of this subsidiary in New York, Melton's responsibilities include training of personnel from foreign subsidiaries and divisions when they come to the United States, and responsibility for people from the American offices who go abroad for temporary assignments. These latter two aspects of his job mean an additional 2,500 people are covered by his work. He supervises a staff of 52 people. In his present position he is four levels below the president of the international subsidiary, and he adds, "There is no line manager between the president and me."

In describing his promotions, Melton said:

> Both these moves have been signficant in terms of increases in responsibility, exposure to top management, and salary. Furthermore, it is clear in the corporation that in order to reach the top rungs of management one must have experience in the international subsidiary as a senior manager.
>
> Both these jobs have been much more "line" than "staff."

The casewriter asked Melton what his attitude was now on the question of playing politics in management.

> It is clearer to me now than ever before that an understanding of and skill at playing corporate politics is integral to one's success. However, the game is different, the play is more sophisticated. The moves made are smoother and one has to be *keener* to play. . . .
>
> I enjoy this competition and feel it is important to be honest about it with myself. . . .

I welcome conflict management as a technique. I don't think of these games as a moral issue, as I may have indicated when the case was written. I see them as a part of the job, since at my level there is roughly equal ability among managers. The difference in who succeeds and who does not becomes a matter of how well one can deal with the politics and come out on top.

There are some 500 people below me who are working to succeed. Some of them are aiming for my job. It is only logical for me to think of where I might go next. I no longer hold the job of vice-president of the parent corporation as an ideal.

For one thing, the guy who now holds the job is younger than I am, and involved in work which takes him away from the daily contact with top management; he has to spend a lot of time covering his flanks and protecting his position. For another thing, realistically it would take me seven years to get there, I would be fifty, and they simply aren't making vice-presidents out of guys that age.

Twenty-three to twenty-four years in this work has made it a very difficult life. I'm not averse to thinking seriously of getting out at age fifty-five. I don't mean retirement. What I mean is getting into something which would again put me into equal opportunity work for minorities. Only a small part of my current work is directed to that effort. I could see myself at that time getting into something in government, for example. And, at that time, I hope the administration and climate will be more receptive to that kind of effort than it is now.

When asked how his present position compares to those of other blacks in the corporation, Melton replied:

There are two aspects to that. In terms of title and hierarchical status, I would say I am among the top five. In terms of policy-making power, in terms of the ability to make things happen, I am among the top two or three.

This is *clearly* not a windowdressing job. I get involved in the release of managers who are higher than I am, who make more money than I do. . . .

# CASE 3
# Growing Pains

John Withrow sat in his dimly lit office surrounded by a week's paper work. He leafed through the stacks of files, occasionally glancing at the pictures of his wife and children that sat on the desk before him. Although he often worked late, this evening was different from the rest. He had left the ball park after his sons had completed their game (he rarely ever missed an opportunity to see them compete) and returned to the office to do "some serious thinking."

A great deal had happened to John in the last few years. Summers were always the busiest seasons for him in the moving and storage business, and this had been no exception. In fact, the summer months had been so complicated by skyrocketing costs, frustrations over state rate control, and problems with hiring and holding a reliable work force that John was convinced he was at a major crossroads in his life.

Earlier that year, he had seriously considered selling his business and entering a different line of work. In fact, such a sale might well have taken place had a prospective buyer not backed out at the last minute. The frustration of long hours that lasted well into the evening, and carrying business problems home with him at night also had led to uneasiness in his home life. Although he had always been a family man, the increasing tensions surrounding his work had become evident to his wife and close friends. John was a regular Jekyll and Hyde during his busy season. On more than one occasion, his wife had confided to friends her deep concern for his physical and emotional wellbeing. And, although he did not show any signs of instability, his moodiness and openly expressed dissatisfaction with the course of his own life had set the stage for this evening.

## The Early Years

John matriculated through what could best be described as a very typical public education. He attended elementary and secondary schools with children from a variety of cultural and socioeconomic backgrounds. However, most came from lower-middle to middle-class families. He did not realize it at the time, but John's early education had exposed him to people from widely varying backgrounds.

From an early age, John tried to make the best grades he possibly could. Good grades served a dual purpose: they were a source of personal satisfaction, and they gave him the reputation of being a "good student." He enjoyed this reputation, and it further strengthened John's self-concept. Additionally, his good marks in school were a constant source of pride for his parents. From

Prepared by Charles W. Hubbard and Donald D. White, University of Arkansas.

an early age, they encouraged him to "do a good job." After awhile, however, the encouragement turned into expectation. Parents and friends and John himself expected him to be one of the top students in the class.

John tended to view himself as a likeable person with an extroverted personality. He related well to most of his peers, but he did have a reputation for being "straight." In junior and senior high school he didn't drink, smoke, or run with the "wrong crowd." He dated only "nice" girls and he didn't attend social gatherings in which "questionable" activities were taking place. The majority of his social life was associated with school athletic programs, the Boy Scouts, and church.

The Boy Scout movement, in particular, exerted a strong and positive influence on John's formative years. He was a very active participant, and, as in school, he strove to be the best in the group. By age fifteen, he had achieved Scouting's two highest awards. The organization to which he belonged was one of the finest in its region, and its members and leaders were instrumental in the development of his character, self-discipline, and self-reliance.

Because of a working-class background, John's family simply could not provide him with *all* the material possessions he wanted. While his basic needs were always provided for, John had an unusually strong desire for money and nonessential possessions—a need which simply could not be met with the financial resources available to the family.

Holding firmly to the Protestant work ethic, the family encouraged and aided John at an early age to perform small tasks and to accept odd jobs in order to "learn the value of a dollar." Indeed, throughout his formative years, the work ethic was strongly encouraged in John. The family found it both desirable and necessary for him to contribute part of his own support. As time passed, he became more financially independent, looking to the family for only basic food, shelter, and medical attention. Increasingly, he provided more of his own clothes, transportation, entertainment, and other extras of a growing, active young man.

In reflecting on his boyhood, John could not overlook relations with his father and mother and the impact which they exerted on his development. Mr. Withrow was forty years old when John was born. This large age difference between John and his father made it difficult to establish a relationship that could be described as warm and supportive. Mr. Withrow found it difficult to accept the value system of John's generation. However, he did subtly implant the Protestant ethic into John's character.

John's mother was sixteen years younger than his father, and John felt better able to identify with her. Her ideas and views seemed to him to be more modern and more closely aligned with his own. She, too, was strongly imbued with the Protestant ethic.

Due to their age differences, it seemed that his parent's personal relationship left things to be desired. As John grew older, Mrs. Withrow increasingly relied on John to perform duties normally thought to be the husband's. Neither John nor his mother realized this gradual evolution in their relationship at the time. However, increased reliance on him tended to have a maturing effect on John. In many ways it seemed to cut short his adolescence and to launch him into manhood well before his time.

## Looking for a Life Style

Even before entering high school, John made the decision to attend the large metropolitan university in his home town. There was really never any question about his attending college. His parents had not been able to go and from his early years they had preached to him the virtues of education and their expectation that John would attend college.

Money for college was short, but jobs in the city were plentiful, so it made good sense to live at home and work and go to school in his home town. Moreover, remaining in the area allowed him to pursue marriage plans with Dina, his high school sweetheart.

John completed his four-year undergraduate program with a B+ average, majoring in business administration. He and Dina were married at the beginning of his junior year. During the final two years of college, both he and Dina were kept busy working, attending school, and maintaining an active social life. At the same time, serious thought was being given to the future. And from John's viewpoint, the future meant more money and more education.

Immediately upon graduation, John was hired by a large, nationally known food processing firm. His initial job responsibility was that of sales to retail food stores and supermarkets. Saleswork seemed to fit his personality and to provide him with the competition and the challenges he enjoyed.

At the same time, John recognized that a master's degree would be helpful to his career. With that in mind, he enrolled in the evening MBA curriculum at his alma mater. Once again, John settled into what by now for him had become a well established life style: working and going to school.

Not long after his new full-time work/graduate school career began, John received his military notice. Fearful of the draft and a lengthy interruption of his career, John scurried to find a way to minimize the interruption. He enlisted in a program of six-months' active duty and six-years' reserve obligation with week-end active duty. While the six months seemed to never end, John soon was back home attending night MBA classes and selling his company's products with renewed vigor. However, the enthusiasm for his job seemed to diminish rapidly, and he found instead a growing interest in pursuing his MBA.

There seemed to be but one course to follow that would bring John the satisfaction and fulfillment he longed for. This course would require certain fundamental decisions, decisions which would have a far-reaching impact on the Withrow's lives, although they did not realize it at the time. He and Dina concluded that he would quit his job, they would sell their recently purchased home, and once again he would become an apartment-dwelling full-time student supported by a working wife. John was able to complete his MBA in one semester, during which he was given an opportunity to teach his first college course.

He was captivated by the teaching experience. He liked the feeling of being at the head of the class, of being the leader—the authority on the subject. He became so fascinated with teaching that new career thoughts began to enter his head—perhaps teaching on a permanent basis. He realized, of course, that full-time college teachers had more education than he; it would be necessary to earn a Ph.D. Simultaneously, he experienced feelings of excitement and uncertainty. Was he Ph.D. material? Were the time and financial commitments really worth it? Was teaching *really* the career for him? Two things he felt were certain: he had never before walked away from a challenge, and he did not have a lot to lose. With these thoughts in mind, and with the assurance of continued support and cooperation from his wife, John was accepted into the doctoral program at a distant university.

The decision to pursue a Ph.D. proved to be the prelude to a series of significant events that developed during his years on campus. These events would have a lasting impact on his life and on his family. John enthusiastically entered his graduate studies. He taught part-time in order to make ends meet, since his wife also had returned to the classroom as a full-time student in pursuit of her bachelor's degree.

Three years on the new campus were highly productive. Dina completed her B.A., graduating as class valedictorian, and John finished his Ph.D. coursework requirements. The most important event to both John and Dina was the birth of twin boys. However, the new additions, along with long hours of work on his dissertation, created additional time and financial pressures for him and Dina.

Upon nearing the completion of his formal studies, John received an appointment as an assistant professor of a recognized university in a city far from the region where he had spent his first twenty-six years. Shortly after moving to his new position, John and his wife began to experience sharp pangs of home-sickness. They did not long for their big city hometown; they sought to return to the small town where he attended graduate school. The longing for that small town not only lingered, but grew. In fact, the feeling became an almost compulsive drive. John and his wife became convinced that their ultimate happiness lay in permanently residing in this one locale.

Although he thought often about returning "home," John was highly motivated in his new job. He became involved in consulting activities and, with a colleague, published a book in his field. His efforts gained him recognition, and after two years he was offered a new position at a major state university. The new position was a step up for John and was somewhat closer to the community to which he and his wife wished to return.

Again he poured himself into his work, developing an innovative program in minority business and continuing to write. However, after two years John and his family were given the opportunity to return to the community where they had for so long wanted to live. He was not to do so as a terminally qualified college professor, but rather as the owner of a small transfer and storage business. John and his wife opted to forego the secure and comfortable world of academia for the uncertainties of entrepreneurship. Some of his friends and colleagues were surprised by his decision, but John explained, "The money was never really good, and the reward systems that I worked under never gave you a fair shake. No matter how hard I worked, I never could get ahead."

## Returning Home

Once back home, John rapidly set about to establish himself as a reputable, dependable, and progressive businessman. He saw his operation as a perfect laboratory in which to experiment with the theories, ideas, and concepts he had so long worked with in the classroom. Dina worked by his side as office manager and head bookkeeper. Together, they quickly became immersed in the business and its challenges. John was thirty-one years old and full of energy and enthusiasm. His persevering nature, his supportive wife, and "lady luck" all combined to create success. The business's facilities and fleet grew in size and quality. The Withrow's lived comfortably, and the company was making money.

Yet John again became restless. He believed that it was time to undertake a major business expansion. He obtained a second freight office in a larger community sixty miles from the original operation. Although the new venture was not yet profitable after eighteen months of operation, he planned to add a third outlet in another nearby community and buy yet another major freight office in the state capitol some two hundred miles away. He envisioned his role as that of a corporate executive, rather than continuing as the general manager of the local operation alone. His business and his plans were growing rapidly.

Unfortunately, John's problems grew, too. Shortages of qualified labor, increased government regulation, and the growing pressures on profits caused by rapidly rising costs were but a few of the problems he encountered. As margins began to slip, so did John's ability to afford additional administrative personnel who could help share the managerial responsibilities and headaches. The second office continued to lose money, and he discarded what was once a priority plan for expansion. In addition to mounting frustration, he had self-doubt that he had never before experienced.

As time passed, John found the pressures of the business becoming more burdensome and his enthusiasm waning. It became more and more difficult for him to get himself and his employees "fired up" about what they were doing. Increasingly, it was beginning to appear to John that he should now, at age thirty-nine seriously reassess his life and career goals.

## Facing the Future

Once he made the basic decision to re-evaluate his career path, John began to discuss thoroughly with Dina, friends, and business associates the options which were open to him.

He asked those around him to give him direct, objective answers to questions about himself and his future. The questions were asked over a period of several months—months that seemed agonizingly long as John searched for the right path to take during the coming years. He felt a sense of urgency in making a decision for, after all, he "wasn't getting any younger." He had to decide how to use the maturity and experience he had gained in the last eight years.

While they seemed to come at a snail's pace, the answers he sought finally began to emerge. Close friends seemed to be saying he would be wise to consider another occupation. Almost simultaneously, possibilities seemed to begin appearing. One such possible opportunity developed in the life insurance industry.

Due in part to his interest and to his "desired personality traits" for the business, one close friend urged John to consider a new career in life insurance sales work. John believed he could handle the job and was curious about an industry test battery that was available. Therefore, he agreed to subject himself to lengthy and intensive set of "career profile examinations" administered by a large, nationally recognized life insurance company. Not surprisingly to his family, close friends, or himself, the tests were returned with very favorable results. While obviously pleased and flattered, John could not firmly convince himself that this was the new direction he wanted to take. A number of obstacles to a new career in life insurance sales lingered in the back of his mind and made him hesitate and ultimately reject insurance as a serious career change possibility.

At the same time that John pondered his decision, Dina concluded that she, too had grown tired of the demands and the problems associated with running and owning a family business. She freely voiced her disenchantment to her friends and to John. John, in response, had encouraged her to reduce drastically her workload in the company office and to stand ready to accept another opportunity should one be offered.

Having at least considered one new position, although he rejected it, John found that the process of thinking about selling his business and changing careers was becoming easier. In fact, he actually enjoyed daydreaming about doing something different. He longed to move into an occupation that was more "professional," something that would let him better use the graduate education and work experiences he had acquired, some of which had lain dormant for nearly eight years. He had thought about how refreshingly different it would be to return to the college classroom; he could surely be more effective now than before thanks to his "real world" experience.

These thoughts were running through his head when one afternoon he received a call from his close friend, Jim Scott. Jim was a faculty member at the university and had been one of John's closest confidantes during his "rough days." Jim knew that John had an interest in returning to the academic community in some capacity, and an opportunity to do so appeared to be on the horizon. Jim told John that it made good sense to have University officials at least contact John. Perhaps both their needs and his could be simultaneously satisfied.

Within a few days, Jim had given John's name to one of the officials, and agreement had tentatively been made for him to occupy a temporary teaching position. The teaching job meant rearranging busy business days and delegating additional duties to employees, and it was understood that his assignment was only temporary, due to university hiring policies. Still, John was excited about the opportunity.

John's life seemed to improve markedly in the following weeks. While he was working hard and logging many hours in his dual role as businessman and professor, he seemed to thrive on the work. Jim frequently commented to John that he seemed like a different person. John actually appeared to both look and feel better. His attitude improved, and it seemed easier for him to cope with problems at his company office. John was thoroughly enjoying his experiences at the university. Sometimes he reluctantly looked at the calendar, noting the last day of the semester approaching.

He was reminded that this pleasant experience would soon end and the diversion from his business would soon be over. He tried not to think about returning full-time to the business; however, his thoughts haunted him. "Perhaps this (the University) really is the life for me."

## The Decision

Shortly before fall semester ended, Jim came to John with news that would complicate John's already confusing and frustrating situation. The Associate Deanship of the College of Business was soon to be vacated. Jim suggested that John consider submitting his credentials. It appeared the position would require an academic background, administrative skills, and a degree of maturity. On the surface, it seemed that John could qualify. There was no way of knowing just what his chances were of receiving the appointment, but one thing was clear—he must make the decision to submit his credentials soon if he wanted to be considered for the job.

John's wife encouraged him to weigh the various options open to him carefully, and, as he sat alone in his office, he was determined to do just that. As he examined the situation, he viewed his first option as completely abandoning a career change and firmly recommitting himself to his moving and storage business. The business did offer the challenges he felt were needed in his life, and he knew it potentially offered him the financial rewards he had always sought. Business conditions had improved slightly, and industry associates had suggested improvements in his operations. If he sharpened his management skills, he was sure the business would produce sufficient profits and income to allow his family to live well.

A second option was to apply for the Associate Deanship. He felt this position would present new and challenging work and would pay a comfortable salary with limited burdens and headaches. Moreover, the job might provide him with an avenue to a permanent teaching position at the university in future years. On the negative side, John wondered if he would enjoy this new type of work. After all, he had never had a position exactly like this before and really didn't know what to anticipate. Additionally, he knew from past experience that salary increases would be limited. Taking the position would mean losing a certain amount of control over his financial future. Finally, he was aware that leaving the business entirely would mean leaving the day-to-day operation in the hands of unprepared subordinates until a buyer could be found.

As he saw it, his third possibility was to make no firm decision at the present time. With respect to an immediate career change, he could simply, for now, keep an open mind and "an ear to the ground." The strength of this position, he believed, was that once it became common knowledge that he was considering a career change, more employment possibilities might soon appear, and he might be able to accept a more attractive offer. However, if he really did feel that the academic environment was where he should be, John had to make a commitment now. In all probability, there would never be another opportunity like this one.

He thought about the need to be rational about this important decision, but he seriously questioned his rationality after "bouncing" from career to career. He confessed to himself that the entire experience was embarrassing, yet he knew he *had* to do something.

# CASE 4
# A Secretarial Gamble

Franklin D. Ward was the director of a 700-member state social service agency. This agency functioned to provide care and training for physically and mentally handicapped individuals from throughout the state. Ward had been working in the field of social service for nearly twenty years, and was dedicated to his work. Under his guidance, the agency was oriented to action. Any activity within the confines of the guiding state law was fair game. Ward enthusiastically advocated programs aimed at providing employment to disadvantaged and handicapped persons. Such persons, his staff was reminded, should be given top consideration in employment decisions.

George M. Simon supervised the public relations department agency. Besides some incidental functions, the department made use of personal and media contacts to establish a positive image with the public. The department staff included two assistants and one secretary. In the past, the secretarial position had been used as a steppingstone to the assistant position. Often, then, the secretary would be asked to do additional tasks to gain experience. For this reason, the secretarial position was among the higher paid secretarial slots in the agency, and applicants for the position were required to have had at least two years of college work. The only skill requirement for the position was that the applicant be able to type accurately and be able to meet and converse well with people.

In April 1971, one of Simon's assistants notified him that she would be leaving the agency. Simon immediately notified the personnel officer, John Williams, and planned to promote the present secretary to the position of assistant. Several weeks passed after the departure of Simon's assistant, however, and no one had been hired to fill the position. The unfinished work was piling up, with the overload placed on the remaining assistant. The secretary was increasingly anxious about receiving her promotion and the accompanying thirty percent raise in pay. Simon inquired and found out that Williams had not been able to locate any suitable applicants for the job. He then called Ward and asked if he knew of anyone. Ward replied that he would see and would call back.

Later in the week Ward stepped into Simon's office with a very attractive young lady, Lisa Kirkpatrick. Apparently Ms. Kirkpatrick had come from a similar position in another city. The former employer and Ward recommended her highly. She had a four-year degree from Leighton University, a nearby institution.

Lisa stated that she would be willing to work as a secretary in Simon's department, since it offered her the eventual opportunity to move into the

Prepared by William Smith and Donald D. White, University of Arkansas.

staff assistant position. The position also offered more in the way of work variety than most secretarial jobs. Ward noted that Lisa had left her previous employer upon hearing of this opportunity and would start work immediately. The necessary personnel action forms were already in process.

Simon was a bit upset at this turn of events. Ward had apparently hired the young woman without asking his prior approval or allowing him to interview her. But after talking with Lisa for a while, he was satisfied that Ward might have judged her wisely. He called in the present secretary and promoted her to staff assistant. The next few days were spent familiarizing Lisa with the the operations of the department.

Several weeks passed. Lisa seemed to be a very capable individual. She was prompt and seemed to be very neat. Her desk was always clear of unfinished tasks. Simon, as was his practice, began to assign a few nonsecretarial duties to her. For example, she initially took visitors on tours of the facility and delivered press releases to newspapers, radio, and television stations in the city. These tasks would help her develop important contacts should she be an assistant later.

Early in June, a personal friend of Simon's telephoned him from another state agency. He was somewhat upset by a letter Simon had sent. Simon was shocked since he was not aware of the letter at all. During the course of the conversation it became apparent that Simon had not written the letter. Simon suspected that the individual responsible for the falsified correspondence might be attempting to disrupt Simon's efforts in public relations. After hanging up, Simon alerted Lisa to increase internal security over the mailing.

Arriving late at the office one morning, Simon passed the mail room just after delivery. He decided to stop in order to save his secretary her usual morning trip to the mail boxes. Scanning the mail Simon noticed that among the letters was one acknowledging the receipt of a letter sent by him. He could not recall having written or authorized such a letter. As he arrived at his desk, he asked Lisa to see if she could locate a copy of the letter in their files.

Simon forgot about the matter until later in the day. Remembering, he buzzed Lisa's desk to remind her. Another department's secretary, Angela Parks, answered because Lisa had gone on her afternoon break. Angela said she would look in Lisa's files for the letter. She unsuccessfully tried to decipher Lisa's filing system, and Simon asked her to send Lisa in after her coffee break.

Lisa reported that she also was unable to locate a copy of the letter. Worried about the mysterious goings-on, Simon again cautioned Lisa about maintaining security of the files and correspondence in the department. Personnel in government agencies were sometimes the target of rather unethical struggles and Simon assumed that something of this sort was going on in his agency.

The remaining days of June uncovered other instances of forgery and mail fraud. He discussed some of his suspicions with Ward. He was rather surprised that Ward had some similar experiences recently. Simon had an uneasy feeling that Ward knew more than he was telling him.

On July 15, Williams called Simon and told him that the agency had been unable to get a copy of Lisa's college transcript. Ward had asked Williams to hire Lisa even though her file was incomplete. But on Ward's instruction and with Lisa Kirkpatrick's promise to obtain a copy of her transcript for the file as soon as possible, Williams had processed the paperwork.

Since then, Lisa had failed to bring a transcript even after several direct requests. Williams then contacted the college registrar's office. The college was unable to locate her file and requested additional information. Apparently they had some troubles in computerizing their records the year before and perhaps additional information would help them locate it. After many tries the registrar's office finally sent him a penciled note saying that they could not locate any record of a Lisa Kirkpatrick.

Simon confronted Lisa with the matter, and she stated that she had experienced this trouble before. She explained that she had been married at the time she was a student, but had since been divorced and subsequently assumed her maiden name. She had forgotten to tell this to Williams. Simon instructed her to take care of the matter immediately.

Two weeks later Williams again called Simon with the news that in a phone call the registrar stated that Lisa had never been a student there. Because it was late Friday afternoon, Simon decided he would put off confronting Lisa until Monday.

The following Monday, however, Simon was called to the state capital on business. While there, he happened to meet Jason Edwards, a new employee in one of the state administrative offices. Upon learning where Simon worked, Edwards commented that he had been dating the director of public relations at that same agency. Since George Simon's title more nearly fit that of director of public relations, Simon asked Edwards who the girl was. Needless to say Simon was surprised when Edwards named Lisa Kirkpatrick.

On Tuesday morning Simon walked briskly past his own desk and went into Ward's office. He told him of his discovery and also hypothesized Lisa's link with the letters:

*Simon:* Mr. Ward, I have reason to believe that Lisa has been misrepresenting her position here to a number of people. I know she has done so to at least one of her friends, and I believe she has been initiating and answering some of my correspondence without my knowledge or permission.
*Ward:* Maybe you should check your files—you may have forgotten some things. After all, quite a bit of correspondence goes through your department.
*Simon:* No, Sir! I thought of that. I came to the office last night to go through the files myself. I found, first of all, that Lisa has not been filing our materials at all. She has been stacking them at the rear of the file drawers, instead. As nearly as I could tell, records of a substantial portion of the correspondence we have processed over the past three or four months are missing.
*Ward:* Lisa has been a secretary before, and she has had a considerable amount of education. Surely she can't be that neglectful.
*Simon:* That brings up another issue. John called the registrar at Leighton. Lisa

has not produced a transcript of her college credits, and the registrar claims she has never been enrolled there. John and I are wondering if she has a degree, or for that matter, any college experience at all.

*Ward:* George, I did not want to have this follow Lisa here, but I can see I will have to tell you now. Lisa worked for my friend, Gordon Stansill, at Corona Corporation before she came here. Gordon told me that Lisa has had considerable difficulty in holding a job because she has relatively minor psychological problems. He said that he was going to have to let her go before long himself. But he felt that she might be able to straighten out things if she were to work for a while somewhere where there was less pressure on her

*Simon:* Exactly what kind of psychological problem did he say Lisa had?

*Ward:* Gordon told me that her marriage broke up a few years back, and she has not been able to deal with it. While she worked for Gordon she continued to maintain that she and her husband were still together. She even went so far as to send roses to herself at the office, saying that they were a birthday present from her husband.

*Simon:* (*Somewhat indignantly*) Exactly how did you expect *me* to help her? I'm not running a psychiatric aid service—she should have professional help if she has that kind of problem! Besides, I certainly cannot carry out my duties using what I consider to be irrational personnel!

*Ward:* (*Also becoming angered*) As you well know, we are a social service agency. I believe that we owe it to the public to help our fellow man in any way we possibly can. Lisa certainly couldn't find help in an industrial concern. The competitive pressure would only make her worse. You and your staff aren't exposed to that kind of day-to-day pressure since yours isn't a line department. It's not likely that Lisa could do any real harm to the organization as the secretary to a staff department. As to your first question, I did not expect you to help her in any overt manner—that's why I did not fill you in on her background. But I did tell Mark Fuller, our staff psychologist, to talk with her occasionally to see if she was improving or needed his advice on anything.

*Simon:* If you could tell Fuller, I don't understand why you couldn't tell me something of her difficulty. I can't be expected to—

*Ward:* (*Interrupting*) I did not tell you because you could not have given her a real chance had you known the situation. Lisa certainly could not be expected to improve if no one around her exhibited anything but complete trust in her abilities. If you and your staff had known that she might let you down in some way, you would have watched her constantly. You would have treated her like a patient instead of a coworker, and she would have sensed your doubt sooner or later.

*Simon:* Well, that may very well be! But I've got to have a secretary who can carry out her duties in an acceptable manner and who knows the difference between her job and the department head's job!

*Ward:* You'll do well to remember who gave *you* the job of department head! Furthermore, I hired Kirkpatrick and I will be the one to dismiss her if I decide she should go. You and your staff can work around her for now if you have to, and I will try to find her another position with a supervisor who is a bit more tolerant of people's problems. You are going to have to learn that we have to help each other in this world sometimes, son!

Feeling that he still had not been told the full truth about Lisa Kirkpatrick and the reasons why she had been placed in his charge, Simon stormed out of Ward's office.

## Appendix: Letters to Lisa

*These are excerpts of correspondence from Lisa's mother to Lisa.*

### Thursday, 21

*Dear Lisa,*   Why don't you answer my letters sweetheart? You know that Dad and I love you very much and only want the best for you. You *do* need help, honey—things haven't been the same since Dad was away those five years with the service. Daddy and I want to help you. Your Dad works very hard and just can't keep straightening things out for you the way he has for so long. A man called from the bank Tuesday and said that you had written over $100 worth of bad checks since the first of the month. You just can't keep hurting your Dad like that Lisa. He's not well. He keeps paying for your bad checks but he's not rich. Why do you keep hurting us this way, darling? It seems like Daddy has pampered you since you were five years old. I love you—

### Monday, 4

... Tommy just doesn't understand, and I don't know how to tell him where you are and why you won't come to see him. It's only an hour's drive here, and he begs to see his mother. I can accept the fact that you don't love us any more, but how can you do this to your own child?? He's getting to be more than I can cope with ... especially his questions ...

### Monday, 18

... Lisa, you are just going to have to face the fact that Henry's not there any more! He took as much of your abuse as he could stand. He loved you so much when you two were married even though Tommy was on the way ... I know he did. I thought sure you would settle down, especially after Tommy was born. I feel sorry for you, but I don't blame Henry for leaving and I think I know exactly why he did ...

### Friday, 22

*Dear Lisa,*   I'm happy about your new job ... Kathy told us you are working for the state now. I don't have your address where you're staying now so I hope you will get this at work. Why don't you write? ...

### Saturday, 27

The man from Leighton called again today. He said he couldn't find your transcript and wanted some additional information on you to help him find it. Why didn't he just call you at work?

I'm so glad you got your degree, honey. Dad and I never were able to finish college and we always wanted you to. I wish you had gone to the graduation exercises, though, even though the college didn't require you to attend. We wanted to see you in your cap and gown. After paying your tuition for four years, we certainly could have managed the $50 graduation fee.

## Some Time Later

You've been out of school for nearly four years now. What happened to your plans to go back to graduate school? We would be glad to pay your way . . .

### Wednesday, 1

. . . people are calling us from all over town about your bad checks and the bills you are running up. We just can't continue to pay for your mistakes. Dad just isn't able . . .

### Friday, 24

. . . try to hold on to this job. You've lost so many the last few years. Why don't you go back to Dr. Herman? I know he could help you if you would just let him. If you give him a chance I just know he could help you see things more clearly . . .

### Tuesday, 4

. . . she said you had listed your parents as being *deceased* on your application and just wanted to call to see if there had been some mistake. You hurt us so much . . . what did we ever do to you, Lisa??

### Wednesday, 22

. . . I know you probably turned Henry against you because you couldn't keep your eyes off other men. Didn't Dr. Herman say you have had trouble since that ugly Billy Bartlett jilted you at the freshmen prom? Will it ever stop, Lisa? I'm praying for you.

# EXPERIENTIAL EXERCISE 1
## The Label Lesson

We sometimes form quick, questionably accurate opinions of people. Then our classification affects our behavior towards those people. Ironically, how we treat others affects how they respond to us. For example, by now you have probably formed an opinion about the professor of this course. You may have judged him or her even before the class started ("the grapevine says . . ."), or you may have formed an opinion after only a few classes. Without realizing it, you have placed a *label* on this person. He or she may as well be wearing a card that says, "treat me this way." Is this label accurate? Let's examine this for a moment.

Suppose you perceive me as being lazy. Since you perceive me as lazy, you treat me as lazy. The more that you treat me as lazy, the more I may act lazy. Why? Maybe I begin doing it to reap some of the benefits along with the blame. Maybe I act lazy to put you on. Maybe it's just that I receive attention (strokes) when I do what you expect. From your perspective, I am lazy. Any lazy behavior allows you to confirm your earlier opinion ("See, I knew he was lazy"); we often see what we want to see. The objective question remains Am I lazy? For you, the reasoning is self-fulfilling. But how do I act in other situations? Around other people? How much have *you* contributed to my actions? Each of us knows some people we like, some we trust, some we ignore, and so on. Are they inherently that way, or have we helped to shape their personality by our behavior?

This exercise exposes you to the use of labels—prescribed mental sets—and the resulting effects of labels on behavior. Several students will have the opportunity to experience some common labels The rest of the class will have a chance to observe, analyze, and relate prior class material to what they see and hear during the role playing.

### Instructions

1. Seven student volunteers are required for this role-playing exercise.
2. Each of the seven students should stand in the front of the room with their backs to the rest of the class.
3. Fix one label to each student's forehead, being careful to ensure each student does not see what is on his or her own forehead.
4. The seven students then walk around the room slowly so the observers (the rest of the class) may write down each student's name and label.
5. There is going to be a party at the apartment (classroom) of one of the seven. Each of you must respond to the others at the party only in terms of what is on the other's forehead. Please follow this rule and do what each forehead says when encountering the individuals.
6. One student is designated by the teacher to play host of the party. The other six must wait outside the classroom. (Do *not* interact and do *not* reveal to

Prepared by J. Kenneth Matejka, University of Richmond.

each other what is on the foreheads). One of the six should arrive at the party (enter the room) every five minutes.
7. Classroom observers should write down their impressions and reactions to what takes place at the party.
8. After the full party has gone on for ten minutes, everyone at the party must freeze. One at a time, each labeled person should explain how he or she feels at the moment. After all seven have responded, they may guess what is written on their foreheads.
9. The class as a whole may now comment on what transpired. Relating the experience to conceptual frameworks such as TA may be helpful.

## Questions

1. How did you feel during this exercise?
2. How do you cope with social interactions when, no matter what you do or say, you are treated the same way?
3. What was the most difficult label to wear? Why?
4. What two labels provided the most frustrating interactions? Why?
5. As a group, could you modify someone's behavior in your classroom by placing a label on them and behaving accordingly? How long would it take? Has this happened in your class already this semester?
6. How do you relate what transpired to the material covered in class so far?
7. What direct and indirect implications does this exercise have for the work situation?
8. What are some common labels placed on people in organizations?

# EXPERIENTIAL EXERCISE 2
## Johari Window

To a large extent, our attitudes and intents are judged by others on the basis of our overt behavior. In the same way, we judge others by what they do. Sometimes, actual reasons for behavior are hidden from others. Events from our past and privately held beliefs may not be known to those around us. Consequently, their actions may not be based on "complete" information. On the other hand, we also might overlook certain characteristics of our own behavior while they are clearly observed by those with whom we come in contact. The net result is that the behavior of individuals toward one another is limited to what they think they see (or perceive) and thus may be inappropriate.

The purpose of the Johari Window is to develop a more complete and accurate awareness of ourselves and those with whom we interact. This exercise will allow you to discover your own assets and liabilities as you as well as those around you see them and to disclose to them certain hidden reasons for your behavior. Through this more accurate awareness of self and others, your relationships with those around you can become more meaningful and realistic.

### Instructions

1. Either on this page or on another sheet of paper list in the left column the major assets and liabilities of your personality. Then place a check mark in front of those aspects that you have revealed so far to participants. (Use the Feedback Sheet to write your impressions of other participants.)
2. When the facilitator collects the feedback sheets and reads them aloud, use the right column of your sheet to record perceptions of you held by other participants.

---

| *Assets* | | *Assets* | |
| *Self-Perceptions* | | *Others' Perceptions* | |

---

| *Liabilities* | *Liabilities* |
|---|---|
| *Self-Perceptions* | *Others' Perceptions* |

Reprinted from *Group Processes: An Introduction to Group Dynamics* by Joseph Luft by permission of Mayfield Publishing Company, formerly National Press Books. © Copyright 1970.

## *Johari Window Feedback Sheet*

Write your impressions of the major assets and liabilities of each participant, including yourself, in the spaces below. These will be read aloud anonymously as feedback.

| Participant | Assets | Liabilities |
|---|---|---|
| | | |
| | | |
| | | |
| | | |
| | | |
| | | |
| | | |
| | | |
| | | |
| | | |
| | | |
| | | |
| | | |
| | | |
| | | |

From J. William Pfieffer and John E. Jones (eds.), *A Handbook of Structured Experiences for Human Relations Training*, Volume 4, La Jolla, CA: University Associates, Inc., 1974.

# CHAPTER TWO

# Learning and Applied Behavior Analysis

Unlike many theories of managing people, those based on principles of learning focus on outward behaviors rather than intangible needs or difficult-to-define goals. Chapter Two explores underlying theories of learning and the systematic application of learning principles in the management of human resources.

## Theories of Learning

Most generally accepted theories of learning include three essential components. First, learning involves a *change* in behavior. Learning theorists are concerned with changes in overt behavior. Second, the change must be *relatively permanent*. A one-time occurrence or temporary change in behavior may not represent true learning. Third, this relatively permanent change in behavior is the result of *past experiences* or practices that have been *reinforced*. Therefore, for our purposes, learning is defined as *any relatively permanent change in behavior that occurs as the result of reinforced experiences*.

### Classical Conditioning

Early learning theorists focused primarily on reflexive behavior. They believed that learned behavior represented a response to a specific stimulus. The classical or S–R approach to learning was characterized by the works of researchers such as Ivan Pavlov[1] and John Watson.[2] In his famous study, Pavlov "conditioned" a dog to respond by salivating (reflexive behavior) to the sound of a bell (stimulus). This was done by causing the dog to associate an unconditioned stimulus (food) with the conditioned (learned) stimulus (bell). The degree of association was measured according to the extent of the dog's salivation. In essence, Pavlov caused the dog to learn, or associate, a specific response with a specific stimulus.

Watson broadened the range of stimulus-response learning situations and popularized behavioristic explanations of why beings behave as they do. In addition to advancing the cause of behaviorism, Watson encouraged those interested in human behavior to deal with that which they could observe (outward behavior) rather than the activities of the mind, conclusions about which could not be scientifically validated. Technically, classical conditioning tended to be concerned with reflexive responses rather than those consciously controlled by the individual. However, as more has been learned about how behaviors are acquired, the distinction between reflexive responses and learned responses has been more difficult to distinguish.

## Operant Conditioning

Whereas classically conditioned responses are elicited from an individual on a seemingly involuntary basis by a stimulus, operant conditioned responses are emitted by the individual in order to influence the environment. In other words, one might say that the behavior (response) precedes the stimulus, which in this case is the desired consequence of the behavior. Advanced by B. F. Skinner,[3] operant conditioning emphasizes that the individual is instrumental in his or her own learning.

Skinner saw the individual as learning behaviors in relation to the immediate environment. The environment is a source of positive and aversive reinforcements that an individual may seek to acquire or avoid. Behaviors, then, can be voluntarily emitted in order to obtain desired consequences from the environment. Figure 1 briefly outlines the differences between classical and operant conditioning.

The operant view of learning has contributed significantly to the application of learning theory in organizational settings. Behaviors are theoretically emitted by employees based upon the rewards (organizational, social, or others) that are desired from the situation. For example, Sandra enters her office (stimulus situation) each morning. She may influence the responses of her co-workers or her boss by varying her behavior in this situation. If Sandra arrives late, her boss may reprimand her. On the other

**Figure 1. Differences between classical conditioning and operant conditioning.**

| Classical Conditioning | Operant Conditioning |
|---|---|
| 1. Responses are elicited *from* a person (reactive). | 1. Responses are emitted *by* a person (proactive). |
| 2. Responses are fixed to a stimulus (no choice). | 2. Responses are variable in type and degree (choice). |
| 3. CS is a stimulus such as a sound, an object, a person. | 3. CS is a situation such as an office, a social setting, a specific *set* of circumstances. |
| 4. Reinforcement is not received by choice. | 4. Person is instrumental in securing reinforcement by "operating" on the environment. |

hand, this may make her more noticed by her co-workers (possibly a desirable consequence). Therefore, Sandra's promptness or tardiness (learned, voluntary behavior) depends upon the consequences she seeks from her environment.

### Principles of Learning

Both classical and operant theories of learning have contributed to our understanding of behavior in organizations. However, before we attempt to apply learning theory in organizational systems, it will be helpful to identify a few underlying principles of learned behavior. Those principles include the conditions which must exist in order for learning to take place, a "law" of reinforcement known as Thorndike's Law of Effect, and reinforcement scheduling.

*Conditions for learning.*   Three conditions must exist in order for learning to take place: (1) arousal and motivation, (2) association, and (3) reinforcement.[4] In order for a behavior to be learned, an individual must be aware that a learning situation exists. Moreover, "in most learning situations, the organism is not merely aroused, it is motivated in some way."[5] Without some awareness that a learning situation exists, an individual may well overlook what is to be learned. For example, an employee may be told that she is to be shown how to operate a piece of equipment. The supervisor turns on the equipment and proceeds to demonstrate the way that it is operated. If the employee is unaware that the machine was first turned on by the supervisor, she will be unable to operate it even though she learns the procedures for doing so. Moreover, if the employee has no motivation to learn how to use the machine, the likelihood that she will acquire the necessary behaviors will also be significantly reduced.

Second, an individual relates learned behaviors in terms of time and place (situation). For example, a salesman learns that a particular sales pitch works best when the buyer shows some reluctance to complete the purchase, and that another approach is more appropriate when the buyer has expressed prior interest in the purchase. A student raises her hand in class when she wishes to speak to the professor. However, the same student encountering the same professor at a local restaurant no doubt would speak directly without first asking permission. Not only do we associate events in learning, but we also associate a given stimulus with the appropriate response. This pairing of events or pairing of a stimulus and a behavior is known as *association*.

Finally, an individual must receive some form of reinforcement for a pairing to be learned. Reinforcement refers to the second stimulus of the pair being presented (classical conditioning) or a reward or punishment achieved as a consequence of a behavior (operant conditioning). In effect, reinforcement strengthens the association that has been formed. Moreover, the more closely the reinforcement follows the association, the more likely it is to be learned.

*Law of effect.*  So important to learning is the concept of reinforcement that virtually all attempts to apply learning theory place special emphasis on it. An appreciation for the significance of reinforcement in learning can be traced back to a proposition known as Thorndike's Law of Effect:[6]

Of several responses made to the same situation, those which are accompanied or closely followed by satisfaction . . . will be more likely to recur; those which are accompanied or closely followed by discomfort . . . will be less likely to occur.

Analyzing the Law of Effect, we find that several responses or behaviors may occur in a given situation. However, not all behaviors will be associated with the situation in the future. Rather, only behaviors that are positively reinforced (rewarded) will be more likely to recur. Conversely, those that are associated with punishment or some other aversive reinforcer will diminish. Although unstated, a careful reading of this proposition suggests that behaviors that are in no way reinforced are *no* more likely to occur in the future. Thus, a supervisor who fails to compliment or otherwise positively reinforce an employee's desirable job-related behaviors should have no reason to believe that those behaviors will be more likely to occur in the future. In fact, without such reinforcement, the behaviors may actually decrease in frequency (extinguish).

*Reinforcement scheduling.*  Reinforcement takes on even greater importance when administered according to some systematic pattern. The 2 × 2 matrix shown in Figure 2 describes important concepts in reinforcement scheduling. The ratio and interval schedules refer to whether a reinforcement is given based upon the occurrence of the behavior or according to a designated time period. Thus, reinforcing an employee for each unit produced would be a ratio reinforcement, while reinforcing an employee every hour on the hour would be an example of reinforcing according to interval. Determination of the type of schedule to be used depends on the job and the immediate work environment. "For example, jobs that can be performed and measured by each piece produced are easily adaptable to ratio schedules. On the other hand, administrative positions may be better suited to interval scheduling." [7]

The terms *fixed* and *variable* schedules refer to the frequency with which reinforcement is administered. A fixed reinforcement is one that is administered on a regular basis. For example, a reinforcement administered every time a behavior occurs (continuous) or every third time a behavior occurs would be given on a fixed schedule. A variable schedule is one that is irregular. The schedule is not predictable, and the reinforcement is administered on a random basis.

The importance of reinforcement scheduling lies in how quickly a be-

**Figure 2. Impacts on behavior of reinforcement scheduling.**

Ratio (event)                                             Interval (time)

**Fixed**

**Fixed ratio:**

High rate of response.
Fairly steady behavior.
Brief pauses after each
   reinforcement.

Example: Piece rate incentive
               systems.

**Fixed interval:**

Low rate of response immediately
   after reinforcement.
Behavior rate increases steadily
   and more rapidly as time for
   reward nears.

Example: Weekly paychecks.

**Variable**

**Variable ratio:**

Stable, vigorous response.
Slow initial learning.
High resistance to extinction.

Examples: Random compliments,
                slot machine.

**Variable interval:**

Stable, vigorous response.
Slow initial learning.
High resistance to extinction.

Example: Irregular periodic
               praise given through-
               out the day.

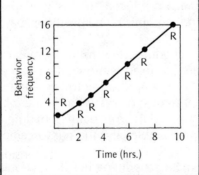

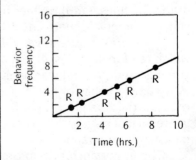

havior is learned, how resistant it is to extinction, and the protracted pattern of the behaviors. For example, a behavior reinforced on a fixed schedule will be learned more rapidly than one reinforced on a variable basis. On the other hand, fixed schedules also may lead to rapid extinction of the behavior if for any reason the rewards are terminated (e.g., the supervisor leaves on vacation). The different combinations of reinforcement shown in Figure 2 may result in highly different learning, performance, and retention patterns.

## Applying Learning Theory in Organizational Environments

Theories of learning have been employed formally in organizations in a form of behavior modification (B Mod) and organizational behavior modification (OB Mod). A more complete and organizationally relevant approach known as Behavioral Contingency Management has been developed and successfully applied in work settings.

### Behavior Modification

B Mod techniques have been used by organizations like General Electric to train supervisors and have been employed on a broader basis by Emery Air Freight, Ford Motor Company, United Airlines, and Chase Manhattan Bank. Successful applications of B Mod also have been reported in smaller organizations, including hospitals and government agencies.[8]

Behavior modification is an outgrowth of operant learning theory. The purpose is to replace undesirable or unwanted behaviors with behaviors that are more acceptable in the situation. Thus, once an unwanted behavior is eliminated, a new productive behavior is learned to fill the void. Organizational behavior modification provides that rewards which are part of the overall organizational reward system (recognition, compensation, special privileges) be systematically withheld or awarded to bring about desired modifications in employee behavior.

### Behavioral Contingency Management

Applied behavioral analysis implies that behaviors be analyzed as to their overt causes and/or consequences. Luthans and Kreitner[9] suggest a series of steps that facilitate such a behavioral analysis and lead to an organizational strategy for bringing about desired changes in performance-related behaviors. The approach, known as behavioral contingency management (BCM), is based primarily on the premise that behavior is a function of its consequences. However, the possibility that certain behaviors are brought about as the result of a stimulus (or cue) is also taken into consideration.

Behavioral contingency management essentially consists of five steps.

*1. Identification of performance-related behavioral events.* Many activities and behaviors occur in the work place. BCM, however, is concerned only with those specific behaviors that contribute to or detract from the accomplishment of an organization's goals. Therefore, it is of critical importance to identify behaviors that are performance-related. Subsequent steps in the BCM process are designed to increase the frequency of such behaviors and/or to decrease the frequency of employee activities that have an unfavorable impact on goal attainment. For example, occasional conversations between employees may not detract from the accomplishment of their work and are of no concern to the supervisor. On the other hand, if conversations interfere with performance of a task, steps should be taken to decrease their frequency and to increase the frequency of task-related behaviors.

*2. Measurement of behavior.* BCM is a data-based technique. Once a performance-related behavior has been isolated, the frequency with which it occurs is recorded and graphed. This initial measurement of the behavior is referred to as a baseline measurement. The data, along with their graphic presentation, may then be used by a manager to determine the extent to which a behavior is occurring and to provide a benchmark for comparing subsequent (post-behavior change) measurements. Comparing baseline to subsequent data may indicate that the initial behavior is either more or less severe than originally thought.

*3. Functional analysis of the behavior.* Understanding the relationship of a behavior to its cause or its consequence is critical to successful behavior change. Behavior occurs under one of two sets of conditions. A behavior may be the result of an antecedent cue (stimulus). For example, the appearance of a fellow employee or a supervisor may elicit a fixed response: stop work and converse, or work more diligently. Other behaviors are contingent upon the anticipated consequence of the behavior. An employee may work slowly if he knows that not finishing his work will require overtime, and he desires the overtime pay. Or, an employee may work diligently if she believes that finishing a distasteful job early will allow her to do a task she would rather be doing. Thus, functional analysis requires the manager to determine whether the performance-related behavior in question is being brought about (or can be brought about) as a result of some antecedent condition, or if the action is tied more closely to the consequences of the behavior.

*4. Developing and implementing an appropriate strategy.* The ultimate purpose of BCM is to bring about, maintain, or increase the frequency of behaviors that will lead directly to the attainment of the organization's goals. The preceding functional analysis of behavior serves as a foundation for developing a specific behavioral strategy. Subsequent behavior change is brought about through the application of operant conditioning principles —specifically, behavior modification. BCM encourages the use of positive reinforcement to accelerate the learning of desirable performance-related behaviors. An employee exhibiting desired behaviors is positively reinforced in order that she or he can clearly see the consequences of the behavior as favorable. In some cases, such reinforcement takes the form of attention or praise. In other cases, special benefits, such as priorities in job selection or work schedules, may be used.

A reinforcement strategy also must consider the timing of rewards and the reinforcement pattern (schedule). As pointed out earlier, the rate of learning and how well the behavior is maintained depend in part on the immediacy of the reward and the selected schedule.

An effective behavior-change strategy does not rely on behavioristic technologies alone. For example, changes in work schedules, work locations, or the composition of work groups may alter both the antecedent cues and the consequences of on-the-job behaviors. BCM merely encourages managers to recognize that work conditions that typically have occupied their attention do have a direct and systematic bearing on subordinate behavior.

*5. Measuring the impact of BCM.* The purpose of BCM is to encourage behaviors that will lead directly to improved performance. Initially, changes may be measured on the basis of the frequency of the desired behaviors by comparing post-intervention performance against pre-intervention baseline measures. Failure to produce desired changes may be followed by re-analysis of functional relationships and a redesign of the intervention strategy.

## Summary

Theories of learning are concerned with the manner in which overt behaviors are acquired or changed. Classical theory focuses on stimulus–response relationships. Operant theory, on the other hand, examines learning based upon the consequences of behavior. In order for learning to take place, a behavior must be reinforced. The timing and pattern of the reinforcement (reinforcement schedule), along with its appropriateness for the individual, influence the rate, strength, and retention (resistance to extinction) of the learning.

Applications of learning theory in organizational systems have been made in the form of behavior modification and organizational behavior modification. A comprehensive approach to changing behavior in organizations is known as behavioral contingency management. BCM combines classical and operant principles with organizational systems analysis to provide managers with specific tools for affecting performance-related behaviors.

## References

1. Ivan P. Pavlov, *Conditional Reflexes,* translated by G. V. Anrep (London: Oxford University Press, 1927).
2. John B. Watson, "Psychology as the Behaviorist Views It," *Psychological Review,* vol. 20, 1913, 158–177.
3. B. F. Skinner, *Contingencies of Reinforcement* (New York: Appleton-Century Crofts, 1969).
4. Clifford T. Morgan and Richard A. King, *Introduction to Psychology,* 4th ed. (New York· McGraw-Hill Book Co., 1971).
5. Ibid., p· 65.
6. Edward L. Thorndike, *Educational Psychology: The Psychology of Learning,* vol. II (New York: Columbia University Teachers College, 1913.)
7. Fred Luthans and Donald D. White, "Behavioral Modification: Application to Manpower Management," *Personnel Administration,* vol. 34, July–August 1971, p. 43.
8. Fred Luthans and Robert Kreitner, *Organizational Behavior Modification* (Glenview, Ill.: Scott, Foresman, 1975), pp. 150–173; Donald D. White and Bill Davis, "Behavioral Contingency Management: A Bottom-Line Alternative for Management Development," *The Personnel Administration,* April 1980.
9. Luthans and Kreitner, op. cit., pp. 68–83.

## Recommended Readings

Readings marked with an asterisk are included in *Contemporary Perspectives in Organizational Behavior,* edited by Donald D. White (Boston: Allyn and Bacon, 1982).

Owen Aldis, "Of Pigeons and Men," *Harvard Business Review,* vol. 39, no. 4, 1961, pp. 59–63.
*Harold W. Babb and David G. Kopp, "Applications of Behavior Modification in Organizations: A Review and Critique," *The Academy of Management Review,* vol. 3, no. 2, April 1978, pp. 281–292.
Fred Luthans and Tim R. V. Davis, "Behavioral Self-Management: The Missing Link in Management Effectiveness," *Organizational Dynamics,* vol. 8, Summer 1979, pp. 52–60.
Fred Luthans and Donald D. White, "Behavioral Modification: Application to Manpower Management," *Personnel Administration,* July–August 1971, pp. 41–47.
*Henry P. Sims and Charles C. Manz, "Self-Management as a Substitute for Leadership: A Social Learning Perspective," *Academy of Management Review,* vol. 5, no. 3, July 1980.
*Donald D. White and Bill Davis, "BCM: A Bottom-Line Alternative for Management Development," *The Personnel Administrator,* April 1980.

# CASE 5
# The Sociable Salesman

Barry Stone worked as a salesman in the Menswear Department of Holt's Department Store. He obtained a degree in retail management from a small state college and immediately took a job with Holt's. He had been with the store about one year.

Barry was raised as one of two children in an upper-middle-class home. He had always been a bright student in school and graduated in the upper ten percent of his class. Barry had purposely chosen to attend a small college. While there, he was well liked by many members of the student body. His popularity and interactions with his fellow students were enhanced by the fact that he was actively involved in many clubs and organizations. He was vice president of his fraternity and a three-year member of the student government association. During his senior year he actively campaigned for and was elected president of the student body. He also was voted "Big Man On Campus" that same year. Barry was a member of the debate team. He attended college on a full football scholarship and was an all-conference tailback.

Holt's was a one-level department store containing 44,000 square feet of floor space, located in the downtown area. The store was organized into four main selling departments, including Menswear, Ladies' Wear, Cosmetics, and Shoes and Accessories. In addition, there were two sub-departments, Young Men's Wear and Young Ladies' Wear (see Exhibit 1). All working departments operated within designated sections of a single, primarily open, area. All employees regularly worked in a particular department. Interdepartment transfer of personnel was sometimes necessary during periods of worker shortages and increased demand. Once on the sales floor, employees were not permitted to leave their assigned departments except on official business or when traveling to and from the time clock area for lunch and scheduled breaks. Each major department operated under the direction of a department manager who also performed the usual everyday functions of all other salespeople.

The store itself was owned and managed by Stuart Rosen. Mr. Rosen maintained an office within the store but generally was not involved in the day-to-day activities of salespeople. He left direct supervision of the salesforce to the department managers and concentrated his own efforts on the overall operation of the store. Rosen was a well-educated man, respected by employees for his fairness and knowledge of the retail business.

Barry was pleasant and sociable on the job. He enjoyed conversing with customers and other employees in the store. His confident, outgoing behavior seemed to draw respect and admiration from his co-workers. This was reflected in his sales, which, on average, were the highest in the department. He had

Prepared by Steven G. Moon and Donald D. White, University of Arkansas.

consistently turned in high daily sales totals, and his value to the store had never been disputed. Lately, however, Barry's sales had been slowly dropping and had become more erratic.

Joe Pennington, Barry's department manager and close friend, noticed the decrease in Barry's sales. As he observed Barry more closely, he also began to recognize certain patterns in his workday behaviors. For example, when Barry came to work in the mornings or returned from his lunch hour, he would "punch in" on the time clock. For several minutes thereafter, he would stand around in the storage room, hall, or office area and joke with the office or maintenance personnel before actually starting work. Often he would find unimportant things to do in the office before going to his department. After observing Barry's regular delays in getting to the sales area, Joe called Barry aside and explained, "Barry, I know you enjoy visiting with the other workers, but in the future, please see that you come directly to the sales area. You know, Christmas is almost here and we need all available personnel on the floor. We need you every minute out there to sell and restock, and we have to keep an eye out for shoplifters! You can't do that from the office or back room." Barry replied, "All right Joe, I'll be on time tomorrow. I just wanted to keep you guys on the floor busy." Barry and Joe then headed back to the salesfloor talking about the basketball game the two had gone to that weekend. Barry reported to work on time the next day and continued to be prompt for almost a week, when he resumed his pattern of procrastination.

As time passed, Barry's backroom conversations attracted a greater number of workers. Delays in personnel getting to their respective departments were evidenced in temporary manpower shortages. Joe Pennington began to hear a growing number of customer complaints most of which reflected the feeling that, "You can never find a salesman when you need one." And several salespeople who had good sales records in the past were submitting lower daily sales, negatively influencing the total sales of the department.

Once again, Joe decided to speak to Barry. Barry, however, seemed undaunted by Joe's friendly reminder. Not only did he not return to the sales floor, but instead he struck up a new conversation with Joe himself. Barry's "sociable" behavior continued even though Joe spoke with him on several different occasions. It seemed that Joe's warnings only affected Barry's behavior temporarily, if at all, and they had no lasting impact. Moreover, prolonged conversations began occurring between Barry and other employees during afternoon breaks. Each worker was allowed one daily break lasting fifteen minutes. Every fifteen minutes in succession one worker would leave as another returned. Employees traveling to and from their work areas during the scheduled breaks would stop and talk as they met outside their departments or around the break room. These sometimes prolonged encounters caused delays in getting back to the salesfloor and thus resulted in worker shortages and increased idle time.

Stuart Rosen's office was located off a hallway adjacent to the employee breakroom. He would occasionally and unexpectedly leave the office while Barry and the other employees were talking. Upon seeing Rosen, the workers

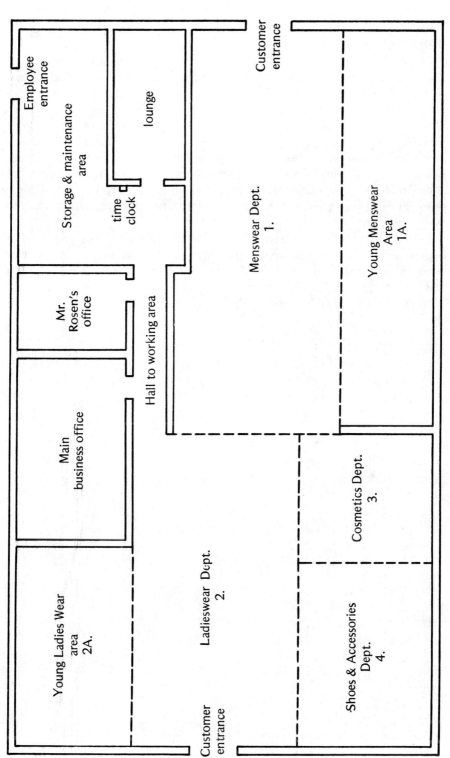

**Exhibit 1. Holt's Department Store plan.**

usually went directly to their departments before he had a chance to detect their loitering. Barry was no exception.

One Friday, Rosen called Barry into his office. "I just wanted you to know, Barry, that we appreciate your fine work around here. Starting today you will receive an increase of ten percent in salary." Barry was elated with Mr. Rosen's praise and the salary increase. "I'm glad you are pleased with my work, sir," Barry said, "and I'll try even harder in the future." "Oh, by the way," exclaimed Rosen, "I'm going to need an extra hand here at the store the next two Saturdays. We need to run a partial inventory. Can you help us out?" Barry gladly accepted Rosen's request. He arrived early both Saturdays. In addition, Barry was punctual the next two weeks and turned in his highest sales totals in two months. Thereafter, Barry's backroom loitering slowly resumed and production again began to slip off.

Joe observed Barry's dawdling, its effect on the efficiency of the various departments and consequently on the store as a whole. With understandable concern, he decided to meet with Barry again to further discuss the problem and any disciplinary action he might have to take. "Perhaps," he thought, "I'm going to have to stop being so friendly with Barry myself."

# CASE 6
## But He's a Damned Good Sports Writer!

Mark Arnold was twenty-four years old and a senior at a small western university. Mark had spent three years in the Marine Corps before deciding to return to the university to obtain a degree in journalism. Although able to finance a good deal of his education through the GI bill, he decided that he could gain valuable experience and pick up a few extra dollars by applying for a job with a community newspaper. The newspaper, the *Evansville Chronicle*, had a distribution of 12,000. Although the paper had been in existence for about eight years, it had only recently tried to compete seriously with other papers in surrounding communities.

Fortunately for Mark, a position as a sports editor opened up at the *Chronicle* shortly before he decided to apply for a job there. The position was particularly attractive to Mark, and he believed his educational background together with some sports reporting he had done for *Stars and Stripes* while in the Marine Corps would give him an edge on other applicants. Mark applied for the job and shortly thereafter received word that he had been selected as the new sports editor for the *Chronicle*.

Mark's first few months on the job were satisfying to him and his employer. Mark felt that he had at last found the type of work that he enjoyed doing. The managing editor rated his work as excellent and gave him a substantial raise after his first six months on the job.

Mark had only minor difficulties learning the ins and outs of the *Chronicle*. The newspaper was run rather loosely, but most of the employees were determined that it would one day be the leading newspaper in the region. However, one employee, Dan Richards, did not seem to demonstrate the same kind of eagerness as many of the other workers at the *Chronicle*. Dan was a reporter in the sports department. Dan was twenty-one and a university student. He had been with the paper for five years and had been a sportswriter for the last three.

Mark and Dan had had an occasional class together while at the university. It was not until Mark took the job with the *Chronicle*, however, that he got to know Dan personally. Mark liked Dan and the two often sat in Mark's office discussing everything from sports events of the day to their futures when they left the university. It was in one of these discussions that Mark found out that Dan had applied for the job of sports editor. The following conversation took place:

*Mark:* I really think this newspaper has a lot of potential. You know, I'd seriously consider staying around after I graduated.

Prepared by Donald D. White, University of Arkansas.

*Dan:* I don't know. I really like being a sportswriter but I'm just not sure that I want to stay around Evansville. You know, I've lived here most of my life.

*Mark:* I know what you mean. If you left, you might have a good opportunity to get a job as a sportswriter at a larger newspaper or maybe even become an editor with another newspaper like the *Chronicle.*

*Dan:* I wouldn't want a job as an editor. At one time, I thought I would. That's why I applied for the job here; but I'm glad I didn't get it, now. Sometimes I'm not even sure that I want to be a sportswriter.

Mark was surprised to hear that Dan had applied for the job as editor. He told Dan that he thought that he was the best sportswriter the *Chronicle* had and that his future surely would be in the newspaper business. Dan said he still wasn't sure, and the conversation ended.

Mark had not been deceiving Dan when he told him that he believed Dan was a good sportswriter. In fact, Mark knew Dan had the talent to become one of the best. In addition, he always showed a great deal of pride in his work. Normally, Dan spent his day writing headlines and picture captions, laying out pages, and answering the phone. He seemed to like the work and particularly looked forward to assignments where he was asked to cover certain sporting events in the area and write feature articles about them. Mark recognized this and occasionally would tell Dan that he appreciated the quality of his work.

Unfortunately, some of Dan's working habits were not as good as the articles he wrote. It was not unusual for Dan to come in late in the morning, especially when he had been assigned a feature article for the day's edition.

For no apparent reason, Dan began coming to work late more and more often. Once he arrived, he did his job as always. However, his tardiness began to wear on Mark. Others in the office asked Mark why Dan could come in late when they were required to be there at 8:00 in the morning. Mark sensed that the other workers thought Dan was receiving special privileges because of his friendship with Mark.

During the next three weeks, Mark made it a point to talk to Dan about arriving to work late. He mentioned the tardiness to Dan on numerous occasions, but Dan continued to come into work late. It was the spring of the year and many of the sporting events in Evansville as well as those at the university required special coverage. Dan had been given these assignments and, as usual, had done an excellent job. However, his feature stories had been turned in late and on as many as four occasions in the last two weeks had caused delays in publication of the newspaper.

Finally, Mark took the problem to the managing editor, George Fairview. He explained the situation, "Mr. Fairview, I just don't know what to do about Dan. If I didn't think we needed him, I'd fire him in a minute. I've tried to talk to him, but he just won't change his ways."

Mr. Fairview listened closely. He told Mark that Dan had been with the paper for a number of years and he felt that he made a valuable contribution to it. He said that he would have a talk with Dan and that he was sure that everything would be straightened out. For the next two weeks, Dan arrived at work on time and continued to do good work. However, the next Monday Dan showed up for work two hours late with a feature article on the weekend's state track finals which had been held in Evansville. Mark said nothing about Dan's coming in late. He took the article from him, looked it over hurriedly, and sent it to the typesetters. He knew that Dan's late arrival would cause a publication delay for the entire newspaper. Before leaving work that evening, he made it a point to compliment Dan on his work. Then, once again, he asked Dan to try to make it in on time the next morning.

During the next three weeks, Dan arrived late with feature articles seven times. Mark again went to Mr. Fairview with the problem. This time, however, Mr. Fairview took a different approach to the problem.

*Mr. Fairview:* Arnold, the sports department is your problem. Dan Richards is a sportswriter, and you're responsible to see that he gets his articles in on time.
*Mark:* Mr. Fairview, this thing has just gone too far. I think we should fire him.
*Mr. Fairview:* But he's a damned fine sportswriter! And besides, he's been around here a long time. Now, these delays are costing the newspaper a lot of money—sometimes as much as $150 a day. You get the matter straightened out the best way you know how. But let's see if you can do it and keep him on the staff as well. Good writers are just too hard to find.

Later in the day, Mark overheard two of the copy boys angrily discussing Dan. He became concerned when he heard his own name mentioned in the conversation. He interrupted the two and asked them what was the problem.

Mark listened carefully. He was surprised by what he heard. Apparently, Dan had left early, but not before telling the two workers that he had just received a raise in salary. Mark went to his office and called Mr. Fairview. He asked about the rumor and was shocked by the managing editor's reply:

I got to thinking about this thing this morning, Arnold, so I called Dan in. After hearing what he had to say, I decided that he just needs a little bit of incentive. He indicated to me that he was planning on taking a job over in Preston because it offered a better salary. I told him that we would match whatever they said they'd pay him. It wasn't much. But I think his performance will improve now.

Mark wasn't satisfied that Mr. Fairview had found the solution. He had known about the job at Preston, but had heard that it already had been filled the previous week. He now had a serious problem on his hands, and it appeared that he was not going to get the necessary help from Mr. Fairview.

That evening, Mark thought back over some of the discussions he had had with one of his professors at the university. When Mark first took the job of sports editor at the *Chronicle,* he decided that he would take a few courses in administration at the university. The subject of one of these courses, "Human Relations in Business," he had found to be quite intriguing.

*Mark:* I thought we were always supposed to find the underlying cause to a problem.

*Professor Howley:* Remember, Mark, I told you that we try to find the cause, but sometimes we just have to work with the behavior as we see it.

*Mark:* Oh, I remember. Work with the symptoms, not the cause.

*Professor Howley:* That's right. Now, what does Dan like about his job? By that, I mean what rewards does he get out of his work?

*Mark:* Well, he has a great deal of pride in the feature articles he writes. I know that he keeps a scrapbook of those articles and whenever he has got something in the sports section, he always grabs the first newspaper he can get his hands on to see what it looks like.

*Professor Howley:* Do you ever compliment him on his work?

*Mark:* Sure! I compliment just about everybody when they do a job. I've tried not to hold this thing about Dan coming in late against him. In fact, the last time he turned in an article late I told him he really did a fine job on it, thinking that that might cause him to think a little bit more about getting them in on time in the future. You know, I was trying to feed his recognition need.

*Professor Howley:* Well, Mark you were awake for part of that lecture, but I'm afraid you missed another very important part of it. What were you reinforcing when you told Dan that he did a good job on the article? If you really want to change his behavior, you're going to have to systematically eliminate that which you don't want and replace it with the kind of behavior you do want. Use some of those principles from learning theory that we talked about in class. I bet Dan's behavior can be turned around inside of three weeks.

# CASE 7
# What's the Problem?

Dale Colson, assistant administrator at Jackson Regional Medical Center, had just finished a two-hour interview with Bonnie, head of the Center's Dietary Department. Problem identification sessions with department heads had become a common occurrence throughout the hospital since the newest administrator, Mrs. Bibbins, had taken over. Bonnie discussed difficulties with Dale such as absenteeism, employees failing to do their work properly, and supervisors that failed to follow her instructions. It seemed to Dale that the answer to these and other situations were related to some of the concepts he had learned in an organizational behavior class he recently had completed at Northeastern State University. However, his lack of practical experience in actually applying the concepts suggested a need for outside help.

He called Carl, who worked at Northeastern State University and set up a meeting for the following afternoon between himself, Carl, and Bonnie. Dale's concern was understandable. He had been the acting administrator when Mrs. Bibbins was hired. During the transition period of eight months, he had become thoroughly acquainted with the operation of Dietary, its goals and its objectives. Moreover, Dale also felt Bonnie, unlike some department heads, would be receptive to help from outside the hospital. A followup meeting with Bonnie was scheduled for the following week.

## Jackson Regional Medical Center (JRMC)

JRMC was a 240-bed hospital in the northeastern corner of a sparsely populated southern state. It employed approximately 500 persons. The hospital had only recently been expanded to its present size. JRMC was the primary health care facility in an area serving approximately 175,000 people. Although somewhat industrialized, the area was primarily a retirement and university community. JRMC had had four administrators in the past eight years. The present administrator, Mrs. Bibbins, had been with JRMC for one year. She had established her credibility with the hospital; however, an aura of uncertainty about the future continued to prevail over the hospital.

### Dietary Department

The Dietary Department had forty-two full-time employees, of which five were supervisory. Two shifts were responsible for serving three meals. The shifts overlapped one another by one hour from 4:00 a.m. to 9:00 p.m. Bonnie

Prepared by Donald R. Latham, University of Mississippi; Daniel S. Cochran, Mississippi State University; and Donald D. White, University of Arkansas.

had been with JRMC for one year in her present position. Lola, her assistant, had been with JRMC for approximately sixteen months (see Exhibit 1 for other employment dates). The organization chart (Figure 2), developed by Bonnie and Lola, represents their perception of the formal relationships within the department. Salaries of the employees ranged from $3.40 to $3.80 per hour. Supervisors earned from $4.00 to $5.00 per hour. Although Bonnie's primary job duties were managerial, approximately fifty percent of her time was spent on operational duties such as inspection of the workplace and employee counseling.

Bonnie's concerns covered a wide range of areas. Turnover in the Dietary Department had been one major source of aggravation. During Dale's and Carl's first meeting with Bonnie she stated, "If a new employee misses one or

**Exhibit 1. Absenteeism tally sheet.**

January 1977

| Name | Date | Job Title | Supervisor | Date of Employment |
|------|------|-----------|------------|--------------------|
| Johnson | 2 Jan | Tray Aide | Jones | Dec 1976 |
| Watts | 3 Jan | Tray Aide | Jones | Dec 1976 |
| Lathum | 5 Jan | Kitchen Helper | Jones | Nov 1976 |
| Cockrell | 7 Jan | Tray Aide | Jones | Nov 1976 |
| Moore | 7 Jan | Cook | George | Jan 1975 |
| Johnson | 10 Jan | Tray Aide | Jones | Dec 1976 |
| Winston | 12 Jan | Kitchen Helper | Waters | Feb 1976 |
| Lathum | 12 Jan | Kitchen Helper | Jones | Nov 1976 |
| McGregor | 17 Jan | Tray Aide | Jones | Jan 1977 |
| | 18 Jan | Tray Aide | Jones | Jan 1977 |
| Watts | 25 Jan | Tray Aide | Jones | Dec 1976 |
| Lawrence | 30 Jan | Diet Clerk | Cochran | Dec 1975 |

February 1977

| Name | Date | Job Title | Supervisor | Date of Employment |
|------|------|-----------|------------|--------------------|
| Watts | 4 Feb | Tray Aide | Jones | Dec 1976 |
| Johnson | 6 Feb | Tray Aide | Jones | Dec 1976 |
| Potter | 7 Feb | Cook | Conners | June 1974 |
| McGregor | 14 Feb | Tray Aide | Jones | Jan 1977 |
| | 15 Feb | Tray Aide | Jones | Jan 1977 |
| Jockel | 20 Feb | Baker | George | Feb 1974 |
| Danley | 24 Feb | Kitchen Helper | Jones | Jan 1977 |
| | 25 Feb | Kitchen Helper | Jones | Jan 1977 |
| Johnson | 25 Feb | Tray Aide | Jones | Dec 1976 |
| Watts | 26 Feb | Tray Aide | Jones | Dec 1976 |
| Winston | 27 Feb | Kitchen Helper | Waters | Feb 1976 |

**Exhibit 1.** *Continued*

March 1977

| Name | Date | Job Title | Supervisor | Date of Employment |
|------|------|-----------|------------|---------------------|
| Danley | 3 Mar | Kitchen Helper | Jones | Jan 1977 |
| Williams | 4 Mar | Kitchen Helper | Jones | Feb 1977 |
| Hay | 6 Mar | Cook | Conners | July 1975 |
| Blancas | 7 Mar | Tray Aide | Jones | Feb 1977 |
| | 8 Mar | Tray Aide | Jones | Feb 1977 |
| Williams | 11 Mar | Kitchen Helper | Jones | Feb 1977 |
| Danley | 14 Mar | Kitchen Helper | Jones | Jan 1977 |
| Montgomery | 21 Mar | Diet Clerk | Cochran | Aug 1973 |
| Blancas | 22 Mar | Tray Aide | Jones | Feb 1977 |
| Winston | 23 Mar | Kitchen Helper | Waters | Feb 1976 |
| Danley | 24 Mar | Kitchen Helper | Jones | Jan 1977 |
| Wooster | 28 Mar | Tray Aide | Waters | Oct 1976 |

two days in his or her first two weeks on the job, they generally don't last too long."

Bonnie also stated, "My supervisors often fail to follow my instructions. It usually takes a couple of reminders to get them to do what I ask." She related several instances where specific instructions were given and not followed until a second or third reminder was used. She felt this problem probably was not as serious as the previous problem. However, it was a source of concern for her.

Employees of the Dietary Department typically were students or housewives who worked to supplement family income. Prior to going to work at JRMC, some had been unemployed due to economic conditions or industrial automation of unskilled work they had performed. They usually had little or no experience in working in a dietary department and adjustment to supervision was sometimes difficult.

Supervisors tended to be the product of tenure and experience rather than formal education. Job criticisms were usually made in the work environment rather than in private counseling sessions.

Bonnie questioned Carl and Dale about the role of personalities in organizational conflict. For instance, she was concerned about having a forty-five-year-old housewife working at the same level as a twenty-year-old university student.

Cleaning problems also were discussed in the initial interview. Bonnie's stated criteria for clean was, "no odor, streaks, stains, nor any unsanitary conditions that are detectable to the eye." See Exhibit 2 for those primarily involved in cleaning activities.

In the meeting it was concluded that Bonnie should observe and quantify

**Exhibit 2. Organization chart.**

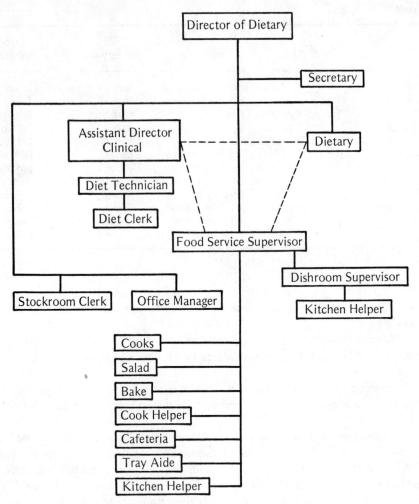

the behaviors she believed were related to the cleaning problem. Carl suggested a tally sheet to provide hard data on what was actually transpiring. The tally sheet would contain such information as where the employee was observed, the cleaning activity, and whether the performance was acceptable or unacceptable. Observations were to be made for a period of four weeks. The results are shown in Tally Sheet 1.

Bonnie also asked to observe and quantify her problem of supervisors not following instructions. The trial period of four weeks again was agreed upon. The chart she was to generate would include such information as subject observed, specific instructions, if the instructions were oral or written, and the performance of the sampled individual. The results are shown in Tally Sheet 2.

Finally, Bonnie was asked to quantify the absentee problem by person,

**Talley Sheet 1. Cleaning problem.**

| Days of Week/ Subject | | Week #1 | Week #2 | Week #3 | Week #4 |
|---|---|---|---|---|---|
| Employee A | M | + F | + A | + C | − B |
| | T | + F | + A | + C | + A |
| | W | + F | + A | + B | + A |
| | T | + A | + A | + D | + C |
| | F | − C | + A | + F | + B |
| Employee B | M | + B | + C | + A | − F |
| | T | + E | + A | + B | + A |
| | W | + E | + B | + C | + E |
| | T | + E | + B | + F | + B |
| | F | − C | + A | + F | + A |
| Employee C | M | + C | + B | + F | + C |
| | T | + C | + C | + F | + B |
| | W | + C | + C | + C | + B |
| | T | + C | + E | + B | + C |
| | F | − C | + F | − B | + B |
| Employee D | M | + D | + F | + E | + D |
| | T | + E | + C | + D | + A |
| | W | + D | + C | + D | + D |
| | T | + E | + E | + D | + C |
| | F | + F | − D | + D | + B |
| Employee E | M | + F | + D | − D | − C |
| | T | + F | + D | + D | + B |
| | W | + C | + D | + D | + D |
| | T | + E | + D | + D | + A |
| | F | + B | + E | + C | + D |

*A—Clean trays.*
*B—Clean wheel carts.*
*C—Clean work area.*
*D—Clean counter top.*
*E—Clean appliances.*
*F—Clean stock room.*
*+ acceptable*
*− unacceptable*
*Returns from cleaning inspections based on acceptable/unacceptable and type of work per-formed.*

date, job title, supervisor, and date of employment. Her findings are shown in Exhibit 1.

A second meeting was arranged with Bonnie, Dale, and Carl to review the findings following the four-week trial period. During this second meeting Bonnie continually asked, "What's the problem?"

**Talley Sheet 2. Following instructions.**

| Subject/Days of week | | Week #1 | Week #2 | Week #3 | Week #4 |
|---|---|---|---|---|---|
| Subject A | M | 1-W–Check menu | 2-W–Asked for report | 3-O–Asked for report | 2-W–Check menu |
| | T | 4-O–Check menu | 2-W–Asked for report | 3-O–Check menu | 2-O–Supplies |
| | W | 2-O–Set up luncheon | 2-W–Check menu | 3-O–Inventory | 2-W–Requisition |
| | T | 5-O–Check menu | 2-W–Check menu | 3-O–Requisition | 3-O–Cleaning |
| | F | 2-W–Brief employees | 3-O–Set up luncheon | 2-W–Brief employees | 1-W–Cleaning |
| Subject B | M | 1-W–Employee orient. | 1-O–Requisition | 1-W–Set up luncheon | 2-W–Check schedule |
| | T | 1-W–Inventory | 1-O–Requisition | 1-W–Set up luncheon | 2-O–Check schedule |
| | W | 1-W–Inventory | 1-O–Requisition | 1-W–Employee counsel | 1-O–Menu change |
| | T | 2-W–Inventory | 1-W–Set up luncheon | 1-O–Brief employee | 1-O–Menu change |
| | F | 2-W–Inventory | 1-O–Cleaning | 1-W–Employee orient. | 2-O–Check prices |
| Subject C | M | 4-O–Employee orient. | 5-O–Check menu | 4-O–Supplies | 5-O–Supplies |
| | T | 4-O–Check menu | 4-O–Check menu | 3-O–Check menu | 4-O–Supplies |
| | W | 3-O–Employee orient. | 5-O–Check menu | 5-O–Employee orient. | 4-O–Employee orient. |
| | T | 2-W–Check menu | 3-O–Check menu | 5-W–Employee orient. | 4-O–Employee orient. |
| | F | 3-O–Employee orient. | 4-O–Check menu | 3-O–Supplies | 4-O–Employee orient. |
| Subject D | M | 2-W–Inventory | 1-W–Requisition | 5-O–Employee briefing | 3-O–Service pricing |
| | T | 2-W–Inventory | 2-W–Requisition | 3-O–Employee briefing | 3-O–Service pricing |
| | W | 2-W–Inventory | 2-W–Requisition | 1-W–Employee briefing | 4-O–Service pricing |
| | T | 2-W–Inventory | 2-W–Requisition | 1-W–Employee orient. | 2-W–Employee orient. |
| | F | 3-W–Inventory | 2-W–Requisition | 1-W–Employee counsel | 2-W–Inventory |
| Subject E | M | 4-O–Inventory | 3-O–Check menu | 3-O–Attend meeting | 2-W–Requisition |
| | T | 1-W–Inventory | 2-W–Check menu | 3-O–Cleaning | 2-W–Requisition |
| | W | 2-W–Set up luncheon | 1-W–Set up luncheon | 3-O–Cleaning | 2-W–Requisition |
| | T | 1-W–Counsel employee | 1-W–Employee orient. | 3-O–Inventory | 2-W–Check menu |
| | F | 2-W–Employee orient. | 1-W–Attend meeting | 1-W–Inventory | 3-O–Change menu |

O = Oral Instructions
W = Written Instructions

1—Did Excellent Job
2—Did Average Job
3—Did Poor Job
4—Partially Did Job
5—Did Not Do Job

# EXPERIENTIAL EXERCISE 3
## Behavioral Analysis: "From A to C"

Organizational goals can only be met when individual behaviors that lead to the attainment of those goals are practiced regularly. As you have learned, behaviors are related to either antecedent cues or specific consequences. That is, a stimulus may cause a behavior to take place, or a behavior may come about in order to achieve some specific consequence or to keep that consequence from happening. If we are to understand why behaviors occur, we must first understand their relationship to these cues and consequences. The purpose of this exercise is to help you identify the relationship of behaviors to antecedent cues and/or behavioral consequences.

*Instructions*

*Part I:* Identify three important performance-related behaviors in your present class. Behaviors are considered to be performance-related only if they contribute directly to the grade you receive in your class.

1. Discuss why these behaviors were selected.
2. These behaviors were identified by you as being important. Does that mean that they are practiced regularly? Why or why not?
3. What consequences do these behaviors have for your organizational unit (this class)?

*Part II:* As we have said, the frequency of these behaviors is related to either antecedent cues and/or consequences of the behaviors.

1. Analyze each behavior as to the reason for its occurrence.
2. In what way could you increase (or decrease) the frequency of these behaviors for (a) yourself, or (b) others?
3. Based upon your understanding of the A → B → C behavioral model, discuss why you and your fellow students either practice or fail to practice those behaviors that will lead to successful class performance.

*Part III:* Formulate a specific strategy for bringing about or maintaining "performance-related behaviors" in your class. Base your approach on the five Behavioral Contingency Management steps described in this chapter. Discuss your intervention strategy with classmates.

Prepared by Donald D. White, University of Arkansas.

# CHAPTER THREE

# The Motivation To Work

Perhaps no question has plagued managers more in recent years than "How can I motivate my people?" Answers ranging from coercion to economic rewards to psychological needs satisfaction have been offered. Yet increasing absenteeism, declining productivity, and a general lack of enthusiasm on the part of employees continue to dominate many work organizations today. Moreover, managers often find that their own jobs lack whatever is needed to sustain their interest and commitment to the enterprise.

Various ideas have been advanced concerning motivation in recent years. The face validity of these theories can be assessed by examining certain real-life situations in organizational systems. Chapter Three presents illustrations in which motivation plays a particularly significant role in the behaviors of organizational members.

## Need Theories of Motivation

There appears to be no single cause of motivation. Yet factors are believed to exist that influence an individual's desire to perform work or to behave in different ways. Many authorities agree that motivation is linked to need satisfaction. This understanding of the concept of motivation is tied closely to a phenomenon known as the need–drive–goal cycle. Motivation is seen as the interrelationship of felt needs (deficiencies) within the individual that arouse behaviors directed by a specific need toward a goal. Achievement of the goal will temporarily satisfy the deficiency, thus causing the behavior to subside until that need or some other need is aroused. (See Figure 1.) The process in its entirety provides a simple, although not comprehensive, explanation of motivation.

The need–drive–goal cycle helps us understand the relationship of motivation to behavior and indirectly to job performance. However, the question of what needs people have and how those needs are related to day-to-day activity still exists.

Abraham Maslow[1] suggested that human needs may be classified

**Figure 1.  Need–drive–goal cycle.**

according to relatively predictable patterns. His need hierarchy has served as the basis for much of the early literature about motivation in organizational settings. Maslow identified five basic needs, or motives, thought to be held by all persons. He concluded that these five needs were arranged in a distinct order of predominance. Any of the five needs could motivate an individual, but lower needs would have to be largely satisfied before higher needs could become important sources of motivation.

Frederick Herzberg[2] added another dimension to motivation theory by classifying factors related to need satisfaction as satisfiers (motivators) and dissatisfiers (hygienes). In his "Two-Factor Theory of Motivation," Herzberg claimed that the use of hygiene factors such as working conditions, pay, and technical supervision could prevent dissatisfaction but not actually motivate an employee. On the other hand, he concluded that motivation was related more closely to such factors as achievement, recognition, work itself, responsibility, and opportunities for advancement. In a sense, Herzberg's model reasserts the distinction between higher order needs (motivators) and lower order needs (hygienes). His contribution is in the suggestion that only the higher order needs can serve as motivators and that lower needs alone cannot contribute to long-run gains in employee productivity.

Herzberg's findings lead us to a conclusion shared by most motivation researchers. Traditional methods of motivating employees in work organizations—such as security, improved working conditions, pay, and more competent supervision—do not bring about sustained increases in productivity.

Both Maslow's and Herzberg's motivation theories have drawn criticism.[3] Methodological questions, along with conflicting findings, have led many to question the extent to which either model can be applied in organizations. Need theorists, therefore, have concentrated their efforts on the study of specific needs and how those needs influence behavior in the work place.

Many motives are believed to underlie behavior. Their number is too great to elaborate on each. However, three motives are generally agreed to

**Figure 2. Maslow's need hierarchy.**

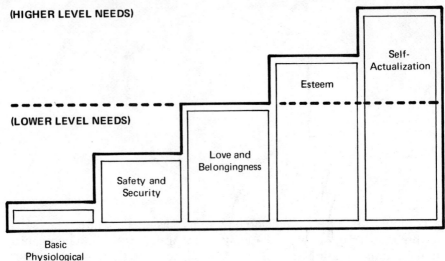

(HIGHER LEVEL NEEDS)

(LOWER LEVEL NEEDS)

Self-Actualization

Esteem

Love and Belongingness

Safety and Security

Basic Physiological

be important in work organizations. They affect the behavior of managers and nonmanagers alike. These motives include the need for affiliation, the need for power, and the need for achievement.

*Affiliation.* The need for affiliation (*n aff*) refers to a person's need for friendly relationships, group acceptance, and being liked by others. Maintaining positive interpersonal relationships within an organization is an important function. Studies have found that managers who were high in the affiliative motive spent more time communicating than did others[4] and were most likely to be found in jobs where maintaining relationships was more important than making decisions.[5]

While promoting and maintaining positive relationships may be an important task of a manager, it is not the sole function. McClelland[6] has suggested that managers who possess high levels of *n aff* may be ineffective in accomplishing organizational goals due to their strong desire to preserve harmony. Nonetheless, managers and non-managers possess varying degrees of *n aff*. Correctly identifying the level of affiliation present in organizational members can help place them in appropriate job positions.

*Achievement.* The need to achieve (*n ach*) is known to be an important managerial need. Central to this is the individual's concentration on goal attainment. Correspondingly, popular management systems, like management by objectives, focus on performance outcomes. Persons who possess a high need to achieve tend to outperform their peers as students and as business people.[7]

Managers high in *n ach* characteristically like to accomplish goals. Equally important to them is the control they have over the goal-setting process. High *n ach* individuals carefully calculate their goals. Goals are set at levels which maximize the sense of achievement rather than the quantity or quality achieved. High achievers set goals that are challenging but attainable. The concern of these individuals is for the achievement itself, and not the reward (pay, promotion) resulting from the achievement. A second important characteristic of the high achiever is that she or he requires immediate, concrete feedback on progress toward goal attainment. Only through feedback of this type can individual performers gauge their accomplishment. Finally, persons possessing high *n ach* are more likely to choose tasks for which they are solely responsible rather than those which require the participation of others.

The implications of *n ach* for organizational behavior are clear. The effectiveness of an organization is partly measured in terms of its ability to achieve its objectives. Persons who are able to align their own personal goals with the goals of the enterprise, and who in turn possess a high need to achieve, can make significant contributions to an organization. Placement of high *n ach* individuals in positions over which they have little or no control in setting organizational goals or goal accomplishment could frustrate such an employee. Placing these men and women in jobs where goal attainment and self-discipline are important could greatly enhance both individual and organizational satisfaction.

It must be remembered, here, that needs are of an individual nature. Because a manager possesses a high level of *n ach* does not ensure that his or her organizational unit will be productive. Alvin Zander[8] has found that the group counterpart to achievement motive, desire for group success (*Dgs*), may be developed within an organization. This unusual blend of *n aff* and *n ach* produces, according to Zander, situations in which a strong sense of group involvement can overcome personal fear of failure or lack of achievement motivation. Interestingly, the characteristics of groups possessing high *Dgs* and individuals who possess high *n ach* are strikingly similar (for example, involvement in goal-setting and the need for concrete feedback).

*Power.*   The need for power (*n pow*) is defined here as a concern for obtaining and maintaining control over others. While a manager high in *n ach* may be expected to try to influence the achievement of a goal, a manager high in *n pow* is more concerned with controlling the resources (human, information, and so on) necessary to accomplish a goal.

Unfortunately, the term *power* too often is associated with those who have misused it. Therefore, it is natural for us to look with skepticism or suspicion at those who possess a high need for power. The manager who possesses a high need for power will not necessarily resort to coercive or autocratic means in order to obtain goals. Instead, this manager may be identified by the fact his or her actions are intended to gain control over the internal or possibly the external environment of the organization.

Research findings recently reported by David McClelland indicate that managers who possessed high levels of *n pow* were judged to be better managers in terms of organizational performance and employee morale than those who were high in *n ach*. Moreover, these *n pow* managers were significantly more successful than were their counterparts who possessed a high need to be liked (*n aff*).[9] According to McClelland, *n pow*—not *n aff* or even *n ach*—is the critical need that should be possessed by top managers.

The needs discussed above are thought to be important in organizational situations, although other motives also can influence individual action. Understanding human needs (or motives) may enable us to more accurately assess underlying causes of behavior. Our ability to recognize our own needs as well as the needs of those we work with can enhance performance and job satisfaction through more appropriate job placement and improved interpersonal relations.

## Motivating Through Goals: Expectancy Theory

Recent studies indicate that the concepts of motivation and effort are closely related. These theories of motivation, known as expectancy theories, suggest that the amount of effort put forth toward a designated accomplishment depends upon the value (reward) of that accomplishment to the individual and the perceived probability that the reward will, in fact, follow.

Expectancy theories are goal (rather than need) oriented. Their central theme is that "an individual's behavior is a function of the degree to which the behavior is instrumental in the attainment of some outcomes and the evaluation of these outcomes."[10] Accordingly, the level of effort expended is a consciously and rationally arrived-at decision. The decision to expend effort is a function of both the value of a desired outcome and the perceived probability that effort and behavior will lead to the desired reward.

The value of a reward may lie in its ability to satisfy a drive-creating need, some innate pleasure it brings, or the extent to which it is seen as contributing to a higher-level goal (secondary outcome). The perceived probability that the value is obtainable by the individual is based on the individual's knowledge of past performance-reward relationships. Lyman Porter and Edward Lawler have set forth the expectancy model of motivation shown in Figure 3. The model illustrates the relationship of both reward valuation (1) and the perceived likelihood that effort leads to reward (2) to effort (3) itself.

Rewards themselves may be classified as being either extrinsic or intrinsic. Extrinsic rewards are those that are only artificially related to an individual's overt behavior. Rewards such as money or better working conditions are examples of extrinsic rewards. Intrinsic rewards come about as a natural consequence of a specific behavior. A feeling of self-satisfaction resulting from accomplishing an important goal, or a feeling of personal growth after solving a difficult problem are examples of intrinsic rewards.

**Figure 3. Expectancy model of motivation. Lyman W. Porter and Edward E. Lawler III, MANAGERIAL ATTITUDES AND HUMAN PERFORMANCE (Homewood: Richard D. Irwin, Inc., 1968, p. 165).**

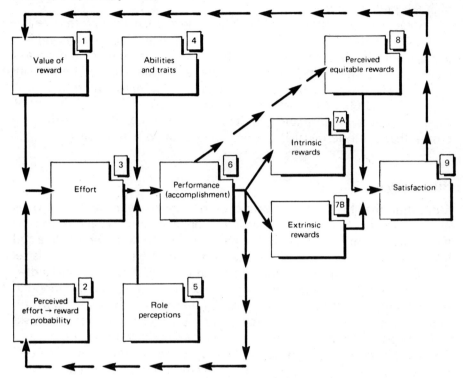

Thus, organizational settings or certain challenging jobs may increase the amount of effort put forth by a worker. Extrinsic rewards, on the other hand, are likely to lead to need satisfaction only when they are tied closely to performance. Efforts to create jobs which will result in a high level of intrinsic need satisfaction often are referred to as *job enrichment.*

Finally, while motivation and effort are closely related, the relationship between motivation and productivity (performance) may be considerably more complicated. An individual may put forth a great deal of effort and fail to accomplish a given task if he or she lacks the necessary ability or skill. The accomplishment of a final outcome is contingent on many input variables. A manager is in a position to control some of these factors, such as equipment, working conditions, or performance-reward relationships. However, the manager may have little or no power to alter others, for instance, intelligence, hand-eye coordination, or emotional state.

Research on expectancy models of motivation has shed additional light on the relationship between motivation and job satisfaction. Findings of Lawler and others discount the traditional belief that satisfaction leads to high performance. Instead, they suggest that performance (6) leads to job satisfaction (9). The latter is related directly to employee behaviors such as absenteeism and turnover. According to Lawler, "Satisfied workers are more likely to remain members of the organization, to go to work regularly, and to get there on time." [11] *However*, "Satisfaction just doesn't seem to lead to high job performance." [12]

Some management systems have been developed which formalize the process of relating rewards directly to performance. One such system is management by objectives (MBO). MBO has received much attention as a management system which enhances long-range planning and performance appraisal. However, the process of involving managers in the setting of objectives and ultimately providing rewards based on accomplishment of these objectives (performance) enriches individual jobs as well as helps ensure that extrinsic rewards are related directly to performance.

## Summary

Motivation may be viewed as a function of internal deficiencies known as needs In particular, needs such as affiliation, achievement, and power may have a significant impact on both a manager's desire to be productive and his or her success within an organization. Alternatively, motivation is seen by some as the result of a rational decision to expend effort toward a desired goal. The value of the goal, together with the perceived likelihood that desired rewards will follow performance, are seen as primary influences on individual motivation. In either case, we must recognize that human skills or knowledge of job requirements are not sufficient to bring about sustained high levels of performance. Employee motivation often is the deciding factor in whether or not an organization successfully achieves its objectives.

*References*

1. Abraham Maslow, "A Theory of Human Motivation," *Psychological Review,* vol. 50, pp. 370–396.
2. Frederick Herzberg, Bernard Monsner and Barbara Snyderman, *The Motivation to Work* (New York: John Wiley & Sons, 1959).
3. J. G. Hunt and J. W. Hill, "The New Look in Motivation Theory Thru to 'The Vroem Model' for Organizational Research," *Human Organization*, vol. 28, Summer 1969, pp. 100–103. Also see Donald D. White and Julio Leon, "The Two-Factor Theory: New Questions, New Answers," *Proceedings of the Academy of Management*, 1977, pp. 356–359.
4. Khalil Noujaim, "Some Motivational Detriments of Effort Allocation and Performance," Ph.D. Thesis, Sloan School of Management, Massachusetts Institute of Technology, 1968.
5. David A. Kolb and Richard Boyatzis, "On the Dynamics of Helping Relationship," *Journal of Applied Behavior Science*, vol. 6, 1970, p. 272.
6. David C. McClelland and David H. Burnham, "Power Is the Great Motivator," *Harvard Business Review*, vol. 54, March–April 1976, p. 103.
7. David C. McClelland, "That Urge to Achieve," *Think Magazine*, November–December 1966, pp. 19–23.

8. Alvin F. Zander, "Team Spirit versus the Individual Achiever," *Psychology Today*, vol. 8, November 1974, pp. 64–68.

9. McClelland and Burnham, *op. cit.*, pp. 102–103.

10. Leon Reinharth and Mahmond A. Wahba, "Expectancy Theory as a Predictor of Work Motivation, Effort Expenditure and Job Performance," *Academy of Management Journal*, vol. 18, September 1975, p. 521.

11. Edward Lawler III, "Developing a Motivating Work Climate," *Management Review*, vol. 66, p. 26.

12. Ibid.

## Recommended Readings

Readings marked with an asterisk are included in *Contemporary Perspectives in Organizational Behavior,* edited by Donald D. White (Boston: Allyn and Bacon, 1982).

Roger J. Howe and Mark G. Mindell, "Motivating the Contemporary Employee," *Management Review*, September 1979, pp. 51–55.

*David C. McClelland and David H. Burnham, "Power Is the Great Motivator," *Harvard Business Review*, vol. 54, March–April 1976, pp. 100–110.

*David A. Nadler and Edward E. Lawler III, "Motivation: A Diagnostic Approach," in *Contemporary Perspectives in Organizational Behavior*, edited by Donald D. White (Boston: Allyn and Bacon, 1981).

B. L. Rosenbaum, "Understanding and Using Motivation," *Supervisory Management*, vol. 24, January 1979, pp. 9–13.

J. E. Stake, "Motives for Occupational Goal Setting among Male and Female College Students," *Journal of Applied Psychology*, vol. 63, October 1978, pp. 617–622.

*Arthur M. Whitehill, "Maintenance Factors: The Neglected Side of Worker Motivation," *Personnel Journal*, October 1976, pp. 516–519, 526.

# CASE 8
## Jack Dobbins' Problem

Jack Dobbins left the vice president's office feeling elated as well as concerned about the new responsibilities he was about to assume. Ralph Barnes, State College's vice president and comptroller, had just told Jack of the executive committee's decision to appoint him Superintendent of Buildings. Jack was concerned because Mr. Barnes had gone into considerably more detail about the many management and morale problems among the college's custodial workers and their supervisors than in any previous interviews.

## The Situation

State College was located in a rural area just outside of St. Louis. It was one of several universities run by the state and was less than ten years old. In this short time it had grown rapidly to 9,500 students, the majority of whom lived off campus and commuted to school each day.

The superintendent's major function was to plan, organize, direct, and control the activities of about eighty employees and supervisors involved in keeping all college buildings, except for the dormitories, in clean and orderly condition. There were ten major buildings ranging in size from 24,000 square feet to 137,000 square feet. Total square footage under the jurisdiction of the superintendent amounted to 1,025,000. This space included classrooms, faculty offices, administration and library buildings, student center, and the like.

Of the eighty employees in the department, sixteen were women and sixty-four were men, including the four supervisors who reported to the superintendent. Starting wages for maids had just been raised to $2,585 per year from $2,300. By some quirk of the state's budgeting system, starting wages for janitors had just been lowered to $2,700 per year from $2,900. Employees could receive only one raise per year, usually on July 1 at the beginning of the fiscal year. It was within the superintendent's authority to grant raises up to a maximum of 10 percent the first year, 7.5 percent the second year, and 5 percent the third year. In order to qualify for the maximum, however, employees had to receive a rating of "outstanding." The work week was forty hours. Vacation leave of ten working days was allowed while sick leave was accrued at the rate of one day per month to a maximum of thirty days. Group life insurance and hospitalization were available by payroll deduction at employee expense. State employees were not covered under Social Security but did participate in the state retirement system under which both the state and the employee contributed. The total budget for the department amounted to about

Contributed by Professor David R. Kennerson, University of South Florida.

$280,000, with $250,000 for wages and salaries and $30,000 for supplies and materials.

Turnover among employees was unusually high. In July and August of 1967, turnover amounted to 15 percent and 20 percent. Typically in this type of work in universities, turnover runs 100 percent per year. Most of the employees were black, and the majority of them were holding down other full-time jobs outside of the college.

## Departmental Work Organization

There was no organization chart for the department, but Jack Dobbins felt it would look pretty much like the chart shown in Exhibit 1. Work was organized on the basis of special tasks. Although supervisors were assigned responsibility for different buildings, work was divided into floor mopping crews, followed up by waxing and buffing crews. Supervisors decided when particular floors were mopped, and waxed and buffed. They coordinated and scheduled the different crews in proper sequence. The day crews worked largely on restroom detail in all buildings, with special groups assigned for carpet cleaning, window washing, and straightening and cleaning meeting rooms.

**Exhibit 1. Organization chart, office of Superintendent of Buildings.**

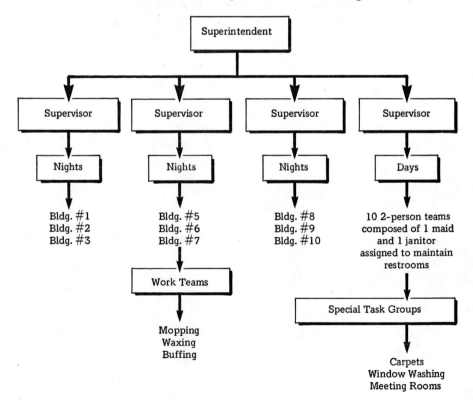

## Jack Dobbins' Background

Jack Dobbins was a retired military man with twenty years' service in various posts as management analyst and operations and training officer. As a young man, he had graduated from a midwestern engineering school. On resigning from the military, he enrolled as a student in a Chicago college of business administration in order to earn an additional degree in management and business administration. At forty-five, he was looking forward to a new career in a new environment in a field where he felt his experience, knowledge, and training could be most effectively used.

During the last hour and one half, in his talk with Mr. Barnes, he had learned much about the current problems of the department. Harry Kraft, the man he was replacing, had come to State College when the first students were admitted. He was about fifty years old, of limited education, and with a varied background as foreman or supervisor in construction firms. When the college was small with only a few buildings and employees, he was reasonably successful. However, four months previously, Harry had fired one of the supervisors with rather disastrous results. Rank-and-file employees were indignant and had sent a petition all the way to the state capitol in an attempt to get Harry's decision reversed. Some were threatening not to come to work. Morale was low, turnover high, and top officials of the college as well as the department itself were being deluged with complaints about the lack of good housekeeping in all buildings. Toilets were not adequately serviced; classrooms and offices frequently went untouched for a week at a time.

Although Jack was concerned, he was not dismayed because he felt strongly that his recent exposure to a wide variety of management courses would make it relatively easy to show substantial improvements in this department.

# CASE 9
# What Ever Happened to Professional Pride?

Air Frame, Inc. is an established producer of small aircraft. As in any aircraft company, the engineering group plays an important role in the company's performance. The service engineering division (SED) at Air Frame is a staff organization whose primary function is to submit recommendations concerning equipment design changes, technical procedural changes, and all other matters requiring analysis and study of an engineering nature. Studies are not instigated by the division. Rather, they are conducted only upon request by project managers. Recommendations that accompany the final reports are nonmandatory.

The service engineering division is organized along two primary lines: (1) according to engineering discipline or specialty, and (2) according to the technical systems serviced.

## Productivity and Job Satisfaction in SED

Productivity within the service engineering division has always been difficult to assess accurately. Quantity is easily measured, but the division's output is closely related to the quality of its final reports. Unfortunately, quality of the reports is not always easy to judge. For instance, the production time for an engineering investigation can be varied or controlled according to the depth of an analysis undertaken. The end product is used by nonengineering line managers. The quality of the reports often is only evident to users in the long run and sometimes not even then.

Most of the engineers recognize the inadequateness of any measure of their own performance. As one senior member of the division stated, "When the work load is heavy, pressures increase to meet deadlines. Quality is ultimately sacrificed as these pressures increase. Our work isn't poor, but sometimes you have to wonder." Some engineering sections have attempted to create a better means for evaluating their own contributions. However, no standard means for evaluation exists throughout the division.

Phil White, the division chief, is pleased with his division's productivity and recently noted:

> Productivity is sufficient; it meets the demand. I suppose it varies substantially among individual workers. However, quality, thoroughness of work, and the extent to which individual projects need be pursued precludes the development of any standards of comparison along the traditional lines of output versus input or output per available man hour.

Prepared by H. William Vroman, Towson State University; and Donald D. White, University of Arkansas.

Neither can productivity be accurately judged by complaints received from the recipients of the final reports. The general policy at Air Frame is not to complain or reject an engineering report. Instead, line managers tend to accept, ignore, or modify the recommendations. Occasionally, an engineering decision or recommendation will result in an accident, failure, or some other easily identifiable calamity. However, the lag time involved between the completion of the report and the implementation of recommendations, together with alterations and changes which normally are introduced, rarely result in the engineering group being held directly responsible.

A recent employee interview program conducted by the Personnel Division at Air Frame indicated that satisfaction among engineers was close to being nonexistent. On more than one occasion, an engineer has been heard to say that accepting a position in "this" organization was like selling one's professional soul to the devil. On the other hand, higher than average salary offers have attracted and helped to hold qualified engineers in the company. Job security at Air Frame is good, and the firm's location in a small community thirty miles east of Kansas City is considered by most employees to be very favorable.

## Personal and Professional Growth

Although an engineering degree entitles the holder to a "quasi-professional status," a truly professional status is achieved only after the engineer has pursued his or her education past the undergraduate level or has acquired a license to practice. There is little recognition at Air Frame of engineers as professional employees except on the basis of their pay differentials. Engineers in the service engineering division are forced to clock in and out of the plant as were production employees up until six months ago when Phil White, under considerable pressure, had the practice discontinued. Neither Phil nor other executives at Air Frame have encouraged their employees to further their education or to obtain appropriate engineering licenses. Two years ago considerable interest was shown by members of the division in a series of engineering seminars conducted by a nearby state university. However, production demands at Air Frame caused requests for time off to be refused.

Last year an evening MBA program was offered by the state university. A large number of engineers enrolled in the program with some departments having as many as 60 percent of their people participating. Shortly thereafter, a small group of engineers from the design department began a movement to encourage a greater number of their associate engineers to obtain professional registration. This was done in spite of the fact that there was no organizational reward for doing so.

A younger engineer who was preparing to leave Air Frame made the following comments to Phil White:

The management here seems more interested in meeting deadlines than with the competence demonstrated on each job. My work in many cases was not even professionally challenging. When it was, I sometimes found facilities like the test laboratory to not be available when I needed them. That resulted in a delay and what I thought was a poor job. You know, no one even told me that my work was under par.

## Phil White's Concern

Phil White was more than a little concerned with the general disinterest among his engineers. He reflected upon the conditions within the division and noted some of the shabby work that had been done of late. Phil recognized that many of the higher level engineering jobs currently were held by persons with no college education. At the same time, he knew that many of these employees would be leaving the firm through attrition or retirement over the next four to six years. He had communicated this fact to younger engineers, but some of them still seemed to be impatient.

Phil believed that one of his biggest problems was the work rules at Air Frame. The same work rules applied to engineering positions that applied to many of the unskilled, hourly, blue-collar employees. It had been a long-standing policy at Air Frame that all employees would be treated alike. Upper management personnel shared the same eating facilities with other workers in the company and no special privileges as far as parking or other fringe benefits were given on the basis of rank or department.

Phil White noted the interest shown by many of the engineers in the MBA program as well as the increased interest in gaining professional registration. Turnover in certain departments within the Division had been as high as 35 percent with the average for the total division being about 23 percent. In his final analysis, he concluded that there were three types of engineers working at Air Frame:

We have a few incompetents who don't care and are doing as little as possible. We also have some professionally minded people here who recognize some of the limitations of their jobs and who make the best out of their situation. Last are those who are using their positions as project engineers as a steppingstone to higher management jobs either here or elsewhere. I'm not really sure what can be done about some of these people. Sometimes I think they've lost their professional pride.

# CASE 10
# The TDIP Committee

Harper Inc. is a large, nationwide producer and marketer of home and office equipment. The management team at Harper has long been aware of the value of a "Theory Y" approach to managing the company. Jane Harper, president of the company, is constantly on the lookout for new employee programs that will "build strong attitudes and a strong company." As an example, Jane refers proudly to the innovative sales and advertising programs that were created with the help of employees from the marketing division. Both ad persons and outside sales representatives were encouraged over a period of six months to contribute ideas toward the design of their own remuneration and fringe benefit systems. The program was highly successful, and a recent university research study indicated that attitudes among sales personnel and those persons in the advertising department were among the highest in the organization.

Similarly, special programs were created for manufacturing employees. Employees were encouraged to tell their supervisors of new ideas that might improve the quantity and/or quality of the final products. Individual rewards were not given to those employees who submitted new ideas. As Jane Harper explained, "How could a supervisor be expected to remember all of the ideas that are given to him or her during that month?" However, a certain percent of cost savings in addition to a share of profits that were attributed to higher quality furniture were passed on to the workers in the various production plants.

Finally, all administrative and office workers have been included in a stock purchase and profit-sharing plan that was designed by department supervisors and top management personnel. Generally, employees throughout the organization have felt that they were well represented in the decision-making activities of top management.

## The University Study

In June of last year, students from the local university conducted a series of research studies within the organization. Their findings generally revealed that employees were satisfied with their work, their compensation, and most of the actions taken by the executive group. Attitudes for almost all divisions and departments were positive and workers apparently were favorably disposed to the company. A noticeable exception to this finding were the members of the transportation and distribution division.

The transportation and distribution division employs about 3,000 people

Prepared by Donald D. White, University of Arkansas; and H. William Vroman, Towson State University.

who work in over sixty locations throughout the United States. In many instances, their terminals are small and not physically connected with either production or sales outlets. Many jobs within the division tend to be uniquely different from one another. The organizational manual showed 128 different jobs in the division. Whereas employees in either manufacturing or marketing came in direct contact with the products being sold, a majority of the employees in the transportation and distribution division rarely ever handled the finished goods themselves. Instead, all furniture moved by division employees was packed in wooden crates and was rarely viewed by the workers. Jobs in the division range from direct product handling and driving to clerical work and sophisticated computer analysis of distribution systems. The jobs and skills of many employees within the division have advanced along with the technological changes of the past two decades. However, the image of the division and its employees is more akin to that of a "burly ex-football player carrying a piano on his back."

Jane Harper was surprised at the finding of the university group that attitudes in the transportation and distribution division were not positive and were sometimes even negative. She called together representatives from various departments within the division and, with the divisional vice president, Gerald McCall, proceeded to outline a program which she believed would positively affect the attitudes of the division's employees.

## The TDIP Solution

Harper began, "We have a lot of people here working all over the country, and nobody knows anybody else. What we need is some kind of central theme, some kind of identity for these men and women. And I want those of you in this room today to help develop that kind of identity." Thus, the TDIP (Transportation and Distribution Identity Program) Committee was launched. The committee was made up of two representatives of each of the division's major departments, plus a member at large from each of the three largest departments. In addition, three union members representing each of the two major unions with whom the firm had contracts were placed on the committee. One committee member explained the consistency of the group in the following manner. "TDIP Committee members were chosen as representatives of all employees in the organization. Whenever possible, peer group leaders were directly or indirectly involved in coming up with ideas for the final program. Although most of these people are leaders, only a few of them are actually supervisors."

The committee met regularly and members maintained close contact with Mr. McCall, one another, and the employees whom they represented. Most of the committee members "felt good about their accomplishments" and believed that the content of the program that was developed would do much to improve the attitudes of employees throughout the division. Among the suggestions of the committee were "meet-the-boss sessions," occasional "open-air meetings" in which employees were free to exchange any and all ideas with their supervisors and other representatives of the company, and the distribution of tie tacks and pocket pencil holders that identified the employee's division and department. In addition, a newsletter and other publicity about the program were distributed on a regular basis.

The meet-the-boss session enabled employees to select a number of representatives who would have an opportunity to meet with Mr. McCall at one of the regional branch offices. Persons were picked at random from throughout the organization to meet with Mr. McCall and his assistant to discuss problems and ideas and to "get to know upper management." At these meetings, Mr. McCall liked to explain to the workers' representatives the new special projects and new programs that had been initiated by top management and the TDIP Committee.

The initial reaction to these programs was very optimistic. A number of employees expressed surprise that a divisional vice-president would bother to sit down with them just to tell them what was going on at the divisional level and to find out what some of their problems were. Several employees said that, although they had worked for the company for twenty years, no one that high up in management had taken the time to speak to them and they were flattered. The reaction to group meetings of all types generally was favorable. A variety of jobs and organizational levels were represented in each meeting. However, the nature of the subjects discussed, as well as the emphasis placed on individual employees, seemed to cause the participants to forget their differences. Projects concerning all levels of supervision, from division to the first line, seemed to congeal the group to a level higher than previously had been thought possible.

A report from Gerald McCall to Jane Harper concerning the effects of the early stages of the program read in part as follows:

Our initial meet-the-boss sessions seemed to be quite successful. Early in the meetings, those in attendance obviously were apprehensive, and I must say that I was a little worried myself. As the meeting progressed, however, everyone became involved in the discussions of problems in their own jobs as well as those of their fellow workers. Specifically, we discussed their concern about personnel cutbacks and training programs. It appeared that everyone left the two-hour meeting feeling better acquainted with each other and with a greater appreciation for other's troubles and responsibilities.

Residual benefits from the meeting included solving some of the problems that were brought to my attention by the participants. In addition, one woman was made aware of the personnel training and career planning program which might help to prepare her for job advancement.

We discussed the possibility of a statewide picnic for approximately 200 employees.

Frankly, Jane, I believe we will see an increase in positive attitudes throughout the division as well as an accompanying increase in productivity. While it is still too early to assess the long-term effect of our program, my people seem to think that our problem is well on its way to being solved.

# CASE 11
# Going Back Home

Jerry Warren had been with the Carrolton Fire Department for only fourteen months. He was twenty-two years old and the youngest fireman ever hired into the department. Now, for the first time, he wasn't sure he wanted to remain in firefighting, at least not in Carrolton!

Jerry grew up in Carrolton, an Arkansas community with a population of about 11,000. He liked the town, but thought he could "make more out of his life" if he got to a bigger city. Once he told his father, "I want to accomplish something in my lifetime. I'd like to be able to look back at what I've done some day and know that I've made someone or something better." Before graduating from Carrolton High School, Jerry was captain of the school basketball and baseball teams and had a B average in his classwork. He attended the University of Arkansas for one year but decided that he was more interested in being a fireman than in obtaining a college degree.

His interest in firefighting had been supported by his service on the Carrolton Auxiliary during his junior and senior years in high school. Before leaving the university, Jerry wrote his uncle who was captain in the St. Louis Fire Department. Jerry thought that if he went to St. Louis his uncle might be able to get him a job with one of the city firefighting units. Instead, his uncle suggested that he apply to the city's Firefighting Academy and "learn to be a modern fire fighter from the start."

Jerry was excited and decided to follow his uncle's advice. He immediately obtained letters of reference from the local fire chief, Frank Hanson, and his uncle and applied to the St. Louis Firefighters Academy. He was surprised and pleased when he received a letter from the Academy accepting him for the fall class. He immediately called his uncle and made arrangements to live in his home during the year he would spend attending the Academy.

Jerry worked hard and graduated close to the top of his class. At his graduation ceremonies one of his instructors approached him and his uncle and said, "You've got a fine boy here, Ted. He not only learns fast, but he also has a lot of good ideas. I'm sure he will make a helluva firefighter before he's through. Why, I'll bet he is a lieutenant in two years."

Jerry remained in the St. Louis area for two years. There he worked with a newly created department in a small suburb and had an opportunity to use much of his training. After two years with the department his name was placed before the city board for promotion to lieutenant. Two days before the board was to make a decision, Jerry received the distressing news that his father was ill and was unable to take care of the farm at home. His mother had written to ask Jerry if he could come home and help out. She thought there was an

Prepared by Donald D. White, University of Arkansas.

opening in the Carrolton Fire Department and he might be able to take job and still have some time to help out around the farm. Jerry was disappointed having to leave what appeared to be a great opportunity. However, he knew that he was needed at home and immediately turned in his resignation.

Shortly after arriving in Carrolton, Jerry went to the fire chief's home. There he explained what had taken place and asked the fire chief if he had an opening in the department. Fortunately, there was an opening. Chief Hanson knew Jerry well from his high school days. In addition, Jerry had kept in touch while in St. Louis by occasionally sending the chief articles about new firefighting techniques and equipment. In his job interview, Jerry asked the chief if he had received the articles. The chief said that he had, but nothing else was said about them. Jerry got the job in the department.

During Jerry's first two months with the department, he quietly went about doing his job. Although he had been considered for lieutenant at his previous position, the opportunity wasn't available in Carrolton. He didn't have any seniority with the department (the average age of his fellow firemen was forty-seven, and most had been with the department twelve years or longer). At one point he asked that his time with the Auxiliary or perhaps that with the St. Louis area fire department be considered as experience on the seniority roster. However, the fire chief stated, "We've never had a situation like this before. I really don't see how we can give you credit when you weren't here with the department."

After a few months Jerry began to get restless. He had continued to take a firefighter's bulletin published in the St. Louis area and on occasion passed on the bulletin to others in the station if an article contained a new idea he thought would benefit the department. From time to time he had made suggestions to the chief and captain concerning training and firefighting techniques. However, few of his ideas were acknowledged and even fewer tried out.

The captain at one point asked Jerry, "Why do you keep taking that paper? It must cost you something, and you know that we can't use those city ideas down here." After fourteen months with the Carrolton Fire Department Jerry was confused. He honestly thought he would like to be a firefighter, but lately he wasn't so sure. That week he received a reprimand for failing to show up for his shift on time. He arrived at the station only to find the last truck pulling out of the garage on its way to a brush fire. Jerry followed the truck to the fire and helped fight it. However, he was still rebuked for his failure to get to work on time.

He decided to discuss the matter with the chief, and the following discussion ensued:

*Jerry:* Chief Hanson, I just wanted you to know that I am sorry about last week. But, I couldn't do much about it. I was looking over the "specs" on the new truck we were considering, and my watch stopped. I'll be more careful the next time.

*Chief Hanson:* You don't need to read about fire trucks or anything else, Jerry. I'll make that decision when the time comes.

*Jerry:* I just thought I could give you some ideas . . .

*Chief Hanson:* You've got a lot of bright ideas—you always did. But I need fire-fighters, not idea men. Wait until you are a chief yourself. That's something I don't understand about you young guys. You're too impatient. You all want to be supervising and changing things before you learn enough about the way things are around here. You know, I had to let a couple of fellas go two years ago for almost the same thing. Just take orders and do your job and everything will work out all right.

When Jerry left the chief's office, he was lost in thought. He knew that his father and mother still needed help with the farm. But he wasn't sure he could remain with the Carrolton Fire Department much longer. "What's the future in it?" he thought.

# EXPERIENTIAL EXERCISE 4
## Understanding Work Motivation

The objective of this exercise is to uncover the many practical dimensions of motivation. As you will see, motivation covers most facets of the work situation.

### Instructions

1. Go through each of the questions and draw upon your experience to support or reject the statement. Place an A or D to indicate whether you agree or disagree with each statement.
2. Underlying the question is an assumption about human nature. In some cases, the questions say that people are basically lazy. In other questions, the assumption is that people are essentially motivated, and stopping them from working hard are bad supervisory practices and too-simple jobs. Try to determine the assumption in the questions and check them against your answer.

### Questions

1. Work that an employee considers interesting is an important source of motivation. _____
2. The opportunity to experience achievement on the job is an absolute necessity if a person is to be motivated at work. _____
3. To be a good supervisor, it is more important to be a good designer of work than to be skillful at human relations. _____
4. Shorter hours of work (for example, the four-day week) is one good motivational tool. _____
5. Incentive pay plans, if tied directly to individual productivity, are an effective motivational tool. _____
6. Improved two-way communications can greatly enhance job satisfaction of employees. _____
7. Plans that push decision-making responsibility down in an organization will be met with resistance by most employees. _____
8. Improved working conditions often affect employee attitudes significantly and contribute to their level of job satisfaction. _____
9. Excessive absenteeism may be due to poor supervision, inadequate pay, or boring work, among other things. _____
10. Elimination of the sources of job dissatisfaction, whatever they may be, will result in improved job satisfaction and motivation. _____
11. A major responsibility of supervisors and managers is to motivate their people to achieve. _____
12. In most cases, extending more decision making to employees involves more risk than gain. _____
13. One effective way to reduce employee dissatisfaction is to see that people are informed about the reasons for decisions that affect them. _____

14. Employees on routine or repetitive jobs are often more motivated and satisfied with their jobs if they understand how their work contributes to overall company goals and objectives. ———
15. Common sources of dissatisfaction at work are personality clashes and disagreements. If these conflicts can be minimized, job dissatisfaction will be reduced, but employee motivation and interest in the work will probably not improve. ———
16. A supervisor's or manager's task is best defined as that of providing people opportunities for achievement so that they will become motivated. ———
17. Most employees would prefer to have their supervisors take over the more complex and difficult tasks in their jobs as long as their pay would not be reduced. ———
18. Boring, uninteresting work may make some employees more demanding about such things as pay, working conditions, holidays, etc. ———
19. Most employees would prefer not to have their work identified because they do not want to receive feedback on their errors. ———
20. Indicators of status and/or longevity such as well furnished offices, privileges of various kinds, and service awards are very important to some employees and provide a strong source of motivation and job satisfaction. ———

# EXPERIENTIAL EXERCISE 5
## What Motivates Me?

Chapter Three discussed a variety of needs that are believed to have an effect on our behaviors. Different individuals may be motivated by different needs. The purpose of this exercise is to discover which needs seem to be most important to us as individuals. We will also see how difficult it sometimes is to understand our own motives—much less the motives of others!

*Instructions*

Following these instructions are sketches of three separate scenes. None of these scenes have any particular meaning in their own right. It is up to you to attach meaning to them. You will be asked to select any two of the three pictures and to write a short story about each. Only select and write about one picture at a time.

*Select and write.* Examine the three pictures carefully for about one minute. Now select one picture and write a story about it. Do not describe the picture; write a narrative about what is happening in the picture. Your story should identify the people in the picture; it should describe what is happening, what has led up to the situation, and what will happen in the future. You may also describe the thoughts of the person or persons shown in the picture.

Once you have selected a picture, work rapidly. Limit your writing to five or six minutes.

When you have completed your first story, turn it over and select a second picture. Examine the picture carefully. Begin writing as before. Do not spend over five or six minutes on writing this story.

*Analyze your stories.* Your instructor will provide you with a guideline for evaluating your stories and the stories of others in your group. Using that guideline, read your story carefully, and write down those motives that you believe are primarily reflected. When you have completed "grading" your own story, each member of the group should read his/her stories in a round-robin fashion. After each story has been read, all members of the group should individually grade the story according to the motives that are reflected in it. Develop a composite evaluation on each person. When all stories have been graded, discuss the questions below.

*Discussion Questions:*

1. Who among you were surprised by the motives that were projected by your stories? Why? Do you believe that these motives are important to you?

Prepared by Donald D. White, University of Arkansas; artwork by permission of Prentice-Hall.

2. If your interpretation of your own stories differed from the interpretation of others in your group, how do you explain those differences? Why are differences in interpretations of your primary needs important to you?
3. What needs seem to be most prevalent (a) in your group? (b) throughout your class? Discuss the significance of any patterns that might exist.
4. Can you describe the reason you selected the pictures on which you wrote?
5. Discuss the validity of this technique. Of what use is it? What are its limits?

Scene sketches begin on page 114.

**Picture A.**

**Picture B.**

**Picture C.**

# PART III

# THE NATURE OF ORGANIZATIONS

Human beings exhibit a variety of personality characteristics, motives, and behaviors, as described in Part II. These characteristics manifest themselves in many ways in organizational life. After all, it is the interaction of human behavior with formal organizations and their processes to which the term *organizational behavior* refers. What, then, is an organization? What factors in organizational life are important to the performance of human beings in organizations?

Part III contains sections on the functions and structures of formal organizations, organizational climate, and effective leader behavior. Through these three areas of study, we will describe and examine the nature of organizations. The concept of formal organizations embraces the goals of the enterprise, its structure, and the related decision-making processes on which it relies.

It is paramount to remember that an organization is an open, social system. Organizations exist in order to unify human activities so that common goals can be efficiently attained. Both the size and complexity of these social systems call for an awareness on the part of managers of the impact of organizational components on organizational behavior.

Structural relationships between various levels and organizational units within an enterprise lead to the attainment of formal goals. They also affect the interpersonal relations of organizational members. Today, modern organizations are experiencing dramatic changes in both their goals and their structures. As objectives and strategies change, new organization structures arise to meet managerial needs and environmental demands. Chapter Four on formal organization examines traditional as well as more recent organization structures and explores their impact on organizational members.

The overall atmosphere within an organization is referred to as its climate, the subject of Chapter Five. Many factors internal to the organization, as well as some related to the perception of organizational members, contribute to organizational climate. Thus, organizational climate is a complex concept in which the interaction of variables—such as size and structure, goal orientation, communication networks, and leadership patterns—influences employee attitudes and output.

Of particular significance to organizational climate and to the ability of an enterprise to reach its intended goal is the leadership ability possessed by key individuals—usually managers—throughout the organization. As such, the subject of leadership has long occupied the attention of management practitioners and researchers. Chapter Six discusses this important topic and explores effective leadership in particular. Progress in understanding what constitutes an "effective" leader has been slow. However, an evolving body of knowledge has resulted in a clearer understanding of the manager's role as a leader and those factors that affect his or her success.

No single leadership style will lead to the effective attainment of organizational goals under all circumstances. Although successful leaders in both political and organizational life may share certain characteristics, leadership research clearly indicates that effectiveness is situational in nature. That is, the impact of a leader on the organizational unit depends upon the leader's personal attributes, other members of the social system, and the type of work or activity in which all are involved.

Analyzing behavior in organizational systems requires a close look at these major leadership variables and the way that they come together in a given situation. Whether a leader should rely more heavily on interpersonal skills or on an orientation to the work that must be done depends upon the situational characteristics of the social system.

Understanding the leader orientation that will lead to goal attainment, along with identifying the managerial roles and corresponding behaviors of managers, is important to you as an organizational decisionmaker. The concepts of management and leadership are distinct. However, they are closely related to one another and are at times (not always accurately) used interchangeably.

The nature of organizations, through formal organizational components, climate, and effective leadership, has a major impact on the behavior of individuals within organizational systems and on the behavior of the systems themselves. Part III of the book presents cases and exercises that allow you to view the impact of organizations and to make decisions involving those crucial organization system elements.

# CHAPTER FOUR
# Formal Organizations and Human Performance

Formal organization may be defined as the activity of a group of persons who are pursuing some common goal through certain formalized structures and processes. Traditionally, formal organizations have been characterized by their structures (the relationships between their members) and by written guidelines (rules and policies) which clarify or enlarge upon those relationships. Organizational structure affects human behavior by providing direction (goals) and means (processes and procedures) that often dictate behavior patterns.

The purpose of structure is to marshall the energies of organizational members in directions that support the system's objectives. These objectives are the organization's stated reason for existing. The success of any enterprise depends on its ability to achieve its objectives while meeting the demands of society and satisfying the needs of organizational members.

The structure of an organization is a means to an end. It is like the automobile one travels in to get to the beach. The mode of travel, like the structure, is one important element in obtaining the sought-after end: arriving at the beach. It is not the only means of travel, nor is it sufficient in itself for us to reach our destination. However, our choice as to structure, just as our choice of a form of transportation, is a critical input which may ultimately affect our goal.

Structure is an important factor in getting the job done in any organization. A broad look at an organization reveals three administrative levels. They are the technological or operational level, the managerial level, and the executive level. Most environmental forces over which organizational participants have little control are dealt with at the executive level (see Figure 1). On the other hand, the authority to make decisions that are largely predetermined, due to the controllable nature of the information inputs, may be delegated to lower managers either at the managerial level or technological level of the organization. Delegation of decision-making authority frees executives to pursue their responsibilities in relation to unstructured or nonprogrammed activities within the organization.

**Figure 1. Environmental forces and the formal organization structure.**

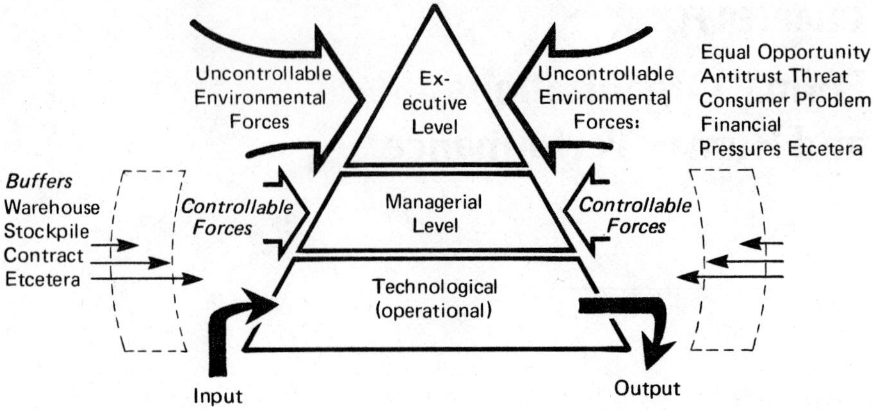

Notice in Figure 1 the blocks that keep the environment from affecting the technological core. These are buffers. They represent such things as inventories of supplies or finished products. Managers do their best to protect the technological core to assure that it continues to function efficiently. Warehouses and stockpiles absorb output when the market will not do so. Stockpiles of raw materials exist to minimize the impact of input shortages. If the technological core does not function and output ceases, the organization's very survival is threatened. Even the largest industrial firms have only a short survival time if they are not producing. The job of executives and managers, then, is to keep the technological core operating regardless of outside circumstances.

Many early management writers focused on improving efficiency at the "shop level" (technological core) as well as on the impact of structure on that efficiency. More recently, attention has been given to examining the behavioral implications of structure and the important role structure plays in linking the organization with its environment.

## Means and Ends

Many problems result from managers using formal organizational tools like rules, regulations, policies, and job descriptions as ends instead of as means-to-ends as they are intended. This misuse of structural tools causes the organization to be rigid and limits its ability to adapt to changing situations. There is a tendency for people in management positions to overemphasize the rule-making function of their jobs. As a manager grows and becomes more effective, he or she sees beyond the trees to the forest. Rules and predefined procedures can be a crutch for the ineffective manager. Many managers are biased toward making decisions within an environmental framework of certainty. They prefer to make decisions only when all possible information about a situation is known. The interests, decisions, and actions of these men and women tend to be based on short-term rather than long-term considerations, on quantitative rather than qualitative data, and on precedent rather than on new and innovative solutions.[1] Preferences such as these are unacceptable when they become obsessions and serve as absolute assumptions that underlie all related administrative activities.

Organization design or structure does set certain operational constraints. Objectives are assumed to be more desirable when they are quantified. Written rules and policies are thought to be more desirable than are unwritten guidelines. These biases toward certainty are particularly noticeable within the technological level of an organization. Objectives at the technological level often are quantitative and are based on what has been achieved in the past. For example, goals such as "increase the number of items produced per hour by 15 percent," or "decrease the cost of patient care by 5 percent" represent decisions related to previous performance based on numerical standards.

### Certainty and Flexibility

Objectives become less certain as we rise in the organizational hierarchy toward the executive level, since the environment itself becomes less controllable. Furthermore, if the enterprise becomes rigid and cannot adapt to the changing forces outside its boundaries, it will become less effective.

Thus, to the extent that structure encourages the organization to emphasize certainty and precedence over the long term, the achievement of the organization's objectives may actually be hindered. A computerized set of rules used to facilitate the processing of patients in a hospital will improve the efficiency with which persons on the patient care (technological) level of a hospital accomplish their day-to-day jobs. On the other hand, a decision concerning the acquisition of a new technology or the marketing of a new product may be made without knowledge of the complete scope of alternatives and constraints.

This necessity for managers on the executive level to make decisions in a somewhat unstructured environment does not rule out the need for goals and a sense of direction. On the contrary, it is at the executive level that is formulated the broad umbrella of objectives which guides the activities of an enterprise. Moreover, executives also require short-term forecasts and short-term feedback to administer their organizations. A manager may operate according to a five-year long-range plan and also require that a quarterly rolling forecast be reported at executive meetings held each month. Needs for certainty are met by the quarterly forecasts, while the five-year plan helps him or her to maintain flexibility.

The way an enterprise meets its needs for certainty and flexibility is shown in the following illustration. Picture a ship (organization) going from point A to point B (accomplishing objectives). The captain (executive) gives the orders (goals, rules, regulations, policies) to the crew (managers). There is short-term certainty about both the goal and procedures. After the ship is under way, a squall (malpractice suit, antitrust proceedings, strike at a suppliers) blows up, forcing the ship off course. If the captain does not re-evaluate the situation and lets the ship proceed under the previous orders, the ship may be broken up on the rocks or may end up at point C.

However, if the captain is aware that unanticipated circumstances (subsystems in operation that he or she does not understand) may arise after the ship is under way, he or she is in a better position to recognize the need for change, re-evaluate the situation, and set a new course toward point B. An executive must know the organization's objectives. But the executive also must also be flexible enough to change plans if forces in the environment so dictate.

## Organization Structure: Traditional Concepts

Organization structures take different forms. Some possess highly rigid formal structures. Others seem to have no stable relationships at all. The term *bureaucracy* was coined by the German sociologist, Max Weber,[2] who observed the inner workings of large, complex organizations and concluded that they possessed similar characteristics. These characteristics taken together are what we refer to as a bureaucracy. They include the following:

1. *Hierarchy of authority.* Organizations have many levels. The levels may be identified by the titles of position holders, for example, president, vice president, division head, department head, work group leader, and so on. Formal organization power is allocated to these positions. Those in high positions are given more power than those on lower levels. Hierarchical arrangements of power are basic to complex organizations. A hierarchy of authority implies that major decisions are made at an upper level and are communicated downward. They are to be followed without question.
2. *Specialization.* Also known as division of labor, specialization refers to identitifying and delimiting a job holder's duties and sphere of authority. On an organizational level, this often takes the form of departmentalization. On the individual level, specific job duties are assigned to those occupying a position. The justification for specialization is that it leads to greater proficiency.
3. *Formalistic impersonality.* Bureaucracies are designed to function efficiently as a result of organizational variables and their relationship to one another rather than because of any personal qualities that position holders may bring to their offices. The term *position holder* has been used intentionally throughout our discussion of bureaucracy. It is positions that are found in organizational hierarchies and positions to which specialized duties are assigned. The activities of bureaucratic office holders are identified through job descriptions rather than personal styles or characteristics of the individuals. The not-too-flattering name given to such position holders is *bureaucrat.*
4. *Rules and records.* Bureaucracies above all else are noted for their stability. This stability is attributable in part to the formalized impersonality described above. The ability of an impersonal organization to continue to function is enhanced through the system of rules and records of past decisions that are maintained by the organization. Such a set of rules, if comprehensive enough,

should provide answers to all questions that a bureaucrat might face. More-over, the guidelines for making day-to-day decisions can be found in the books of regulations and files of past cases that are maintained by the organization.

Organizations which possess these characteristics are known as bu-reaucracies. Clearly, most organizations that we encounter reflect some bureaucratic characteristics. On the other hand, few if any organizations are bureaucracies in the purest sense of the word. Modifications in the way in which bureaucratic organizations are administered leads MacKenzie to label these enterprises as *buroids*.[3]

The bureaucracy lends itself to a pyramid or line form of organization. The line structure shown in Figure 2 clearly reflects the hierarchy, speciali-zation, and impersonality. The bureaucratic structure exemplified by the figure has undergone numerous modifications through the application of management theory. Introduction of concepts like decentralization and staff authority have modified the way traditional bureaucratic structures operate.

*Decentralization.*   Centralization is associated with bureaucratic organiza-tion. It is sometimes assumed that power concentrations at the top of or-ganizations are consistent with bureaucracy. Technically, the terms central-ization and decentralization refer to the location (by level) of decision-making within the organization. A concentration of decision-making power at the top of an organization might classify it as centralized. A

**Figure 2. Simple project organization.**

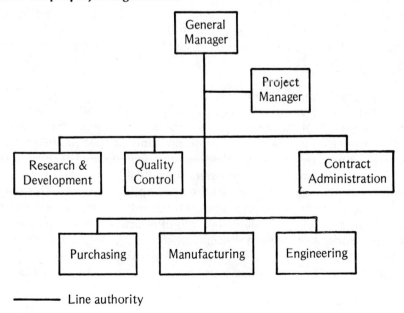

——— Line authority

decentralized organization, on the other hand, is one in which decision-making authority has been placed in the hands of lower-level managers.

Of course, all managers make decisions. Therefore, a more accurate measure of whether an organization is centralized or decentralized may be the location of *important* decisions, the number of functions affected by a manager's decision, and/or the extent to which decisions made must be reviewed by superiors before they are implemented.[4]

The terms *centralization* and *decentralization* should not be used in an absolute sense. An organization does not concentrate all of its decision-making power at the top or at the bottom. Instead, we might say that an organization tends to be highly centralized if decision-making authority is not freely or extensively delegated to lower-level managers. Moreover, certain functions may be tightly controlled while other functions are more decentralized. Alfred Chandler, in his classic study, *Strategy and Structure*, found that major American corporations tend to centralize their control functions (finance, planning, policy making) and decentralize their operations (day-to-day production activities).[5] In the past, any delegation of authority was viewed as a move toward decentralization. However, some writers now foresee a return to more centralized organizations in order to meet weighty environmental demands such as government regulations and antitrust activities.[6]

There are behavioral consequences to either concentrating or delegating authority. A strategy of decentralization would affect the nature of the manager's work by expanding the significance of the manager's role as a decision maker. Such a move would affect day-to-day activities as well as vertical interactions with superiors and subordinates. Finally, the responsibilities and power held by a manager would be altered significantly. How individual managers handle changes in authority depends upon their personalities, the support of their organizational members, and on their preparation for increased decision-making authority. The loss of authority through recentralization likewise would have significant implications for a manager's security and self-esteem.

*Staff authority.*   Staff authority may be a contradiction in terms. Technically, staff members provide information, assistance, and/or advice to line personnel. Their authority is restricted to their own departments and cannot be exercised in the line organization. Only in specific instances (e.g., quality control) or for designated functions (e.g., financial) do staff persons exercise control over line operations. Realistically, however, staff managers may have significant implied or implicit authority. This may be due to their elevated positions, usually reporting directly to a key line manager, or to their elevated status by right of education or professionalization. Staff positions often require specialized knowledge that is held by persons with advanced degrees, special licenses, and professional status.

Line and staff organizations are hybrids of more traditional bureaucratic structures. The actual or perceived reallocation of authority when the staff concept is introduced into organizations results in interpersonal and intra-organizational conflicts. Conflicts may be linked to the different perspectives held by line and staff managers as a result of the particular output pressures placed upon them. The classic confrontation of line/quantity output as opposed to staff/quality output has long been recognized. Educational backgrounds and differences in working conditions also may underlie the friction between line and staff managers. By and large, however, most line/staff conflicts can be traced to the influence, or lack of influence, on important organizational decisions. Therefore, both output and egos affect line/staff relationships.

## Contemporary Organization Structures

Modifications of basic bureaucratic structures, like decentralization and staff authority, have changed the face of modern organizations. However, there are some who believe that bureaucracy itself cannot survive under certain environmental conditions. Some writers have concluded that bureaucracy hinders interpersonal relations and fails to provide for human needs in organizations. They also suggest that bureaucracy is unable to adapt to rapid changes in the environment. These shortcomings necessitate new and alternative organizational structures. Three such structures are discussed below. They include project, matrix, and organic-adaptive structures.

*Project organization.*   In a project organization, units have been formed to accomplish specific goals, such as finding or designing a product or producing a limited quantity of output. These units, also known as project teams or groups, are characterized by the interfunctional composition of their membership, their highly specific task or goal, and the fact that they are disbanded upon completion of their intended purpose. Project organizations gather the necessary resources and place them under the direction of a single individual, the project manager. Organizations that adopt a project structure often do so in order to improve their responsiveness to the environment. This is accomplished through better horizontal coordination. Such coordination is difficult to achieve in the more vertically oriented bureaucratic organization.[7] The life of a project unit normally is defined in terms of some definite time frame or until project goals are accomplished. Therefore, project organizations result in temporary rather than permanent adjustments to the organization structure.

Project structures vary widely in terms of the resources committed to project managers. In some cases, the project manager may be given little more than a desk and a promise of cooperation from other unit (e.g. functional) managers throughout the organization. (See Figure 2.) In other cases, the project manager may be provided with staff groups, limited functional line support, or even line authority over all personnel needed to complete

**Figure 3. Aggregate project organization.**

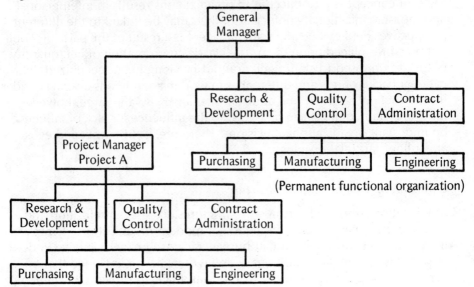

(Permanent functional organization)

the project (aggregate project organization). (See Figure 3.) The dependency of project managers on other departments or persons over whom they have no direct authority may lead to confusion for the project managers and employees. Conflicts arise due to temporary or implicit dual lines of authority as well as questions concerning the priorities of conflicting goals. Project organization results in the decentralization of decision making through the project manager level. At the same time, concentration of authority for project-related activities allows top management to more easily monitor projects and centralize their control.[8]

*Matrix Organization*

The project structure enables an organization to meet the demands of its environment efficiently. Some industries experience greater need for such adaptability than do others. If the technology of an industry or the consumer that a firm attempts to satisfy requires this type of flexibility on a broad scale, a more permanent and extensive project-type structure may evolve. This structure, known as the matrix organization, exists when project management permeates the entire organization. Figure 4 shows how a matrix organization involves overlaying a project structure on a functional structure. Rather than the enterprise organizing on the basis of either function or project alone, matrix structure allows the organization design to accommodate both. Dual lines of authority become the structural rule rather than the exception.

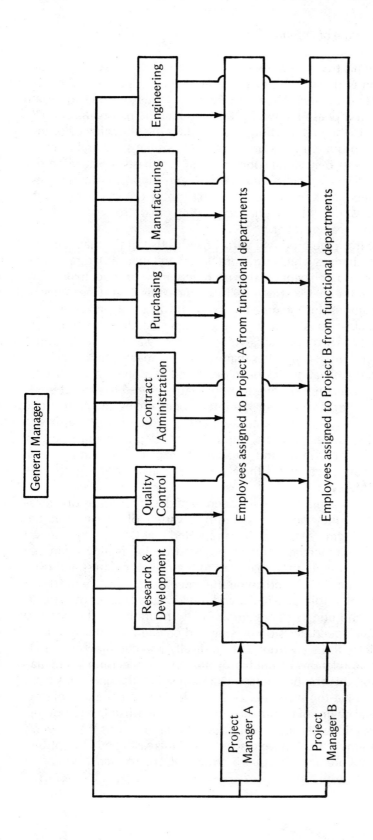

**Figure 4. Matrix organization.**

Kolodny, in his treatise on the evolution of a matrix organization, provides us with an understanding of the structural and operational matrix organization.[9] He concludes that an organization tends to evolve to a matrix structure through a phase known as the "product/matrix organization." During this phase, the organization tries to attain the permanency of the matrix form. The product/matrix organization takes the structural form of a matrix but lacks its behavioral sophistication. Emphasis is placed on building the structural devices, behavioral patterns and support systems necessary to sustain the matrix organization. Such support systems include dual evaluation and reward systems, dual accounting or control systems, team building, and role reassessment.

Movement from the product matrix phase to that of the matrix organization results in changes which are more behavioral than structural. Many of the processes and behaviors that existed under the product matrix form reach maturity in the matrix structure. In essence, this final stage is reached when matrix relationships become an accepted way of organizational life. The matrix organization is characterized by high flexibility and adaptability, intensive boundary transactions, resource sharing and multiple team memberships, and proactive rather than reactive management behavior.

The matrix organization has been described as a permanent, stable structural form. A second, shifting form of matrix geared to project work also exists. In such organizations, "the interdependencies, the market unit, and the people in them shift around frequently."[10] Permanent matrix structures are found in General Motors, International Telephone and Telegraph, General Electric, and Johnson and Johnson. Perhaps the best known user of the shifting matrix structure is the National Aeronautics and Space Administration (NASA).

While matrix organizations have been heralded by some as organizations of the future, they can be plagued by a variety of management and interpersonal problems. Managers have reported that working in matrix organizations often is accompanied by power struggles, feelings of insecurity, and conflict. These, in turn, may lead to high levels of stress and over-involvement in team, group, and committee meetings, excessive overhead due to dual staffing (project manager and functional manager) of management positions, and unnecessary complexity.[11] Theoretically, the matrix organization should speed decision making and enable the enterprise to react more quickly to its environment. Ironically, the complex structural and interpersonal relations of the matrix along with "decision strangulation" may inhibit this responsiveness. Decision strangulation results from the desire to involve too many persons in a decision, frequently referring decisions up dual chains of command, and individual frustration resulting from a manager's inability to make fast, unilateral decisions.[12] Yet even with the limitations that we have discussed, an increasing number of business organizations are adopting matrix structures or find themselves on the evolutionary path to that end.

*Organic Organization (Adhocracy)*

The final organization structure to be discussed is that of the organic form. The organic structure first described by Bennis (organic-adaptive) can be thought of as a "structureless" structure. Bennis describes such an organization as an "adaptive, rapidly changing temporary system . . . organized around problems that will be solved by relative groups of strangers who represent a diverse set of professional skills." [13] Such organizations are termed organic in that they continually adapt themselves on the basis of needed functional inputs rather than along traditional bureaucratic lines of authority. While it might be difficult to envision an entire organization that operates on such a basis, organizational units such as research and development teams, consulting groups, and medical teams already adhere to the description.

Henry Mintzberg, borrowing from Alvin Toffler's best-seller, *Future Shock,* has expanded on this structural theme through his writings on "adhocracy." [14] He states that adhocracies avoid the sharp divisions of labor, unit differentiation, highly formalized behaviors, and emphasis on planning and control systems that characterize bureaucratic structures. They do not rely on standardized skills, but rather use their members' knowledge and skills as a basis on which to build new ones. Mintzberg's description of an adhocracy is somewhat broader than that of Bennis. Moreover, the conditions and characteristics of adhocracy tend to overlap those of project and shifting matrix organizations. In fact, although stages of structural evolution may be identified, distinct differences in these organization designs are sometimes difficult to observe. All are characterized to varying degrees by the organizational instability and uncertainty that bureaucratic organizations are designed to minimize. Consequently, structural ambiguity, relative power relationships, and varying levels of inefficiency due to communication and decision-making obstacles become fertile ground for interpersonal differences. Still, the desire and necessity for organizations to provide enriched jobs and rapid innovative responses to environmental change lead an increasing number of organizations toward these contemporary structures.

The purpose of our discussion of organization structure has been to create an awareness of differences in structure as well as to point out their behavioral implications. No single structure is best for all organizations. And only recently have researchers come to appreciate more fully their operational and behavioral implications.

## Summary

Formal organization refers to the structure and relationships within an enterprise. Written guidelines lend further support and explanation to those relationships. Structure adds to organizational stability by channeling the human and material resources into task- or goal-directed activity. However, flexibility also must be built into the enterprise; it must change in response to the changing forces in the environment. Precedent-oriented and programmed decisions usually are made on the technological and the managerial levels of the firm. However, it is the men and women on the executive level who must make decisions dealing with the uncertainties of a changing environment.

Organizational structures continue to evolve in order to meet technological requirements, human needs, and the demands of the environment. Although bureaucratic structures are prevalent in most organizations, newer forms such as project, matrix, and organic organizations are gaining acceptance in many modern enterprises. The positive and negative impacts of traditional and contemporary structures must be recognized and dealt with by managers in order to accomplish organizational objectives most effectively.

## References

1. J. D. Thompson, *Organizations in Action* (New York: McGraw-Hill Book Co., 1967) pp. 144–158.
2. Max Weber, *The Theory of Social and Economic Organizations*, trans. A. Henderson and Talcott Parsons (New York: Oxford University Press, 1947).
3. Kenneth D. MacKenzie, *Organizational Structure* (Arlington Heights: AHM Publishing Corporation, 1978) p. 260.
4. Ernest Dale, "Planning and Developing the Company Organization Structure," Research Report 20, American Management Association, 1952, p. 118.
5. Alfred Chandler, *Strategy and Structure* (Cambridge: The MIT Press, 1962).
6. Fred Luthans, *Organizational Behavior*, 2nd ed. (New York: McGraw-Hill Book Co., 1977) p. 134.
7. Harvey F. Kolodny, "Evolution to a Matrix Organization," *Academy of Management Review*, October 1979, vol. 4, pp. 543–545.
8. Ibid.
9. Ibid., pp. 543–553.
10. Henry Mintzberg, *The Structuring of Organizations* (Englewood Cliffs: Prentice-Hall, 1979) pp. 172–173.
11. Ibid., p. 175.
12. Stanley M. Davis and Paul R. Lawrence, "Problems of Matrix Organizations," *Harvard Business Review*, May–June 1978.
13. Warren G. Bennis, "Organizational Developments and the Fate of Bureaucracy," *Industrial Management Review*, Spring 1966,
14. Mintzberg, op. cit., pp. 431–465.

## Recommended Readings

Readings marked with an asterisk are included in *Contemporary Perspectives in Organizational Behavior*, edited by Donald D. White (Boston: Allyn and Bacon, 1982).

Jay R. Galbraith, "Organization Design: An Information Processing View," *Interfaces*, vol. 4, no. 3, May 1974, pp. 28–36.

Ralph H. Kilmann, "An Organic-Adaptive Organization: The Maps Method," *Personnel*, May–June 1974, pp. 35–47.

*Harvey F. Kolodny, "Evolution to a Martix Organization," *Academy of Management Review*, vol. 4, no. 4, October 1979, pp. 543–553.

Lyman W. Porter and E. E. Lawler, "Properties of Organization Structure in Relation to Job Attitudes and Job Behavior," *Psychological Bulletin*, vol. 64, no. 1, July 1965, pp. 23–51.

*Joel E. Ross and Robert G. Murdick, "People, Productivity and Organizational Structure," *Personnel*, vol. 50, September–October 1973, pp. 8–18.

*Zahid Shariff, "The Persistence of Bureaucracy," *Social Science Quarterly*, vol. 60, June 1979, pp. 3–19.

# CASE 12
# Waterloo Prison

Professor Arlington entered the office of the Supervisor of Training of the State Department of Prisons. Douglas Jones, the supervisor, had requested that the professor meet with him to discuss a teaching assignment within the prison. The professor was a manager by profession and held a Ph.D. in business administration with a specialization in management. The following discussion took place at the meeting:

*Jones:* Professor, what we would like for you to do is to teach a course in administration for members of our staff who are working toward an associate degree at Cresco Community College. For the most part the students are high school graduates, although some of the men will have one or two years of college, and one of them is even a college graduate who is interested in further learning. Their experience is varied; however, most have never worked in any other organization or environment. The course is for the staff, not the inmates.

*Professor:* Mr. Jones, your proposal is interesting, but I know nothing about the environment of prisons. Before I could teach such students, I would have to spend at least two weeks in a prison so that I can have some appreciation of their problems and their organization. The basic fundamentals of management are the same, but there may be some variables in the application as we look at the entire community of the organization. The two weeks will provide me an indoctrination as well as an opportunity to instill some confidence in prison officials as to my capacity as a manager and a teacher. I suggest that you arrange with one of the prisons for me to discuss with their staff just what they are doing.

*Jones:* As a matter of fact, I have already made arrangements for you to visit a prison. The superintendent has agreed to give you complete freedom to do what you want. Superintendent Blake at Waterloo prison expects a call from you at your earliest convenience.

*Professor:* Let's not go so fast! Just why did you pick Waterloo Prison?

*Jones:* Waterloo Prison was built by the state during the late 1800s, and frankly, I doubt if it has changed much in the last fifty years. The prison is located in a rural area and many employees have never worked anywhere else. For example, Mr. Oberg, the Associate for Custody, started working at the prison as a guard twenty-five years ago and has worked his way up to his present position. I know that you are a management consultant in addition to your teaching. Furthermore, I have heard from some of the members of the department who have attended your classes that you are action-oriented and want to shake up staid bureaucracies. Prisons must meet the new demands of society and they cannot do this with their existing, old procedures. Waterloo Prison needs to move into a posture of change. I hope that you can help them.

Prepared by Vernon L. Stintzi, Pacific Lutheran University (adapted).

*Professor:* Seems to me that you are rather slippery. You ask me to teach a course in administration and I end up with the task of a consultant. Exactly what do you want me to do?

*Jones:* Maybe I did wander a bit, but we need a course that will assist the institution to move into change. You can help us. Other actions will be necessary. Perhaps during your indoctrination at the prison you can discuss the problems related to change and some possible solutions.

*Professor:* You mentioned that Superintendent Blake is in charge. Tell me about him.

## Interviews at Waterloo Prison

Later that week  Professor Arlington drove to Waterloo Prison for the first of a number of interviews he would have with prison officials and other personnel. Upon arriving at the prison, he was escorted to Superintendent Blake's office. The associate superintendent for treatment, Mr. Graham, and the business manager, Mr. James, also were present.

*Blake:* Welcome to Waterloo. Mr. Jones told me that you were coming and I have been looking forward to meeting you. How about some coffee?

*Professor:* Coffee sounds like a good idea. Glad to meet you, Mr. Graham and Mr. James. Certainly a beautiful setting you have in the countryside.

*Blake:* The prison has been here for seventy years and much of the environment remains with its original beauty. That's the way we want to keep it, too. (*Pleasantries followed until a lull*).

*Professor:* Superintendent, I have been asked to teach a course in administration for your staff at the local community college. Before doing this, I want to spend a couple of weeks in your organization trying to find out what is going on. All I want to do is listen. My only questions will be about things I know or understand. I will not write any report to anyone at any level. Also, I would like to have an exit interview with you when I am through.

*Blake:* I assure you that we will make the entire institution available. The personnel officer will meet you at 9:00 A.M. and have a suggested schedule.

*James:* I am going to be leaving tomorrow for two weeks. I wonder if I could talk to you before I leave?

*Professor:* That would be fine. Is there something that the three of us should discuss at this time?

*Blake:* There are two areas that I am concerned about. The first is the fact that I never seem to have time to sit down and reflect or really concentrate on the future. The daily routine packs the day—until there is no time left. Second, we need help in making the changes.

*James:* I would certainly agree on the busy days that we have. Seems like it is go-go-go all the time and there is not time to look ahead or reflect.

*Graham:* I seem to have the same problem.

Later that same day the professor met with Mr. James, the Business Manager.

*Professor:* I think it would be helpful for me to have you tell me about your background before we go any further.

*James:* I am a retired army officer. I spent most of my work career as a controller.
I came here ten years ago and have been the business manager since that
time. I have eight departments under my supervision. Outside of the custody
staff, I have the largest group. The eight supervisors report directly to me.
They are well qualified, except for one, and I am hoping that I will be able to
fire him in the near future. His problem is that he cannot handle the inmates
and he has little, if any, understanding of human beings. I have told him
about his deficiencies, but he makes no attempt to improve himself. The
supervisors have been here from five to fifteen years. This small amount of
turnover is real good—lots of stability in the organization. I should add that
all members of the work crews of the eight supervisors are inmates.

*Professor:* Do you see any problems in the organization, either in your own department or outside, where I could be of assistance?

*James:* You can see that with no turnover and a rather constant workload, things
go along quite smoothly. I do have to follow the gyrations of the budget;
this means close coordination with other departments, but this hasn't been a
real problem. Of course, no one likes to be cut, either in dollars, supplies, or
personnel. If I can't work out a solution, I go to the superintendent. I am
busy as hell, but I like it this way. Even though I have a college degree, I
plan to attend the course you are going to teach. We need to upgrade the educational level of the entire staff.

*Professor:* You commented in the superintendent's office that you never have
time to plan or look ahead because of the heavy daily work. From what you
have told me, this is of your own making more than from any other cause.

*James:* I am afraid that I will have to agree with you. I complain about this lack
of planning, but I don't know what I could do differently if I *did* plan.
Seems like most events or problems fall into patterns for solutions. The organization has made some changes over the past ten years, but these have
been gradual and planning was not really necessary. Sometimes I wonder if
we are drifting rather aimlessly, reacting in a passive manner to the forces
of circumstance. We're a sheltered organization. We live—at least most of us
—in this rather provincial farm community where life changes—but slowly.
Maybe that is why the staff is here; they like it the way it is.

*Professor:* What does the state office do for you?

*James:* For the most part, they leave us alone. Basically, I like this. But there are
occasions when I would like help and guidance. Generally, the assistance is
forthcoming, but there are times when I don't even receive a reply. On
occasions the answer is so late or wish-washy that it is useless.

*Professor:* When the latter happens, what do you do?

*James:* I go to the superintendent for the decision. He is on board about the
issue if the request is significant. I can usually get an answer from him right
away, even though both of us feel that it should come from the state office.
On some occasions, I will ask my counterpart in other prisons to see if they
have had similar problems, the actions they took, etc.

   I think that I should mention to you another area where a problem will
develop. The superintendent, the two associates, and myself are all about
fifty years old. I have been here the least number of years—ten. The others
have been here for fifteen to twenty years. This represents almost their entire
work history. It certainly will be a shock if all the key people leave within a
year or two.

The following day Professor Arlington was back at Waterloo. His first meeting was held in the morning with Mr. Walters, the Personnel Manager.

*Professor:* Superintendent Blake told me to report to you at 9:00 A.M. this Monday.

*Walters:* Glad to meet you Professor Arlington. I have a schedule of people that you may want to visit, but you can change this as you see fit. Just come here at 9:00 A.M. and 1:00 P.M. and I will have everything arranged—appointments, where to go, etc. I thought maybe you might want to talk to me for a while this morning.

*Professor:* Good idea. There are a few things I was curious about. First of all, why this education emphasis? What is the level of education of the staff and why Cresco Community College?

*Walters:* Except for the counselors in treatment, the staff have high school educations. The superintendent and several others have bachelor degrees, and there is an occasional year or two of college training among the staff. There is no financial or promotional incentive to attain more formal education. You are not hired at a higher pay rate if you have more than the minimum required education. The associate superintendent for custody and his captain are high school graduates. The training officer for the custody staff is a retired army type. Recently he stated in a meeting that he could see no advantage for himself in going on to school—there would be no increase in pay; he had made lieutenant and he was satisfied with himself. The training lieutenant reflects the views of the captain and the associate superintendent for custody. Needless to say, with these ideas floating about there is no mad rush by the custody staff to get into the community college program. You asked why the training emphasis? For some reason or other, the training supervisor at the state office is pushing it. Of course, the money to support the tuition comes from federal funds, so it doesn't cost the state anything. Staff attends at night after duty hours. My problem is to get the staff to enroll and stay in the program. There isn't any need for self-improvement in the minds of most staff members. No one has failed to get a promotion because of failure to seek additional formal education. We use the community college because it is the closest. As personnel officer, I have formal education under my jurisdiction.

*Professor:* You have a staff of about 270. How many are enrolled in the community college program?

*Walters:* About thirty were enrolled and I think there are about fifteen still active.

*Professor:* Let's move on to another area. Since there is a minimal turnover, there aren't many personnel actions, so what do you do?

*Walters:* Seems to me you over-simplified my job real quickly. It is true that over-all there is not too much turnover, but this varies with the employment conditions in the shipyards. If they are hiring, we lose people to their higher wages. If they are laying off, we can take our pick. Even when we can choose, we must be careful not to overhire. For example, right now we could hire some engineers and other degree types for custody, but at the first upturn of the economy they would leave us.

*Professor:* Do you have oral examinations for newly hired people and those to be promoted? I am thinking specifically of people hired for custody and subsequent advancements to sergeants and lieutenants.

*Walters:* The oral examinations for new hires are conducted by Mr. Oberg, the associate superintendent for custody. I sit in along with the captain from custody. The promotional examinations for sergeants and lieutenants are conducted by personnel from outside this institution.

*Professor:* Is there anything that you could tell me about the oral examinations for new hires in custody?

*Walters:* I think the most significant fact is that we pass those who think like Oberg. The captain never disagrees with him and I act as recorder. This means I arrange the details and take care of the paper work.

Toward the end of Professor Arlington's conversation with Mr. Walters, the professor expressed a desire to meet with various members of the Treatment and Custodial staff. At first, Walters was reluctant. However, he recalled that he had been instructed to cooperate fully with the professor. Therefore, he proceeded to arrange a series of interviews for him. Subsequently, the professor was able to interview Lieutenant Johnson, the chief training officer; Captain Watkinson, the assistant to associate for custody; Dr. Griffith, a consulting psychiatrist attached to the division of treatment; Mr. King, the Plant Manager; and finally, Mr. Oberg, the Associate for Custody.

*Professor:* Good morning, Lieutenant. Mr. Walters told me that you were expecting me.

*Johnson:* Nice to meet you, Professor. I am at your disposal, so what can I do for you?

*Professor:* I guess the best approach is for you to tell me just what you do. You know, this is my first time in any sort of a correctional institution.

*Johnson:* Briefly, I am in charge of training with particular emphasis on the six-month probationary period. We have a program for new hires and I monitor it in conjunction with concerned supervisors. If there are problems, I take the matter up with Mr. Oberg. I also work closely with the captain. I'm also available for special projects that Mr. Oberg may assign to me.

*Professor:* Is there any kind of ongoing training for the custody staff, like upgrading their skills to meet new demands of the system?

*Johnson:* This question should be answered by either the captain or Mr. Oberg. The new demands of the system and resultant skill changes, if any, would come from them. I have been here seven years; skills have not changed during this period of time. As you know, we have a relatively stable staff with very little turnover. Certainly the sergeants and lieutenants know what is expected of them, so why do we need additional training?

*Professor:* I understand there is a program through the local community college where interested staff can obtain an associate's degree. What do you think of it?

*Johnson:* I thought I just answered this. I don't really know what the objective of the program is. I enrolled, but then decided not to continue after a few weeks. The courses were pretty dull and seemed to me to be for an eighteen-year-old high school graduate. I have had over twenty-five years working with people. When a longhaired sociology professor, under thirty, who has never been in a work group tells me how to act—I get turned off!

*Professor:* You certainly have a point there. I would think the courses would be practically oriented—you take the learning from the classroom and use it in your daily work. On the other hand, there may be some fundamentals that should be discussed.

*Johnson:* If education is important, why isn't there some reward for attaining it? As a matter of fact, if a staff member really pursued education, he would educate himself out of a job in this institution. It might be a good idea for some. However, it's not for me. Then, if you did take a lot of courses and learned some new skills, where and how would you use them? About the only result would be that you would be known as "that smart ass!"

Since Mr. Oberg is not in this week, why don't I take you to see the captain?

Professor Arlington interviewed a few of the remaining staff members during his two-week visit at Waterloo. In substance, the remaining interviews were similar to those first described.

*Professor:* Good morning, Captain Watkinson. Mr. Walters, the personnel officer, arranged for me to see you. Perhaps we could start our discussion with your telling me what you do.

*Watkinson:* Nice to meet you, Professor. I guess the best way to explain my duties is to say that I am the assistant for custody to Mr. Oberg. Either the superintendent or Mr. Oberg set custody policy and I insure that the policy is followed. I pay close attention to new custody staff to be sure that they are compatible with our methods of operation at the end of their probationary period. Additionally, inmate violation of rules may come to my attention, depending upon the seriousness of the offense. These are my duties, broadly speaking. Is there anything you want in more detail?

*Professor:* What do you think of the program at the community college?

*Captain:* It's a waste of time. Nothing is learned that is useful. There is no real reason why a member of the custody staff should take formal education training. We have experienced supervisory personnel who can train people on the job for whatever is necessary. My convictions are based on personal experience. A sociology professor explained to me the intricacies of group interactions. He was trying to teach me principles that I have been practicing for twenty years. I doubt that the guy had ever practiced what he was preaching. He was just repeating words from the textbook. (*The captain's response was heated, and he spoke in excited and sharp tones. He was angry.*)

I've had a high school education, the same as Mr. Oberg, the associate superintendent for custody. To be very frank with you, I don't think further formal education can help me on the job.

*Professor:* I am not sure that we should condemn all education based on one unproductive experience. I share with you the fallacy of professors teaching youngsters and experienced supervisors with the same approach and content. The department should design the course and select professors to match the participants.

Moving on to another area, do you see any difference in the youth today that enter the prison as compared to fifteen to twenty years ago? I understand that the average age in this prison is in the early twenties.

*Watkinson:* I think the major difference is that the inmates are less structured.

There does not seem to be anything that we can work with. Instead of a firm character, there is a wishy-washy, bland sort of nothing. Whichever way the wind blows, they move.

*Professor:* Maybe this is because you became more structured yourself as you matured. Could it be that you have changed and not the inmates?

*Watkinson:* I suppose to some extent this could be. But if they are going to succeed in society, they have to develop fiber of some sort. The inmates learn conformity from our strict control methods. Besides, these aren't your normal people; 50 percent of them are returned here after they had been released.

*Professor:* Why do so many of them return?

*Watkinson:* Why don't you ask the treatment staff that question?

Some time later, the professor and the Associate for Treatment meet in the latter's office.

*Professor:* Mr. Graham, you know what I am doing here, so why don't we commence with any obstacles you may see in the way of providing more and better treatment to the inmates.

*Graham:* Treatment, in a general context, attempts to do what it can toward better preparing the inmate to be a meaningful part of society upon his release. Others in the prison focus on this same goal. There are differences in philosophy as to how best to proceed toward the goal; as a result, conflict does arise. Conflict is good if it will clear the air by open discussion—we would know where everyone stands and why. But we don't have open discussion.

   Unfortunately, we are a closed system as I see it. We do not react to changes in society and the environment that are outside of the prison system. We follow the procedures of fifteen to twenty years ago and are reluctant to change. Over the long term there are some changes; quick reaction on the part of prisons can come from enlightened leadership and a supporting society. I am not sure that either of these two conditions exists right now.

*Professor:* Is there anything that I can do to help you?

*Graham:* How can you change a limited and narrow outlook into one that is broad and all-encompassing?—Particularly when your system is aired in long-standing bureaucracy? It is not *im*possible though, and I think there are some actions we can take right now.

   Let's start group meetings with participants from every function of the prison—counselors, custody officers, teachers from vocational training and academies, supervisors in plant maintenance, superintendents, and inmates (that's a real shocker). Really open discussions; for example, what mistakes did each of us make last month?—Or, just how is each of us proceeding to correct mistakes? Are there areas where one impedes the progress of another? What can we do about it?

   We would need outside help to make these meetings productive.

*Professor:* You just mentioned that the prison is a closed system; your group meeting approach suggests that within this system you have smaller closed systems. Yesterday I was an observer during an oral interview for a promotion to sergeant. The custody officer had been in the institution for six years. He stated that he had no idea what treatment was doing. He did seem to be able to answer the custody questions quite well—he was qualified and knowledgeable in his specialty and his own system.

*Graham:* You have given a good example of what exists throughout the organization. But quietly and without fanfare I am getting through—treatment is being heard and progress is being made.

*Professor:* How much time do you have?

*Graham:* That is not the right question. It *should* be, how can I progress more rapidly?

*Professor:* I can't answer your question because I don't know your problems in detail. From my brief encounter, it appears that you need the enlightened leadership, on your own behalf, that you have said is essential for quick reaction.

There seems to be a general consensus in the state office as well as within the institution that Mr. Oberg is the true authority and both you and Superintendent Blake follow. Your analysis of moving quietly and without fanfare in treatment is interpreted as abdication.

*Graham:* Just because Oberg is loud and boisterous and I am quiet, doesn't mean that he dictates to me.

*Professor:* What spiritual guidance do you receive from your counterpart in the state office?

*Graham:* None.

*Professor:* How do you keep up-to-date with the latest innovations in your profession?

*Graham:* I do some reading. Occasionally I talk to my peers in the other institutions.

*Professor:* Is there any program offered by the University that could help you?

*Graham:* No. We have never asked for one.

*Professor:* Are there workshops or meetings with recognized leaders in the treatment disciplines?

*Graham:* No. But two years ago while I was on leave I stopped by a neighboring state and talked to the treatment staff.

*Professor:* Are you keeping up-to-date in your profession?

*Graham:* No. But I am doing as much as the rest. I would like to do more but there is no real incentive. Nobody seems to care and the possibility of using new knowledge is remote. After fifteen years of such an atmosphere, I have difficulty in assuming any sort of self-generating attitude.

I know the picture that I have portrayed to you of myself and treatment in this organization isn't good. This open conversation has been helpful. Maybe I can. . . .

## Later

*Professor:* Dr. Griffith, I have been looking forward to meeting you. I understand that you have been in correctional work since medical school, some thirty years ago. What is your specific job here?

*Doctor:* I am a consulting psychiatrist attached to the division of treatment, but I work for the superintendent. Two months ago he gave me a specific assignment of figuring out how to make the disciplinary unit less destructive. I have not taken any action and don't expect to. Nothing would change, regardless of what I would recommend.

*Professor:* If you are not accomplishing anything, why do you remain?

*Doctor:* Sometimes I wonder. But I do help some individual inmates. I am not a consultant who is concerned with programs where I would be more effective. I am a doctor working with individuals. I spend about 40 percent of my time interviewing inmates and 20 percent interpreting these interviews. In other words, 60 percent of my efforts is directly with inmates. The remainder of the time is taken up with paper work such as reports to the parole board.

*Professor:* The prison has one psychiatrist for two days a week. Is this because of the small workload, lack of funds, or what?

*Doctor:* There is one psychiatrist on a part-time basis because the correctional system is not directed to the individual.

The resources of the prison are expended towards the inmates as a mass. They are controlled as a group; they must earn their moves from close custody—to intermediate—to minimum custody. They must learn good work habits in order to hold a job outside. Everyone should have a high school education, so they all attend formal classes. By "they" I mean everyone is treated the same when he enters the prison. Of course, each inmate is an individual and he should be treated as the situation demands.

It is only by chance—a very small chance—that the inmate receives individual treatment. They are here because of personal problems. These problems caused them to violate a control established by society, and additionally, may have contributed towards poor work habits and inadequate formal education. The prison does nothing about the basic personal problems.

*Professor:* You mean that inmates should have psychiatrists available for treatment? This would take all of the qualified psychiatrists in the state for just one institution. I wonder, even with this approach, if you would solve the personal problems?

*Doctor:* You missed my point. Obviously this would be impractical and I doubt that all the problems would be solved. What I *am* suggesting is that we change the direction. Instead of the same approach to all inmates—control, work habits, and education—let's look at each individual and do the best we can with our existing resources.

*Professor:* I asked Mr. Oberg about more individual treatment for incoming inmates. He indicated that changes had been made.

*Doctor:* There have been two inmates in the last six months who have entered the prison and gone directly to minimum custody. Mr. Oberg sees this as a drastic change.

*Professor:* You mentioned that you wanted to be more concerned with programs. What programs do you suggest?

*Doctor:* Inservice training for inmates should be intensified and improved. In other words, give it more emphasis. Use custody in a manner conducive to helping this training. The positive gain by custody as a helping unit is minimal.

I don't deny the value of good work habits and education, but the real value comes when the inmate is motivated to really want them—to see that they are essential for his success. The value is minimal when they participate to please and impress the parole board or to conform to the system.

In the industry program or other areas where the inmate works, the emphasis is placed upon the value of the work, whereas it *should* be on the development of the man.

In the past, the prison literally dumped the inmate back into society. There should be more effort to soften the shock upon the individual when he returns. Work release and halfway houses are steps in this direction, but more action should be taken within the prison, or at least the problem should be recognized.

*Professor:* Why aren't such programs in existence?

*Doctor:* We need leadership in treatment. Much of what I have mentioned can be done within existing resources providing the staff wants to. Behavioral science theory exists to give the necessary guidance.

*Professor:* Given a free hand, what would you do?

*Doctor:* The first step is to get the prison going in the right direction—treatment. To do this, everyone must understand, be willing, and cooperate toward moving in this direction.

    Second, custody/control must be downgraded to a supporting service—not the primary objective. This will not be easy because the most militant are selected as lieutenants. Custody does not know what they are doing to the inmates—they must not only be shown but also accept their new role.

    Changing direction and changing the attitude of custody is not impossible. I would start with group sessions led by behavioral experts who are knowledgeable in corrections. Visit institutions that have moved in this direction and find out firsthand how they did it and the mistakes they made.

*Professor:* Do you have contacts with other institutions in the state or the central office?

*Doctor:* No.


Later . . .


*Professor:* Mr. King, as plant manager, what is your most critical problem?

*King:* The most difficult and time consuming part of my job is the continual counseling of foremen about their work relations with the inmates. If the inmate force is not effective, the prison is not maintained properly. The entire maintenance work force is from the inmates except for the foreman. He is the supervisor, teacher, work habit counselor, and he may have the closest—sometimes the only—personal contact with the inmate.

*Professor:* The treatment division of the prison provides counseling. Is your work with the inmates important adjunct to their counseling?

*King:* I am not sure *what* they do in treatment. I know that their case loads are heavy—sometimes a hundred or more. They cannot give the personal contact that our foremen can on a daily basis.

    There is one area that really upsets the foremen and myself. That's the rapid turnover. I don't have accurate figures, but I think the average length of time an inmate is on a job would be three to four months. This causes continual training.

    This is further aggravated by the disappearance of the inmates from the work force without prior notice. Transfers are never coordinated with us; they just happen. The foreman could be making real progress in his training and teaching role and this can be uncomfortable to the inmate. He goes to his counselor and wants to be removed from his present assignment. I suppose there are other reasons for the transfer, but the counselor should talk to the foreman before taking action.

    But in spite of our problem, I think we are about sixty percent as effective as our counterparts on the outside.

*Professor:* Why don't you take the matter up with the associate for treatment?
*King:* I am the plant manager. There is no indication that treatment is interested
   in the relations we have with the inmates, at least they never contacted me.
   I guess that they assume we are teaching good work habits.

The professor was especially pleased to hear that Mr. Oberg, the Associate for Custody, had returned to Waterloo. He phoned him and received an
invitation to come to Mr. Oberg's office "as soon as it is convenient for you."

*Oberg:* Come in, Professor. My training officer and captain have told me of their
   conversations with you. I don't know what I can add. Let's face it, I am
   from the old school. I believe in control—strict control. Society can't or
   hasn't been able to cope with our inmates. They find themselves here and
   we do what we think is best for them. I don't believe in big brother, leave
   of absence, work release, or any other method that takes inmates from this
   environment. If they prove themselves in our system and they earn relaxation of control they receive it; from close control at entry—to intermediate
   —to minimum. If the new programs I've mentioned or others are implemented, I will comply; but I don't agree with these methods.
*Professor:* I am not in a position to agree or disagree with your ideas about how
   to handle inmates. My only hope is that I can conduct a training course in
   administration that will result in better using resources to prepare inmates
   to cope with society upon their return to it. As a layman, I can see merits
   in your control methods; however, when I am confronted with the return
   rate of inmates to your own prison—maybe changes in methods should be
   considered.
*Oberg:* Professor, let's broaden our scope in looking at inmates. What does
   society want? Historically they want law breakers confined—out of sight.
   Suppose that our superintendent comes up with a good idea to improve the
   system—lessen the return rate. We try it—it fails. Whose head falls? The
   superintendent for sure, and perhaps mine—because control was relaxed.—
   Not the poor misguided sociologist who thought up the idea in the first
   place. Would the director of prisons back us? The executive branch of state
   government? The legislative branch? They *will* support saving money, but
   will they back "risk" in returning inmates to society? I have been in this institution for twenty-five years, and the answer is still the same—*no risk!*
*Professor:* What can I do to help you?
*Oberg:* Our greatest problem is communications. Do something about that.
*Professor:* Communications to me is twofold: the passing of information and
   understanding. I see lots of information flowing, but I don't see a great deal
   of understanding—like your failing to understand any procedure that is contrary to control. I am unable to teach a course to remove mental blocks.
      But let's move on to another area. It seems to me that your custody
   staff has more direct contact with inmates than anyone else. At the administrative review board you noted from the cell card of a particular inmate
   that he had been counseled eleven times by custody. You may have been
   using the term "counsel" loosely; perhaps it was just a warning or truly
   counseling. If the amount of contact is this great, it would seem to me that
   the more expertise your personnel have in interpersonal relations, the better

would be the result of custody contacts with inmates. So, why are you against more formal education?

*Oberg:* The treatment division of the prison has all the education. What does *it* achieve?

*Professor:* There seems to be a consensus among people, both inside and outside the institution, that you call the shots and really run things. Blake is your puppet and Graham does only what you permit him to do? What about it?

*Oberg:* I am outspoken. In addition, I speak loudly. I speak frankly and there is no doubt as to the meaning. If I am convinced that an issue should take a certain course, I go all the way to the superintendent. The timid would view my approach as a steam-roller—crumbling all resistance.

# CASE 13
# A Simple Problem of Communication

Chicago Chemicals is one of the three largest producers of chemicals in the United States. Due to the size of the organization and nationwide scope of its activities, Chicago Chemicals relies on a regional system for recruiting future personnel. Each regional office is responsible for locating, screening, and hiring all persons to be employed in that area. Depending on the part of the country, this may include engineers, production staff, and marketing personnel, in addition to persons employed in other supporting departments. The North Central Regional Office is responsible for recruiting in Wisconsin, Illinois, Michigan, Indiana, Ohio, and Pennsylvania. In addition to the North Central main office, there are seven smaller district recruiting offices that in turn, employ sixty-seven full-time recruiters.

There are thirty-five persons currently working in the regional office under the management of Richard Thompkins. The office itself is composed of four departments: Administration and Personnel; Scheduling; Advertising and Publicity; and Recruiting Operations (see Exhibit 1).

## Departmental Responsibilities

Director of the Administration and Personnel Department is Mary Charles. The department is responsible for coordinating activities at the regional office, designing and printing all recruiting materials, and developing specific programs for all recruiting activities in the region. In addition, the department maintains a reporting and control system and initiates security checks on potential employees when necessary. The department is responsible also for selecting and training all recruiters and for assigning them to individual offices.

The Advertising and Publicity Department, under Terrence Reddin, directs the advertising and publicity program for the regional office in support of its recruiting function. Members of the department provide guidance and assist recruiters on special projects. Mr. Reddin has initiated a high school education information program and a widely based public relations program in the region. These two programs are not directly related to activities of the individual recruitment offices. An internal information program for the region has been initiated by the department.

The Scheduling Department is a small but powerful unit under the direction of Ben Holdridge. Holdridge's department prepares, maintains, and monitors all contracts and contract agreements for office space, vehicle rental and maintenance, and other forms of transportation. The time frames for all

Prepared by H. William Vroman, Towson State University; and Donald D. White, University of Arkansas.

**Exhibit 1. Organization chart, Chicago Chemicals North Central region.**

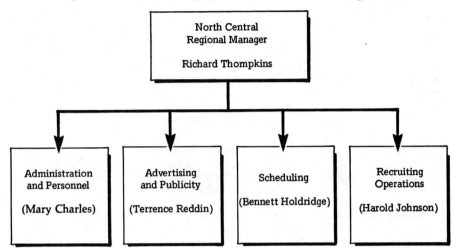

recruitment trips must be cleared through the Scheduling Department. In addition, the Scheduling Department provides staff assistance to the regional director and to each recruitment office supervisor.

Work in the Scheduling Department is often exacting and requires a considerable amount of detailed paperwork. Staff members find it necessary to be thorough and deliberate when completing assigned tasks. An expansion at the Chicago office which took place one year ago drained off many of the "older hands" from the department. Therefore, existing members of the department average a little over two years' experience in their jobs (see Exhibit 2). The department received a rating of "excellent" in the last regional office evaluation. Some of the group norms are: Strive for accuracy; pay attention to detail; do the job right the first time.

Recruiting Operations, under Harold Johnson, is responsible for a wide range of activities. Principally, it directs the development of plans and programs pertaining directly to personnel selection. The department establishes policies and carries out plans from the Chicago office to achieve personnel procurement objectives. Johnson's staff formulates and initiates recruitment programs and policies for the region. Evaluation of the performance of individual recruiters is handled by the department, and certain personnel programs, such as a recent incentive awards program and a safety program, were initiated there. It is not unusual for Johnson or individual department members to recommend additions, changes, or new programs to other departments or to Mr. Thompkins himself.

No serious problems have ever arisen between Recruiting Operations and the other departments. However, some members of other departments have complained of interference from Operations. For example, all divisions are required to make staff assistance visits into the field. Recruiting Operations often exhausts its travel money prior to the end of the quarter. The depart-

**Exhibit 2. Department members (Recruiting Operations and Scheduling).**

| Position | Name | Age | Years' experience on the job |
|---|---|---|---|
| *Recruiting Operations Department* | | | |
| Manager | Harold Johnson | 52 | 18 |
| Staff | Gerald Thomas | 34 | 8 |
| Staff | James Lawson | 38 | 7 |
| Staff | Betty Jennings | 36 | 3 |
| Staff | Richard Horn | 44 | 14 |
| Staff | Joe Sutton | 46 | 11 |
| Staff | Gene Maddox | 46 | 14 |
| Staff | Gordon Edwards | 49 | 14 |
| Staff | Tom Campbell | 36 | 7 |
| *Scheduling Department* | | | |
| Manager | Ben Holdridge | 48 | 9 |
| Staff | Gary Ford | 22 | New employee |
| Staff | John McGee | 34 | 4 |
| Staff | Robert Webb | 35 | 3 |
| Staff | Barbara Peterson | 24 | 2 |
| Staff | Jan Owens | 21 | New employee |

ment claimed that there were numerous unanticipated changes in requirements. On the other hand, many persons outside the department suggested
the difficulty was the result of poor planning. Additional travel funds eventually were obtained from Chicago, and the matter was dropped.

A final function of the department is to analyze district operations and
investigate "slow employment areas" or unduly large numbers of unsuccessful placements. Reports concerning these investigations are forwarded directly
to the regional manager.

The members of the department averaged over eleven years' experience
and each had served in the field for up to three years as a recruiter (see Exhibit 2). In fact, their appointment to the Recruiting Operations Department
was based on "outstanding performance" as a recruiter. Department members
take pride in their appointments. They are a cohesive group and often socialize off the job. Norms of the operations group include: keep the recruiters in
the field well informed; delays hamper accomplishment.

## Personnel Problems at Home

In recent months, word of conflict between the Recruiting Operations and
Scheduling departments filtered up to Mr. Thompkins. Symptoms of conflict
were numerous and varied. For example, he noted that members of each department seemed to avoid having conversations with one another whether on
or off the job. On more than one occasion, he had observed a group of employees from one of the two departments quickly disperse when members of

the other department entered into the discussion. Moreover, activities of the two departments have been marked by a noticeable lack of communication. On three separate occasions during the last six months, directives from the Operations department to local recruiters in the field have instructed those recruiters to move out of old facilities and into new ones before the Scheduling Department had finished the paperwork on the move. On another occasion, field offices were instructed by the operations department to have additional telephone lines installed in their offices before approval had been received from Scheduling. Scheduling had an extremely difficult time justifying them after the fact, since expenditures of this nature were closely scrutinized by the Chicago office.

Richard Thompkins decided that steps must be taken to discover the underlying cause of the interdepartmental difficulties. After talking with members of each of the two departments on an informal basis, he began to make some notes to himself about the conversations. His findings are summarized as follows:

1. No one really wants to talk about the other department; most do not complain readily.
2. Members of each department believe that they are doing their job, but they claim that the other department hinders their work.
3. Attitudes of Scheduling and Personnel about the Operations Department is best summed up in comment of Scheduling supervisor: "Those guys just seem to me to be pushy and self-centered. They're too much rah-rah and go-go-go. Who do they think they are, anyway?"
4. Operations Department members describe the Scheduling Department as "slow as hell"; "They never want to cooperate with us"; "We really care about this recruiting operation, but those guys just don't seem to understand the importance of getting to these people (potential employees) the fastest with the most!"
5. A comment from Harold Johnson: "My people know the importance of their job and I think they have real company loyalty. To tell you the truth, I can't say the same for the fellows in some of the other departments."

After reading over the list a couple of times, Thompkins leaned back in his chair and smiled knowingly. Later that day he called into his office the two department heads. He began his discussion by saying, "Bess, Harold, I think we have a bit of a communication problem here. It's as simple as that."

# CASE 14
# Electelon

Electelon, a medium-sized electronics firm, is primarily engaged in the manufacture of subassemblies for the space administration (NASA). These subassemblies are designed for use in rockets and capsules. The primary technological process (line activity) is highly precise and complex. Consequently, there is a necessity for the organization to provide engineering services and support to all electronic systems maintained in an operational status by their customer, NASA.

Due to the complexity of the systems and the great variety in their nature and application, responsibility for service/support is assigned according to function. As a whole, the organization of the engineering branch has the responsibility of providing engineering management, direction, and control to all operational electronics systems.

The engineering branch is composed of four sections corresponding to the currently operating systems. The sections are the Electronic Communication Section, the Radar Section, the Computer Section, and the Satellite Transmissions Section. Within each section are several functional engineers depending on the number and size of the projects undertaken at any one time by the section. Having different functions but equal organizational rank are the section chief and the engineering manager. The section chief is expected to provide a communications link with the whole organization. In addition, he or she is expected to perform the traditional functions of job appraisal, system assignment, and workload monitoring and prediction. The engineering manager, on the other hand, has minimal administrative duties and is primarily engaged in professional engineering activities. Consequently, he or she works closely with the engineer assigned to the project.

Exhibit 1 illustrates the offices of the engineering branch. The functional engineers are in the appropriate section in bullpen fashion. The engineering managers and section chiefs are in the branch office, which is divided into separate offices.

Projects are formally started when an engineering manager forwards information regarding action to be taken to the integration section. This section is charged with the planning activities of the branch. The paperwork authorizing manpower from the engineering manager "establishes" a project. The authorizing paperwork includes an outline of the project and the specific engineers needed for the project. All projects are then forwarded to a particular section chief for review and assignment.

Charles Hildreth is the section chief of the electronic section. Charles, 48, has been in charge since the reorganization seven years ago. He has had super-

Prepared by H. William Vroman, Towson State University.

**Exhibit 1. Physical relation of offices to one another.**

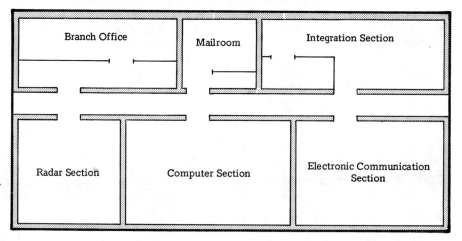

visory experience in other line positions prior to that. His experience has served him well and he seems to understand engineers. His philosophy with new engineers is to allow them to progress as fast as they can. He starts them on short, routine tasks which can be clearly defined and judged upon completion. The general evolution toward more complex and general tasks is achieved through demonstrated success with previous tasks. Reliance on superiors diminishes as the engineer attempts the more complex tasks. His or her professional orientation is expected to guide behavior. All is not well in the branch, as the following incidents illustrate.

## Incident 1

The following conversations took place at ECS between Charles and Bud Mason, an engineering manager.

*Hildreth:* Here's the project list I got from I. S. [Integration Section]. I had to make a couple of changes in the engineers you'll get.

*Mason:* Wait a minute, Charles. I specifically requested Murphy and James. They aren't here.

*Hildreth:* I know. I wanted them on Project W.

*Mason:* Hell, that's not going to challenge them! They have the expertise I need for this job—that's why I wanted them. Anyway, Charles, we've already started this project.

*Hildreth:* What?

*Mason:* The project came up while we were testing on ECS. Before I made out the information papers for Integration, I checked on the availability of and interest of the relevant engineers.

*Hildreth:* I'm sorry you did that, Bud. Projects are not supposed to start until I give the authorization.

*Mason:* I'm the engineer, Charles. I know the expertise of the people here. I'm with them all the time. Whenever there's a project at any NASA installation, we go as a team. You're always in Washington or corporate headquarters. In addition, I know my systems and what it takes to get the job done. I'm sorry that we don't see eye to eye on this. Also, Charles, don't pull rank on me; we're both equal on this totem pole.

*Hildreth:* My job description clearly states what my duties are, Bud. You and I have been through this before. The division of labor is clear-cut. I respect your engineering knowledge, just don't make commitments that are in my realm.

## Incident 2

Chuck Bradley, engineering manager of receiver systems, has six engineers assigned to him. He is talking with Belle Gradman, one of the assigned engineers.

*Gradman:* Hey, Chuck, did you get the specs from Huntsville?
*Bradley:* Yeah, they're in my basket in my office.
*Gradman:* Duplicate a copy and send it over for our files, will you?
*Bradley:* Sure. This reminds me, the chief engineer of Teledyne is going to call this afternoon at 2:00 at my office. I guess we'll have to arrange a conference call. It's sure too bad that we're not on the same line. Say, do you guys have a copy of blueprint 340S in your file? I don't have a set in mine. You people weren't there yesterday and I needed them for Washington. Damn, we ought to have rooms just for projects. This duplicate file stuff is rotten.

## Incident 3

Jim Tate, a two-year man, talking with a new recruit, Tom Urban.

*Urban:* I understand you're leaving, Jim?
*Tate:* Yes, Tom, and I'm pretty bitter too.
*Urban:* Really?
*Tate:* It's a problem you'll have to contend with, Tom. I guess I can fill you in on it. This is an extreme view, but I guess I'm tired of just sharpening the pencils of the "favored few." I've been out of school five years now. It's time to start my move. Home, kids, work on the MBA, age—all these things are beginning to sap my energy. With the challenge on this job, I'm going to wake up one of these days technically obsolete. I think they want you that way so you're not so much of a threat. This garbage about increasing your responsibility as fast as you can handle it is a myth. Billingsley got a start in establishing a track record. But he also came from the same school as Mason. Hildreth's signature is on everything, but the guys you have to play up to are Bradley and Mason. Hildreth doesn't know engineering, or at least he doesn't have the credentials—and around here that is half the battle. That's the scene. I hope you contend with it better than I have.

# CASE 15
# The Case of Two Masters

The Adamson Aircraft Company has in the last decade expanded its product line to include the design, development, and production of missiles for the United States government. For this purpose a missile division was established, and over 5,000 personnel were gathered to man this portion of the firm.

The traditional type of organization in aircraft manufacturing calls for functional specialization like that found in the automobile industry. Aircraft are made up of such items as engines, radios, wheels, and armament. The manufacture of component parts was standardized and the aircraft put together on an assembly line. It was quickly recognized that such a simplified approach would not meet future requirements, as the demand for greater capability and effectiveness increased and forced the designers to insist upon optimum performance in every part or component. Several components, each with an operational reliability of 99 percent, may have a combined reliability of only 51 percent. Even with the most judicious selection and usage of standard parts, a system could end up with a reliability approaching zero. To overcome this reliability drop, it became necessary to design the entire system as a single entity. Many of the parts that were formerly available off the shelf must now be tailored to meet the exacting demands of the total system. Thus, the "weapons system" concept was developed, which necessitated a change in organization and management.

For each weapons system project, a chief project engineer is appointed. He assembles the necessary design personnel for every phase of the project. In effect, he organizes and creates a small, temporary company for the purpose of executing a single weapons system. On his staff are representatives of such functional areas as propulsion, secondary power, structures, flight test, and "human factors." The human factors specialist, for example, normally reports to a human factors supervisor. In the human factors department are men with training in psychology, anthropology, physiology, and the like. They do research on human behavior and hope to provide the design engineers with the basic human parameters applicable to a specific problem.

James Johnson, an industrial psychologist, has been working with the missile division of Adamson for six months as a human factors specialist. His supervisor, George Slauson, also has a Ph.D. in psychology and has been with the firm for two years. Johnson is in a line relationship with Slauson, who conducts his annual review for pay purposes, and prepares an efficiency re-

From *Principles of Personnel Management (Fourth Edition)* by Edwin B. Flippo. Copyright 1976 by McGraw-Hill Book Company. Used with permission of McGraw-Hill Book Company.

port on his work. Slauson is responsible for assembling and supervising a group of human factors experts to provide Adamson with the latest and most advanced information in the field of human behavior and its effect on product design.

Johnson has been assigned to a weapons system project, which is under the direction of Bernard Coolsen, a chief project engineer. In a committee meeting of project members, Coolsen stated, "I am thinking about a space vehicle of minimum weight capable of fourteen days' sustained activity, maneuverability, and rendezvous with other vehicles for maintenance and external exploration. How many men, how big a vehicle, and what instruments, supplies, and equipment will we need?" Johnson immediately set to work on his phase of the project. The data for the answer to this request were compiled and organized, and a rough draft of the human factors design criteria was prepared in triplicate. Johnson took the original to his supervisor, Slauson, for review, retaining the other two copies. Using one of the copies, he began to reedit and rewrite, working toward a smooth copy for presentation to Coolsen. A week later Johnson was called in by Slauson who said, "We can't put out stuff like this. First, it's too specific, and secondly, it's poorly organized." Slauson had rewritten the material extensively and had submitted a draft of it to his immediate superior, the design evaluation chief. In the meantime Coolsen had been calling Johnson for the material, insisting that he was holding up the entire project. Finally, taking a chance, Johnson took his original copy to Coolsen, and they sat down together and discussed the whole problem. An illustrator was called in, and in two days the whole vehicle was sketched up ready for design and specification write-up. The illustrator went to his board and began converting the sketches to drawings. Coolsen started to arrange for the writing of component and structural specifications, and Johnson went back to his desk to revise his human engineering specifications in the light of points brought out during the two-day team conference.

Three days later the design evaluation chief called Johnson into his office and said, "Has your supervisor seen this specification of yours?" Johnson replied that he had and that this was Slauson's revision of the original. The chief then asked for the original, and Johnson brought in the third original copy. Two days later the chief's secretary delivered to Johnson's desk a draft of his original specification as modified by Slauson as modified by the design evaluation chief. Johnson edited this for technical accuracy and prepared a ditto master. Slauson and the design evaluation chief read the master, initialed it, and asked for thirty copies to be run off. One copy was kept by Johnson, one by Slauson, one by the chief, five put into company routing, and the balance placed in file. Those in company routing went to the head of technical staff, head of advanced systems, and finally to the project engineer, Coolsen. Coolsen filed one copy in the project file and gave the other to Johnson. The latter dropped it in the nearest waste basket, inasmuch as several days previously, Coolsen had combined his, the illustrator's, and Johnson's material and submitted it to publications. Publications had run off six copies, one each for Coolsen, the illustrator, Johnson, the head of advanced systems, the U. S. Patent Office, and one for file. Also, by this time, the vehicle had been accepted by the company management as a disclosure for patent purposes. Johnson breathed a sigh of relief, since he thought that he had gotten away with serving two masters.

# EXPERIENTIAL EXERCISE 6
## Organizing

The purpose of this exercise is to increase your awareness of the importance of structure in organization. In addition, the exercise focuses on the importance of management in organizing a venture.

### The Problem

Select one of the following situations to organize. Then read the background material before answering the questions.

a. The registration process at your university or college.
b. A new hamburger fast-food franchise.
c. A Jetski rental in an ocean resort area.

Do steps 1 to 7, below, as homework. In preparing your answers, use your own experience, or think up logical answers to the questions.

### Background

Organization is a way of gaining some power against an unreliable environment. The environment provides the organization with inputs, which include raw materials, human resources, and financial resources. There is a service or product to produce which involves technology. The output is to be sold to a client, a group that must be nurtured. The complexities of the environment and the technology determine the complexity of the organization.

### Planning Your Organization

1. In a few sentences, write the mission or purpose of your organization.
2. From the mission statement you should be able to write down specific things that must be done in order to accomplish the mission.
3. From the list of specifics that must be accomplished, an organizational chart can be devised. Each position on the chart will perform a specific task or is responsible for a specific outcome.
4. Add duties to each job position on your organizational chart. This will form a job description.
5. How would you ensure that the people that you placed in these positions worked together?
6. What level of skill and abilities is required at each position and level in order to hire the right person for each position?
7. Make a list of the decisions that would have to be made while you planned

**Prepared by H. William Vroman.**

and built the organization. Make a second list of those decisions you would have to make just after your organization began operating.

## *In Class*

1. Form into groups up to three members that organized the same project, and share your answers to the questions.
2. Come to agreement on the way to organize utilizing everyone's responses.
3. Present the group's approach to the class.

# CHAPTER FIVE

# Organizational Climate

Elsewhere in the book we discuss organizational structure, leadership, and conflict and stress. Each of these concepts is important to study in its own right; however, each also contributes to an organizational phenomenon called climate.[1] Many other terms are used to refer to climate, for example, internal environment or atmosphere.

Climate is used in organizational analysis in a way similar to our everyday reference to the weather. Climates change because pressure areas, winds, or one of many other factors shift; some climates are better for human functioning than other climates; and climate changes are reasonably well understood. Similarly, in organization theory climate is a characteristic of the entire unit and is a result of the many forces operating in that environment. As a result of the evolution of a climate, the response of that organization to outside influences becomes predictable.[2] The organization as a whole has a climate or "personality."[3] However, individual departments or units in the organization also may generate their own unique climates. For example, the research and development laboratory has a different climate than the boiler room. However, units with similar functions in the same geographic setting probably have similar climates in which their employees work.

Climate is a complex concept. Campbell and his colleagues define climate as "a set of attributes specific to a particular organization that may be induced from the way that organization deals with its members and its environment."[4]

## Influences on Climate

### System Influences on Climate

Figure 1 shows the relationship between climate and organizational system input and output factors. The factors labeled as input factors in the figure

**Figure 1. Climate as an intervening variable.**

| Input factors | Intervening factor | Output factors |
|---|---|---|
| External<br>  sociopolitical<br>  technology<br>  size | | |
| Internal (organizational)<br>  leadership<br>  roles<br>  rewards<br>  communication<br>  power | ----▶climate ----▶ | Organizational performance<br>  production<br>  satisfaction<br>  absenteeism<br>  adaptiveness |
| Group<br>  processes | | Group performance<br>  production<br>  morale<br>  cohesiveness |
| Individual<br>  attitudes<br>  personality<br>  learning | | Individual performance<br>  production<br>  satisfaction |

Feedback

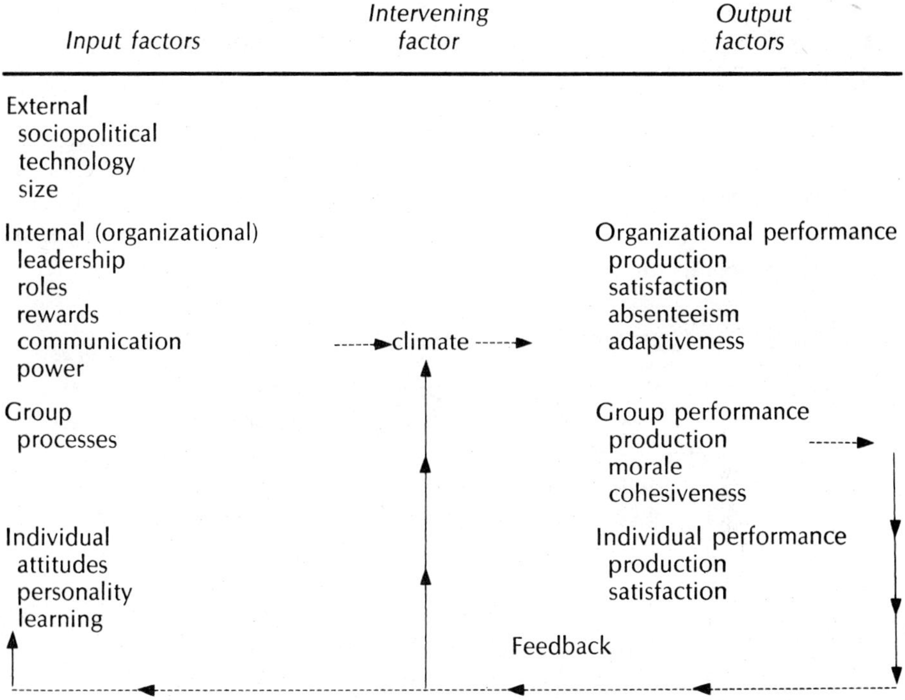

lead to the output of the organization. Climate is an intervening variable that mediates the impact of inputs on the organization. If the climate is favorable, influences from input factors will result in positive changes in outcomes. If the climate is unfavorable, input factors will be moderated so they do not have a positive influence on output factors. The feedback cycle completes the picture. Results of the input–climate–output interactions are fed back to climate and to the input factors. Climate is enduring (ongoing). However, it does change as a result of the dynamics of the system.

*Input factors* are broken into external factors and internal factors. Internal factors include organizational, group, and individual components. Each component has several sub-components. All these are inputs to the organizational climate. Once established, the relationship of these inputs to the organizational functioning becomes enduring and somewhat resistant to change.

*External forces* emanate from sources outside the organization. For example, a social force might be a change in consumer taste. A political force might include a new set of social responsibility laws. Internal forces are generated within the organization and include leadership behaviors as well as those behaviors engaged in while acting out organizational roles (e.g. communicating, conflict, and planning). These factors change and force reactions from organizational participants and organizations themselves, creating certain response patterns (i.e., characteristic ways the organization perceives things that happen to it). Moreover, the influence of any single factor may be difficult to diagnose, since many factors combine to create the organizational climate.

*Output factors* are broken down into organizational, group, and individual components. Major sub-sets are listed for each component. Organizational performance as a whole is emphasized at the expense of group and individual components. A strong case can be made for the importance of all three levels in the performance of an organization.

### Societal Influences on Climate

Forces external to the organization are major determinants of organizational climate. Managers used to be considered the major influence on an organization's climate because of their control over reward and role systems. Today, however, societal influences are believed also to have a highly significant impact in the organization. Some of the pervasive external factors are listed below.[5]

*Educational levels.* Workers enter the job market today with a higher level of education and higher awareness of the opportunities that can fully utilize their skills and talents than was previously true. A result is an increasing demand for greater autonomy and respect and more challenging work.

*Diversity of the workforce.* Many forces have converged to open the workplace to minorities and women. Maintaining organizational vitality and creativity under the pressure of increasing diversity is difficult as established on-the-job behaviors undergo challenge and change.

*Technological advances.* World War II signaled a technological revolution. Computers, satellites, and moon walks are only some of the glamorous results of these technological advances. Organizations spend significant amounts of time and other resources to ensure that they are abreast of, and able to use, technological advancements that will contribute to the attainment of their goals.

*Union contracts.* Union contracts constrain management's ability to unilaterally affect job design and reward systems, two major tools that directly affect organization climate.

*Government regulations.* Governmental agencies directly affect the workplace in numerous ways. Their net effect is to limit managerial options to deal flexibly with such influences as the changing technology and workforce diversity. Resources must be allocated to internal recordkeeping and compliance activities directly associated with government regulation.

*Organizational growth.*   Increasing organization size has made it more difficult for the worker to see where his or her efforts fit into the overall performance of the organization. Dissatisfaction and low performance may result when individuals feel "lost" in organizations.

*Attractiveness of nonwork.*   The increasing attractiveness of leisure and other nonwork activities adds pressure on the workplace to provide human value that cannot be achieved off the job.

Each of the external factors mentioned above exists independently and lies either outside the organization (e.g., government regulations) or inter-dependently with outside agencies (e.g., union contracts). Moreover, the factors combine in unique ways to affect organizations; for example, the diversity of the workforce has increased the amount of government regulation through equal employment legislation.

## Macro Organization Characteristics

A number of internal characteristics have been identified which explain variances in climate from organization to organization. These characteristics are relatively enduring and are a major influence on the behavior of people. Forehand and Gilmer maintain that these factors interact to largely create the organization climate.[6]

*Size and structure.*   Size is a major influence in determining the nature of interpersonal interaction as well as the authority structure. Large organizations often have many levels between the employee and top management. This creates an air of impersonality. Authority and the trappings of authority are usually very important in large organizations. Smaller organizations are less likely to have elaborate authority structures. In small organizations people at all levels are likely to know one another, and rules and policies are less likely than in larger organizations to be evident.

*Leadership patterns.*   Early studies focused on the importance of leadership as a prime determinant of climate. For example, task-oriented and people-oriented leadership were associated with autocratic and democratic climates, respectively. Leadership is an important factor in climate, but many other factors have been found to be equally important under differing conditions.

*System complexity.*   Organizational systems include departments, processes, information flows, roles, and activities. Each of these variables depends on the action of other variables. The larger the number of variables and the more highly they are interdependent, the more complex the system. The organization that assembles plastic toys is not as complex as the organization that develops space-age equipment. Attention to organization matters increases considerably as system complexity increases. In addition, the degree of required employee competence increases as the complexity of the technology increases.

*Goal direction.*   Public versus private, voluntary versus nonvoluntary, organizations often have different goals. Although there are many similarities across organizations, differences in goals may mean major differences in reward systems. Working in a private, bottom-line-oriented firm creates different pressures on managers and employees than does working in a nonprofit agency. Voluntary organizations (Girl Scouts, Chamber of Commerce) motivate workers differently than do nonvoluntary organizations. The authority of nonvoluntary organization managers is much more than that of the voluntary organization managers, because the volunteer can just walk away. The motivational program must be positive and encouraging, hoping to retain the volunteer. Even within a category the direction of goals may be quite different. A commercial firm in a growth phase of development may emphasize goals to increase market penetration, while a more mature firm may emphasize product development. Different goal directions create differing climates in organizations.

*Communication networks.*   Openness and trust play a role in how individuals react to their positions. The networks of horizontal and vertical communication channels available to an organization affect both status and the effective exercise of authority. The adequacy of information channels also is related to system complexity. The more complex the system, the more information that generally flows between decision centers. Finally, communication networks influence the nature and importance of informal groups in the organization.

### Climate Influences on the Individual

Climate uniquely affects individuals in an organization. The influence is subtle but commanding.[7] Environmental characteristics—such as the size of the organization, technology, or economic conditions of the industry—are critical in the definition of the *stimuli that influence the behavior* of organizational participants. For example, if economic conditions are poor, there may be a demand to cut costs. This orientation determines many of the pressures, regulations, and leader behaviors that guide worker behavior. When profits are high, the orientation is probably less inhibiting.

*Constraints upon freedom* is another effect of climate on the individual. Hierarchical rules and regulations clearly limit freedom of behavior. Subtle influences like the political nature of the organization may cause managers to limit their openness with one another. Finally, climate defines opportunities for *reward and punishment* within the organization. For example, in some organizations subordinates can make broad decisions without consulting their superiors and will be rewarded for their creativity; in other organizations the same type of behavior is punished.

### Dimensions of Organizational Climate

Factors discussed thus far are major variables in the determination of organizational climate. Participant perceptions of these organizational properties also affect their behavior. Litwin and Stringer emphasize the leader's impact in fashioning the climate closest to the worker.[8] Their research resulted in a taxonomy of factors which contribute to organizational climate and which are perceived by participants as relevant stimuli, constraints, or reinforcements. In this view, climate has eight dimensions. The properties of each dimension evoke certain feelings in people.

1. *Structure* affects the feelings participants have about the constraints in their work situation. Examples include the rules governing employee behavior and constraints explicit in job descriptions.
2. *Challenge and responsibility* affect the feeling of being "your own person" and not having to doublecheck everything with a superior. Challenge and responsibility usually result from jobs that are significant and sufficiently reinforcing. The emphasis on specialization in large organizations forces individuals to do jobs that use only limited skills and therefore create only limited challenges.
3. *Risk* refers to the sense employees have when they do things on their own as part of their job. In some organizations the political nature of career advancement requires limited risk-taking and "safe" work behavior in order to get regular promotions. In other organizations, people are encouraged to take moderate risks without the threat of retribution.
4. *Reward* refers to the positive feelings experienced for a job well done. A rewarding environment is one which places emphasis on positive reinforcement as opposed to criticism and punishment. Rewards raise an individual's level of aspiration. In addition, "get-even" behaviors are minimized in climates characterized by reward.
5. *Warmth and support* imply feelings of "good fellowship" and helpfulness from others that prevails in some organizations. This feeling is ordinarily evoked because sufficient time is given for informal activities in the organization.
6. *Conflict* is a condition of tension in an organization. If conflict is settled openly, it generates a feeling that management is not afraid of differing opinions. In such a case emphasis is on settling differences here and now instead of suppressing or delaying the confrontation. Many conflict cycles are generated because not enough time is allowed to deal effectively with all conflicts. If the organization stays under control, it is because the employees feel they can openly discuss difficulties and errors will not be used against them. Where conflicts are suppressed or conflict participants are punished, the tension that develops causes additional mistrust and further conflict rather than solutions.
7. *Identity* is the feeling of loyalty to the organization. The feeling of being a

needed member of the organization results from activities in a cohesive work group or informal group. Respect and encouragement of superiors, peers, and subordinates naturally result from this situation.

8. *Standards* refer to the extent to which company goals are challenging and the degree to which excellent work is expected. Many organizations attempt to encourage high standards through incentives, management by objectives, and other programs. Transmitting clear and noncompetitive goals is the desired outcome of standards.

### Individual Motive Patterns

Climate dimensions can be motivating or discouraging to individuals depending on their individual motive patterns. Organizational climate should be designed to complement the motive patterns of the participants. Litwin and Stringer,[9] following research by McClelland (see Chapter Three in this text), use three motive patterns: the need for achievement (*n ach*), need for power (*n pow*), and need for affiliation (*n aff*). A person having one of these motive patterns will function best in a climate designed to arouse that motive. For example, people with high *n ach* have needs including medium risk, rewards for effort, and clear organizational expectations about standards. High *n aff* people need democratic, supportive atmospheres where feelings of loyalty are emphasized. Those individuals with high *n pow* will be motivated where they have decision-making control, a high degree of structure, low conflict, and a high degree of loyalty. Each of these descriptions emphasizes certain dimensions of climate and minimizes others.

## Summary

Organizational climate is multidimensional and situationally related. Many forces operate to create an organizational climate. Once established, climate tends to cause the organization to react in characteristic ways. Some major environmental forces affecting climate are the general educational level of workers, the diversity of the workforce, technological changes, union constraints, government regulations, growth incentives, and the attractiveness of leisure. These factors operate on the overall organization and combine in unique ways for each organization depending on such activities as their hiring patterns and technology.

Some organizational level factors that influence climate include organization size, leadership patterns, systems complexity, goal direction, and communication networks. Climate has an impact on individual behavior in the workplace by defining stimuli, constraining the freedom of employees, and creating reward-punishment contingencies for behavior.

Employee perceptions of climate dimensions significantly contribute to the impact of climate within the organization. Eight climate dimensions include: structure, challenge, risk, reward, warmth and support, conflict, identity, and standards. The number of unique climates is large, given the variance and possible combinations of the eight dimensions. Finally, all employees in organizations have their own motive patterns. The interaction of individual motive patterns and stimulus patterns created by organizational climate will influence both employee morale and productivity.

*References*                                                              $STOP$

1. Benjamin Schneider, "Organizational Climates: An Essay," *Personnel Psychology*, Winter 1975, pp. 447–480.

2. B. S. Georgopoulos, "Normative Structure Variables and Organizational Behavior," *Human Relations*, 1965, pp. 18, 115–170.

3. Andrew J. DuBrin, *Fundamentals of Organizational Behavior*, (New York: Pergamon Press, 1974), p. 331.

4. John Campbell, M. D. Dunnette, E. E. Lawler III, and Karl E. Weick, *Managerial Behavior, Performance, and Effectiveness*. (New York: McGraw-Hill Book Co., 1970), p. 389.

5. Edward E. Lawler III, "Developing a Motivating Work Climate," *Management Review*, July 1977, pp. 25–28, 37–38.

6. Garlie A. Forehand and B. Von Haller Gilmer, "Environmental Variation in Studies of Organizational Behavior." *Psychological Bulletin*, vol. 64, no. 4, December 1964, pp. 361–381.

7. Ibid.

8. George H. Litwin and Robert A. Stringer, Jr., *Motivation and Organizational Climate*, (Harvard University Press: Boston, 1968), pp. 45–65.

9. Ibid.

*Recommended Readings*

Readings marked with an asterisk are included in *Contemporary Perspectives in Organizational Behavior*, edited by Donald D. White (Boston: Allyn and Bacon, 1982).

H. K. Downey, D. Hellriegel, and J. Slocum, Jr., "Congruence Between Individual Needs, Organizational Climate, Job Satisfaction and Performance," *Academy of Management Journal*, March 1975, pp. 149–155.

*Lee Ginsburg, "Strategic Planning for Work Climate Modification," *Personnel*, vol. 55, November–December 1978, pp. 10–20.

L. R. Jones and A. P. Jones, "Organizational Climate: A Review of Theory and Research," *Psychological Bulletin*, December 1974, pp. 1096–1112.

R. L. Payne, S. Fineman, and T. D. Wall, "Organizational Climate and Job Satisfaction: A Conceptual Synthesis," *Organizational Behavior and Human Performance*, June 1976, pp. 45–62.

*Benjamin Schneider, "Organizational Climates: An Essay," *Personnel Psychology*, vol. 28, Winter 1975, pp. 447–479.

R. W. Woodman and D. C. King, "Organizational Climate: Science or Folklore?" *Academy of Management Review*, October 1978, pp. 816–826.

# CASE 16
# The Letter

## Part I

*Company History*

Pearl's is a retail department store in a large Eastern city. Established 120 years ago by the Pearl family, it is still family owned.

The Main Store is in the heart of the city on the site of Pearl's original building. Beginning in the early 1950s, Pearl's expanded to include four additional stores located to the north, south, east, and west of the city close to the beltway system of highways which ring the city. Three years ago a sixth store was established at the far end of the state.

The changing fortunes of center city areas, with the flight in the 1950s and 1960s of middle- and upper-income families to suburban communities, provided the new locations with a ready source of consumers. The trade at the Main Store, however, dropped precipitously. Once the cornerstone of the company, by 1976 it had slipped to the third-highest volume producer and to last place as a profit center.

The Pearl family had taken an active part in the operation of the company until 1974, when the management decided that the decline of the company due to changing consumer patterns and a general economic crunch had reached critical proportions. A major reorganization was needed to save the firm. Financial and managerial executives from other retail and nonretail organizations were brought in to head various divisions of the company. For the first two years after the reorganization, not many of the changes affected lower-level employees.

Beginning in 1976, however, the impact was felt throughout the organization at all levels. More than half of the middle managers were either released or relocated, and new executives were brought in from outside the company. Most positions open by retirements and resignations were not refilled, with the responsibilities of those positions dispersed to the remaining managers.

The general sales force in all stores was reduced by approximately 35 percent, with the greatest reduction in the Main Store. Of those retained, most had their work schedules reduced 7 to 10 percent. The previous emphasis of customer service at any price was replaced with a more profit-oriented plan of regular sales coverage during peak hours and minimal coverage at other times.

Prepared by H. William Vroman.

164

The Pearl family had maintained high visibility throughout the years when they were active in the management of the store. The company "felt like a family." Many employees had spent their entire working lives within the organization. Most managers had begun with the company as stock clerks or salespeople. Strong social ties were formed through frequent social events such as dances, picnics, trips, and sports teams. Three generations of the same family employed at the same time was not an unusual situation. Most employees felt a strong personal loyalty to the Pearl family directly, not just to the company.

Management, in turn, was extremely visible in their concern for the individual employee. Some member of the Pearl family was seen in virtually every work area each day. Personal messages of congratulations, condolence, and recognition were usual. Access to top management was possible for any employee who was not satisfied with the response of the organization to questions or problems through normal channels. Discipline and performance standards were set more by mutual understanding than by actual enforcement. Few instances of dismissal occurred because of poor performance or low productivity. Employees were generally retained unless repeated offenses occurred or major infractions were discovered.

The new management style introduced by Mr. Kagle, who became president of the company in 1976, was greatly different. Contact between levels of employees was generally limited to direct superiors and subordinates. The president and vice presidents of the company as well as most divisional managers were rarely seen outside of their immediate work areas. After three years, the majority of employees had not met Mr. Kagle, and many did not even know him by sight, even though his office, and all corporate offices, were located in the Main Store.

A general feeling of unease and uncertainty, particularly at lower levels, existed for a time while the adjustment to the more distant managerial style was made. While the uneasy atmosphere did diminish, the previous company loyalties and feelings of collective involvement in the future of the organization never returned in full and the gulf between management and employees was never completely bridged.

## Sales Audit

The Sales Audit Department was responsible for processing all documents related to sales, changes in inventory, status of merchandise, and services. As a part of the Control Division, this department was under the direction of Neil Follet, the accounting manager until March 1978. After a realignment of responsibilities, the Sales Audit Department was given to James Johnston, manager of Corporate Informations Services. Mr. Johnston was a data processing expert and had previously been responsible only for the Electronic Data Processing (EDP) services. Since the work output of the Sales Audit Department was to a great extent the input for the EDP division, this alignment seemed to streamline the workflow of these areas and increase the speed with which vital real-time reports were processed.

Mr. Johnston's office was located in Building B within the EDP complex. The majority of his time was spent in this area. The Sales Audit Department was located on the seventh floor in Building A. It was headed by Barbara Knight, the section supervisor, who had held the position for the previous seven years. She had been a member of the department for twelve years before that.

Mrs. Knight was an extremely competent manager who was both respected and liked by subordinates. She had an excellent reputation as a leader among superiors and peers. She was familiar with all work that passed through her area and was frequently called upon to assist other areas whose workflow passed through the Auditing Department. She was a very personal supervisor, concerned with problems that affected her employees. She was outspoken to management about the needs of her department, and her communications were usually answered by whomever she addressed.

The Audit Department had thirty-one employees, whose average length of service was five years. Most jobs involved keypunching, comptometer operation, and basic computer programming. A change to POS (point of sale) terminals was anticipated within a few years, and many employees were concerned with the possible resulting staff reduction.

The workload within the unit was always high, but during the months of October through January, the peak retail season, it nearly doubled. Most regular employees worked overtime during the Christmas season. Normal working hours for the department were from 8:00 a.m. to 5 p.m. Some members started as early as 7:00 a.m. to process in-house media, while the balance of the work force arrived in time to receive the sales media from the suburban stores which arrived by store bus between 7:30 and 8:00 a.m. The work week was generally Monday through Friday except during peak periods.

The Audit Department was in a large, L-shaped area with rows of desks facing the supervisor's office. It had the only open work area on the seventh floor; the rest of the floor consisted of small cubicles and managerial and merchandising offices. The area was completely visible to all employees in the area and at times served as a shortcut from the Pay Office to the General Ledger offices.

It had been the general practice for radios to be permitted within the department. It was felt that, as long as the workload was being met, this practice was not a hindrance to the operation of the area. No employee from another area on the seventh floor objected to this, as most offices were similarly equipped. Many members of the unit were heavy smokers, and this, too, was permitted.

In general, the performance of the department met all production standards set by the company, and the change of management to Mr. Johnston's area scarcely made a ripple in the day-to-day operation of the department. Mrs. Knight was effectively in control of the department, with Mr. Johnston exercising only a supervisory role as manager.

# Part II

*The Letter*

Beginning in March 1978, a series of changes were announced which affected the benefits and working conditions of nearly all Pearl's employees. Some of the first changes were:

- Elimination of the store's medical offices. Instead of a nurse on call at all times, public medical facilities near each store were to be used for all on-the-job ailments.
- Elimination of the quarterly publication of an in-house magazine which highlighted employee activities, personnel changes, and organizational objectives.
- Reduction in the hours that cafeteria and lounge facilities were available.
- A change in the sick benefits policies which eliminated the sick pay benefit for the first two days of any illness, while extending the length of coverage for major absences.
- Elimination of the discount privilege on purchases made by layaway or charge card and on certain types of merchandise whose initial markup fell below a certain percentage.

These and similar announcements were made primarily through the use of departmental meetings and were supplemented by publications in weekly store bulletins. While each change created a stir in certain circles, no real objection was voiced from any area that could not be handled by the department managers.

Beginning in September 1978, however, a series of announcements were made that led to a major problem in Sales Audit. The events that follow are a chronology of the time between September and December.

This announcement appeared on September 12 in the weekly store bulletin:

MEMO TO ALL MAIN STORE EMPLOYEES

Effective immediately, games such as checkers, chess, and all card games will no longer be permitted in any area of the store. This includes employee cafeterias and lounges. Those employees who wish to do so may, of course, leave the store at lunch break and use outside facilities (e.g. the library or the YWCA). Violation of this policy will be considered a serious matter.

In response to the questions from members of the Sales Audit group, Mrs. Knight explained that lunch breaks had been extending beyond the one hour permitted, in some cases, and that management had decided to ban the games for that reason. Since all members of the group were TRs (time recording), their lunch breaks had always been monitored by using the time clock. Department records showed that the one-hour break had not been abused by the women who participated in the daily pinochle game. When the statement was made that the probable participants who had caused this ban were employees who did not have to punch a timecard (NTNs—anyone in a managerial job), Mrs. Knight replied that it was management's position that, although they were aware that many employees were not improperly extending the lunch hour, the problems that had been caused by the games could not be tolerated and the ban was final.

For a few days, the group tried using the YWCA building a few blocks away, but it took too much time to eat and travel there, and the practice was abandoned within the week. The general feeling expressed was that they were being punished for someone else's behavior.

In a bulletin of September 26, management announced that the cafeteria would no longer be available for coffee breaks, because it was too far from the work area for employees to return in just twenty minutes and they were taking too much time.

Aside from a few comments such as "I wonder what they'll knock out next week," the restrictions seemed to be accepted, with reluctance. Comments were made, however, as different group members left the area for their work break, sarcastically asking if they were permitted to go to the ladies' room, leave the floor, walk through the store, and so forth. Some were said with humor, but many had an edge of sharpness until Mrs. Knight said to a small group a few days later, "I got the message the first time, so let's not beat a dead horse. Just go on and take your break and stop all this noise." No further comments were voiced.

At the departmental meeting on October 13, Mrs. Knight read a memo from the vice president saying that to improve working conditions no smoking or radios would be permitted except in private offices. This restriction would apply to most women in Sales Audit. Since nearly all of them had been listening to individual radios tuned to various stations, the reaction was uniformly unpopular. The noise of the machines which were operated constantly within the area was annoyingly obtrusive to many workers. The din of conflicting types of music mixed in with the soap opera stations had become a normal part of the work environment, and no member had complained of distraction or annoyance. Also, the radios helped relieve the monotony of most tasks performed in Sales Audit. Mrs. Knight approached Mr. Johnston with the request that, since all members were assigned individual desks within the area, they be permitted to continue the use of the radios if they used earphones. She stated that the annoyance of background noises might be a possible cause of a reduction in productivity. Mr. Johnston said that as long as the productivity of the group was maintained, he would permit this arrangement.

The modification was greeted with great delight, tempered only by the continuing displeasure of the smokers in the group. Many smokers still felt uncomfortable "chained to the desk" as one of them put it, and the frequency of trips to the ladies' room increased considerably for a few weeks. Mrs. Knight, a smoker herself, told them that she would overlook the frequent trips for a short time until they adjusted to the ban, but that she fully expected the workload to be maintained. She gave the smokers the option of taking these brief breaks for a few days or weeks in place of the twenty-minute work break but said it would not be a permanent exception. Most of the workers who accepted the alternative eventually returned to the regular break schedule, but some "quick trip" arrangements still continued even after three months. Since virtually every other unit on the seventh floor was an individual office or one in which only two or three people worked, the restrictions seemed to affect only the Sales Audit Department. This did not go un noticed.

The continuing problem of sales at the Main Store had been the subject of many discussions in the managerial offices of Mr. Kagle, the president, and other major executives. Because of the Main Store's proximity to large office buildings located in downtown, the bulk of the traffic in the store was during the lunch period. Although the sales force had been rescheduled to peak at this time, complaints were still being received by the store manager of shoppers' inability to receive quick service during this time.

The suggestion was made that the influx of Pearl's own employees as customers during the lunch hours might be making a problem situation even worse. The suggestion was made that employee purchases not be permitted at all in the Main Store, but this was rejected on the basis that there were many slow periods of the day in which employees could shop without delaying Pearl's regular customers. A time schedule was discussed briefly at one of the managers' meetings early in October, but no decision was made.

During the week of October 23, as the holiday business began to pick up, the number of complaints from customers did, too. Some of these were directed not to the store manager but to Mr. Kagle directly. His concern became even greater as he realized that he would shortly be leaving for two weeks, and by the time he returned the business would be in the thick of the Christmas season. Rather than delay a change in policy, he decided to issue a statement limiting the hours when an employee could receive a discount in the Main Store. This, he felt, would relieve the problem. He prepared a letter to all employees and instructed his secretary to distribute them to the stores on Friday, November 3.

MEMO TO ALL MAIN STORE EMPLOYEES

It has been determined that the traffic patterns in the main store are concentrated between the hours of 11:00 a.m. and 2:30 p.m. We have received periodic complaints that shoppers, especially those on their lunch break, are forced to wait too long for service. As a result they often leave the store without making a purchase.

To alleviate this problem and to render the best possible service to customers who are paying full retail price for a purchase, we are asking that all Pearl's employees and their dependents refrain from shopping in the Main Store during the hours of 11:00 a.m. to 2:30 p.m. Accordingly, effective November 6, the courtesy discount extended to all Pearl's employees and their dependents will not be granted during the hours of 11:00 a.m. to 2:30 p.m., Monday through Friday.

To make additional time available to you at the end of each day, the lunch period for all *corporate* employees will be changed from 60 minutes to 45 minutes, effective November 6. Upon implementation of this change, these corporate employees whose work day currently ends at 5:00 p.m. will have 45 minutes during which to shop (4:45 to 5:30). As a positive byproduct of this change, your shopping should be easier and you should receive better service than usual, because it is during the end of the day that our traffic pattern is traditionally at its lowest level. You are invited to shop in the Main Store on Saturday or, of course, in any of our suburban stores.

It is of vital importance to us that Pearl's find ways to make shopping convenient and pleasant for our downtown customers, or they will cease to patronize us. The Main Store can ill afford to lose profitable business.

Please be assured that your shopping business is, however, most certainly valued by Pearl's. Your understanding and cooperation will be greatly appreciated.

Sincerely, John Kagle, President.

Upon reading this letter, the Sales Audit area immediately erupted into a loud complaining session. Mrs. Knight had gone on vacation and would not return for ten days. Some members of the unit tried to call Mr. Johnston for clarification as to just how this would affect their area. Since the media with which they worked made their schedules fairly rigid, they did not see how they could be rescheduled so as to take advantage of the last forty-five minutes of the day to shop. Also, through experience they were aware that sales coverage was low at that time. However, Mr. Johnston was not in his office nor would he be for three more days. Since no one in top management was aware that the area was without an official leader who could have voiced the complaints to higher levels of the company, they were ignorant of the problem.

Reassembling Monday morning, after having had the weekend to mull over the new policy, three outspoken group members began to list their complaints on paper. By Tuesday evening, they had four pages of questions, statements, and demands.

When Mr. Johnston arrived at his office the next morning, the three employees were waiting for him. None of the three had had any real contact with him prior to this meeting. Even though Mr. Johnston told them that he could only spare a short time with them, they proceeded to list the complaints that had been compiled, and they said that they wanted a quick response. Some of their comments follow:

- The discount "privilege" was not just a courtesy but part of the salary package promised when they were employed. Lack of it at any time would be considered a pay cut.
- Just when can we shop? We are all scheduled to work overtime till Christmas.

- Managers can still receive discounts at any hour because the deduction is made from their bill rather than at the time of sale.
- Workers at other stores are not being penalized with restricted shopping hours.
- The discount benefit is one of the reasons I work here. If I can't use it as much as I need to, I'll go somewhere else at a higher regular salary and buy what I need from any store.

Mr. Johnston replied that he would take the group's complaints to Mr. Kagle when he returned. He stated that he could not make an exception for only one area, and they would have to wait to see if modification of the policies could be made.

The women were not satisfied and said so. The reaction of the rest of the Sales Audit group upon the return of the three spokeswomen was anger. The most common statement was "Just what I expected—nothing." They decided to use their twenty-minute breaks to shop. When the next store bulletin came out, it included this notice:

A REMINDER TO ALL EMPLOYEES

It is Pearl's policy that employees are not permitted to shop during their working hours (i.e. any time for which they are being paid). Breaks, if granted, are taken during time for which employees are being paid and are not to be used for shopping.

Mrs. Knight returned to work on the following Monday to face an angry department.

## CASE 17
## National Brickworks

National Brickworks was organized in 1866 and has developed into a leading producer of fire brick and high-temperature mortar. The company now has thirteen plants throughout the United States. The St. Louis plant, built in 1900, produces fire brick, high-temperature mortar, and brickram, a packing used to fill cracks in high-temperature kilns.

Employees under Frank Trouse, plant supervisor, work in one of six locations. All clerical and other administrative workers are located in the Main Office Building. Shipping and receiving of goods takes place in an area referred to as "the Docks." Production is housed in two separate plants, with brickram and high-temperature mortars being made in Plant #1 and fire brick being made in a second building—the Hill Plant. Quality control personnel are located in the Laboratory, and machinists' equipment is located in the Shop. The Shop and Laboratory are adjoining buildings (see Exhibit 1).

**Exhibit 1. Brickyard layout.**

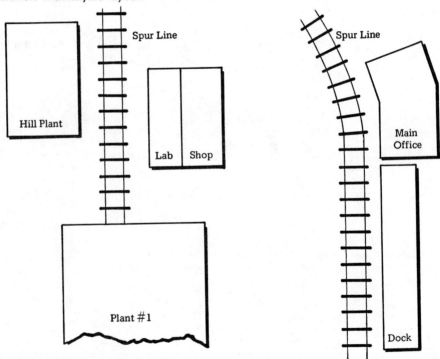

Prepared by Donald D. White, University of Arkansas.

Most of the laborers employed at the St. Louis plant have been with National Brickworks for more than fifteen years, the oldest worker having forty-six years' seniority. Although many laborers were in their late thirties or early forties, the strenuous work involved kept the men in excellent physical condition. The work of the plant employees ranged from unskilled to semi-skilled in nature.

Most of the laborers lived in the same or similar housing areas. All but six were black. Their incomes put them in a lower-middle income group. Shop, laboratory, and clerical employees were all white.

A problem arose in early 1968 when, despite the availability of work in the plant, the workforce hit an all-time low. Turnover among new workers was particularly high, and the number of men applying for jobs as laborers was negligible. Plant supervisor Trouse took note of the problem and decided it needed immediate attention. On Tuesday morning, he called his foremen together to present the problem to them and get their reactions (see Exhibit 2). When everyone was assembled, he walked to the head of the table and said:

We have a problem on our hands. We've all seen its physical symptoms, but we mistakenly thought they would go away if we let time take its course. Well, time has revealed only one thing, and that is that the problem will have to be met head-on. Let's start by getting the physical symptoms of our problem down on paper.

Thus began a brainstorming session which lasted many hours. After the men had exhausted their resources trying to pinpoint the symptoms of the problem, the following list was read:

1. A high rate of turnover exists in the two production plants, especially among the newly hired workers.
2. Turnover tends to remain low in the quality control group as well as among the dock workers (only four men actually worked full-time on the dock).
3. Safety violations in the two plants are becoming more numerous, and more hours are being lost to on-the-job injuries than ever before.
4. Conditions in the two plants, such as excessive heat and dust, are being complained about more frequently by both younger and older workers, yet these conditions have always existed to some extent and have actually been improved during the past two years.
5. Complaints about wages have increased recently. (Even though base rates were below average in the field, a piece-work program gave most of the workers a weekly wage that was far in excess of the average wage in the field.)
6. Talk of a possible strike is in the air, but no reasons are being mentioned by the men.

The list was studied by those attending the meeting. After lunch, a second phase of the meeting was begun. During the afternoon sessions, the men discussed specific occurrences and reasons why particular problems arose more frequently in some work areas than others.

**Exhibit 2. Organization chart, National Brickworks.**

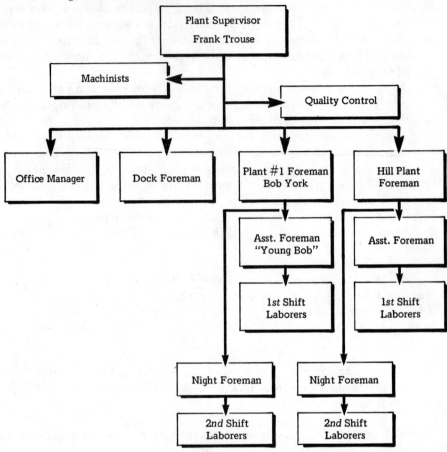

The foreman of Plant #1, Bob York, was the first to bring out important factors. The symptoms listed found their origin in Plant #1 and the Hill Plant, although they were beginning to spill over into the quality control group and some of the clerical staff. Both of these production plants had large work forces compared to the number of personnel in the other locations; those workers with the most seniority also worked in these two areas. York mentioned that his relations with the men in his plant were, in his opinion, extremely good. Only two major and six minor grievances were turned in to him during his seven years as foreman, and all were effectively handled immediately. York said he believed that the older workers had recently tended to segregate themselves from the new personnel, yet neither group, young or old, associated themselves with the plant or the company.

At this time, John Norton, foreman of the Hill Plant, interrupted. He agreed that he found conditions in the Hill Plant to be similar to those in Plant #1, but said that he found a different atmosphere existing on the second shift. Workers on the second shift, he said, seemed to "work more harmoniously" and he considered them to be a "cohesive group." Although working conditions were similar for both the first and second shifts, the men on the evening shift considered themselves to be a team and often referred to each other as the "Night Riders" or the "Late Oil Burners." Bob York agreed that Norton's observations were consistent with those of his own concerning the second (night) shift.

Foremen from other areas felt that the problems mentioned by York and Norton were not nearly as serious as in the two production plants but admitted that they felt the uneasiness in the air. The cohesiveness of the other work groups was beginning to break down. Not only were they losing their teamwork attitudes, but loyalty to the company seemed to be losing meaning, as evidenced by the machinists and quality control personnel who had stopped wearing their company shirts regularly and had recently been removing National "morale posters" from the area bulletin boards.

After this information had been accumulated, Mr. Trouse pointed out two factors that he had discovered from personnel records kept during the previous twelve months. "These factors," said Trouse, "indicate possible underlying aggravation of the workers." He went on:

During the end of 1967, a rash of accidents occurred in the shop, on the dock, and in the Hill Plant. As you remember, it was at this time that we began to crack down on horseplay in all locations. A form letter went out to each department indicating that punitive action would be taken against any worker engaged in horseplay while on company property. The new rules were strictly enforced; some workers received docks in pay, while others were laid off work for up to one week.

As you remember, in mid-1967 we received notice from the home office that unnecessary costs were getting out of line in a number of the plants throughout the country. We were asked to cut back wherever we felt it would be feasible to do so. Our cutback was in the previously planned modernization of facilities. We hated to do it, especially after explaining our plans to the union, but we discarded our proposed program since it seemed to be the only answer. A union grievance was filed, but we knew the cost conditions and just let time heal the unrest.

At this time, Bob Wulff, the head machinist, spoke up.

You know, this may not have seemed important at the time, but we made one other change when the memo on cost came through. The men had quite a company softball team in 1972. They took second place in the Industrial League and often talked about how they were going to clobber Universal, the league champs, in the upcoming season. Unfortunately, there won't be an upcoming season for our ball club and the men in the shop have recently been commenting about the fact.

All of the men agreed that they had heard comments about not having a team this year, and about how the men would miss the big turnouts when each department would cheer for their fellow workers.

Wulff was referring to the abandonment of the National softball team when the cost cutback was announced. The team members were occasionally let out of work early, with pay, to attend away games; this appeared to be an undue expense. It was also felt that afternoon practices might be tiring to the workers and could have an adverse effect on individual performance during working hours.

No other comments were made by the assembled group of foremen regarding the discussion topic, so Mr. Trouse once again took the floor.

Men, I think that this meeting has brought many of the problems here at National to the surface. A summary of today's discussion will be printed and sent to you tomorrow. Look it over carefully. We'll meet back here at 9:30 Thursday morning. We'll decide on a course of action at that time.

That afternoon, as Bob York was planning to leave the plant, Henry Johnson, the union president approached him. Johnson asked Bob about the meeting. Bob decided that most of what had been said should be kept confidential. However, he did say that termination of the company softball team had been discussed and that he, Bob, believed that there was a good chance the team would be active again in the spring.

The following morning Bob and the other foremen were called into Frank Trouse's office. Frank looked disturbed. His message was brief and to the point:

Henry Johnson just stopped in here and told me that the union met last night. They voted to give their officers the power to call a strike when the contract ends next Friday. That's the first time this has happened in fifteen years.

# CASE 18
# The Atlanta Sanitation Strike

## Part A

The fall (1969) election in Atlanta found four candidates for the mayor's office: Rodney Cook, Sam Massell, Everett Millican, and Horace Tate. These four candidates represented widely divergent views. Cook was a wealthy young Republican; Massell was a dynamic young former vice-mayor under the outgoing mayor, Ivan Allen; Millican was a perennial candidate for the mayor's office; and Tate was a prominent and respected member of the black community.

The political positions of these candidates are evident from the press statements they made before the elections of October 7. Massell claimed that Cook should be considered the frontrunner since he had the backing of "the heads of larger business" behind his campaign. As for himself, he stressed the position that he could "deal with blacks and whites on their separate as well as common interest" (Atlanta had, for the first time in history, an equal population of the white and the black races.)

As the campaign progressed, important individuals and groups began to align themselves with the candidates. The *Atlanta Journal* endorsed Rodney Cook, while Mrs. Martin Luther King, Jr., State Representative Julian Bond, and Ralph Abernathy of the Southern Christian Leadership Conference (SCLC) endorsed Horace Tate. Labor and prominent leaders of the black community endorsed Sam Massell.

The black leaders' rationale for supporting the white instead of the black candidate was, "We cannot elect a black man mayor. So, we have decided to endorse a man who can be elected mayor." The application of this reasoning generated great controversy which caused, by election eve, a split in the black community between the supporters of Horace Tate and Sam Massell.

The October election resulted in no candidate receiving a majority of the popular vote for mayor. A young black, Maynard Jackson, garnered 58 percent of the vote and won the position of vice-mayor. Massell received 31 percent of the total vote and 45 percent of the black vote forcing a runoff with Cook (26 percent of the vote) on October 21.

The retiring mayor, Ivan Allen, entered the campaign for the first time on October 13, appearing on local television to endorse an "operation vote" campaign. The Massell camp saw this as a subtle push to increase votes for his adversary. On October 16, labor backers of Sam Massell specifically charged: "The Chamber of Commerce has converted the excellent idea of Mayor Allen into a partisan effort on behalf of their candidate, Rodney Cook."

Prepared by H. William Vroman, Towson State University.

The tempo of the campaign increased when Allen went on television to ask Massell to step out of the campaign because of "misuse of power." His brother had pressured nightclub owners to contribute to his campaign. Sam Massell subsequently admitted that his brother had used bad judgment in soliciting contributions from the nightclub owners; however, he stated that the accusation that his brother had put pressure on the owners was a fabrication and part of a smear campaign against him because he was Jewish.

Despite the frenzy of activity before the election and before the runoff, the campaigns ended on a rather low key the night before the runoff when Cook and Massell met on television. Cook emphasized community togetherness and his experience, while Massell stressed human relations. It was a remarkably unemotional meeting.

Sam Massell won the runoff with a 54.97 percent plurality. The composition of the vote was very interesting. Analysis revealed that Massell had received 18,500 white votes (approximately 27 percent) and 43,000 black votes (93.5 percent), while Cook had received 47,000 white votes (68.5 percent) and 3,000 black votes (6.5 percent). Clearly, when he took office in January 1, 1970, it was largely because of the black voters of Atlanta.

Even while the election and runoff were occurring, other events were taking place in Atlanta that could greatly affect the course of the political lives of Massell and several others. In January 1970, the Aldermanic Finance Committee had approved a pay increase for the city's employees. The employees were represented by the American Federation of State, County, and Municipal Employees (AFSCME) on the basis of an informal agreement between the city and the union. The reason for this casual relationship was the state law that excluded formal recognition of governmental employees unions. At any rate, the city had granted a $5 million raise to the city employees in January of the same year.

On October 23, 1969, the lame-duck chairman of the Aldermanic Finance Committee, Milton Farris, publicly proposed that the new administration give all city employees an additional two- or three-step raise in pay at an estimated cost to the city of approximately $3 million. He based this proposal on an anticipated increase in revenues for the coming year.

The AFSCME (American Federation of State, County and Municipal Employees), representing the black sanitation workers and headed locally by Morton Shapiro, was encouraged by the election of Massell. Based upon his platform the black vote, the appointment of a black to chair the finance committee, they renewed the clamor for an additional increase; specifically demanding a one-step increase retroactive to January 19, 1970. As time progressed, the political inexperience of the finance committee chairman, Joel Stokes, began to show as: (1) legal constraints in the city's budget cycle threatened an immediate increase (March 31 deadline); (2) he evidently agreed with the union on the retroactive one-step increase on March 10, only to have the Finance Committee vote on March 16, to deny the union demand because the city lacked funds and, in addition, denied giving a raise at the next legal opportunity, fall, 1970. The reason was the same—lack of funds.

Enraged and disappointed at the decision, the members of the union voted to take a "holiday" on St. Patrick's Day, March 17, 1970, to protest it. Twenty-five hundred of 7,200 city workers and most of the sanitation men remained home on March 17. Coming as it did directly after a legal three-day weekend, the uncollected garbage was already a problem.

*1. Assume Mayor Massell's shoes. What would be your reaction to this strike?*

## Part B

Jesse Epps, assistant to Jerry Wurf, national president, AFSCME, started the verbal battle with, "There ain't no wheels gonna turn in this city, the villain is down at City Hall. Massell is a boy in a man's job. I hope he grows up." Massell's retort was, "I will not let the union run the city."

As could be expected, action on the problem came immediately. Sam Massell offered the workers an increase aggregating to $400,000, if they returned to work immediately. If they stayed out, they faced being fired. The union, however, rejected the increase as trifling and countered with the demand for the two- to three-step increase mentioned by the former finance committee chairman, Milton Farris.

Evaluated, the demand and counteroffer looked like this:

*Union demand:* $2.5 million used to raise the salary of over 7,200 employees.
*City offer:* $400,000 resulting in a raise in minimum pay from $1.67 to $2.13 per hour, plus $5,000 in free life insurance for all employees.

That afternoon, Massell showed the public a copy of a letter that was part of the informal understanding between the city and the union. The city had agreed to submit to binding arbitration any issue over which an impasse was reached in return for a no strike provision. The local AFSCME leader, Shapiro, countered that the letter was a summary of the provisions for negotiations after the employees received a one-step pay increase. He contended that had the agreement of the mayor's appointee Stokes stood, the letter would have too, but as the agreement fell through, the substance of the letter was void.

In final defense of the union's position, Shapiro alleged that the new administration was not taking the union's demands seriously—the union had worked hard to elect the present administration and deserved some consideration for it. Specifically, Shapiro claimed that they had gone out and personally registered some 8,000 blacks to vote.

All of the offers and counteroffers and threats did not ease the burden of the Atlanta community dwellers or the business districts. On March 18, it was estimated that garbage was piling up at the rate of 1,000 tons per day.

The mayor took a hard-line stand Wednesday evening, March 18, and issued the following ultimatum: Either those city employees out on strike return to work on Thursday or they would be fired. When Massell issued this ultimatum there were approximately 2,500 city employees on strike. Of these 2,500, some 1,400 were from the Public Works Department of which more than 800 were from the sanitation division. Following this ultimatum, Jesse Epps, a national union representative, implored the city to make contracts with the striking workers, but with little positive response.

However, on Thursday morning Mayor Massell did postpone sending out dismissal notices. Although some 1,400 city employees stayed out, there were encouraging signs of a return to work and Massell agreed to allow a citizens' committee to bring the two parties together.

By the end of the third day, March 19, the major issues surrounding the city employees' strike seemed clear. The union and its members, led by Morton Shapiro, were disenchanted with the existing pay scales and had relied upon the new administration to grant a one-step pay raise in addition to the pay raise the city employees received at the beginning of the year.

The city, led by Mayor Massell, felt the union had breached negotiations by condoning a strike which the union had supposedly agreed not to condone while negotiations were still in progress.

1. *Can the situation be saved now? How?*
2. *Assume negative results from the citizens' committee. What are Massell's alternatives?*

## Part C

On Friday, March 20, 1970, after the citizens' committee had failed to bring the parties together, Mayor Massell sent special delivery dismissal letters to those workers still involved in the walkout.

In response to this action, Morton Shapiro issued the following statement: "National President Jerry Wurf has declaired he will put the full resources of the union behind the striking Atlanta employees." Shapiro went on to charge the mayor with union-busting tactics, claiming the mayor was undermining the union and the city employees by allowing the supervisors throughout the Public Works Department to decide which employees could go back to work.

The union's main argument was still that the city had reneged on a promise of a one-step pay increase for all city employees. However, Shapiro found a new cudgel in the mayor's paradoxical action—while the mayor claimed to be a friend of labor he fired some 1,500 city labor workers, mostly blacks. The union official further pointed out that Massell admitted workers had the right to strike. In talking to this union, Shapiro put it like this: "The mayor says you've got the right to strike, but you're fired."

The mayor's defense to this argument was to refuse to recognize that a strike existed. Instead, he considered it a work stoppage as the city had no contract with the union, therefore the city employees could not legally strike.

At this point the city versus the AFSCME controversy moved in a physical direction, i.e., no longer was it just at the negotiation level. Saturday, March 21, Mayor Massell opened the city personnel office to take applications for the strikers' jobs. He also ran an advertisement in the newspapers calling for applicants. As applicants began arriving at the personnel office so did a picket line begin to form. Saturday's attempt at hiring new city workers culminated in a virtual jamming of the process by union members. They crowded the application lines, discouraged those who were genuinely applying, and falsified applications to make it as difficult as possible for the city.

Threats of violence began circulating and when Shapiro was confronted with this possibility he claimed that any talk of violence was emanating from the mayor's office. He even accused Massell of carrying a gun, which the mayor subsequently denied.

The city issued a statement over the weekend saying that an estimated 1,100 of 2,500 original strikers had already returned to work.

Raleigh Bryans, an *Atlanta Journal* correspondent, took time to reflect upon the events of the first week of the strike: "It is reasonable to deduce from all this that Massell may be treading on dangerous ground politically— that he stands in some danger of being accused of pleasing his enemies and critics while displeasing his friends and supporters." Bryans draws a comparison experienced by Ivan Allen in 1968, saying that at this early stage of Massell's strike the difference between the two is:

1. In this current strike there is no massive civil rights involvement as there was in Allen's, and;
2. In sitting down at the negotiating table with the city officials, the union officials (mostly blacks) are confronted by a black man—Joel Stokes, chairman of the finance committee.

The confrontation between the city and the union was not without its effect upon the citizens of Atlanta. Atlanta's daily garbage pick up was in excess of 1,000 tons and at the beginning of the strike it was obvious that something had to be done quickly regardless of how fast a negotiation settlement might come about. So, the mayor distributed some 750,000 heavy-duty plastic bags throughout the communities of Atlanta and implored the people to use these bags for their garbage and to place them out in front of their curbs, where he had arranged for consolidated pick-ups. This makeshift set-up appeared to run more smoothly than anyone had anticipated and its success definitely seemed to hurt the union's bargaining power.

As the strike moved into its second week, Vice-Mayor Maynard Jackson publicly voiced his sympathy for the strikers and called for binding arbitration of the strike without Shapiro's taking part in any of the negotiations. However, the mayor, as part of his tough stance in failing to recognize the strike's existence, had already rejected such a possible solution. In addition, John Dougherty, Assistant District Attorney, stated that this would be impossible (binding arbitration) as it would be tantamount to delegating the power of the mayor and the aldermen, which the state law prohibited. Dougherty emphasized that only the mayor and the aldermanic committees could make city policy.

On March 25 the AFSCME rejected the city offer which consisted of the following two conditions (not unlike the initial proposal):

1. Take back all strikers but without pay for the time lost.
2. Grant an increase in minimum wage from $1.67 an hour to $2.13 an hour and a free $5,000 life insurance policy.

Mayor Massell's reaction to the rejection was predictable: "It would be a terrible mistake for the poor employee if he is used as a tool by some out-of-town official who is just trying to build some power base." By "out-of-town official" the mayor was referring to Jerry Wurf, the national AFSCME leader, who had come to Atlanta to bolster the union's demands following the kidney ailment and the consequent hospitalization of the regional representative, Morton Shapiro, on March 25. The mayor charged that Wurf had packed the union meeting, which voted down the city's offer, with nonunion members to insure the continuation of the strike.

Massell asked for and got television time the evening of March 25 to state, to the citizens of Atlanta, his facts and the city's position on the strike. Essentially, the mayor emphasized the following:

1. City employees got a $5 million raise in January 1970.
2. The city did not have the additional $2.5 million requested; however, the city did honor the request by seeking additional revenue from the legislature—but unsuccessfully.
3. The union promised not to strike and struck without a request for arbitration.
4. The union had no contract with the city, therefore, the strike was illegal.
5. The union signed an agreement with the city whereby the union was supposed to have recommended initial settlement negotiations to its members on March 17, when in fact, at the meeting, the union refused to endorse the settlement to its members.
6. The city, a week after the strike had begun, was willing to hire back all the strikers (reportedly at the request of the union) with no lost benefits.

On Saturday, March 28, final checks were sent out to some 925 striking city employees of which 660 were in the sanitation department.

In spite of Mr. Bryans's comparison earlier, this strike did take on civil rights overtones as it became clear that the workers were the group suffering. The meager strike fund with which the national AFSCME was supporting the workers was already nearly exhausted. Influential civil rights leaders, Ralph Abernathy, (SCLC) and Jesse Hill (SCLC), echoed Vice-Mayor Jackson's sentiment, calling for immediate arbitration. Abernathy described the urgency of the situation in the following metaphor: "I realize the city is filthy now with uncollected garbage, and we all want Atlanta to be clean and beautiful, but filth is not only measured in terms of garbage. It is also measured in terms of man's exploitation of his brother and the destruction of human dignity."

Atlanta NAACP leader, Lonnie King, rapped the mayor by saying, "You don't kick people in the behind who put you in office. . . . The subtle issue here is, is there going to be a union? I believe that if Massell could find a way to give money and get rid of the union, he would do it."

A black coalition of Jesse Hill, Vice-Mayor Jackson, and State Senator Leroy Johnson continued to urge the mayor to submit the strike to arbitration, but they were still unable to get the mayor to admit there was a strike. Instead, he continued to refer to it as a work-stoppage.

The relations between Massell and Wurf continued to go down with a televised meeting on March 31, ending up in a shouting match. Typical of Wurf's comments were:

You lie! You're a contemptible, irresponsible little man! You're playing games with human beings! How sick you must be. You're a little man who suddenly got power and can't handle it.

and

You ugly, vicious rumor-monger! You contemptible strike-breaker! You are a sorry example of a human! You're not fit for the synagogue. You're the type that was a concentration guard for the Germans.

Mayor Massell accused Wurf of trying to destroy the city. After two meetings which degenerated to shouting matches the mayor avowed to avoid Wurf. And he did so for the duration of the strike.

As the city and union continued to remain far apart on a settlement in the beginning of April, overtones and warnings of violence became more pronounced. Surprisingly, though, the strike in its entirety was marred very little by any major violence. The following is a brief, chronological account of those demonstrations and confrontations between the city and the union that did occur:

*March 21*   Strikers picketed the city personnel office in reaction to its opening on Saturday to accept applicants for the strikers' jobs.
*March 23*   Six strikers were arrested for not allowing employees to cross picket lines.
*March 28*   A large march was planned with Mrs. Ralph Abernathy to speak at its conclusion. The march was apparently ineffective; only 200 out of an expected 10,000 participated; it began two hours late; and Mrs. Abernathy never showed.
*April 4*   A mass rally/march was held this Saturday on the anniversary of the assassination of Martin Luther King, Jr., at his tomb. His father delivered an address urging nonviolent action in the strike. Ironically, the day was marred when a worker on a city garbage truck shot a sanitation striker in the leg after a fight broke out between members of the SCLC march and the crew of the truck (both the individuals involved, incidentally, were charged with battery).
*April 6*   Six strikers were arrested for blocking entrances used by garbage trucks.
*April 9*   Black strikers, headed by Hosea Williams, hurled abuse at the black leaders who were pleading with the strikers to return to work. Williams

labeled Senator Johnson, Jesse Hill, Martin Luther King, Sr., Reverend Williams, and others as "egghead, handkerchief-head niggers." Irony lends itself here too as Hosea Williams was a member of the SCLC, an organization Martin Luther King, Sr.'s son founded.

*April 12*  One hundred twenty-five protesters, led by Hosea Williams, kicked off a boycott campaign by marching on some of Atlanta's bigger businesses and stores, exhibiting signs such as "Things go bad with Coca-Cola until city workers get a raise," "Rich's starves garbage men," and "Stay out of Sears until we get a raise."

*April 13*  Thirty-six strikers were arrested during a mass picketing disturbance. Signs carried such epithets as "Sam sleep in dread, until my children are fed" and "Think Massell, a hungry man is a dangerous man."

*April 20*  Picketing begins again as the truce during the garbage talks ended when negotiations once again broke down. That evening the relationship between the city and the union reached its most strained point. Strikers marched from the union hall to the city hall where an aldermanic committee meeting was in session. Mayor Massell called out the riot squad, some 120 policemen, to prevent the strikers from marching back to the union hall (the union had not obtained a license to legally march that evening), but the aldermen averted possible major violence by convincing the mayor to back down and allow them to march back.

Two days after this confrontation, the realization of the major violence posed by the mayor's hard-line stance caused those black leaders who were sympathetic to the strikers, e.g., Vice-Mayor Jackson and Ralph Abernathy, to put added pressure on the union to accept the city's latest offer.

The following is an abbreviated listing and discussion of negotiations throughout the strike now lasting thirty-seven days:

1. *March 18*  Union rejected an increase in minimum pay from $1.67 to $2.13 an hour and a free $5,000 life insurance package.
2. *March 25*  Union rejected essentially the same proposal.
3. *March 31*  Since this was the legal deadline established by the city charter for granting city employees a pay raise, Mayor Massell called a special meeting of the aldermanic council to consider a last-minute offer to the union. The council considered two proposals:
   a. A $5 weekly bonus for the city's lowest paid employees (some 2,300) for perfect attendance.
   b. a 10¢ per hour increase for the waste collectors.
   The aldermanic council approved the former, but the union rejected this offer. One striker's reaction was that accepting the bonus would take away his pride.
   Senator Leroy Johnson also found the bonus offer to be demeaning—that it implied that the lower echelon employees, mostly black, were lazy and would not show up for work.
4. *April 7*  Union proposed the following to the Finance Committee:
   a. That the city agree to give a one-step pay raise to about 3,600 of the lowest paid employees on January 1, 1971.
   b. That the $5-a-week bonus be converted to a one-step pay raise effective

January 19, 1970, with the union lending the money (estimated at $400,000 by Wurf) to make up the difference between available city funds and the cost of the raise.

c. That the city have only a "moral understanding" with the union to repay them for the borrowed money (this last proposal was worded this way because the city could not legally contract with the union to repay such an outlay).

The city rejected this offer of using union funds to bankroll a city pay raise and Chairman Stokes of the Finance Committee counter-offered:

a. to convert $5 bonus to a one-step pay raise for the 2,300 lowest paid employees;
b. to promise a one-step raise January 1, 1971;
c. to reinstate all fired workers;
d. to not prosecute any striker arrested during the strike.

The union did not agree to these terms either.

5. *April 20*   A new city proposal was offered:

a. to grant a one-step pay increase to those 2,300 lowest paid employees on July 1, 1970;
b. to request a study to see if some 550 employees could be reclassified beginning July 1, 1970, thereby possibly increasing their pay.

As was becoming the habit, the union rejected this proposal as well. By April 22, 1970 the union and the city were still at a stalemate, after thirty-six days of fruitless negotiations.

1. *What are the major forces preventing an agreement at this time?*
2. *What are the mayor's alternatives?*

# Part D

On April 23, 1970, the city garbage workers were back on the job, ending a thirty-seven-day holdout. The union accepted the following city proposal:

1. Conversion of the $5 bonus proposal to a one-step pay raise for the 2,300 lowest paid employees, effective May 1, 1970.
2. A reclassification study to be completed by May 9, 1970, to determine if approximately 550 city employees could be placed in a higher pay scale.
3. Reinstatement of all fired workers.
4. Amnesty of those arrested.

# CASE 19
# Western Vanlines

Bill Weston graduated from Auburn University with a bachelor's degree in aeronautical administration. He joined the Air Force to become a pilot but was disqualified from pilot training for medical reasons. He spent four years in the Air Force as an aircraft maintenance officer. Upon discharge he decided to return to school to strengthen his background in business administration. During that time he worked with Lockheed Aircraft and attended night classes at the University of California.

Bill didn't feel challenged by his job at the plant. Although he held the title of Manufacturing Engineer, he soon discovered that the job was little more than that of a minor problem-solver for several production supervisors. He began to look for other employment opportunities. One day while browsing over a bulletin board at the university, he noticed an advertisement for a position of accountant. He called in response to the advertisement and arranged for an interview.

## The Interview

Bill entered the office building at Western Vanlines. The building was old and the office was modestly furnished and somewhat dirty. However, Bill reasoned that the type of business—moving and storage—did not lend itself to new buildings and fancy fixtures. The interview turned out to be a very encouraging session. The president, Ralph Wiley, was a neat, middle-aged man. He explained that the company was a family held corporation and that he was the owner. In addition, he elaborated the advantages of working in a small company and repeatedly stressed that when the company prospered so did its employees. Mr. Wiley made a point of describing a large Christmas bonus given to the employees during the previous year. He also informed Bill that the position he was interviewing for was more than simply that of an accountant. Bill was assured that he could one day become controller of the company if his performance was satisfactory. Bill was enthusiastic after the interview. He saw an opportunity to move from a huge organization where he was just a number to a small company where everyone knew everyone else. In addition, he felt that he would have an opportunity to actually achieve something.

Mr. Wiley recognized that Bill had been favorably impressed with the company in the interview. As Bill was about to leave, Mr. Wiley stated:

The opportunities with this company are endless. I joined the company twelve years ago as an assistant to the president and today I *am* the president. In fact,

Prepared by Donald D. White, University of Arkansas; and H. William Vroman, Towson State University.

Sam Donaldson, from whom I bought the company, today works for me. I've helped to build this company and I'm proud of it. I can honestly say that I wouldn't want to be doing anything else. Working in a company like Western can cause you to go home every night knowing that you're doing the kind of work you are cut out for.

## On the Job

Bill's salary was modest by most standards. However, after his first day with the payroll, he realized that he was making almost as much as the top two employees in the company. Both of these men had been with Western for many years. In addition, Bill was making considerably more than other workers in the company and was not required to punch a time clock as most of them were.

At first the other employees seemed to keep him at arm's length. He reasoned that most of the other workers viewed him as an outsider and as a possible threat to their own advancement in the company. In addition, he thought that the workers might be envious of his new position and the opportunities for rapid promotion that he had been promised. He learned that Mr. Wiley had, on several occasions, mentioned that he intended to hire someone to "come in and straighten out the company."

Bill soon realized that his job was not all that it had been described in the interview. Instead of being an accountant, he functioned as a bookkeeper and clerk. Mr. Wiley had suggested in the hiring interview that Bill would be supervising the bookkeeper and the posting machine operator and that the billing department would be placed under his control. However, no formal restructuring of the company took place. The billing department continued to operate separately from Bill's office, and the bookkeeper continued to work almost exclusively for Mr. Wiley. Eventually, Bill was given the title of Controller. However, his functions remained unchanged.

In time, Bill became an accepted member of the group. As he was told by one long-time employee, "It just took us a while before we realized that you were just another employee around here like the rest of us." Soon Bill found that many of the employees were dissatisfied with their work. The jobs which they performed often were regarded as monotonous and unchallenging. Although Mr. Wiley attempted to maintain the cordial atmosphere in the office, little in the way of formal recognition of work ever was received by the office workers. Employees complained, sometimes bitterly, about the inadequacy of the present building and equipment. One day while a group of employees were having coffee, the comment was made that Western Vanlines was a "second-rate" company. Another worker quickly added, "Mr. Wiley acts like a nice guy around here, but we all know that where he's concerned the company profit comes first. He doesn't care what the circumstances are, and he doesn't mind letting us know it either." No one spoke in defense of either Mr. Wiley or the company.

## Weekly Staff Meetings

Each week Mr. Wiley conducted a staff meeting. The meetings were held after regular working hours, and attendance generally was restricted to several top-level employees. One hourly employee also attended the meetings for a few months. However, he was told that his attendance would no longer be required when it was discovered by Mr. Wiley that the employee was not clocking out until after the meetings were over. About one month after starting work, Bill asked if he was supposed to attend the meetings. He was interested to see what took place in the meetings and thought that by participating in them he would become closer to the other managers at Western. In addition, several employees with whom he had been associating encouraged him to go so that they might have more information about what was happening at the top. There was a periodic rumor that the business was to be sold, and many employees were worried about the possibility.

After attending several meetings, Bill realized that he had made a mistake. Normal office hours ended at 5:00. Mr. Wiley required those attending the meetings to remain at the office until the dispatcher had finished his communications with all drivers on the road. Sometimes, this meant that the meeting itself would not start for thirty to forty-five minutes. During this time, Mr. Wiley remained in his office making long distance telephone calls to his friends on a newly acquired WATS line.

The meetings were structured along committee lines, but most participants conceded that they were little more than "listen-to-the-president sessions." Little pertinent business was conducted during the meetings. However, they often lasted for several hours. Most of the meeting time was taken up by discussions between Mr. Wiley and various individuals in the room concerning their individual problems. Some felt that Mr. Wiley enjoyed dragging these problems out in front of the group.

The person who was most often maligned by Mr. Wiley was Sam Donaldson, from whom he had purchased the company some years back. At first, Donaldson was kept on the staff as an adviser. But Mr. Wiley thought that it would be "better for everyone concerned" if Donaldson was given a title within the formal organization. Officially, Donaldson was referred to as Administrative Vice President. However, his duties were ill defined, and during the meetings he was designated to record the minutes. Donaldson had talked about leaving Western, but at sixty years old, he knew his opportunities elsewhere would be limited. Most of the employees believed he would remain with Western or permanently retire.

## The Last Straw

From time to time, Bill received special assignments from Mr. Wiley. He attempted to apply many of his newly learned ideas and techniques, but generally Mr. Wiley rejected them in lieu of more traditional approaches to solving the problems. For example, Bill was once told that he should begin digging into the financial records of the company and do everything possible to find ways of decreasing costs. Bill worked hard on the cost analysis, comparing costs incurred in several preceding months to those of the present month. He believed his investigation revealed some interesting trends in rising labor costs in one of the departments. He was excited about his findings and eager to show the results to Mr. Wiley. When he did so, however, Mr. Wiley gave the materials a casual glance and proceeded to enumerate reasons why they were not valid.

Another frustrating situation concerned having Mr. Wiley's wife work in the same department with Bill. Mrs. Wiley worked in the accounting department once or twice each week for several hours. She was a likable person and willing to do any work she was asked to do. Unfortunately, her work was substandard and generally required extensive review and correction. Complicating the problem was that Mrs. Wiley was formally designated as a vice president of the company. (Bill was later to find out that it was through Mrs. Wiley's personal fortune that Ralph Wiley was able to purchase Western Vanlines.)

Morale in the company seemed to be slipping daily. While various employees seemed to cooperate well with one another on an informal basis, they very often disagreed when it came to business matters. At the same time, few of the workers felt free to express their opinions and make suggestions to one another for fear their opinions would be transmitted back to the president.

A final incident late in the year caused Bill to reflect seriously on whether or not he wished to remain with Western Vanlines. Mr. Wiley continually reminded workers both on the job and in the staff meetings that "whenever the company prospers, you'll prosper, too." It seemed that the more often he made the comment the more skeptical the workers became.

Mr. Wiley paid himself what was thought by most to be an extravagant salary. In addition, he had placed his wife, one son, and a daughter on the payroll as part-time employees. None of them did much work when they were present, and the son rarely was around when he was supposed to be. During the year, Mr. Wiley had purchased a houseboat, charging a large part of its operating expenses to the company under the pretense that it was used to entertain prospective clients from large companies. By the end of the year, Western Vanlines showed very little profit.

Mr. Wiley instructed Bill to go to the store and obtain fruit cakes which were to be distributed as Christmas bonuses at a party he had planned for Christmas Eve day. In addition, he handed Bill a number of small cards that were to be attached to each of the cakes.

After Mr. Wiley left Bill's office, Bill looked at one of the cards. It read:

*Please accept this gift as a token of my appreciation for your work this past year. Remember, if we work even harder next year a bigger and better bonus may be yours!*

*Merry Christmas, R. M. Wiley*

# EXPERIENTIAL EXERCISE 7
## Organizational Climate Survey

Climate is sometimes difficult to identify clearly. Yet, as you have found out, it plays a role in most organizational behavior situations. This exercise points out the more personal dimension of climate. How do I react to things around me? Are there organizational environments in which I would be more effective?

### Instructions

1. Place yourself in several different group settings in answering the questions. Would your answers be different if you were in a family group? What about your last job? Think of a class in which you felt close to your classmates.
2. How important is the idea of trust?
3. Pick out at least four questions. Give to each question the answer that would yield to the worst possible climate. Have you ever experienced such an inhospitable organization? Give each question the best possible answer. Where have you been in a scene like this before?
4. Assume the role of a supervisor who minconstrues things, interrupts, acts judgmental, and is less than frank. While two students are acting out the roles, the rest of the class acts as process observers reflecting their feelings about what is going on.
5. Lay out a plan that will allow you to generate the type of climate you think is best.

### Questions

Think about how your fellow group members as a whole normally behave toward you. On the blank in front of the items below place the letter that corresponds to your perceptions of their behavior.

A  They can always be counted on to behave this way.
T  Typically I would expect them to behave this way.
U  I would usually expect them to behave this way.
S  They would seldom behave this way.
R  They would rarely behave this way.
N  I would never expect them to behave this way.
I would expect my fellow group members to:
———— 1. level with me.
———— 2. get the drift of what I am trying to say.

From J. William Pfeiffer and John E. Jones (eds.), *A Handbook of Structured Experiences for Human Relations Training*, Volume 1 (Rev.), La Jolla, Ca.: University Associates, Inc., 1974.

——— 3. interrupt or ignore my comments.

——— 4. accept me for what I am.

——— 5. feel free to let me know when I "bug" them.

——— 6. misconstrue things I say or do.

——— 7. be interested in me.

——— 8. provide an atmosphere in which I can be myself.

——— 9. keep things to themselves to spare my feelings.

——— 10. perceive what kind of person I really am.

——— 11. include me in what's going on.

——— 12. act "judgmental" with me.

——— 13. be completely frank with me.

——— 14. recognize when something is bothering me.

——— 15. respect me, apart from my skills or state.

——— 16. ridicule or disapprove of my peculiarities.

# CHAPTER SIX
# Effective Leader Behavior

Leadership has preoccupied observers and researchers for a long time. The leadership of small groups and a wide variety of complex organizations such as churches, armies, businesses, and nations has been studied. Throughout the years investigators have tried to answer the question, "Why are certain people successful leaders, while others are not?" Successful leaders were sometimes described as being charismatic. A charismatic leader is one to whom followers respond based upon some indefinable qualities (charisma) the leader possesses. Successful organizations in complex societies seem to place less of a premium on charismatic leadership qualities and more importance on bureaucratic or managerial behaviors. Yet even today our knowledge of what truly constitutes an effective leader is limited.

Leadership is a complex subject. It has been approached from different points of view and generated numerous theories and prescriptions.[1] Lack of agreement concerning leadership comes, in part, from the beliefs of some that leadership may not have a major impact on the course of events in modern organizations. For example, Hall [2] suggests that most managers are selected for positions, and that the selection procedure may be biased against "leader" behaviors in favor of a more limited managerial style. Second, rules, regulations, policies, and informal norms limit what the manager can do in a role as leader. Finally, the complexity of large modern organizations may overwhelm the ability of any single individual to affect the course of events in such an enterprise.

Leadership and managerial components of executive positions are explored in Chapter Six. We define leadership as the "behavioral process of influencing individuals or groups toward set goals; leadership effectiveness will be defined by how well these goals are achieved." [3]

A number of theoretical schemes are presented because they are useful in examining leadership and managerial positions in organizations. The first to be examined is the trait approach. Although still in use by lay managers, the trait approach largely has given way in the literature to leader behavior approaches (what successful managers actually do), such as those growing out of Ohio State and Michigan studies, and more contemporary leadership theories. Among the more recent theories of leadership we examine are Fiedler's contingency theory, which examines the relationship of situational variables and leader style to leadership effectiveness, and House's path-goal theory, which describes the influence potential of a leader over subordinates by clarifying goal paths. Finally, we will look at Mintzberg's theory of management roles and the relationship of certain roles to successful management.

## Theories of Leader Behavior

### The Trait Approach

Early studies of leadership attempted to identify and define physical, intellectual, or personality traits that distinguished leaders from followers. The approach was accepted because of the great reliance that large institutions such as the army and the Catholic Church placed on leadership traits over the years. However, two researchers, Bird and Stogdill,[4] analyzed over one hundred studies of leadership traits in 1948, and found that less than five percent of all the traits thought to be important were common in four or more of their studies. They concluded that it was not possible to pin down the traits common to all successful leaders.

### Styles of Leadership Approach

*The Iowa studies.*   In a classic series of experiments at the University of Iowa in 1938, Lewin, Lippitt, and White[5] observed some significant differences in leadership styles. They identified three styles of leadership: autocratic, democratic, and laissez-faire. The basic difference in the three styles was the location of the decision making function in the group. Authoritarian leaders made decisions for their groups and communicated those decisions to group members. Democratic leaders allowed the group to make decisions that would affect their activities; the leader merely helped the group arrive at a "decision point." The role of the laissez-faire leader was less clearly defined. Individuals under the leader made decisions that would affect their own activities rather than those of the entire group. The laissez-faire leader did not take an active guiding role, offering assistance only when asked by a group member.

Findings of the Iowa studies were favorable to the democratic approach and directed many students of leadership to endorse democratic and other participative styles. Loose interpretations and applications of Lewin's work caused many to question the value of production-centered managers, equating their approach with an "authoritarian" style.

The classifications used in the Iowa studies simplify our view of leadership styles. However, later research indicated that the "either-or" scheme did not accurately reflect leadership behavior.

*Ohio State leadership studies.*   A number of researchers at Ohio State University were disappointed by the results of trait research and attempted to document what leaders actually did and how they did it. Using questionnaires, they found two major leader behaviors strongly related to effectiveness. These behaviors were called *initiating structure* and *consideration*.[6]

Initiating structure is the orientation of the leader to the task. A person who is high in initiating structure is one who is oriented to scheduling work, assigning people to tasks, and determining performance levels. Consideration, on the other hand, deals primarily with a leader's concern for the needs of group members. People have a need to be near others, to talk about problems, to laugh, and to release tensions. Ideas such as friendship, mutual trust, respect, and warmth are important to a person high in consideration.

The fact that initiating structure and consideration are independent of one another is particularly important to our understanding of effective leadership. The finding implies the existence of at least four leadership styles:

Style 1: high initiating structure, high consideration.
Style 2: high initiating structure, low consideration.
Style 3: low initiating structure, high consideration.
Style 4: low initiating structure, low consideration.

Research on the two leadership dimensions suggested that high consideration (employee-oriented) leaders could expect low turnover and low absenteeism. High task orientation was found to lead to improved employee performance. However, recent studies have produced some contradictory evidence. Contingency and path-goal theories of leadership have subsequently been offered to explain some of the inconsistencies in earlier findings.[7]

### Leader Effectiveness

The question of what constitutes leader effectiveness is critical to understanding the impact of leaders on organizations. Leader effectiveness may be defined as the ability of the group to reach its goal as a result of the leader's style.

The work of Fred Fiedler[8] and his colleagues at the University of Illinois has provided a breakthrough in the area of leadership research. After nearly three decades of carefully studying the relationship of leadership style to leader effectiveness, he has evolved an empirically based "contingency theory" of leadership.

The approach taken by Fiedler is two phased. First, the present style of the leader is assessed, using a questionnaire known as the "esteem for least preferred co-worker" scale (LPC). According to Fiedler, the scale reflects whether a leader is "relationship-oriented" (high LPC) or "task-oriented" (low LPC). Leader style is seen as being relatively stable and resistant to change.

Next, three variables believed to be most important in the group (organizational) setting are measured. They are (1) leader/member relationships, (2) task structure, and (3) position power of the leader. These variables, in effect, measure the leader's influence or control over the group in a given situation. A specific combination of these variables constitutes the "situation." (Eight distinct situational settings exist based upon high/low measures for each variable.)

*Leader/member relations* refers to the willingness of group members to follow a particular leader. If there is little conflict or strain in the relationship between the leader and his or her members, then the situation is favorable. If conflict and strain exist in the relationship, the situation is unfavorable. Leader/member relations is seen as the most important of the three situational variables.

*Task structure* describes the clarity or ambiguity of the task. Assembling a watch is very routine, while putting together a company policy on ethics is ambiguous. If the correctness of the task can be determined quickly, then the task is clear. If a number of approaches can be used to accomplish the task, and time is required to determine its effectiveness, it is ambiguous.

*Position power* is related to the authority vested in the leader because of his or her position in the organization. Ability to hire, fire, and reward gives a leader high position power.

Numerous empirical studies of Fiedler's contingency theory have resulted in a clearer picture of the appropriate match between leadership style and situational control. Specifically, Fiedler found that task-motivated leaders (low LPC) perform best in situations of high or low control. Relationship-motivated leaders (high LPC), on the other hand, perform best in situations of moderate control.[9] High control refers to situations in which leaders have a predictable environment (e.g., support of group members, high task structure). Low control situations include those in which the task is unstructured or unclear, where definite procedures do not exist, or where leaders lack group support. Moderate control refers to situations that lie somewhere between the extremes of high and low control. Situations vary according to the combinations of high/low situation variables (leader-member relations, task structure, and leader position power). Figure 1 describes the behaviors and likelihood of effectiveness of task- and relationship-oriented leaders to various control situations.

Once the appropriate match is determined, a decision must be made as to how it can be brought about. Fiedler views leader style as being relatively stable and resistant to change. Therefore, he asserts that effectiveness can best be obtained by engineering the job to fit the leader rather than expecting leaders to change personal styles which may be deeply ingrained. Organizational or situational variables can be adjusted with relative ease. For example, the leader's degree of authority can be altered under certain conditions to moderate the position power available. Additional changes in

**Figure 1. Leadership style, behavior, and performance under varying levels of leader control.**

| Leadership style | Situational Control of Leader | | |
| --- | --- | --- | --- |
| | High control | Moderate control | Low control |
| Relationship-Motivated | Behavior: Somewhat autocratic, aloof, and self-centered. Primarily concerned with task. Effectiveness: Poor. | Behavior: Considerate, open, and participative. Effectiveness: Good. | Behavior: Anxious, tentative, overly concerned with interpersonal relations. Effectiveness: Poor. |
| Task-Motivated | Behavior: Considerate, and supportive. Effectiveness: Good. | Behavior: Tense, task-focused. Effectiveness: Poor. | Behavior: Direct, task-focused, serious. Effectiveness: Relatively good. |

Adapted from Fred Fiedler, et al., *Improving Leadership Effectiveness: The Leader Match Concept* (New York: John Wiley & Sons, 1977) p. 136.

position power can be brought about by altering the degree of participation required for certain unit decisions.

Task structures can be adjusted by allocating projects to appropriate leaders according to the degree of routineness. Production problems may be assigned to the low LPC (task-oriented) leader. Leader/member relations can be changed by increasing or decreasing group homogeneity or altering group composition through selection and placement. On the other hand, it may be possible for leaders who become more aware of their own styles to vary those styles as different situations arise within the group.

To date, the significant contribution made by Fiedler has been through his evolution of an empirically based contingency theory of leadership that may be used to determine leader style and organization situation. How best to arrive at the most effective style/situation match will no doubt be the subject of much future research.

### Path-Goal Theory

Path-goal theory is a situational theory[10] that focuses on the leader behaviors necessary to motivate a subordinate to work more effectively. The job of the leader is seen as that of increasing personal payoffs to the subordinate for attaining work objectives. When the subordinate most clearly sees the behaviors necessary to attain the payoffs, the leader has cleared the path to goal accomplishment in the subordinate's mind. Leader behavior is seen as effective if it: (1) is seen by subordinates as an immediate or future source of satisfaction; (2) makes subordinate rewards contingent on performance (work-goal attainment); (3) supports the attainment of goals by removing roadblocks to goal attainment.

Path-goal research has explored four specific types of leader behavior: supportive leadership, participative leadership, instrumental leadership, and achievement-oriented leadership. These show the effects on the dependent variables—satisfaction, acceptance, and productivity—under various task conditions. The leader styles are defined as follows:

Supportive leadership. one which shows concern for subordinate well-being and comfort and attempts to make the climate supportive of these concerns.
Participative leadership: one which encourages subordinate influence in decision making and sharing of information.
Instrumental leadership: one which emphasizes formal activities such as planning and organizing.
Achievement-oriented leadership: one which determines results-oriented, challenging goals in a climate where subordinates are expected to assume responsibility.

The behavior adopted by the leader is one that most effectively clears the path to goal accomplishment in the subordinate's mind. In other words, the subordinate must perceive the leader behavior as aiding goal attainment.

Figure 2 outlines some of the research findings about path-goal theory.

**Figure 2. Some contingency variables for goal-path clarification.**

| Leader style | Environmental variables | Personality variables |
| --- | --- | --- |
| Supportive | Stressful, frustrating tasks | No clear relations evident |
| Participative | Ambiguous, ego-involving ——▶<br>and<br>Unambiguous, clear tasks ——▶ | Internals and<br>non-authoritarians<br>Personalities predisposed<br>to participation (non-<br>authoritarians) |
| Instrumental | Unambiguous, clear, ————▶<br>routine (at technological<br>level)<br>Ambiguous, non-routine ———▶<br>(upper management<br>levels) | Dogmatic, authoritarian<br>personalities<br><br>Both authoritarians and<br>nonauthoritarians |
| Achievement | Unambiguous ——————▶<br>non-repetitive tasks | No clear relations evident |

These concepts are just beginning to be explored, so the findings should be regarded as tentative. Effective leader style is contingent on the environmental and personality variables listed opposite the style. For example, participative leadership is likely to be effective in either ambiguous, ego-involving tasks or in unambiguous tasks providing internal or non-authoritarian personalities are involved. Figure 2 can also be used to select the characteristics of a situation to see what leader style is likely to be effective. For example, predominantly dogmatic personalities in ambiguous tasks call for an instrumental leadership style.

*Managerial Roles*

The concept of leadership takes on additional significance when viewed in relation to the broader activities of managers. Henry Mintzberg[11] has defined the activities of business executives into nine distinct categories. Each of these categories suggests an organizational role that executives play. Although separate from one another, the activities associated with each category are closely interrelated. Three groups of roles were formed out of the nine individual roles. The first group is called interpersonal and is made up of the figurehead, leader, and liaison roles. The second group is made up of the information processing roles, labeled monitoring, disseminating, and spokesman. Third, the decision-making roles include the entrepreneurial, the disturbance handler, and the resource-allocator roles.

These roles help to form a picture of managerial behavior. For example, the manager uses the interpersonal roles to get information for making wise decisions. If the manager's decision making is ineffective, attention can be focused on the other roles in the category which support decision making. In this case, the manager may be weak in information processing or interpersonal roles necessary to gather data. These roles would need to be improved to make him or her more effective.

Mintzberg's figurehead role is perhaps one of the more critical functions for leaders. Leaders may become "targets" because people attribute great influence to them, whether they have it or not. The discussion starting this chapter questioned the actual impact leaders have. If subordinates and peers attribute influence to a position, then leadership becomes important —if only because people believe it is. When the business or sports team does badly, the president or manager is fired. The leader becomes the target largely because of the power attributed to the leader's role and title, not because of the control he or she actually has in a situation. Besides, it is easier to fire one person than the entire management group or baseball team!

## Summary

Trait research was an early attempt to understand leadership. Other investigators followed different paths when this approach failed to satisfactorily explain leader effectiveness. An important contribution to leadership research was made by those who focused on leadership styles. The Iowa leadership studies identified three styles of leadership: autocratic, democratic, and laissez-faire.

Investigators at Ohio State University attempted to document what leaders actually did and how they did it. They found two major leader behaviors strongly related to effectiveness: initiating structure and consideration. Initiating structure is the orientation of a leader to a task. Consideration deals primarily with interpersonal relations between a leader and group members. The researchers found that leaders who are high on both of these dimensions tend to be more effective.

Fiedler's situational approach hypothesizes that leaders tend to have predominantly task-oriented or people-oriented styles and consequently are effective only in certain situations. His contingency theory of leadership theorizes that appropriately matching leader style to the situation will result in higher performing groups. Fiedler concludes that the job should, if necessary, be engineered to fit the leader's style to enhance his or her effectiveness.

Path-goal theory focuses on the way leader behavior enhances subordinate performance. Leader behaviors are effective to the extent that they help a subordinate to see that intrinsic and extrinsic rewards are directly related to performance. Different styles of leadership are effective under different circumstances.

Manager behavior has been explored by Mintzberg. He uncovered nine distinct roles that focused on critical behaviors of a manager. Three groups of roles evolved: interpersonal, information-processing, and decision-making roles. The interpersonal symbolic role is particularly important to the manager-leader, because its functioning affects subordinate perceptions of the amount of influence the leader has.

Leadership is complex and multifaceted. Leaders must carefully assess the situation in which their group is functioning and must determine whether or not their style is compatible with that situation. Alterations in either the situation or leader style may then be undertaken, if necessary, to enhance the likelihood of group success.

### References

1. Jeffrey Pfeffer, "The Ambiguity of Leadership," *Academy of Management Review,* vol. 2, no. 1, January 1977, pp. 104–111.
2. Richard H. Hall, *Organizations: Structure and Process* (Englewood Cliffs: Prentice-Hall, 1972), p. 248.
3. Jeffrey C. Barrow, "The Variables of Leadership: A Review and Conceptual Framework," *Academy of Management Review,* vol. 2, no. 2, April 1977, pp. 231–252.
4. C. Bird, *Social Psychology* (New York: Appleton-Century-Croft, 1940); and R. Stogdill, "Personal Factors Associated with Leadership: A Survey of the Literature," *Journal of Psychology,* 1948, pp. 35–717.
5. Ralph White and Ronald Lippitt, "Leader Behavior and Member Reaction in Three Social Climates," in *Group Dynamics,* edited by D. Cartwright and A. Zander (New York: Harper and Row, 1968), pp. 318–336.
6. Ralph M. Stogdill and Alvin E. Coons, eds., *Leader Behavior: Its Description and Measurement* (Columbus, OH: Ohio State University Bureau of Business Research, 1957).
7. Steven Kerr, C. Schriesheim, C. Murphy, and R. Stogdill, "Toward a Contingency Theory of Leadership Based upon the Consideration and Initiating Structure Literature," *Organizational Behavior and Human Performance,* 12, 1974, pp. 62–82.
8. Fred E. Fiedler and Martin M. Chemers, *Leadership and Effective Management* (Glenview, Ill.: Scott Foresman, 1974)
9. Fred E. Fiedler, Martin M. Chemers, and Linda Mahar, *Improving Leadership Effectiveness: The Leader Match Concept* (New York: John Wiley and Sons, 1977) pp. 134–136.
10. A. C. Filley, R. House, and S. Kerr, *Managerial Process and Organizational Behavior* (Glenview, Ill.: Scott Foresman, 1976), esp. ch. 12.
11. Henry Mintzberg, *The Nature of Managerial Work* (New York: Harper and Row, 1973).

### Recommended Readings

Readings marked with an asterisk are included in *Contemporary Perspectives in Organizational Behavior,* edited by Donald D. White (Boston: Allyn and Bacon, 1982).

B. J. Calder, "An Attribution Theory of Leadership," in *New Directions in Organizational Behavior,* edited by B. M. Staw and G. R. Salancik (Chicago: St. Clair 1977), pp. 179–204.
Tim R. V. Davis, and Fred Luthans, "Leadership Reexamined: A Behavioral Approach," *Academy of Management Review,* vol. 4, no. 2, April 1979, pp. 237–249.

*Raymond A. Gumpert and Ronald K. Hambleton, "Situational Leadership: How Xerox Managers Fine-Tune Managerial Styles to Employee Maturity and Task Needs," *Management Review,* vol. 68, December 1979, pp. 8–12.

*"How To Be a Successful Leader: Match Your Leadership Situation to Your Personality," An Interview with Fred Fiedler, *Leadership,* November 1979, pp. 26–31.

*Robert J. House and Terence R. Mitchell, "Path-Goal Theory of Leadership," *Journal of Contemporary Business,* vol. 3, Autumn 1974, pp. 81–97.

J. G. Hunt and L. L. Larson, eds., *Leadership: The Cutting Edge.* (Carbondale: Southern Illinois University Press, 1977), pp. 84–93.

# CASE 20
# Out of the Frying Pan

"How in the world am I going to untangle the situation that has developed in the Purchasing Department?" wondered John Sterling, the president of a paper products distribution firm. "Did I read something more than I should have when Pete Brown said he could handle it? Was I too quick to agree with him because the problem needed so badly to be solved? But, really, what choice did I have? Clearly, there was a need for action—prompt action. My God, the department was disintegrating! So—"

No one in the company doubted that there were significant problems in the Purchasing Department, for there were few secrets in this small organization. At the same time there was little sympathy among other employees, many of whom thought that the three buyers in purchasing considered themselves a cut above the rest. Company salesmen grumbled frequently about out-of-stock to the company's own warehouse. The order-takers who worked downstairs from purchasing and in another department had believed for some time that the buyers had certain working privileges not available to others. Not only did this belief rankle them, but also the fact that they, as order-takers, had to take flack from customers who were not always gracious when told the items they wanted were not available. As the buyers dealt primarily with suppliers, they therefore were buffered from any direct heat emanating from disgruntled customers. Not surprisingly, the order-takers did not relish such a role and tended to compensate for this harassment with frequent criticism of any real or imagined shortcomings on the part of the buyers.

Over thirty years ago, John Sterling and subsequently Tom Fenton bought the fledgling company organized a year before as a branch office of a much larger firm in another city some two hundred miles away. As a consequence of astute and aggressive operations, the company grew and prospered in the very competitive paper products distribution industry, largely due to the drive and stimulating example of the president. From the outset Sterling concerned himself with overall company operations, while Fenton narrowed his attention to sales. Over the years, this arrangement prevailed without major alteration. While a principal stockholder and member of the board, Fenton never questioned who was the boss. He seemed content with his subordinate and much circumscribed role in the company. Within broad policies and goals set by Sterling, Fenton was expected to proceed on his own initiative. Operating in a city of over 200,000 the firm not only expanded within the municipality, but also was able to extend its business to roughly a hundred-mile radius in all directions. In seeking national accounts, the company commenced a concentrated effort to develop institutional type accounts as opposed to the

Prepared by George Eddy, University of Texas.

smaller retail customers previously solicited. With some one hundred employees, the firm's annual sales were about $25 million, offering such products as matches, toilet and facial tissues, paper towels, packing material, business forms, paper cups, plates and napkins, and the like. Having acquired twenty acres of highly suitable commercial property serviced by rail, the company had built its own warehouses adjoining the office facilities. Deliveries to customers were accomplished by its own fleet of trucks. Company salesmen were divided into local and regional components. Exhibit 1 portrays the organization chart.

Now that the company's business had risen sharply and rather abruptly, Sterling had become increasingly concerned about the performance of the buyers. Their decisions and actions determined whether the company obtained the right products in the right quantities at the most favorable cost. With profit margins at two percent or less, there was little room for inventory mistakes. Some time ago, Sterling thought that he had made a needed change when he turned the Purchasing Department over to the Sales Manager, who said he was willing to take on this added responsibility. A member of the firm for more than fifteen years, Pete Brown had always been in sales in one capacity or another. He was confident of himself, and now that he had acquired two principal assistants and a most competent secretary (primarily an administrative assistant), Brown told Sterling he was sure he could improve the unstable situation in purchasing.

One of the difficulties in making this new assignment was the circumstance that Sterling would have to tell Tom Fenton, the senior vice president and one of the major stockholders in the company, that he would have to relinquish his authority over purchasing after considerable time as the chief of that function. Another complication was the fact that Fenton previously had been Brown's supervisor for several years. Sterling had placed Fenton in charge because of his extensive knowledge in this area and his passion for detail. Fenton also was well known to all the company's major suppliers and respected by the top managers as well. He liked working with figures and was especially intrigued by the challenge of developing new procedures, especially if they could be put on the company computer. He was not, however, a programmer or an analyst, depending on reasonably well what a computer was suited to do. As a superior management tool, the computer impressed Fenton, as he observed, "In today's environment, we can't function without it."

A working supervisor, Fenton applied himself strenuously, never complaining about the time he spent beyond normal working hours. He liked to write numerous short memos to his subordinates whenever he wanted to bring something to their attention:

"Harry, I've been checking on your purchases for the last month and they are way off base. I want you to tell me why you haven't been following the recommended buys programmed into our computer, and what you are going to do about it. We've spent a lot of money on this program and it *works*. Let me have this tomorrow."

"Peggy, you are making far too many errors in computing these supplier

**Exhibit 1. Organization chart.**

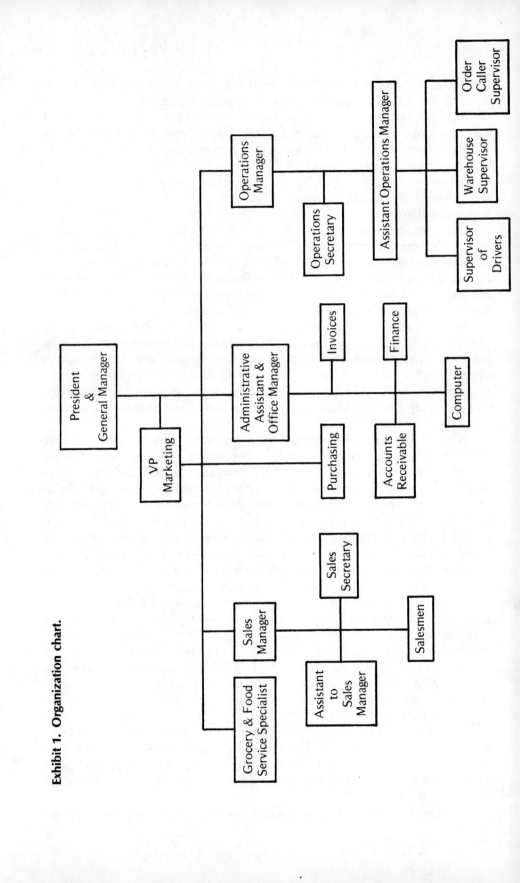

**Exhibit 2. Purchasing Department.**

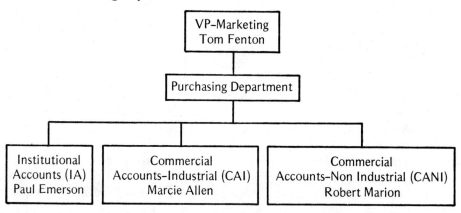

invoices. Here's a sample of what I've found in just the last week. You've got to be more careful, for these mistakes are costing the company money. I've been over this with you three times in the past month. . . . Come and talk to me about this."

If Fenton decided to talk with a buyer directly, he typically would approach the buyer in this fashion:

"Charley, I just don't know what's the matter with you! Just look at this! I've forgotten now how many times I've been through this with you, and you keep screwing up. Are you ever going to get it straight? What does it take to penetrate your brain?"

"Gee, I'm sorry, Mr. Fenton. I thought I had it right. I . . ."

"Well, it isn't, damn it! I figured you could understand something as simple as this purchase. Maybe you'll never get it—I don't know. . . ." At that point Fenton would turn away and go back into his office. Picking up a stack of computer print-outs, he would resume an item-by-item review.

A newly hired secretary, having overheard this exchange, went over to another, nearby buyer and asked:

"Mr. Bixby, is Mr. Fenton like this always?"

"Oh no, he's pretty calm today."

"You mean—"

"Wait, let me say this: Mr. Fenton is an expert, and he expects us to follow his instructions—"

"Exactly?"

"You get the idea."

"But, isn't there a lot to remember? I was told that each of you buyers handles nearly four hundred items—is that right?"

"Yes to both questions. Weren't you told about the book of instructions, where all the individual tasks are listed? Mr. Fenton wrote those himself."

"Book? No, I don't remember that. Do you have one?"

"No, there's only one and Mr. Fenton keeps that in his office."

"Oh."

"Now, don't get the wrong idea. When I came here for this job, Mr. Fenton called me into his office and went over all of it with me. If I have a question, I can always go in and ask him."

The Purchasing Department consisted essentially of three elements: institutional accounts and two commercial accounts. Generally, the three buyers shared the same workload, although the 1,200 line items the company carried were not neatly divided into three equal parts. Computer programs provided the basis for decisions on what and when to purchase, with a variety of printouts. Among these were the Recommended Buy Report, Expedite Report, On Hand Report, Daily Receiving, Stock Adjustment, and other reports (i.e. weekly, biweekly, monthly, and so on). The Recommended Buy Report contained specific quantities to be purchased on a standard pack basis; it also reflected recent customer usage rates by company identification number, work description, and the like. The quantities to be purchased were computed automatically in accordance with a special Economic Order Quantity (EOQ) formula, which was updated periodically.

Pointing to the EOQ column on this report, Fenton declared to the buyers: "This is what you will order."

Orders were placed by telephone and confirmed by Purchase Order, subsequently produced by the computer, based on punched card input from a form completed by the buyer. Occasionally the buyers were expected to adjust item quantities to be ordered from a supplier to constitute a full realcar load to minimize freight charges. A special computer program was called upon to assist the buyers in making such a determination, yet buyers did alter some computer recommendations on their own initiative. Another important duty each buyer had to complete was to record and keep track of the increasingly frequent price changes that suppliers submitted. Fenton also expected each buyer to seek special promotions from as many suppliers as possible and as often as feasible. A promotion involved a limited period when price reductions applied as an incentive to increase sales.

Concerning a typical day for these varied tasks, one buyer commented, "I estimate that I spend about 50 percent of my time placing orders, with followup on delivery status accounting for 10 percent of my total effort. The balance of my time is consumed by troubleshooting for 20 percent and about the same for administrative demands."

When asked how much time was devoted to studying the market for his commodity area, he replied, "I don't have time for that."

On the subject of personnel turnover, this same buyer remarked, "Well, there's been a lot. For example, shortly before I came here, and I guess that was about nine months ago, Peggy was on non-industrial commercial accounts, Charley on industrial commercial, and Mary on institutional. Mary quit and was replaced by Stella. That didn't seem to work out, so Rozella switched from being a secretary to industrial accounts when Stella quit. A few weeks later, Rozella was fired, and I found myself as the new institutional buyer. I tried to pick up the pieces as best I could, and—well, I'm still here."

"Did the department settle down after that?"

"No, it didn't. Three months after I came, why, Charley—he was the grocery industrial commercial buyer—was fired. About the same time, Peggy quit and Marcie became the industrial buyer. We had to sort of juggle things around to cover all the accounts, and finally I ended up as the industrial buyer and Ron moved into Purchasing from Sales to take over the frozen foods desk. Thinking about the time involved when all this was happening, I'd say that it was from May to October."

This was the period when Fenton was in charge of the Purchasing Department. These circumstances led Sterling to seek a change by asking Pete Brown if he would assume the responsibility for Purchasing in addition to his position as the Sales Manager. "I need someone who gets along with people," Sterling mused, "and certainly Pete fills that bill."

So he called Tom Fenton to his office and told him that he needed him to work on some high priority matters that only Fenton could handle. Further, Sterling told Fenton he believed that Brown could step in and assume Fenton's role. While Fenton may not have entirely agreed that Brown could handle the complexities of that department, he finally acquiesced to Sterling's urging.

Accordingly, Brown moved into the front office in Purchasing and assumed the full responsibility for it. As he viewed what he thought was a chaotic situation in the department, he decided to bring in Ron from his Sales Department to take over the industrial accounts. Since this position already was occupied by a buyer named Paul who had been in that function for approximately five months and the fourth one in somewhat less than one year, Brown realized that initially this move would not ease the unrest which prevailed for so long. Nevertheless, he considered that this action should be taken.

After he summoned Paul to his office, Brown said, "Paul, I need to talk to you about the industrial accounts, which you've been breaking in on for the past several months."

"Yes, Mr. Brown, is there something wrong?"

"Well, let me say that things could be better."

"Could you explain what you mean, Mr. Brown?"

"Well, I've been observing your work, and it seems to me that you are having more trouble with it than you should. There still are instances where you order too much of an item on the one hand, and too little of something else on the other. Perhaps it's because you've never been a buyer before. I don't know. . . ."

"Could you give me some specific example, Mr. Brown?"

"Of course I can, but I don't think it's necessary to repeat what I've discussed with you before on the cups and the plates. Let's just say that the job is too much for you at this time." Brown hastened to add, as he noticed a puzzled look spreading across Paul's face, "So, I've decided to make a change and move you over to non-industrial commercial which is not so complicated. I'm going to bring Ron in from Sales to work the industrial desk."

"Ron Fisher? Has he ever been a buyer?"

"Yeah, that's right—Now, Paul, I want you to spend some time with Ron, helping him get adjusted as fast as possible—and, of course, you'll also be handling the non-industrial desk at the same time. I don't think you'll have any real trouble. Okay, Paul?"

"If you say so, Mr. Brown."

For a few months matters in general appeared to improve in the department, and the buyers apparently were more content than under Fenton's control. The working atmosphere gradually became quite relaxed, almost gay at times. At least this was the impression gained by some employees in other, nearby offices. One, perhaps envious worker was overheard exclaiming, "Why, that place has turned into a (expletive deleted) country club!"

Unfortunately, in Sterling's opinion, performance in the department did not match his expectations. His concern mounting as reports continued to reach him that the buyers were more interested in their own well-being than in doing a better job, Sterling began to press Brown for details. At this juncture, Sterling's suspicions were confirmed that discipline was overly lax and that Brown tended to let too many details get by him. The deeper Sterling probed into the circumstances developing in the Purchasing Department, the more acute was his apprehension that Brown really was not cut out for that job.

What appeared at the outset to be a welcome change when Brown moved to Purchasing was now turning sour. Initially successful in curbing the anxieties of the buyers under Fenton which were adversely affecting their performance, Brown apparently was more pleasant than demanding. Sterling was convinced that it was imperative that the buyers recognize immediately that they had to knuckle down—or else. The inventory situation remained in an unsatisfactory state: too many dollars tied up with dormant stock concurrently with too many out-of-stock items. After discussing this state of affairs further with Brown, Sterling concluded that the Purchasing task was beyond Brown's abilities or interest.

# CASE 21
# Davis Regional Medical Center

Davis Regional Medical Center is an acute care, general hospital located in Charlesville, a community of 35,000 in the southwestern United States. The organization began in 1950 as a 35-bed facility known as Davis County Hospital. The hospital grew to a capacity of 55 beds after its first three years of operation. Economic growth in the region along with a rapid influx of people resulted in additional expansions, and by 1968 the hospital had reached its present capacity of 166 beds.

The population in the region has grown steadily over the last fifteen years. (The population of Davis County was approximately 56,800 in 1960 and 86,600 in 1975.) However, the hospital size has remained unchanged. Approximately 500 people are employed at Davis. The medical staff consists of 75 doctors and dentists. A substantial majority of the medical staff are specialists. Therefore, the hospital offers a wide range of medical services. Current estimates are that the hospital serves 10,000 inpatients and approximately 16,000 outpatients each year.

## Regional Medical Center

In 1972, the board of directors of the hospital concluded that it was necessary to undertake a major expansion of the hospital's physical plant if it were to continue to adequately serve residents in and around the Charlesville area. Hospital managers and board members had received numerous complaints concerning overcrowded conditions in the hospital. Beds for patients often were found in the halls and waiting rooms, considerable delays were experienced by new patients registering at the hospital due to the lack of available space, and numerous offices and hallways had become storage points for inventory material and equipment. At one point, hospital administrators were informed by State Health Department officials that if equipment and cartons of supplies were not removed from various hallways, the hospital would not be licensed for the coming year and therefore could not be accredited by the Joint Commission (a national accrediting agency).

The situation had become critical by the time the final decision was made on the expansion. It was decided that a major building effort costing twelve million dollars would be undertaken. The number of beds in the medical facility were to be increased from 166 to 248, and a number of existing services were to be expanded in the new facility. Shortly after the expansion decision was made, the board also changed the name of the hospital from Davis County Hospital to Davis Regional Medical Center. The purpose of this name change

Prepared by Donald D. White, University of Arkansas.

was to more accurately reflect the services available and the population served by the growing medical complex. A fund raising drive in Charlesville managed to provide a base of one million dollars with which to begin the expansion. However, a feasibility study completed during the drive suggested that the performance of the hospital (based on past figures) could not financially support the total planned expansion. Therefore, a revised plan was decided upon.

## Administrative and Organizational Background

Davis Regional Medical Center, like similar county hospitals in the state, is governed by a seven-member board of directors. State law provided that the board be appointed by the local county judge. As with any political system, appointments are based on a combination of individual qualifications and the political postures of board members. Historically, the board had not provided strong leadership to the hospital. However, recent appointments, together with strong leadership from a new board chairman, had greatly increased the activity and contribution of the board to the operation of the hospital.

The administrator of any county hospital is placed in a unique position of having to respond to political pressures and medical needs of the people whom he serves. In addition, he often finds himself between pressures created by his medical staff, employees, and the public. The toll which these pressures create sometimes is quite high. Such was the case at Davis Regional Medical Center. Within the ten-year period from 1965 to 1975, the hospital had four separate administrators. Three of those administrators along with the one acting administrator served in the position during the last five years.

Reasons for the turnovers were numerous. One administrator, Frederick

**Exhibit 1. Past administration at DRMC.**

| Administrator | Years | Reason for Termination |
|---|---|---|
| G.B. | 1949–53 | Under pressure to resign (personal) |
| B.C. | 1953–55 | A series of problems both financial and political; asked to resign |
| H.M. (R.N.) | 1955–62 | Considered to be a good administrator; resigned under positive circumstances; she may have felt that the job was becoming "Too Big" for her |
| F.H. | 1962–67 | Hospital showed a $250,000 loss; was asked to resign |
| G.E. | 1967–71 | Illness; under mild pressure to resign |
| R.W. | 1971–74 | Was asked to resign |
| C.B. | 1974–present | Currently the DRMC Administrator |

Harold, was asked to resign after the hospital lost over $250,000 in a period of two years. His replacement, Glen Easton, was charged with the responsibility of putting the hospital back in the black. Within one year Easton had done so. However, during the end of his term as administrator, his decisions affecting patients and employees alike became more and more autocratic and seemingly unrealistic. For example, he once forced an orderly to enter the room of a critically ill patient to collect a dollar-a-day charge for TV service. He had instructed the employee to collect one dollar from each patient each day that the patient was in the room. Acts such as these received considerable attention throughout the community. Later, it was discovered that Easton had leukemia, and he retired from his position as administrator. (A number of his later decisions were attributed, in part, by those around him to his illness.) His replacement was Robert Winston who had served as assistant administrator under his predecessor for a period of two years.

The board appointed Winston as administrator of the hospital in 1971. He served in that position until he was asked to resign in 1974. Persons who worked with the hospital during his tenure as administrator (outside consultants and hospital managers), described him as unimaginative and unwilling to put in the necessary work to develop and maintain a strong medical facility. In his final months as administrator, he was on the hospital premises from four to six hours a day. Although reasons for his requested resignation were never made public, personal problems which were believed to interfere with the fulfillment of his administrative responsibilities were cited by the board.

Due to the suddenness with which Winston had been asked to tender his resignation, the board had not yet begun its search for a new administrator. In the interim period of five months Donald Dale, who served as assistant administrator under Winston, was named as acting administrator. He was closely assisted by Larry Engels, the Director of Personnel. The two men worked closely as a team making day-to-day operating decisions.

Dale and Engels were aware of acute employee morale and motivation problems within the medical center. They attributed these problems to the lack of leadership under which the hospital had been operating and employee concerns about what the new administrator would be like. Both recently had attended a seminar for hospital administrators in which the importance of employee attitudes and participation had been a major subject. In particular, they had been impressed by the discussion and illustration of a Management by Objectives (MBO) system designed for health care organizations. They were convinced that such a system would help create greater *esprit de corps* at Davis Regional Medical Center and improve the exchange of ideas and information between department heads within the hospital. Furthermore, the director of personnel believed that supervisory and department head training programs would have to be conducted in order to prepare management personnel throughout the organization for the hoped for MBO-type system.

In July 1974, the director of personnel contacted Dr. John Connors, a university professor and management consultant. It had been Dr. Connors who earlier that year had presented the administrative seminar that Engels and Dale attended. They arranged to meet together and to discuss the present situation at Davis Regional Medical Center. During the next month, the two administrators and Dr. Connors met on numerous occasions and discussed the problems and needs of the hospital.

Both Dale and Engels were emphatic about wanting to develop a more employee-oriented administration. For example, they created a non-supervisory employee council which met once a month to discuss with the two men problems and conditions throughout the hospital. The intended purpose of this council was to provide a means by which Dale and Engels could enhance two-way communication between the hospital administration and the employees at Davis. Each department elected one person to represent them in the council. Initially, most of the communication was from, the top down. However, shortly after the council had been created, a core of employees rose to take leadership of the group. They elected a spokesman and requested that they be permitted to meet once a month without either Dale or Engels present. Thereafter, the employee representatives met twice monthly, once with the administrators and once without them.

Dale and Engels also shared the view that some form of management training should be developed and conducted for department heads and hospital supervisors, whom they saw as the key to hospital effectiveness. There was some hesitancy on the part of Dr. Connors and Mr. Dale to initiate such a program prior to the selection of a new administrator. Both men believed that it might be unfair to saddle a new administrator with a program that he might not favor. The director of personnel, however, felt strongly that the program should be initiated "as soon as possible."

Such a program subsequently was designed by Dr. Connors and agreed upon by the three men. Shortly thereafter, Mr. Dale was informed that a new administrator had been selected by the Board of Directors. The new administrator was scheduled to take over his post at DRMC in approximately four weeks. Mr. Dale told Dr. Connors that his discussions with the new administrator, Mr. Benson, led him to believe that Mr. Benson would be favorable to a management development program. However, both men decided to wait until a formal meeting could be held with Mr. Benson before proceeding with the actual program.

## A New Leader for the "Troops"

Arnold Benson came to Davis Hospital from a multi-facility complex in St. Louis, Missouri. He had been selected out of seventy applicants for the position of administrator at Davis County Hospital. Benson was a young man, 33 years of age. He held bachelor's and master's degrees in business administration and had considerable experience working in hospital organizations. In his words, "My objective was to become a professional hospital administrator. I realized that since I did not yet have a master's degree in hospital administration I would have to go with a 'back door approach' by working my way up the ranks."

Thus, Benson's first position in a hospital was that of director of purchasing and personnel in a 118-bed facility. He next took the position of assistant administrator in a 156-bed Catholic hospital. In a period of two years, he rose from assistant administrator to associate administrator and finally to that of administrator of the hospital. Finally he became administrator of a 144-bed and a 134-bed multi-hospital complex in St. Louis, Missouri. He remained in the hospital for four years "gaining exposure, experience and expertise." Prior to his hospital experiences, Mr. Benson had worked for a year and a half on a General Motors assembly line while going to college. He also had spent four years in the Marine Corps, having enlisted when he was 17 years old.

In the summer of 1974, Arnold Benson began looking for a new position as a hospital administrator. He believed that he had learned a great deal in his present job; however, he was anxious to relocate in a smaller community. The St. Louis Hospital of which he was administrator was located in a predominantly black, low-income, ghetto area. His hospital had been a prime target for numerous union drives (none of which were successful) and he had overseen a major expansion of the hospital facilities. He wanted to relocate in a community of less than 50,000 population somewhere in the southwestern United States. His salary requirements were rather stringent due to his experience in administration. Therefore, he was very pleased when he was selected as the new administrator at Davis Regional.

Benson was a tall, athletic-looking man whose mild manners and easygoing Texas drawl tended to hide his "down-to-business" approach to administration. Soon after arriving, he realized that he would be facing many problems inside and outside of the hospital in the next few months. He knew that the most pressing of these was the hospital expansion. Moreover, it was clear to him that the first concern of certain members of the board of directors was the financial position of the hospital.

Financial concerns plagued Mr. Benson from the moment he arrived at Davis Regional Medical Center. During his first weeks on the job, the building program finances consumed almost 50 percent of his time. In addition, two particular decisions, both of which would have a direct impact on hospital employees, had to be made.

The first of these decisions concerned a 10-cent across-the-board pay increase that was due to all hospital employees in January. Mr. Benson had not been told of this promised increase until he had been at the hospital for some time. Immediately upon learning of the proposed increase, he sat down and calculated its impact on his budget. The total cost to the medical center appeared to be well in excess of $200,000. Feeling the need to hold the line on expenses, Mr. Benson decided not to put through the wage increase. In his words, "When I 'came aboard' the board charged me with the financial responsibility of the medical center. If the troops were to get their pay increase in January, it would throw the entire budget out of kilter. I have only been here three weeks, and quite frankly the '75 budget didn't get the attention it deserved." After making his decision, Mr. Benson dictated a memo announcing that while employees at Davis could expect to receive up to a 6 percent increase for the new year, the 10-cent across-the-board increase would not be given. Mr. Benson also stressed that the total financial posture of the hospital would have to be re-evaluated. The memo was posted on the employee bulletin board.

Soon after the memo was posted, a rumor circulated throughout the hospital that the board of directors was about to purchase a new automobile for Mr. Benson. Pictures of Cadillacs and Mark IV Continentals were placed on the bulletin board on an almost daily basis. His memo concerning denial of the pay increase was slashed with a knife and various comments were written on it. (The hospital-owned automobile which Benson actually used was a Ford Galaxy driven by the previous administrator.)

Recognizing the discontent over his decision, Benson met with members of the employee advisory council to discuss the pay question. Several members of the group quoted statistics showing that on the average blue-collar workers throughout the United States were being paid more than were most hospital employees. Mr. Benson replied that he thought it was unfair to quote blue-collar statistics and that he believed the most that a hospital employee at the medical center could look forward to would be to live comfortably. He then asked the members of the advisory council if they would work harder if they received a 10-cent per-hour increase. According to Benson, "When all responded negatively, I told them point blank that it appeared that it would be foolish to reward people ten more cents per hour with no increase in productivity." He did go on to tell those present that he would do his best to see to it that they received some pay increases (up to 6 percent based on merit) as soon as the necessary funds became available. In addition, he told them that he hoped to put in effect a new wage and salary administration program in the near future.

The employee council also voiced complaints about other conditions at Davis hospital. Over a period of the next few weeks, Mr. Benson saw to it that many of the problems were dealt with to the group's satisfaction. However, when the last "demand" was met he announced that he believed that there was no longer a need for the advisory group. A question was raised by one of the employees concerning whether or not the group would be permitted to reform if subsequent problems arose. Mr. Benson replied that it would not be permitted to do so.

Benson was confronted by a second important decision not long after the incident involving the pay increase memo. The hospital had been able to obtain the money necessary for expansion through tax exempt revenue bonds. However, the building program itself did not include much needed parking lots. Arnold Benson, therefore, found it necessary to take his request for an additional 1.3 million dollars to the local banking community. Although the bankers agreed to underwrite the project, the feasibility study on which their decision was based indicated that the parking lots would have to be income-generating entities in their own right. Prior to this time, all parking in hospital lots was provided without charge to the medical staff, employees, and visitors. Now however, it was clear to Benson that *all* parties would in the future be required to pay a parking fee.

Although he expected resistance on the issue from the doctors, he was more concerned about the reactions of general employees to the decision. The fact that he had been confronted by this second decision so shortly after his refusal to grant the across-the-board pay increase further aggravated his situation. As far as Benson was concerned, the decision had been made. However, he and Dr. Connors agreed that its announcement should be temporarily postponed.

## Management Development

In early January, department heads from throughout the hospital began meeting with Dr. Connors as part of an overall management development pro-

**Exhibit 2. Managerial personnel on payroll when Benson was hired.**

| Name | Department | Tenure with DRMC Years Employed | Years as Department Head |
|------|-----------|-----------|-----------|
| J.C. | Physical Therapy | 25 | 21 |
| D.T. | Nuclear Medicine | 18 | 6 |
| D.D. | Assistant Administrator | 11½ | 11½ |
| B.G. | Housekeeping | 9 | 2 |
| G.H. | Radiology | 8½ | 8½ |
| K.F. | Nursing | 7 | 2½ |
| L.H. | Dietary | 7 | 7 |
| L.E. | Personnel | 5 | 4 |
| J.H. | E.M.S. | 5 | 1 |
| P.G. | Purchasing | 4 | 1 |
| L.C. | Child Care | 4 | 3 |
| T.M. | Pharmacy | 4 | 2 |
| E.B. | Laboratory | 7 | 2½ |
| D.B. | Medical Records | 2½ | 2½ |
| J.G. | Maintenance | 2½ | 2½ |
| L.P. | Respiratory Therapy | 2 | 2 |
| E.I. | Social Service | 1 | 1 |
| M.R. | Volunteers | 1 | 1 |
| M.K. | Comptroller | 1 | 1 |

Explanation:
1. Two new departments, EKG and EEG, were added shortly after Benson's arrival. Previously, their functions and personnel were under Nuclear Medicine.
2. Of those department heads listed above, the following persons left DRMC within six months after Benson's arrival. K.F. (resignation requested); L.H. (resigned following demotion); L.E. (resignation requested); P.G. (resigned, but was to have been replaced); E.B. (resigned to take promotion elsewhere); L.P. (resigned to take a similar position elsewhere, was dissatisfied at DRMC).

gram. Those participating met in a series of seven two-hour sessions. The total program took place over a period of approximately one month. (A similar program was conducted for supervisors during the following month.)

According to Mr. Dale, the purpose of the management programs was twofold. He believed that it was necessary to provide those hospital employees in management positions with some form of supervisory training. He also felt that the program would be a good way to single out the department heads and supervisors for "special attention."

The sessions were recommended to the department heads and supervisors by Mr. Benson, however, participation remained voluntary. All but two department heads attended the series of sessions. (Although Mr. Benson and Mr. Dale requested that they be permitted to attend the classes, it was agreed that their presence might inhibit the participation of department heads. Both men were provided with copies of all materials distributed, but neither attended the formal sessions.)

The content of the programs included traditional subjects such as the elements and techniques of supervision. However, emphasis also was placed on achieving improved interpersonal relations between department heads and improving the exchange of information between the departments themselves. (See Exhibit 3)

One event which took place during the sessions dramatized that a certain amount of distrust and lack of cooperation existed between many department heads throughout the hospital. During one of the early sessions, the participants were asked to complete evaluation forms that were to be used in con-

**Exhibit 3. Outline of supervisory development program, Davis Regional Medical Center.**

| Session[1] | Assignments |
| --- | --- |
| 1　Introductory Comments and an Icebreaker Supervisory Functions: Models and the Environment Preparing for our Sessions | Case Study |
| 2　The Hospital Organization: Authority, Power and Informal Relationships | Case Study Ch. 15[2] |
| 3　Understanding Ourselves and Others | Case Study |
| 4　Leading and Motivating Employees | Case Study, Film Ch. 1, 2 |
| 5　Improving Interpersonal and Interdepartmental Communications | Ch. 4, Nominal Grouping Exercise, Role Play |
| 6　Setting Goals and Making Decisions | Case Study, Role Play, Ch. 6, 9 |
| 7　Evaluating and Handling Employee Conflict | Ch. 11,12, Case Study, Role Play |

[1] Sessions—(1 hour and 50 minutes; last 15–20 minutes spent answering questions and dealing with problems on an individual basis.)
[2] Chapters were taken from a hospital supervisory management book selected for the program by Dr. Connors.

nection with an exercise known as the Johari Window. The purpose of the exercise was to help the managers see themselves more clearly as others saw them and to help others in the group in a similar manner by providing them with "image feedback" information. The theory behind the exercise together with its purpose was explained to those present. Each manager was asked to write the name of every department head (including him/herself) and to list at least one asset and one liability of that person. Dr. Connors requested that the completed forms be returned to him at the beginning of the next session. The name of the individual providing the "feedback" information was not to be placed on the sheet itself. Dr. Connors explained that he would facilitate the exchange of feedback at the next session by reading the name of a participant followed by the assets and liabilities which were identified by his/her peers.

As he had planned, Dr. Connors began the next session by asking that all feedback sheets be passed in to him. Much to his surprise only about half of the sheets were returned and most of them were insufficiently completed. After a short pause, he asked those present to explain why they had failed to complete the assignment. Following a brief discussion, it was evident that the department heads had decided in another meeting that they would not complete the feedback sheet. Reasons for not wanting to complete the assignment ranged from claims that the participants did not know one another well enough (prior to the management program many of the department heads did not know one another by name, although a "get acquainted" exercise was used in the first session) to fear that the information assembled on each individual would in some way be used against him or her. One woman openly expressed concern that other department heads at the meeting might misuse the information. Another head privately suggested that some of those in attendance thought that Dr. Connors, himself, might take the information to the administrator. The discussion that followed the failure to hand in the assignment had a cathartic effect on the group. For the first time, many of those in attendance "opened up" and talked about the lack of communication and trust that existed between the department heads and between the department heads and the administrator.

Dr. Connors ended the session by again explaining that the purpose of the exercise was to "improve our understandings of ourselves as well as of those with whom we associate throughout the hospital." After another brief discussion, it was agreed by all that the feedback sheets would be completed and returned at the following session. At that next session, the exercise was completed smoothly. Many of the managers commented afterwards that they believed that the exercise had been beneficial and had helped to open up the group. One department head did comment, however, "To tell you the truth, I think our refusal to complete the feedback sheets helped to break the ice between us. You know, it is the first time we really ever got together and agreed on something."

Subsequent sessions of the department head development program produced numerous positive comments and favorable evaluations of the overall program. Upon completion of the program, each participant received a certificate signed by Mr. Benson and Dr. Connors.

## Followup

A few days after the department heads' program was completed, Mr. Benson asked Dr. Connors to meet with him. He began their conference by stating that he was pleased with what he had heard about the sessions and was anxious to insure that the momentum which had been created would not be lost. He asked Dr. Connors what he thought of bringing all of the department heads together for a weekend retreat at a resort area not far from Charlesville. Dr. Connors was pleased with Mr. Benson's suggestion. He told the administrator that he had seriously considered recommending that such a retreat take place, but was hesitant to do so because of the financial situation at the hospital. Mr. Benson replied that the money for the retreat could be found since he anticipated that the outcome of the retreat would have a positive impact on the operation of the facility.

The following week Mr. Benson told department heads at their weekly meeting on January 31 that the retreat had been scheduled for the weekend of February 14 and 15. He went on to explain that the department heads would gather on Friday morning at the hospital and would drive directly to the resort. All expenses would be paid by the medical center. He told them that he hoped that the meeting would permit a free exchange of ideas.

During the week before the scheduled retreat, Dr. Connors received an invitation from Mr. Benson to meet with the department heads in their meeting on Thursday. Dr. Connors agreed to do so as long as neither Mr. Benson nor Mr. Dale would be present at the meeting.

The meeting itself brought quite a surprise. It was immediately evident to Dr. Connors that the mood of the department heads was not what he had expected. As he walked into the room he heard the men and women present voicing numerous complaints to one another. When they saw Dr. Connors the group immediately quieted down. It was not clear to him whether or not they had been told he would be attending the meeting. Therefore, he explained his presence and told them that he was interested in how things had been going the two or three weeks since their last session. Much to his surprise, the grumbling began immediately. Some of the complaints were minor. However, one complaint in particular took Dr. Connors by surprise. That complaint focused on the upcoming retreat. A few department heads stated that they did not know whether or not they would go to the resort with the rest of the group. One newly married woman stated that it was Valentine's Day and her husband did not want her to leave. Two other heads said they had previous plans to attend a Valentine's Day dance at the Country Club that Friday evening. As discussion continued, it became apparent that the department heads had been told rather than consulted about the retreat. Some expressed displeasure with being "forced" into going to the retreat and using part of their weekend without first being asked their opinion.

Dr. Connors listened carefully and explained to the managers that he himself believed that the retreat was a good idea. He told them about how he had planned on suggesting such an activity to the administrator, but how Mr. Benson had come up with the idea on his own. Moreover, he told them that he believed that they should give Mr. Benson "a chance" during the weekend to see what might come out of the retreat. There were a few supportive comments made by one or two department heads and the meeting broke up.

Dr. Connors left the meeting disturbed. He had not expected to find the level of dissatisfaction which existed among the department heads. As he walked toward the entrance of the hospital he asked himself whether or not he should try to provide any further assistance to Mr. Benson before the group left for the retreat the next morning. He decided to stop in and see the administrator before leaving the hospital.

# CASE 22
## Instrument Data Corporation (IDC): Engineering Branch

The first few hours of my new job consisted of filling out insurance, tax, and any other kind of form that can be thought of. It was now lunch time and one of the secretaries directed me to the plant lunchroom. After going through the lunch line, I spotted a table with an empty chair. "Hi, I'm Bill Casey. I'm new here and—well—would you mind if I sat with ya'll?"

The big guy sitting across the table immediately said in a curt manner, "Where ya' from?"

"The University of Texas. I just graduated and this is my first day here."

I sat down and there was immediate silence. As if to answer the suspicious, cold glances of the other men, the big guy said, "He's all right, he's from Texas."

After talking to the men for a while, I realized that I would be working in a section with these same men. Steve, the big guy, decided to show me around the plant and introduce me to some of the other engineers. "Don, this is Bill. He just graduated from Texas and is going to be working with us."

"That's great," said Don. "It will be nice to work with you. There is plenty of work, so I'm sure you won't have any problem finding something to keep you busy." While I was looking around, I heard Don say, "I sure am glad he is not one of those troublemakers from Mobile. I just can't stand those guys."

I didn't know what to think when I heard this. I thought it was just some kind of joke between Steve and Don. However, I would soon find out that this was no laughing matter.

It took only a few days to find out that Don's comment was indicative of trouble within our branch. The problems had not been present very long.

About three months before I was hired, IDC transferred two other branches to Albany, Georgia. Work loads were consolidated at this location in an effort to improve efficiency and effectiveness. The two branches that were closed were located in Mobile, Alabama and Dayton, Ohio. It was the company's policy to offer a transfer of personnel when work loads are transferred. Several engineers had come from Mobile, but none had transferred from Dayton. I was one of twenty engineers recruited from other industries or colleges to handle the increased work loads.

When the Mobile branch transferred to Albany, some of the men, including their branch supervisor, had more seniority than the men in Albany. It was also a company policy to make transfers within the company on the

Prepared by H. William Vroman, Towson State University.

basis of seniority. The Mobile branch supervisor replaced the Albany supervisor. The branch was then divided into three sections, in anticipation of the arrival of the new recruits. Tom, the old Albany supervisor, was put in charge of one of the sections. Another engineer from Albany was to be in charge of the second section, while Jim, a guy from Mobile, would be in charge of the third.

The first two sections were to be composed of Albany engineers and new recruits, while the third section was to be composed entirely of Mobile people. Dissatisfaction with the new arrangement became apparent. The old supervisor was well respected by the other Albany men and they were not satisfied with his subtle demotion.

Needless to say, there was instantaneous conflict. The Albany men did not like the apparent take-over of their branch by the Mobile people. The conflict worsened when Jim was promoted, or as the men in my section said, "handpicked by the Mobile supervisor," to section supervisor. The Albany workers felt that their advancement opportunities were being devoured by the men from Mobile and there was an immediate hatred formed for these men.

The Mobile workers felt that they should make the best of the situation. After all, they had to transfer from their branch to come here. They felt that they should have the same opportunities to advance here as they did in Mobile.

During my first month on the job, ten of the other recruits arrived. After all the new men arrived, the branch tripled in size. By now the building we were working in was getting overcrowded. There were two other divisions in this building, and they too were experiencing overcrowding due to increases in personnel.

I started playing golf on Saturdays with a few other guys in my section. While walking to the green, Bob and I were talking about the working conditions. He said, "I just can't get anything done. I feel like a sardine packed in a can. I wasn't even used to this when I worked for Apex in New York."

I replied, "You would think that they would provide us with a respectable place to work under respectable working conditions. After all, we are professionals."

It soon became evident that all of the engineers coming from other companies were dissatisfied with the working conditions. These men began to be absent from the office with great regularity. When they did come in, they complained so much that they were unable to get very much work done. Most of the older IDC workers did not seem to be bothered with the crowded conditions. It was as if they expected only minimum facilities and accepted this.

Because of the continuous complaints received from the new engineers, management had come to realize that working conditions were poor and facilities were overcrowded. In an effort to ease the overcrowding, it was announced that the engineering branch would be moved into a "new" building. I soon discovered that this "new" building was not so new. It had been condemned no less than three times in the past fifteen years. It was not air conditioned and was in need of many repairs.

At first, everybody in our branch questioned the reasons for our branch having to move into the building rather than one of the other divisions. Everyone thought that our work was just as important as that of the other divisions. I thought to myself, "Why shouldn't we have working facilities that are as good as those of the other branches?" It soon became apparent that the other workers had common sentiments. The men soon realized that the move was inevitable and nothing could be done about it.

Tom, our section supervisor, continually complained about the conditions of the old building. He arranged a meeting with the other two section supervisors, the branch supervisor, and the plant managers. It was finally decided that IDC would furnish the material if the engineers would furnish the labor necessary to remodel the old building. The engineering branch agreed to make the best of their situation and remodel the old building. Never before had I seen all of the engineers work together with such energy and cooperation. Everyone seemed determined to remodel the building so that we could have the facilities and working conditions we thought we deserved.

It took about two months to make the necessary repairs and move into the old building. However with the constant influx of new people, work loads were assigned and/or re-assigned as required. These constant changes prevented any system of coordination or organization being efficient. Workers were moved from one task to another and efficiency was low.

After all of the new men had arrived, things began to settle down. These men were accepted as a part of the new organization and were soon to become friends with the men in their sections. The reason the new men were accepted was that they did not pose any threat to the security of the older workers. They could not exercise any seniority rights and displace any of the older workers because they had not accumulated any such rights. Routines were re-established and everything seemed to be going all right.

A few weeks later I noticed that the production in the first two sections was considerably higher than that of the Mobile section. It was now evident that none of the Albany workers liked any of the Mobile workers. The typical comment about the Mobile section was, "They are nothing but lazy bums. All they ever do is flirt with the secretaries or go to the pub and get soused after lunch. Just let us goof off the way they do and *their* branch supervisor would jump down our throats. They get all of the easy assignments anyway. If something difficult comes up, we are the ones who have to do it."

Even our supervisor disliked the Mobile branch supervisor. Any time our supervisor had a problem, he would go straight to the plant managers for help. Tom's reason for this was he "couldn't work with the new branch supervisor because of his authoritarian manner."

Production in the Albany sections was at an all-time high. The older workers seemed to be trying to show up the Mobile workers, while the newer workers were trying to show and prove their capabilities. The Mobile section seemed to be unaware of our obvious challenge. No one in our section ever talked to them. It was almost like an unwritten law that you could not talk to any one of the men from Mobile.

The men from Mobile probably wouldn't have cared if they knew of the challenge. Tom told me that they did just enough to get by and they didn't care about anything else.

Things have really been bad lately. One of the "goof-offs" from Mobile was promoted to another division. Everybody in my section resented this. I heard many people comment, "Why should he be promoted? We all work twice as hard as he does. All he ever does is flirt with the secretaries in the morning and drink beer in the afternoon." Others would reply, "Well, you know how those Mafia people stick together. Their section supervisor ought to be shot for giving him a good recommendation."

About three weeks later, a large government contract was lost and fifteen men were laid off. All of these men worked in the Albany sections. The union has been called in to settle the problem. Unfair labor charges have been filed against the Mobile section supervisor and the branch supervisor. I really don't care what happens now because I am looking for another job. I was one of the men who was laid off.

# CASE 23
# Robertson Rubber Products, Inc.

Many people see the man who owns his own business as "having it made." To them, he is his own boss, and can come and go as he pleases. There are no set hours in which he must report for or stay at work. He can tell people what to do, and they had better do it if they want their jobs. They also believe that he is making bushels of money.

In reality, small, independent, owner-managed businesses are not the panacea commonly thought. The following case illustrates the growth and development of one such firm, Robertson Rubber Products, Inc. (RRPI) by its present owner-manager, Mr. Fred Engle. To all who want to be their own bosses, it would be wise to reflect a moment on the pros and cons of owning that "dream venture."

## Early Company History

Isaiah Robertson founded the company that still bears his name in 1893. Mr. Robertson perceived an opportunity to serve industrial customers with a limited line of rubber products as a manufacturer's representative. His son-in-law joined the firm in 1915; the business began to prosper, directing its activities to the "after-market" rubber products customer.

In 1930, Mr. Robertson hired an experienced rubber products salesman, who convinced him that great opportunities were available in "jobbing" operations.

World War II saw a greatly increased demand for rubber products of all kinds, and the firm expanded operations by adding a manufacturing job shop to produce those small specialty items that large rubber manufacturers were not interested in producing. The company developed a reputation as a place to go with a problem that larger firms considered to be of too limited potential volume to warrant the tooling expenses incurred. When the war ended, Robertson Rubber Products had annual sales of nearly $1 million, and had found its niche between the little company that lacked RRPI's skills and the big company that was not interested in the volume of job that Robertson manufactured.

## Recent History

*Market and Competitive Environment.* At present, Robertson sales are generated 30 percent from jobbing, and 40 percent from distributing. Of these,

Used with the permission of the authors, Jeffrey C. Susbauer and Donald W. Scotton, both of the Cleveland State University.

the manufacturing operations are the most profitable, while distributing has the least margin. Intense distributor and jobber competition exists in the market area currently served by the company, which is generally confined to the state of Missouri.

Manufacturing competition is less intense, since the manufacture of rubber products is a specialized business requiring considerable skill and expertise. Most smaller rubber firms do not have the skills or resources to manufacture, and therefore, elect to stay out of this facet of the business. RRPI concentrates on specialized, shop type operations with relatively frequent low-volume runs. The well-equipped shop area of the Robertson plant contains almost no special-purpose machinery.

Larger manufacturers cannot compete with Robertson's expertise and overhead rates, and are generally uninterested in attracting the types of jobs Robertson performs. Some competition does exist within the market area served by RRPI from other small rubber products manufacturing concerns, but the impact of over twenty-five years of experience in this field has contributed to a solid list of satisfied customers. Opportunities generally exist for further manufacturing, jobbing, and distribution expansion of the enterprise without expanding the market territory boundaries.

## Mr. Fred Engle

Mr. Fred Engle held a variety of jobs after graduating from Purdue University, with B. S. and M. S. degrees in Metallurgical Engineering in 1937. Among other occupations, he had been a mining engineer and an assistant production manager for a medium-sized corporation prior to serving as a major in the U. S. Army during World War II.

Shortly after the war, he came to work for RRPI. He was to go on to become the next president of the firm. One major factor leading to this position was the fact that he married the boss's daughter, but it was by no means his only asset.

When Mr. Engle assumed control of the company in 1949, it had gone through several changes. From its early stages of strictly being a distributor, it had diversified into manufacturing, jobbing, and distribution. His major contribution to the continuation of this diversification was to change the primary direction of the firm from the after-market to the "Original Equipment Manufacturer (OEM)" market. The firm continues to supply the after-market to this day; over 1500 items for this portion of RRPI's business are stocked.

Mr. Engle felt that the company could best develop through the use of the manufacturing facilities. He apparently made the proper decision, because the firm has grown from about $1 million in annual sales when he became president, to nearly $3.5 million in sales in 1972. In addition, Mr. Engle has made major modifications to the structure of the firm internally during his twenty-four year tenure as owner-manager.

## Present Organization Structure

The Robertson organization, currently housed in a satisfactory two-story building downtown in a large mid-central city, employs forty-eight people, including Mr. Engle. Mr. Engle and his wife own 90 percent of the stock of the concern. A simplified organization chart is shown in Exhibit 1.

Mr. Engle feels that his company is relatively unique, and that this is a direct result of his planning and operating philosophy. He noted that most small, closely held, owner-managed firms do not really provide for the succession of the enterprise in the event of the death or retirement of the owner-manager. (It is not unusual for such firms to simply dissolve when the principal owner-manager retires or dies.)

The board of directors of the firm includes Mr. Engle and his wife. One long-time employee, who is also a stockholder, is the only other inside director of the firm. Mr. Engle has placed several outside directors on this body to advise him and serve as devil's advocates to his plans and whims, including other businessmen, the dean of the local college of business administration, an economist, and a lawyer. Mr. Engle believes that if his board does not thwart at least one of his ideas at each session, they are not doing their jobs. It should be noted that Mr. Engle is free to accept or reject the advice of the board, given his ownership position.

**Exhibit 1. Organization chart, Robertson Rubber Products, Inc. (RRPI).**

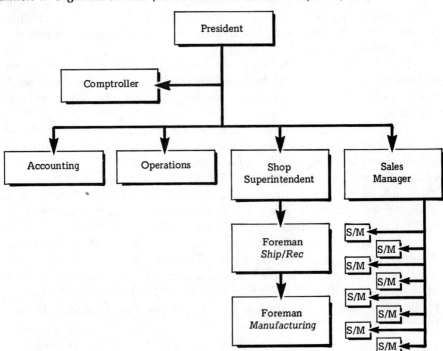

*Financial and Fiscal Controls*

Though his formal academic background was obtained in engineering, Mr. Engle considers sound financial control systems essential to the success of his firm. He hired a staff comptroller for the corporation in 1964 to insure that he was receiving timely information upon which to make decisions and gauge the performance and direction of the firm. It has proven to be a wise decision, in his estimation.

As Mr. Engle explained:

The large firm can make many mistakes, but it is insulated from the shock effect of those errors. In the small firm, a major mistake can have catastrophic effects because there are few buffers, checks, and balances. At the same time, a properly responsive control system can provide me with the means of finding out about the mistake, and the small size of my operations pays the dividend of being able to respond more quickly than the large firm can.

*Employee Relations: Philosophy*

Until 1971, the company did not differ from many small firms. It was run in a paternalistic fashion, with fairly lax work rules, no unionization, and a "happy family" atmosphere. Mr. Engle became concerned that perhaps the family was *too* happy when he noticed his cost of overhead and manufacturing labor rising in relation to previous years' performance.

His corrective action—replacing the manufacturing operations foreman with a more hard-nosed supervisor—produced the reverse effect anticipated. He had hoped the new foreman would make people more conscious of the need to be productive and improve the manufacturing margin. Instead, the new foreman managed to alienate the hourly employees; they, in turn, sought a union to represent them as their bargaining agent.

Like most managers, Mr. Engle viewed this unionization attempt with uncertainty; he dragged his feet as long as he could and mounted a counter-campaign. Finally, when he could not legally postpone recognition further, the union became the workers' representative in his shop.

After the shock had worn off, he reflected on what was accomplished by unionization:

Prior to 1971, there were no strict work rules that were really enforced. Everyone in this company had the right to come to me and complain about their problems. I had to figure out all the wage rates, merit increases, percentages of profit sharing for each employee. We had an inhouse grievance system, but it always included my negotiation with the worker and the foreman. When the union came in, I suddenly found out that I no longer had to perform most of these functions. The labor contract set the wage rates, fringe benefits package, and laid out procedures for handling disputes. Strangely, the two workers who most agitated for union recognition were not backed by the union when we fired them shortly after the union took over for infractions of the work rules. All of a sudden, the union became the enforcer, and made the employees "toe the line." Also, in exchange for a $.15 per hour raise, we negotiated the end of merit increases and profit sharing for the hourly workers. There are several of the hourly workers that now wish they did not have to pay the initiation dues to the union and those monthly dues. The union also makes sure that production quotas are achieved.

## Salaried and Officer Personnel

Of the forty-eight people employed by Robertson Rubber Products, thirty-one are included in these categories. Salaried personnel (twenty-eight) are distributed among the accounting, operations, and sales functions of the business. All of these people share in any profits the company makes each year.

For thirty years, Robertson has had an employee bonus plan keyed to profitability. In these thirty years, only in 1971 has the company failed to distribute some portion of profit to these employees. In recent years, this distribution has ranged from a high of 24 percent of pre-tax profit to a low (excluding 1971) of 10 percent of the profits.

Prior to Mr. Engle's ascendancy to the presidency, profit sharing was the only fringe benefit the company had for employees. Mr. Engle believed that:

... in order to retain those good employees and attract competent new ones, there had to be a better fringe package. Therefore, over the years, I have added additional fringes of full hospitalization, a group life insurance policy, and a sickness and accident policy to what the employees could receive from the company. Of course, they have been covered by Social Security for many years.

Under the charter of the company, as amended, Mr. Engle is required to pay a *minimum* of 5 percent of profits before taxes into the company profit sharing fund. This is a deferred compensation to employees covered. It takes three years of continuous employment, full time, to be eligible for any benefits, and the employees' rights to the noncontributions fund becomes fully vested after thirteen years of continuous employment.

Compensation in the company is perhaps unique when compared to similar practices in government and large private corporations. Mr. Engle commented:

We have several salesmen who work for the firm who have not grossed less than $30,000 for years. Their compensation is geared to their productivity, on a commission basis. As a consequence, there are a handful of individuals in this company that earn more than I do. I think this is healthy, and I encourage it. After all, the more they sell, the more worth I have in the company. But you don't find this condition in your run-of-the-mill, *Fortune 500* firm.

## The "Comfort Stage"

One of Mr. Engle's problems is the fact that he has been owner-manager of this company for over twenty years. He has guided its growth and development from a corporation doing slightly less than $1 million annual sales to one doing in excess of $3.5 million—a growth rate, compounded over 10 percent annually. It currently takes about $25,000 in additional working capital to generate growth at the rate previously obtained. He has reached what he describes as the "comfort stage"—a position where he obtains sufficient remuneration from the company to support his material needs and desires. Increasingly in the past few years, he has been able to do what he wants, within limits, and still keep the company on an even keel. In recent months, for example, he has felt sufficiently comfortable about the competency of his subordinates that he has been able to take off a week at a time to pursue his golfing in various places around the country.

What do I do now? I've mastered the job. What directions should the company pursue? The corporation is perfectly capable of expanding market territories, if desired. Present accounts can be maintained and new ones can be acquired through normal business expansion without excessive efforts on my part. Should I take more remuneration from the business? Should I sink more into the venture, even at this mature stage? Should I retire, turn the firm over to someone else with more need to succeed at this point?

I have felt no great need to expand this company at more than the inflationary rate—about 5 percent a year. If we are to get ahead of the game that we currently play in this economy, it must expand at more than this rate, yet I am very comfortable at the 5 percent pace, and can live very adequately on that kind of expansion. My goals are no longer driven by the need to achieve that kind of success, and these may be incompatible with my employees' needs—particularly the newer ones. At the same time, I am still in charge, the one who makes the ultimate decisions upon which the company sinks or swims. I think the corporation has done right by me. The weight of the decision making will not really pass out of my hands until I relinquish the reins of control. Unfortunately, although the invitation is open, my son-in-law is not interested in joining the firm, and I have some hard decisions to make. I am not independently wealthy, yet my ambition is somewhat less urgent than it was ten, fifteen, or twenty years ago.

As Mr. Engle told the case writer his story, he turned to an article in that morning's *Wall Street Journal* that described a small company in South Dakota that also was suffering problems similar to his firm's.

Here, this is exactly my dilemma—the locale is different, but the problems are still the same. These people [in the article] have been successful, but they can't interest their children in following in their footsteps. I've still got some years before I would have to retire, but if I wanted to step down tomorrow, the business would have no one to step into my shoes.

# EXPERIENTIAL EXERCISE 8

## Situational Leadership

This exercise is designed to accomplish the following objectives. First, it illustrates the necessity of adaptability in leadership style because of situational requirements. Second, it focuses on behaviors associated with commonly accepted theories.

### Directions

1. Divide the class into groups of four to eight members. Take no more than ten minutes for the first three steps.
2. Each individual reads the background material (Section A).
3. Then read the Key Behavior material (Section B). These are behaviors that may be required of the leader in order to manage the situation.
4. Read each Situation (Section C), and rank the top four appropriate key behaviors on Answer Sheet D.
5. Share your rankings with the groups and arrive at a group consensus on the appropriate key behaviors.
6. A spokesperson from each group will explain the group's consensus on each situation to the class. Take no more than twenty minutes for steps 4–6.

### Section A: General Setting

You have been hired as the manager of a retirement community which will open its doors in two years. The community will deliver comprehensive care, addressing the social as well as the medical needs of the clients. A philosophy of management will be emphasized that encourages retirees to be independent. Therefore, key managers who share these values must be carefully chosen.

You are to watch over the construction of the physical plant, assemble a management team, and attract a clientele to fill the 315 units. In the first four months the management team grew from four to seven members. The team consists of four women and three men. The men occupy the roles of Director, Purchasing Manager, and Grounds, while the women hold the positions of Accounting Assistant, Assistant to the Director, Client Representative, and Secretary.

After the team has been assembled, the next step is to prepare the community for opening. The incidents occur over a span of one and a half years.

### Section B: Key Leader Behaviors

1. Strongly emphasize task accomplishment.
2. Decide which tasks are to be done and how those tasks are to be carried out.

Prepared by H. William Vroman.

3. Request subordinate suggestions on problems.
4. Input personal suggestions to task group decision making.
5. Help subordinates overcome barriers to task accomplishment.
6. Support and reinforce subordinates in their work.
7. Provide feedback, develop standards on task accomplishment.
8. Consult with subordinates about task.

## Section C: Key Leaders Situations

As you read these situations, read between the lines because these are only headlines; there are many details behind headlines.

1. Initially take your three new employees and explain what the project will entail and explain the fact that additional employees will be hired over the next several months. In particular, you want to hire the Medical Director and the Social Director very carefully to ensure the right philosophy is carried on to those departments.
2. Three months later, you hire three additional employees and simultaneously move to new quarters. Each person now has an office situated on two floors of an old mansion on the construction site. The old location was a single room where every transaction took place in front of everyone. Lois, an experienced employee, now is upstairs doing accounting, while Judy, a new employee, is right next to the manager's office. Lois in particular, and others to a lesser extent, feel left out upstairs.
3. Six months later, the complexities of keeping the construction on schedule, unanticipated difficulties with the Board, relative inexperience of the employees, and interpersonal difficulties between the old and new employees make the situation seem like it is coming apart.
4. Six months later, the situation has successfully come together. Construction has largely been completed. Ordering furnishings, hiring blue-collar help, and recruitment of retirees have been accomplished. The remaining tasks include moving the clients into the apartments and organizing the social-medical aspects.

## Section D: Answer Sheet

*Situation 1*

| Key behaviors | You | Group |
|---|---|---|
| | | |
| | | |
| | | |
| | | |

*Situation 2*

| Key behaviors | You | Group |
|---|---|---|
| | | |
| | | |
| | | |
| | | |

*Situation 3*

| Key<br>behaviors | You | Group |
|---|---|---|
| _____ | _____ | _____ |
| _____ | _____ | _____ |
| _____ | _____ | _____ |
| _____ | _____ | _____ |

*Situation 4*

| Key<br>behaviors | You | Group |
|---|---|---|
| _____ | _____ | _____ |
| _____ | _____ | _____ |
| _____ | _____ | _____ |
| _____ | _____ | _____ |

# EXPERIENTIAL EXERCISE 9
## Leadership Style and Group Effectiveness

Through his studies of leadership effectiveness, Fred Fiedler has designed a set of questionnaires to (1) determine a leader's style and (2) assess the leadership style that should lead to the successful attainment of the group's goal. In other words, he has refined the concept of leader-organization match. The purpose of this exercise is to give you experience in using the research tools developed by Fiedler and in comparing the differences in leader styles and organizational requirements. On the following pages are copies of the questionnaires developed by Dr. Fiedler. Follow the instructions provided below in order to administer and evaluate the instruments.

### Instructions

Locate three separate leaders (or managers) in three distinct leadership positions (e.g., different types of organizations, different industries, and the like). First, ask the leader to complete the questionnaire entitled, "Least Preferred Co-Worker." When the questionnaire has been completed, write the number indicated for each scale under the column headed, "Scoring," and total that column. According to the Fiedler theory, LPC scores of 64 and higher indicate a high LPC (relationship-motivated) leader. Scores of 57 or less indicate a low LPC (task-motivated) leader.

The remaining questionnaires are intended to reflect the group situation. That is, how good are leader-member relations, how structured is the group's task, and how much power does the leader actually have? Ask the selected leader (manager) to complete each of the questionnaires.

### Analyzing the Results

When the three questionnaires are completed, add together the numbers for each item and obtain a total score for each questionnaire. Now, add together the three scores (Leader-Member Relations, Task Structure, and Position Power) in order to obtain a "situational control" score. The amount of situational control can be described as follows:

51–70  High control.
31–50  Moderate control.
10–30  Low control.

A leadership style-situation match is obtained by comparing the leader's LPC score to the situational control score. Thus, a leader with a high LPC score (64 or higher) should be in a Moderate Control situation (31–50). A low LPC leader will

Prepared by Donald D. White with questionnaires used by permission of John Wiley & Sons.

be most effective in High Control (51–70) or Low Control (10–30) situations. Refer back to Figure 1 in Chapter Six's introduction for additional information about the leader-situation match.

## Questions for Discussion

1. Did you find similar or different leader styles in your three subjects? What is the significance of this finding?
2. Did you find similarities or differences in the situational control of the leaders studied? Of what significance is this finding?
3. Discuss the nature of the leader-situation comparisons you made.
4. Describe the advice that you would give to a manager whose leadership style and situational control were not congruent. What changes should be made?

### LPC Instructions

Of all the people with whom you have worked, think of that person with whom you could work *least* well. This is not necessarily someone that you did not like. Rather, it was that person with whom you had the most difficulty getting a job done. Now, describe the person using the Least Preferred Co-Worker Scale that follows.

**Least Preferred Co-Worker (LPC) Scale.**

*Scoring*

| | | | | | | | | | | |
|---|---|---|---|---|---|---|---|---|---|---|
| Pleasant | | | | | | | | | Unpleasant | ___ |
| | 8 | 7 | 6 | 5 | 4 | 3 | 2 | 1 | | |
| Friendly | | | | | | | | | Unfriendly | ___ |
| | 8 | 7 | 6 | 5 | 4 | 3 | 2 | 1 | | |
| Rejecting | | | | | | | | | Accepting | ___ |
| | 1 | 2 | 3 | 4 | 5 | 6 | 7 | 8 | | |
| Tense | | | | | | | | | Relaxed | ___ |
| | 1 | 2 | 3 | 4 | 5 | 6 | 7 | 8 | | |
| Distant | | | | | | | | | Close | ___ |
| | 1 | 2 | 3 | 4 | 5 | 6 | 7 | 8 | | |
| Cold | | | | | | | | | Warm | ___ |
| | 1 | 2 | 3 | 4 | 5 | 6 | 7 | 8 | | |
| Supportive | | | | | | | | | Hostile | ___ |
| | 8 | 7 | 6 | 5 | 4 | 3 | 2 | 1 | | |
| Boring | | | | | | | | | Interesting | ___ |
| | 1 | 2 | 3 | 4 | 5 | 6 | 7 | 8 | | |
| Quarrelsome | | | | | | | | | Harmonious | ___ |
| | 1 | 2 | 3 | 4 | 5 | 6 | 7 | 8 | | |
| Gloomy | | | | | | | | | Cheerful | ___ |
| | 1 | 2 | 3 | 4 | 5 | 6 | 7 | 8 | | |
| Open | | | | | | | | | Guarded | ___ |
| | 8 | 7 | 6 | 5 | 4 | 3 | 2 | 1 | | |
| Backbiting | | | | | | | | | Loyal | ___ |
| | 1 | 2 | 3 | 4 | 5 | 6 | 7 | 8 | | |
| Untrustworthy | | | | | | | | | Trustworthy | ___ |
| | 1 | 2 | 3 | 4 | 5 | 6 | 7 | 8 | | |
| Considerate | | | | | | | | | Inconsiderate | ___ |
| | 8 | 7 | 6 | 5 | 4 | 3 | 2 | 1 | | |
| Nasty | | | | | | | | | Nice | ___ |
| | 1 | 2 | 3 | 4 | 5 | 6 | 7 | 8 | | |
| Agreeable | | | | | | | | | Disagreeable | ___ |
| | 8 | 7 | 6 | 5 | 4 | 3 | 2 | 1 | | |
| Insincere | | | | | | | | | Sincere | ___ |
| | 1 | 2 | 3 | 4 | 5 | 6 | 7 | 8 | | |
| Kind | | | | | | | | | Unkind | ___ |
| | 8 | 7 | 6 | 5 | 4 | 3 | 2 | 1 | | |

Total ___

**Leader–Member Relations Scale.**

| Circle the number which best represents your response to each item. | strongly agree | agree | neither agree nor disagree | disagree | strongly disagree |
|---|---|---|---|---|---|
| 1. The people I supervise have trouble getting along with each other. | 1 | 2 | 3 | 4 | 5 |
| 2. My subordinates are reliable and trustworthy. | 5 | 4 | 3 | 2 | 1 |
| 3. There seems to be a friendly atmosphere among the people I supervise. | 5 | 4 | 3 | 2 | 1 |
| 4. My subordinates always cooperate with me in getting the job done. | 5 | 4 | 3 | 2 | 1 |
| 5. There is friction between my subordinates and myself. | 1 | 2 | 3 | 4 | 5 |
| 6. My subordinates give me a good deal of help and support in getting the job done. | 5 | 4 | 3 | 2 | 1 |
| 7. The people I supervise work well together in getting the job done. | 5 | 4 | 3 | 2 | 1 |
| 8. I have good relations with the people I supervise. | 5 | 4 | 3 | 2 | 1 |

Add the numbers for each item in order to obtain the total score

*Total* _____

**Task Structure Rating Scale—Part 1.**

| Circle the number in the appropriate column. | Usually true | Sometimes true | Seldom true |
|---|:---:|:---:|:---:|
| *Is the goal clearly stated or known?* | | | |
| 1. Is there a blueprint, picture, model or detailed description available of the finished product or service? | 2 | 1 | 0 |
| 2. Is there a person available to advise and give a description of the finished product or service, or how the job should be done? | 2 | 1 | 0 |
| *Is there only one way to accomplish the task?* | | | |
| 3. Is there a step-by-step procedure, or a standard operating procedure which indicates in detail the process which is to be followed? | 2 | 1 | 0 |
| 4. Is there a specific way to subdivide the task into separate parts or steps? | 2 | 1 | 0 |
| 5. Are there some ways which are clearly recognized as better than others for performing this task? | 2 | 1 | 0 |
| *Is there only one correct answer or solution?* | | | |
| 6. Is it obvious when the task is finished and the correct solution has been found? | 2 | 1 | 0 |
| 7. Is there a book, manual, or job description which indicates the best solution or the best outcome for the task? | 2 | 1 | 0 |
| *Is it easy to check whether the job was done right?* | | | |
| 8. Is there a generally agreed understanding about the standards the particular product or service has to meet to be considered acceptable? | 2 | 1 | 0 |
| 9. Is the evaluation of this task generally made on some quantitative basis? | 2 | 1 | 0 |
| 10. Can the leader and the group find out how well the task has been accomplished in enough time to improve future performance? | 2 | 1 | 0 |

Add the numbers for each item in order to
obtain the total score.                                            Subtotal _____

**Task Structure Rating Scale—Part 2.**

*Training and experience adjustment*

*Note: Do not adjust jobs with task structure scores of 6 or below.*

(a) Compared to others in this or similar positions, how much *training* has the leader had?

| 3 | 2 | 1 | 0 |
|---|---|---|---|
| No training at all | Very little training | A moderate amount of training | A great deal of training |

(b) Compared to others in this or similar positions, how much *experience* has the leader had?

| 6 | 4 | 2 | 0 |
|---|---|---|---|
| No experience at all | Very little experience | A moderate amount of experience | A great deal of experience |

Add lines (a) and (b) of the training and experience adjustment, then *subtract* this from the subtotal given in Part 1.

Subtotal from Part 1. ——

Subtract training and experience adjustment ——

Total Task Structure Score ——

**Position Power Rating Scale.**

*Circle the number which best represents your answer.*

1. Can the leader directly or by recommendation administer rewards and punishments to his subordinates?

| 2 | 1 | 0 |
|---|---|---|
| Can act directly or can recommend with high effectiveness | Can recommend but with mixed results | No |

2. Can the leader directly or by recommendation affect the promotion, demotion, hiring or firing of his subordinates?

| 2 | 1 | 0 |
|---|---|---|
| Can act directly or can recommend with high effectiveness | Can recommend but with mixed results | No |

3. Does the leader have the knowledge necessary to assign tasks to subordinates and instruct them in task completion?

| 2 | 1 | 0 |
|---|---|---|
| Yes | Sometimes or in some aspects | No |

4. Is it the leader's job to evaluate the performance of his subordinates?

| 2 | 1 | 0 |
|---|---|---|
| Yes | Sometimes or in some aspects | No |

5. Has the leader been given some official title of authority by the organization (e.g., foreman, department head, platoon leader)?

| 2 | 0 |
|---|---|
| Yes | No |

Add the numbers for each item in order to obtain the total score.     Total ____

# PART IV
# ORGANIZATIONAL DYNAMICS

The term, *dynamic,* refers to a state of motion or change and implies an active rather than static situation. The title of this section, *Organizational Dynamics,* has been chosen carefully. The dynamics of organizational life have been characterized in this book through organizational communication systems, the nature and activities of group behavior, and conflict and stress that organizational members experience. The section includes cases, exercises, and discussion concerning these dynamic behavioral forces and processes at work in formal organizations.

Communications between individuals in organizations may be planned or unplanned. Formal organizations are designed to enhance information flow so that managers will have the inputs necessary to make important decisions. Communication systems may dictate the lines and the form that information flow takes. Thus, an organization's design may be a function of planned information flows; and a design that fails to consider information flows may have a counterproductive impact on communication and goal attainment.

Of course, not all communication is planned or intended. Informal communications between organizational members may support or even replace a formal system. In either case, human, perceptual biases influence both the sending and receiving of information. No matter how carefully a system is designed, keep in mind that human qualities influence the ability of the communication system to accomplish its goal.

A second, important dynamic force in organizations is the social relationships among members. Organizations are social systems that have formalized their goals, structures, and processes. Informal organizations arise within the system to satisfy individual and organizational needs. Such groups may form in response to needs for friendship or prestige or to advance some common cause. In any event, their impact can be felt on individual and organizational behavior alike.

Early writers believed that small groups inhibited individual productivity. Today, we recognize that such groups may contribute significantly to organizational output. In addition to recognizing the positive force they may bring to organizations, the unique energies of small groups have been harnessed to accomplish organizational goals. Problem solving groups such as brainstorming, delphi, and nominal groups represent three such efforts. As with any dynamic force, groups, too, may experience friction internally or externally. As such, group-related conflict is a concern of the modern manager.

*Organizational dynamics* also addresses a variety of types of conflict within organizations and the forms conflict may take. Organizational conflict is treated as a potentially positive force in organizational life. Understanding the sources of conflict and the ways it is manifested will enable you to make conflict work for you rather than against you.

On a personal level, conflict often results in a disease known as stress. Stress is a physical and psychological reaction to certain environmental stimuli (stressors) that create imbalances within us. Stress is a highly significant force in individual and organizational life. It may lead to physical and mental exhaustion or may take the form of debilitating illness that results in low productivity and time lost from work. Managed properly, however, stress can contribute to personal well-being and on-the-job performance.

Understanding these dynamic forces in organizations—communications, group behavior, and conflict and stress—will provide you with additional insights into the complexities of organizational systems. The cases which accompany each of the following chapters illustrate situations where organizational dynamics play an important role. In addition, you will be called upon to make decisions concerning the management of these forces in a manner that will lead to organizational goal attainment as well as individual satisfaction.

# CHAPTER SEVEN

# Communication
# in Organizational Systems

Information circulating between individuals and organizational units is the lifeblood of an organizational system. The process by which information is exchanged is known as communication. Communication of sometimes necessary and other times irrelevant information is initiated and interpreted by human beings throughout the enterprise. Whether formal or informal, communications between parties convey facts, sentiments, and beliefs by senders and receivers alike.

Perceptual biases resulting from different patterns of individual development and different perspectives on the immediate situation affect the accuracy and completeness of the information we exchange. The quality of information exchange is essential to an organization's ultimate goal attainment. Therefore, managers direct a large part of their efforts toward increasing the efficiency of information processing through better communications.

The model in Figure 1 describes the context in which communication takes place. The stimulus context includes three categories of stimuli affecting the communication: group influences (norms, pressures to conform, and cohesiveness), organizational influences (structure and management control systems), and personal influences (perception, learned behaviors, and motivation). Expectations are communicated from one party to another. For example, Person A attempts to influence Person B by verbally or nonverbally communicating an expectation (information). Party B receives the information and reacts by either following, avoiding, or rejecting the expectation. Person B's reaction (a behavior) is perceived by A, who then decides whether it is necessary to further influence B, or if the flow of information should be terminated. The facts, sentiments, and beliefs communicated by A have been influenced by the way A perceived the situation and the extent to which he or she believed it necessary to influence B. B's reaction to the communication of expectations depends upon his or her interpretation of the information received.

Misperception refers to an interpretation of stimuli in a context other

**Figure 1. Communications model.**

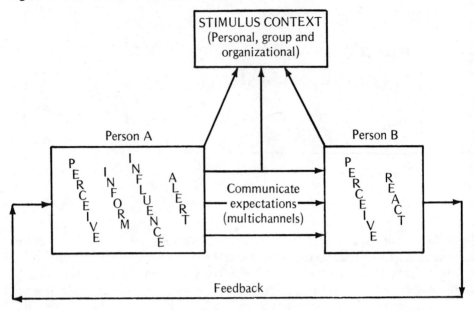

than that intended or actually presented. However, "misperception" is in-accurate. Perception is primarily a psychological process that lies within the organism and therefore is relative to each individual. We may miscon-strue the *intent* of a sender, but our perception of the stimuli we receive is our own. Nevertheless, potential breakdown in communication between two individuals is enhanced by the complexity of the stimulus context.

Any interference with the communication of expectations is known as *noise*. Failure of B to perform in the manner desired by A may be due to the situational noise. However, assuming minimal noise in the stimulus con-text and clearly articulated expectations from A, B can follow or reject the expectation. In some cases B may even choose to avoid the expectation rather than commit to a course of action. Avoiding an expectation may be accomplished by saying one forgot or was too busy, or by not being present when the expectation was to be fulfilled. It is clear that the response or lack of response to A can further complicate communications, as both rely on unique personal interpretations of the information being communicated.

In some cases, multiple channels of communication are used at the same time. For example, in addition to familiar written and verbal channels used to convey expectations, nonverbal channels of paralanguage, kinesics, and proxemic modes may be used. Often, a combination of these com-munication channels may be used at a single time.

Multiple-channel communication may overcome communication noise or in some other way may bring sender and receiver closer together. On the other hand, a verbal channel may say one thing, while a nonverbal mode says something quite different. For example, in the midst of writing a report,

Phil approaches his supervisor, Maryann, to ask her advice. Although Maryann may provide the necessary answers, her quizzical frown may indicate to Phil that she herself is not sure about the answer.

Paralanguage refers to the pitch, range, intensity, and the like of one's voice. A superior who lowers his usual pitch when gaining the attention of a subordinate may indicate to the subordinate that an unpleasant topic is about to be discussed. The impact of emotional exchanges is often accentuated by paralanguage.

Kinesics refers to an individual's total body activity while communicating to another party. Such factors as body position (crossing the arms or legs, looking away from the person with whom we are communicating, and so on), posture, and gestures (a raised eyebrow, the hint of a smile, or the pointing of a finger) all indicate our involvement in the content of our communication as well as our feelings toward the other party. For example, a professor may reprimand you in class for joking about the subject matter. However, if she cracks a smile while doing so, it is unlikely that serious repercussions will result. On the other hand, as was pointed out earlier, a confusing double message may be sent to the receiver: "It was funny, but don't do it again!"

Finally, proxemics, or the distance between communicants, may convey the way that people feel toward one another or the privacy or openness with which they believe certain information should be discussed. Proxemics is actually the study of territorial needs. "Each of us carries around a sort of invisible bubble of personal space wherever we go." [1] We think of the area inside this bubble as our private territory. The area is almost as much a part of us as our own bodies. We may become uncomfortable when someone moves too close to us, because this person has invaded our private space. On the other hand, we may desire to share our own private space in varying degrees. For example, young lovers wish not only to be close but also to touch. Anthropologist Edward T. Hall [2] has suggested that four proxemic zones exist. They include intimate distance, personal distance, social distance, and public distance. These distances are relative rather than absolute, and they vary according to culture and personal preference. For example, the personal distance in some Mediterranean cultures more closely approximates the intimate distance in our own culture. It might not be unusual, therefore, to see a Westerner literally walk into a wall trying to maintain his personal distance with a Greek acquaintance whom he is accompanying down the street.

In some instances, the arrangement of inert objects, such as chairs, desks, and even salt and pepper shakers, is used to define territorial distances. An interview conducted between an interviewer and interviewee who are each sitting in chairs angled in toward one another seems to be conducted on a more personal level than one in which the interviewer sits behind the desk while the interviewee sits in front of it. On the lighter side, persons eating in restaurants often arrange their dishes, glasses, and other table items in a way so as to define their table space. For example, you may find that placing a sugar shaker or some personal item in the territorial space of a luncheon partner may make the partner uncomfortable. Ultimately, you may find the sugar shaker back on your side of the table. In some cases, a subtle game of territorial expansion and protection may ensue.

In summary, a variety of communication channels exists and is used by senders and receivers. In some cases, these channels may be used unintentionally. A sender may "give away his true feelings" or a receiver may "read something into" expectations which have been communicated to him. The result may be any number of barriers to effective interpersonal communications. Removal of these barriers must begin with an individual's awareness of himself or herself as a sender and/or a receiver as well as with the limitations of the channels of communication available.

One serious barrier to communication is the meaning we attach to words or groups of words. An associate related the story of a new secretary who was having difficulty picking up the office jargon. At one point, she was asked to burn a copy of a letter for a client. Later that afternoon, her boss walked out of his office to find her preparing to incinerate the carbon copy of the letter in her ashtray. Only at this point did the businessman realize that she had not been told that "burn a copy" referred to photocopying a letter, not igniting it! Eliminating barriers to communication requires a conscious effort on the part of both sender and receiver to iron out perceptual differences between them and to recognize the impact of their verbal and nonverbal exchanges of information.

### Organizational Influences on Communication

The very purpose of organizing puts a high premium on communication. Departmentalization, chains of command, and spans of control are designed (or evolve) largely due to their impact on information flows. Rogers concludes that "Communication . . . is the very essence of the social system or an organization." [3]

*Structural influences.*   Organizational structure affects both formal and informal communication in that it increases, and in some cases restricts, members' contacts with one another. Moreover, in many instances, it defines the actual *or expected* nature of those contacts. In addition to bringing together the necessary resources to obtain the organization's objective, structure designates the required relationships, task to task and person to person, that lead to the objective's accomplishment.

Formal communication channels have two purposes. First, they provide decision makers with information necessary to accomplishing a task. The nature of the task determines the information processing demands made on a work group. These demands, in turn, influence the patterning of communication within the group. Thus, variations in organizational forms are partly a reflection of attempts to meet task center information needs. [4] Second, communication channels are designed to integrate task units (e.g., departments, work groups) so that all organizational participants may work toward a common end. Whether or not an enterprise accomplishes its goal depends in large part on how well information flows from one area in the organization to another. Thus, communication is facilitated by organizational structure and is a primary determinant of organization design.

*Direction of flow.* Information may be communicated vertically, horizontally, or diagonally. However, traditional bureaucratic organizations emphasize superior-subordinate relationships. Therefore, they are designed with vertical communication flows in mind. Downward communication is characterized by organization and procedure manuals, memos, posted notices, pay inserts, and in-house publications. Upward communication, on the other hand, may take the form of personnel, sales, or financial reports and other "paper" media. Katz and Kahn suggest five types of downward communication:[5]

1. Specific task directives—*job instructions;*
2. Information designed to produce understanding of the task and its relation to other organizational tasks—*job rationale;*
3. Information about organizational *procedures and practices;*
4. *Feedback* to the subordinate about his or her performance;
5. Information of an ideological character to inculcate a sense of mission— *indoctrination of goals.*

Note that all five types of downward communication are task oriented— that is, how one does the job, why one does it, details about the job, how one is doing on the job, and attempts to motivate. Job instructions dominate downward communication due to a perceived need for expediency along with the traditionally held belief that subordinates do not have to know "why," only "what." Such a belief is reminiscent of Tennyson's poetic admonition concerning troops in battle: Theirs not to reason why, theirs but to do and die.

Both formal and informal communications are responsible for upward flows of information. While formal channels are more clearly visible (e.g. production reports, attitude surveys, and so on), informal communication often is used to inform higher-ups about difficulties indirectly related to the performance of the task. On the surface, interpersonal channels for upward communication would appear to be identical to those for downward flows of information. However, organizational practices are steeped in the bureaucratic philosophy of downward communication (order-giving). Moreover, communication from subordinates to superiors may contain information for which a subordinate might be penalized, further discouraging the free flow of information up the hierarchy.[6] The result is impeded feedback up the channel and increased reliance on an *informal network* for "getting the word up the line."

Upward communication falls into four distinct categories, which concern, "what the person says (1) about himself, his performance, and his problems, (2) about others and their problems, (3) about organizational practices and policies, and (4) about what needs to be done and how it can be done." [7] Upward communications generally are limited to the immediate supervisor unless the organization's structure provides direct channels to higher levels. Open door policies, grievance systems, and other formal suggestion systems may be adopted by organizations to enlarge an employee's feedback loop beyond the immediate supervisor.

Contingency theorists have suggested that an organization's environment plays a major role in determining its structure and the way it is managed. This is particularly true for businesses and other endeavors affected by rapidly changing technologies (e.g., chemicals, electronics, medicine) or are advocates of the "marketing concept" (consumer-oriented). Keeping the organization "fingers" on the pulse of a dynamic environment requires structures (and therefore, communication channels) to meet special information needs. These needs have in fact led some observers to conclude that "the combined demand for more information at faster speeds is now undermining the vertical hierarchies so typical of bureaucracies." [8]

More contemporary organizational forms recognize the need for horizontal and diagonal communication and therefore formalize those types of interaction. For example, the matrix structure discussed in Part III of this book encourages the flow of administrative information along one axis and the flow of functional (technical) information along a second axis. Organic-adaptive structures go one step farther by encouraging the free flow of information in all directions.

The introduction of multi-directional information flows through modern structures like matrix and organic-adaptive organizations focuses the attention of organizational members on their common goal and allows for the direct communication of unfiltered information to decision makers. Furthermore, joint decision making is enhanced through shared information. On the other hand, Knight points out that such structures may be inefficient due to the high cost of communication.[9] The encouragement of many if not all organization members to contribute or be consulted prior to making a decision may be time consuming. As Mintzburg concludes, "finally, a decision emerges . . . although it is typically late and will probably be modified later." [10] Thus, there is still a great deal to be learned about the impact of these newer organizational configurations on information exchange and their effect on organizational decision making.

### Auditing the Organizational Communication System

A variety of conditions precipitate information flow in organizations. Whether formal or informal, the communication may serve to inform, clarify, influence, or diminish the uncertainty between organizational members. Of course, some messages may confuse the receiver or muddy the waters. Managers have the responsibility of auditing (examining) the total communication system and its subsystems to ensure that it contributes to the efficiency of the enterprise and does not inhibit the attainment of objectives.

Such an audit entails an evaluation of the extent to which the present communication system facilitates the accomplishment of organizational goals. The structural elements of the system (the organizational units, functional communication networks, communication policies, and specific communication activities) must be identified and individually evaluated.[11] The extent to which they are effective in their own right and to which they systematically complement one another in support of the primary objective should be measured on a continuous basis.

Level and Galle[12] have identified five distinct categories of communication that should be monitored through the organizational audit:

1. Intraorganizational set—communications that flow between members of the organization as they seek to accomplish some unit goal (e.g., between an engineer and a production foreman concerning product tolerances).
2. Interorganizational set—communications that move from output subsystems to input subsystems or vice versa (e.g., point-of-service terminals that send sales data directly to those responsible for inventory maintenance).
3. Input/organizational set—information flows between the firm and the input set (e.g., between a purchasing department and suppliers).
4. Output/organizational set—communication flows between the firm and its output set (e.g., between salespeople and buyers or manufacturing and the Environmental Protection Agency).
5. Interactions exclusively between environmental elements—information that flows between parties who lie completely outside the organizational set (e.g., between consumer protection groups and consumers).

Figure 2 illustrates how a complete communication system (all five categories) might be evaluated relative to its structural elements. Such an approach would provide a complete, although admittedly complex, framework for a total organizational communication audit.

## Summary

The exchange of information between individuals and organizational units is critical to the effectiveness of an enterprise. We communicate our attitudes, opinions, and knowledge verbally and nonverbally, formally and informally. The intended or inadvertent use of multiple channels of communication may accentuate and clarify a message. However, conflicting signals may confuse a receiver and result in misunderstandings between persons.

A first step to eliminating barriers to effective communication is to increase one's awareness of oneself as a sender and a receiver. Formal communication is facilitated by organizational structure. Structures change in response to the information processing demands of task units as well as to environmental demands. Finally, the total communication system should

**Figure 2. Proposed framework for a communication systems audit.**

|  | Intra-organiza-tional set | Inter-organiza-tional set | Input-organiza-tional set | Output-organiza-tional set | Environ-mental set |
|---|---|---|---|---|---|
| Organizational unit/s goal(s) | | | | | |
| Functional communication networks | | | | | |
| Communication policies | | | | | |
| Specific activities | | | | | |

be audited to ensure that it and its elements contribute to the attainment of the organization's objective.

*References*

1. Ron Alder and Neil Towne, *Looking Out/Looking In* (New York: Holt, Rinehart and Winston, 1978), pp. 239–240.
2. Edward T. Hall, *The Hidden Dimension* (Garden City: Anchor Books, 1969), pp. 110–120.
3. Rolf E. Rogers, *Organizational Theory* (Boston: Allyn and Bacon, 1975), p. 51.
4. Jay R. Galbraith, "Organizational Design: An Information Processing View," *Interfaces,* vol. 4, May 1974, p. 28.
5. Daniel Katz and Robert L. Kahn, *The Social Psychology of Organizations,* (New York: John Wiley & Sons, 1966), pp. 239–242.
6. Ibid., p. 246.
7. Ibid., p. 245.
8. Alvin Toffler, *Future Shock* (New York: Random House, 1970), p. 139.
9. Kenneth Knight, "Matrix Organization: A Review," *The Journal of Management Studies,* vol. 13, 1976, p. 126.
10. Henry Mintzburg, *The Structuring of Organizations* (Englewood Cliffs: Prentice-Hall, 1979), p. 463.
11. Harold Greenbaum, "The Audit of Organizational Communication," *Academy of Management Journal,* vol. 17, December 1974, pp. 740–745.
12. Dale A. Level and William Galle, *Organizational Communication: Theory and Practice* (Dallas: Business Publications, 1980), p. 317.

*Recommended Readings*

Readings marked with an asterisk are included in *Contemporary Perspectives in Organizational Behavior,* edited by Donald D. White (Boston: Allyn and Bacon, 1982).

*John E. Baird and Gretchen K. Wieting, "Nonverbal Communication Can Be a Motivational Tool," *Personnel Journal*, vol. 58, September 1979, pp. 607–610.

*Howard H. Greenbaum, "The Audit of Organizational Communication," *Academy of Management Journal*, vol. 17, no. 4, December 1974, pp. 739–754.

*A. G. Kefalas, "Human, Social and Organizational Communication," in *Contemporary Perspectives in Organizational Behavior*, edited by Donald D. White (Boston: Allyn and Bacon, 1981).

Dale Level and William P. Galle, "A System Framework for Organizational Communication," *Business Communication: Theory and Practice* (Dallas: Business Publication, 1980), pp. 311–330.

C. D. Porterfield, "Toward the Integration of Communication and Management," *Journal of Business Communication*, vol. 17, no. 2, Winter 1980, pp. 13–21.

Barry E. Woodcock, "Characteristic Oral and Written Business Communication Problems of Selected Managerial Trainees," *Journal of Business Communication*, vol. 16, no. 2, Winter 1979, pp. 43–48.

# CASE 24
# The J. R. Reston Company, Inc.

## Background

The J. R. Reston Company, Inc., like many of today's giants of American industry, had a modest beginning. It all started back in 1915 when John Reston, known in later years in the company as "the old man," quit the bank for which he was working over a dispute about the way stocks, bonds, and other securities were physically being transferred from the bank to other banks, customers, brokerage houses, and other financial institutions.

Reston opened his own private currier service, specializing in fast, dependable, and confidential transferring of various types of important printed documents between all of the banks in Denver and the various places to which these instruments needed delivering. Reston expanded rapidly and opened the first branch office in Los Angeles in 1920. By this time the name "John Reston" had become synonymous with integrity and confidentiality in Western financial circles. Using this well-deserved reputation, Reston hired several of his former colleagues away from their banking positions and incorporated the first of several wholly owned subsidiaries—J. R. Reston & Partners, Ltd., a stock brokerage firm.

About the time Reston had completed negotiations to purchase all of the outstanding stock of Bowles & Son, Inc., a printing concern, he started getting some feedback about the need for another type of business which would fit in well with his rapidly growing company. It seemed that many of the banks for which the Reston company delivered were approached from time to time by parties with whom they were unfamiliar, who would ask for financing. The prevailing practice at the time was for the bank loan officer to forward the request to the bank's "new business" department. This department would then begin an investigation to determine the credit worthiness of the applicant.

It appeared that this was taking too long for most of the banks, and they were losing some business from impatient businessmen, many of whom turned out to be excellent credit risks. If ever there was a man with a "nose for opportunity," it was Mr. J. R. Reston. He called his board of directors together and asked their opinion of the forming of a third wholly owned subsidiary. The corporate title suggested was Reston Services Company, Inc. A motion was made to proceed, a person was hired to lead this new venture, and thus Reston was launched into the providing of information to financial institutions.

The venture proved profitable and led Reston to expand his services to

Prepared by Scott Markham, University of Central Arkansas; and Dale A. Level, University of Arkansas.

include all types of businesses that might have need for the same data he had been furnishing exclusively to banks. The expense had been incurred by the time the report went to a bank, so Reston thought why not make extra copies of the report, lower the price to all customers, and share the data with other parties who had legitimate business reasons for needing it?

The stock market crash ruined J. R. Reston & Partners, Ltd.; the printing and delivery and business information companies managed to break even. By 1935 they were going strong once again. With the general boom in American industry following World War II Reston decided to retire. John, Jr. was ready to take the helm. His first major decision was to "go public." The stock issue was well accepted. It sold out within three weeks of its issue date.

With this increased capitalization, J. R. Reston Company, Inc. moved into other fields, including a 20 percent ownership of a small western railroad, a 50 percent ownership of a large California farm, and another wholly owned subsidiary—Reston Real Estate, Inc.

## Organization

Transportation, communication, information, food, and shelter—five industries that J. R. Reston felt would always be winners in the U. S. economy. One way John, Sr. had rewarded "his people" was to give them a title. Thus, the organization had "grown up" and been expanded with each new division. Lines of authority and responsibility often overlapped. John, Jr. kept most of the men who had worked for his father, and, in fact, he observed the same basic management style: "give them the ball and tell them to run with it as far as they want to." A partial organizational chart is shown in Exhibit 1.

## Take the Ball and Run

Ben Smith, VP Marketing for all of the Reston Companies, called a 10:00 a.m. meeting in his office for Tuesday. Present at the meeting were Glen Humphrey, Walter Brown, and Smith.

Smith opened the meeting cordially: "Gentlemen, glad you could make it. What we have to talk about today could be the thing that really puts the name of Reston Services Company on the tongue of every business person in the country. You are both aware that we have completed putting all of the information on all of the companies in our files into the computer—there are over 1,000,000 companies—the businesses America does most of its business with. What I am proposing is that we develop a program whereby any organization can use our data for purposes other than just checking to see if someone is a good credit risk."

"What sort of uses did you have in mind, Ben?" Glen Humphrey asked.

"I was especially thinking of uses in the area of prospecting for new business. We could have our computer programmers develop programs to print-out the critical information on each business; name, address, who to see, what they do, and size. Instead of the long reports we are now selling, I could

**Exhibit 1. Organization chart.**

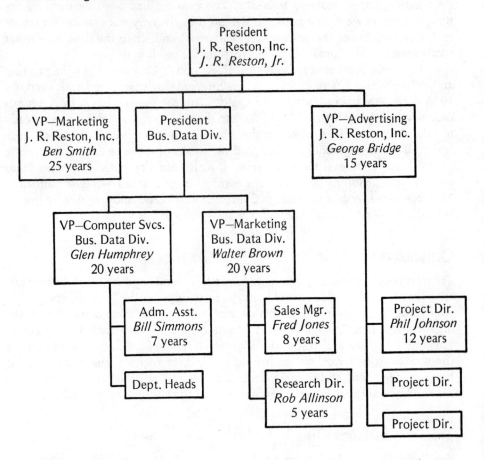

see this new service being offered on punch cards, 3 × 5 cards and tape, where our customers could plug our data directly into their data processing equipment, or give it directly to their salesmen in the field."

"Sounds tremendous to me," Walter Brown added.

"I'm glad we're all in agreement. Walter, I'd like you to develop some ideas for promotional tools to push this concept, and Glen, you will be in charge of developing the computer programs. All clear?" Smith asked.

"Clear to me," responded Brown.

"Yes, quite clear," Humphrey echoed.

For the next several months, rumors were running rampant throughout the company's headquarters, based initially upon the meeting just described.

One of the rumors was that the basic information division of the company was going to be completely "computerized" and that many of the lower level jobs now being performed by high school graduates with some experience, and recent college graduates, would be eliminated.

Bill Simmons, administrative assistant, brought this to Humphrey's attention during coffee one morning: "Mr. Humphrey, I've heard quite a bit of talk lately, from several sources, that a lot of the people who gather our raw data are afraid there is some move afoot to discontinue their jobs. I know this is because of the work we're doing to develop computer programs and formats for Smith's new product idea, and that, when completed, it won't affect their jobs one way or the other, but they don't know that. Do you think it would be a good idea for you to distribute a memo to that effect to the department heads in our division, and maybe ask Mr. Brown if he would like to do the same in his division?"

"Hell no, Simmons, the less we pamper those people on the bottom, the better off the company will be. If we start sending out memos every time we hear a rumor, that's all this office will end up doing: sending out memos. And as far as Brown is concerned, we'll let him make his own mistakes, understood?"

"Yes, sir." replied Simmons.

## Who's in Charge?

A formal letter outlining what a great opportunity this was for the company was issued from Ben Smith's office about four months after the initial meeting. It was addressed to the department heads in the information division. Humphrey was a bit miffed, as he received his copy at the same time the department heads who reported to him received theirs. But this was not unusual.

When Humphrey was leaving work, it was inevitable that on some afternoons he would be in an elevator with some of the line people in his division. Even though these people all worked for the same company, Humphrey never carried on much of a conversation with any of them. A few of the men, who had been with the company almost as long as Humphrey, would always try and talk with him anyway. On the few occasions when he would respond with more than a "yes" or "no," it really "made their day." Humphrey's general attitude and his "great stone face" only served to reinforce the younger line employees' opinion of him.

Even though an unusually large number of employee turnovers hampered the progress of developing the computer outputs, Humphrey managed to make headway on his part of the project. Walter Brown, in the meantime, was forging ahead on the promotional tools which he hoped would be a major factor in causing the success of this program. His first step was to call a meeting between himself, George Bridges, in advertising, and Fred Jones, sales manager. In the meeting, Bridges seemed distracted, even though it would be his department's responsibility to actually produce the physical promotional items.

"Is it O.K. with Smith if we bring in the ad agency guys on this one?" Bridges asked.

"I don't really know, George," Brown responded. "I just don't know."

"Well, this looks like a helluva lot more work than I can handle—especially considering the other projects we're working on," Bridges added. "What did Smith mean when he said 'promotional tools' anyway?"

"He didn't really spell it out, George. I suppose pamphlets, brochures, some 'leave-behinds' for the salesmen, some direct mail, you know, that sort of thing."

"Yeah, my guys will need all the help they can get when they go into this area. You know, it will be a whole new ball game out there. They may be calling on the same types of firms, but they'll be talking to different guys once they get inside," Jones added.

"I know, I know, but let's get back to Smith's 'promotional tools,'" Bridges stated. When he pronounced "promotional tools," he had an unmistakable smirk on his mouth.

"He doesn't want any radio, or magazine, or newspaper, is that what you're saying?" Bridges asked. "Not even the *Journal (Wall Street Journal)*?"

"I don't know for sure, George. Why don't you go up there and ask him?" Brown retorted, this time raising his voice just a bit.

"Anyway, George, if you would work on some ideas for us I would appreciate it, and I'm sure Fred and his people would too. If you need to talk to Smith, just go up there and talk to him, or if you think he would say he's too busy, then just work up what you think is best. At any rate we've got a meeting with his people, my people and your guys and Humphrey's crew in the Board Room, June 1. O.K.?"

"O.K." Bridges grunted.

George Bridges didn't return directly to his office. Instead, he walked around the block a few times. His mind was racing. "Why didn't Smith invite me to the initial meeting? Why didn't he put in writing what kind of promotion he wants, or at least why didn't Brown put in writing the kind of promotion he would like to see. If either, or both of them had, that would at least give me something more concrete to go on." He returned to his office and called in Phil Johnson, one of his project directors.

"Phil, we've a real job coming up. What it involves is producing some direct mail and some pamphlets for Smith's latest brainstorm."

"You mean the computerized sales aids Humphrey's people have been working on?"

"One and the same. You get down to Humphrey and find out what you can about the product and the market, and write me up some stuff. Have one of those girls in the art department 'dummy up' some samples of what you think the brochures should look like."

Phil Johnson followed through on his part of the assignment, collecting most of the data from various people in Humphrey's area, not getting much help from Humphrey himself. Johnson developed a direct mail campaign consisting of three letters, each accompanied by a different brochure. The brochures could also be used separately as "leave-behinds" by the sales force, or could be used with personal letters written by the sales people to preferred customers. He went in to explain what he had developed to George Bridges. About midway through, Bridges stood up from where he had been seated and looking out of the window and asked Johnson to leave the material on his desk and that he would get to it as soon as he could. Johnson left Bridges' office a very confused young man.

## Hidden Agendas

June 1 rolled around and found Ben Smith and his top two assistants in the Board Room on the twentieth floor thirty minutes before the meeting was to start. Smith had seated himself at the end of the table farthest from the door. His two people flanked him.

Brown, Jones, Allinson, Bridges, and Johnson arrived at about the same time. Brown, Jones, and Allinson seated themselves on the side of the table nearest the door, with Brown sitting nearest Smith. There was one empty chair between Brown and the person on Smith's right. Johnson followed Bridges to the opposite side of the table and they arranged themselves similarly to Brown and his people. Humphrey, Simmons and two more business data people arrived about five minutes after 1:00.

Humphrey reported that work was progressing nicely on the computer programs. He passed around samples of what the 3 × 5 cards would look like, and explained what data would be available on the punched cards and magnetic tape. Brown reported on the field work he and Jones had done with their sales force, working through their department heads, as well as the instructions he had given Bridges in regard to promotion.

Bridges then passed around Johnson's letters and brochures, never mentioning who did them. They were well received. Bridges then asked Smith's opinion of some ads in the *Wall Street Journal.* Smith responded favorably and also mentioned he thought some "things in the business sections of the *Los Angeles Times* and *New York Times,* plus *Fortune* would be nice." Bridges mentioned that he had been thinking the very same thing.

Humphrey then mentioned that what he saw and heard was good but that it seemed to him something was missing. Some type of brochure that was more extensive, something that would contain some useful data that would really whet the businessman's appetite for more. Smith consented and asked Brown and Bridges to work on it.

Bridges and Brown met. Brown tried to give the project to Bridges. Bridges said that it was Humphrey's idea, so "why didn't he do it?" In the end, it was delegated as a group project to Johnson from Advertising, Simmons from Business Data, and Rob Allinson from Marketing Products.

During their first meeting, Simmons suggested their second meeting could easily be held in his division's conference room, as it was in the center of the building, and accessible for both Johnson and Allinson. Allinson countered with the statement that "Yes, but our place has the new video equipment, and it might make it easier for Phil if we met there, because he will probably want to have slides made of his stuff anyway, and that way he would have all the equipment he needs already in the room."

Simmons did not make a verbal reply, he simply raised the palms of both hands upward and shrugged his shoulders.

It was decided that the booklet would contain grouped data on the businesses in the Reston file. The data were to be arranged first by type of industry and secondly by geographic area, namely by each of the fifty states. The data were compiled after several more months' work, and rough copies were hand-delivered to Smith, Brown, Bridges, and Humphrey.

## Success in Spite Of?

In a subsequent Board meeting, Smith, Humphrey, and Brown were present. The computer programs, formats, and all promotional materials (letters, brochures, newspaper and magazine advertisements, and the booklet) were presented. All met with the Board's approval, with minor modifications.

The product and its accompanying promotion were presented later at a major meeting at the Denver Hilton. All of the parties previously mentioned were present, as was J. R. Reston, Jr., and all of Reston Service Company's Regional Managers. Brown, Bridges, and Humphrey each was thinking to himself, "There must be a better way. . . ."

# CASE 25
# Loran State University

Loran State University is a small liberal arts university with some 6,000 students. There are 250 full-time faculty members and another 25 part-time faculty. Loran is presided over by the university president who is an appointee of the state governor and serves what amounts to a lifelong term of office. Edicts and announcements from the president are usually sent via campus mail to the office of vice president for further dissemination.

The vice president runs the day-to-day affairs of the university. He is a powerful individual on campus. The vice president screens most matters before they reach the president. The vice president will act on and settle the majority of such matters. Matters of strategic importance will sometimes be passed on to the president with a recommendation from the vice president. Immediately accountable to the vice president are the seven academic deans of the various schools on campus.

On matters internal to a particular school the individual dean may use discretion in arriving at a resolution. As a group the deans comprise the Deans' Committee. The Deans' Committee screens recommendations originating at the department head level and from the Faculty Government. The Deans' Committee may reject a recommendation brought before it or may pass it along with its approval to the vice president for consideration.

**Exhibit 1. Abbreviated organization chart for Loran State University.**

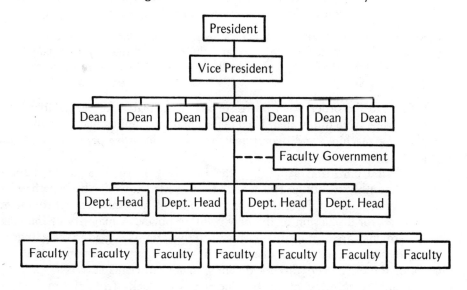

Prepared by Michael Budden, Southeastern Louisiana University.

The Faculty Government is an elected group of thirty full-time faculty members who represent the faculty of the various departments on campus. Membership by department heads or other administration personnel is forbidden. Members are elected by their respective department's faculty and serve three-year staggered terms. The purpose of the Faculty Government as stated in its constitution is to "recommend and advise" the administration on matters pertaining to university and academic policy. The constitution was endorsed years earlier by 90 percent of the faculty and had also been approved and signed by the previous president of the university. The Faculty Government meets the third Tuesday of each month during the school year to discuss business. The Faculty Government periodically makes recommendations to the administration in the form of written resolutions passed by a majority of the members. By custom, resolutions are then forwarded to the Deans' Committee, which meets the fourth Wednesday of each month. The Deans' Committee then studies the proposals and either rejects them outright, studies them in detail (which generally takes several months), or approves the recommendations immediately and passes them along to the vice president with the Committee's endorsement.

The majority of faculty representatives could not recall the last time a resolution had passed the deans' scrutiny. Only two faculty members, who had been reelected several times, could remember the vice president approving an action of the Faculty Government, and that had been some five years previous. No one could remember what the last approved resolution pertained to.

On Tuesday, October 16, at 3:00 p.m. a letter from the president's office was delivered via campus mail to all faculty mailboxes. The brief edict announced a new university policy pertaining to the printing of tests, syllabi, and other teaching materials that required duplication. It stated:

Beginning October 17, all such materials needing duplication are to be taken to the university's central printing office and the personnel there will prepare the copies and return the finished work to the professor. There are to be no exceptions to this policy.

Prior to the order, each professor was responsible for seeing that his or her materials were duplicated. Each department on campus had its own mimeo duplicating machine, and department heads would order paper as needs dictated.

At 4:00 p.m. that same day, the Faculty Government gathered for its regular monthly meeting. The meeting was called to order by the chairman and proceeded smoothly until the introduction of new business when a member moved for discussion of the new printing policy. A majority of the members were unaware of the announcement so the letter was read to the gathering. The group was shocked and dismayed. In the ensuing discussion several criticisms of the order were discussed. Three major criticisms surfaced.

First, the printing office was located two blocks from the majority of classroom buildings. Second, the printing office required a three-day lead time to complete work brought in for duplication. A third and major criticism was the fact that four student workers assisted the two full-time printers, causing concern about the security of printed tests. This serious discussion lasted over one hour. Two ensuing resolutions were quickly passed by unanimous vote. One called for the chairman to write a letter to the president of the university asking for an immediate postponement of the implementation of the policy and an explanation of the reasoning behind such an order. This unusual decision to send the recommendation directly to the president was made because of the lack of time before implementation of the policy was to take place. The letter also was to include the major criticisms of the policy. The second resolution called for an emergency meeting of the Faculty Government the following week to discuss the results of the letter to the president.

The next morning the letter from the chairman of the Faculty Government was hand-delivered to the secretary of the president. The president had not yet arrived. In the ensuing week anger and dissent grew among the faculty. Even department heads were outwardly displeased with the order but seemed to prefer to defer action until the results of the Faculty Government recommendation had come in. Expensive printing equipment in the individual departments sat idle during the week. At the packed emergency meeting a week later the chairman sadly announced that no communication from the president's office had been forthcoming. The members and faculty left shocked.

The next three weeks saw faculty morale fall. Some faculty announced in classes that remaining tests would be administered orally. A few canceled tests until further notice, indicating that student grades would be dependent on work other than written tests. There were indications that some faculty were sneaking into the buildings late at night, duplicating their own materials. Paper supplies in the departments were disappearing. Other faculty followed the new policy and allowed the central printing office to duplicate their teaching materials. Students, too, became visibly upset. Student discussions in the cafeterias centered around the "new" testing policies of some of the faculty. These student discussions were often noisy and angry. The Student Government passed a resolution supporting the Faculty Government and requested a quick end to the problem.

The next regular meeting of the Faculty Government came to order on November 17. The chairman excitedly deferred regular business so that a letter he had received moments earlier could first be read to the members. The letter was from the vice president. It stated that there was no cause for the low morale and dissension among the faculty due to the duplication policy of October 16 because the order had been rescinded by the president on October 18. The vice president's letter included a photostatic copy of a letter from the president dated October 18, addressed to the vice president. It stated:

... Under advisement of the Faculty Government, I am rescinding my duplication policy order of the 16th and will study the matter further.

The letter was signed by the president of the university.

The meeting was silent.

# CASE 26
# The Chief

"I never thought that b—— would try a stunt like that!" Alex Brown angrily exclaimed, striking his desk with a clenched fist so hard he winced.

Startled by the outburst, Anne Stevens looked up from her desk where she had been trying to type the minutes of the last Safety Council meeting. Astonished and concerned by this unexpected action from her boss, Anne realized that something quite serious must have occurred in the plant manager's office. Mr. Brown had rushed over there as soon as Mr. Arrowsmith called over the office intercom. She had always regarded Mr. Brown as a quiet and fairly restrained type of person who never "blew his top." She believed most people would agree with her view of Mr. Brown as a competent and highly motivated individual whose considerable energies were devoted to developing ways to increase the efficiency of the Plant Safety Office at Southwestern Arsenal.

As his secretary, Anne knew Mr. Brown was experimenting with some new approaches that he was confident would resolve a number of problems created by the newly organized firefighter-guard force at Southwestern. For several weeks, Mr. Brown had been trying to define responsibilities and authorities of several new supervisory positions. The force was an amalgamation of two formerly separate organizations: a security force and a firefighting force. Both had existed for several years. Selected to head this new combination was William Sprague, who had been the Chief of the Fire Department at Southwestern almost since the organization's inception at the commencement of World War II. An aggressive, outspoken person, Sprague's substantial physique seemed particularly consonant with a brusk, authoritarian manner.

Constructed in the early 1940s, Southwestern Arsenal was typical of scores of industrial plants the federal government built to produce explosives of all sorts and to load, assemble, and pack (lap) a great variety of small arms, artillery shells, and bombs. Encompassing some 15,000 acres of relatively flat and treeless terrain, this installation was divided into two principal areas: one devoted to administrative purposes and the other designed to provide the extensive areas needed for working with explosives. Each area was separately fenced, with entrance and egress controlled by guards of the internal plant security force. Activities in the explosive operational areas were closely supervised and performed in accordance with detailed written procedures commonly referred to as Standard Operating Procedures (SOPs).

Because of the potential catastrophic results which might ensue from a fire involving explosives, the plant firefighting personnel required special knowledge of the important characteristics of explosives and principal chemi-

Prepared by George Eddy, University of Texas; and Jerry Saegert.

cal reactions to high temperatures associated with conflagrations. Training and drills for such personnel received continuous emphasis, and frequently the plant manager, Henry Arrowsmith, either participated himself or observed in the company of the safety officer. Supplementing these drills, detailed critiques were held with the objective of improving performance. During World War II, all firefighting was the responsibility solely of the Fire Department, while the separate Guard Force concerned itself with the aspects of physical security of the administrative and operational areas of Southwestern. Not considered qualified to fight fires involving explosives, the guards did get some training in the subject of explosives characteristics and were expected to assist the Fire Department during emergencies.

After the war, Southwestern continued in production (the majority of such government facilities were closed and sold) under the same general management, although the scope of its activities was substantially reduced and there was considerable turnover of personnel. Included in the numerous organizational realignments necessitated by the significantly lessened need for the plant's products was the decision to merge the Guard Force with the Fire Department. Shortly after Henry Arrowsmith chose William Sprague to become the chief of this new organization of some fifty men, Alex Brown joined the staff as the plant safety officer. After reviewing the organization chart (Exhibit 1), Mr. Brown realized his arrival was coincidental with probably the maximum degree of turbulence engendered by the considerable shifting and reassignment of both former guards and firemen.

Following his initial meeting with Chief Sprague, a tour of the firefighter-guard facilities and an opportunity to talk with most of the supervisors and men on duty, Mr. Brown began to assess what he had observed. When he first visited the central station, located about the middle of the Restricted Area, Mr. Brown noticed that Mr. Arrowsmith was in the kitchen pouring himself a cup of coffee. Each station had sleeping quarters, a small kitchen and eating

**Exhibit 1. Southwestern Arsenal organization chart.**

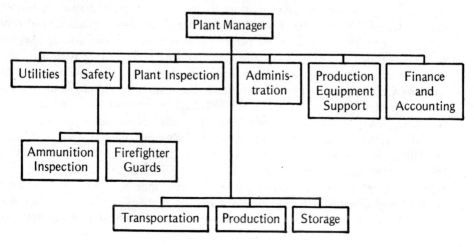

area, an office, supply and armory facilities, general equipment area, washing and toilet facilities, and an area that could be used for a variety of purposes, such as conferences, classes, and the like. Operated on a twenty-four-hour basis, there was always a coffee pot brewing.

"Hello, Alex," greeted Mr. Arrowsmith, "I see you are making the rounds. What do you think of our setup?"

"I think I've seen just about everything that's under the Chief's control, Hank. Of course, I'm trying to sort things out, but it shouldn't take long. Already, I can appreciate this reorganization of security and firefighting elements requires a 'new look' in a lot of aspects," replied Mr. Brown, as he concluded with a comment that he thought that the realignments would place a premium on flexibility in attitudes.

"Well, okay, Alex," Mr. Arrowsmith noted as he got up to leave, "I've got to get back to the office. It sure makes a nice break to get out in the area and stop off here and shoot the bull with the Chief. It'll soon be hunting season again, so I'll be out here a lot."

As the Chief walked out to the car with Mr. Arrowsmith, Mr. Brown noted that the conversation seemed quite informal and jovial. He wondered how often the plant manager visited the station and what sort of relationship existed between them. Recalling that each time the Chief had come to visit him in the Administrative Area, some six miles distant, the Chief had yet to come on his own initiative. Further, that he either stopped by Hank's office before coming to see him or went there right after Mr. Brown had concluded their discussion about some matter on firefighting or security.

Soon after Mr. Brown had proposed a major change in the training schedule to the Chief, the subject was mentioned by Mr. Arrowsmith. Surprised at first by the extent of Hank's knowledge of some of the details which he had not discussed with the plant manager, Mr. Brown quickly learned that the Chief had spoken to Hank about it, voicing various apprehensions of certain provisions. Mr. Arrowsmith told Mr. Brown that he had agreed with several of the Chief's concerns. Due to the manner in which Mr. Arrowsmith related his conversation with the Chief, Mr. Brown was convinced that the plant manager did not know these were matters that originated with the safety officer, not the Chief. "Yeah, Alex, I told him the idea to increase the amount of time spent on security training by 40 percent was screwy," remarked Mr. Arrowsmith offhandedly. "After a bit, the Chief said he had to agree with me."

It was about this time that Mr. Brown recognized with growing irritation that the Chief seemed to be getting more disputacious on changes or innovations that Mr. Brown proposed. As he reflected on the past three sessions with the Chief, Mr. Brown had to note that the Chief disagreed with every new idea the safety officer suggested was worth trying out. He gathered that while the Chief did not say so directly, he managed to convey the impression he felt these recommendations were absurd. The Chief began to emphasize that since his long tenure as the Fire Chief had run smoothly, there was no need to get tangled up in schemes of questionable merit. Clearly, the Chief was nettled by what he believed was meddling in his affairs by a newcomer who had not been at Southwestern when "things were really tough" and who furthermore had probably never even held a firehose in his hands.

Even Hank suggested that perhaps he was pushing the Chief too hard, and that Mr. Brown should give him a little more time to adjust to the requirements of the new firefighter-guard organization. The hunting season had commenced, and Mr. Brown learned that the plant manager spent several hours every day "out in the area." While some of these hours occurred right after daybreak, and thus were before the normal working day started, it seemed apparent that Mr. Arrowsmith stopped at the firefighter-guard station at least once every day for coffee and conversation. Mr. Brown was convinced the Chief always managed to be present when the plant manager appeared. Not a hunter himself, Mr. Brown never went out with Mr. Arrowsmith, who did not lack for company. Usually he took the mayor of Midvale, a small town nearby, as his guest.

"That must be quite a chore, Hank, to clean all those birds you seem to shoot so expertly," Mr. Brown remarked at the height of the season.

"Oh hell, Alex, I don't do that!" exclaimed Mr. Arrowsmith, "the Chief always takes care of it for me."

Some four months after he assumed the duties of safety officer, Mr. Brown was dismayed to recognize that whatever changes he had succeeded in getting implemented in the firefighter-guard organization had been "by direction." It no longer seemed possible to discuss matters of importance with the Chief, who never failed to find something wrong with anything new or different—Mr. Brown concluded—and who had become so intractable that Mr. Brown was weary in his repeated attempts to get the Chief to focus on central issues instead of personalities. Even the relatively simple matter of determining the vacation schedule for supervisory personnel had become a contentious matter. The schedule the Chief had presented bothered Mr. Brown as he believed it unduly "favored" the supervisors with the longest tenure, giving them a disappropriate share of the most desirable vacation periods and simultaneously leaving the force under the newest and least experienced hands. After a heated discussion, the Chief reluctantly agreed to modify the schedule, but remained vague concerning his own plans.

Pointing to the wall calendar, Mr. Brown remarked that there were several periods available to the Chief. "Just let me know when you want to take off, Chief," Mr. Brown declared as the Chief got up to leave. "Yeah," replied the Chief and departed.

Mr. Brown picked up the latest training schedule and tried to concentrate on those portions that pertained to leadership and the general aspects of how to improve supervision. Based on his observations of the firefighter-guard organization Mr. Brown was convinced the supervisory personnel, both relative newcomers and most oldtimers, were significantly deficient in performance in that capacity. Technically, they seemed reasonably proficient, and the continuing program to upgrade the force in this respect had progressed without major difficulty. He had spoken at length on leadership matters with the Chief, but since the latter had not shared his concern about such an emphasis, Mr.

Brown went ahead and prepared a detailed and comprehensive program. At the time of the session on the vacation schedule, Mr. Brown had just concluded the last details, including lesson plans and the preparation of reference material he proposed to hand out for further study by the firefighter-guard supervisory personnel. Scheduling himself as the instructor for the majority of the lessons, Mr. Brown believed he had developed something significant that was long overdue.

Still smarting over his last discussion with Hank Arrowsmith about the Chief who had complained again directly to the plant manager over a matter that Hank seemed disposed to regard as minor but was considered by Mr. Brown as most important, Alex was astounded by this contention:

"The Chief says you are trying to get him, Alex," Hank began, "He claims you've never stopped attacking him since the day you first arrived. He does not understand why this is happening as he has done his job for years without prior criticism. Then you appear and nothing is right? Why? Suddenly he figures it out. You are trying to act like your father!"

"What?"

"Let me finish, Alex," continued Hank Arrowsmith. "That's the way the Chief looks at it. He thinks you are so impressed with your father's methods that you can't help imitating him."

"You've got to be kidding, Hank. He's never even met my father, who has never been to Southwestern. I know that my father is fairly well known as a forceful plant manager elsewhere. I'm not trying to 'get' the Chief—unless you regard trying to persuade him to follow reasonable instructions as something intolerable. I've given him every chance to cooperate, Hank, and he has chosen to fight me instead."

"Now, Alex, I don't think it's quite that," interjected Hank.

"Yes it is, Hank. The Chief has decided that he's going to override my authority and that he doesn't have to listen to anyone but you! It's now gotten to the point that it's either him or me . . ."

Mr. Arrowsmith had risen from his chair while Mr. Brown was speaking agitatedly. Now he went over to the window, turning his back to Mr. Brown in silence. After a few minutes of waiting for Mr. Arrowsmith to turn around, Mr. Brown abruptly left the office.

When he returned to his own office, Mr. Brown required some moments to regain his composure. Finally he picked up the telephone and dialed the number of the central firefighter-guard station.

"I want to speak to the Chief," he said to the person who answered.

"Golly, Mr. Brown, I thought you knew."

"Knew what?"

"That he's gone on vacation."

"Oh . . . ah, yes. Must've forgot." He hung up, fuming.

The day the Chief returned he found a message to report to Mr. Brown's office right away. Just as he started to leave the central station, the telephone rang. He picked it up and recognized Hank Arrowsmith's voice: "Say, Chief, glad you're back. I've got an errand I'd like you to run for me. It's quite important and you'll have to go right now."

"Sure, Mr. Arrowsmith, just tell me what you want and I'll be on my way."

"I feel like a damned fool, Chief, but I know I can count on you. You see, I just realized that when I sent my suit to the cleaners in Midvale this morning I forgot to take out the master key I have to all the gates at the plant. You've got to get it back immediately and quietly without tipping anybody off what the key is. Got it?"

"I understand, Mr. Arrowsmith. I'll get it, you can be sure. Don't worry about a thing. I'm on my way."

Wondering what was keeping the Chief, Mr. Brown reread the letter of reprimand he had prepared to give him as soon as he arrived.

It was the strongest disciplinary letter he had ever written, and he thought grimly it would probably lift the Chief right out of his chair.

# CASE 27
# The Invisible Colleague

## Part A

Eight men and one woman were seated at a cloth-covered, rectangular table in a small meeting room of the kind typically provided by large downtown hotels. They were participants in an invitational workshop exclusively for directors of privately funded educational reform grants.

The workshop was designed to help the grant directors produce well written case reports illustrative of the problems they encountered in educational change that could be considered for inclusion in a yearbook published by a prestigious national institute on educational futures. The participants were assigned to five-person teams to critique case reports by members of several presentation teams. Midway through the workshop the members of the critique teams were assigned to presentation teams while those who had already presented reconstituted the critique teams. Thus, by the end of three and one-half days of tightly scheduled meetings, all participants had read and reacted to many case reports as well as presented their individual reports and obtained rigorous feedback. Each participant received extensive encouragement to rewrite the case and submit it to the editor of the institute's yearbook.

It was now the morning of the last day, and Dr. Erica Howe along with the other three members of the presenting team were meeting the five-person critique team. Because of her scheduled afternoon departure, Dr. Howe had asked the critique team's chairman to schedule her presentation earlier rather than later in the morning session.

Dr. Howe was conscious of her peculiar status in the group both as the sole woman and as a person who, with a Ph.D. in experimental psychology, had little formal preparation in the fields of higher education, educational administration, and curriculum that comprised the backgrounds of most of her peers at the workshop. Despite her experience as a co-professor of a special master's degree course in educational administration, Howe remained somewhat skeptical about educational disciplines that lacked a rigorous experimental base. Dr. Howe, a full professor holding joint appointments in psychology and educational psychology, achieved her present position with no small effort and personal sacrifice. Like most universities, hers had institutional practices that systematically discriminated against women irrespective of their positions. Professor Howe, in concert with other feminist women on the campus, had engaged in a long and sometimes bitter fight to equalize promotion, salary, and other considerations for women. Howe felt her career had

Prepared by Ellen Kimmel, University of South Florida.

blossomed since her early involvement in the feminist movement on the campus. She published extensively in her disciplines, was a much sought after consultant on sex equity practices in both the public and private sectors, and was a recipient of state and federal grants. By any standard, Professor Howe judged herself to be academically productive, a superachiever, and "workaholic" who managed as well her roles as a mother of four daughters and wife of a distinguished scholar.

As one who attended a similar conference in the preceding year, Dr. Howe was aware that her case report was different in its emphases from the concerns and interests of most of the people at the workshop. She had been restless while listening to the critiques of others' cases. In many instances she had felt poorly informed about the "finer points" of interpretation in matters such as school law, budget management, and planning formats that had been presented to her critique team. Howe had not been comfortable in such a passive, silent role within the workshop meetings. To better inform herself about the views and special interests of fellow participants in the workshop, Howe had actively initiated discussions with them during the breaks and at meals.

Dr. Howe had found her new colleagues, 95 percent of whom were male, generally friendly and willing to talk with her. However, for the first time in her career, she had a gnawing feeling that their responses to her were more social than professional. Aware, perhaps for the first time, of an intense sexual interest in a male participant at the workshop, she had wondered whether her behavior around men had betrayed her interest. As a "young" 38, slim and attractive, she had systematically sought to avoid any of the flirtatious manner that served her so well when much younger. She wished now that she had a videotaped record of her behavior to see if traces of the flirt were yet visible.

Professor Howe was greatly relieved that the person who so strongly appealed to her was not on her presentation team or on the critique team she faced today. Despite his absence, she experienced some difficulty attending to the discussions of the case reports, forcing her to renew her efforts at concentration. Howe's new sense of vulnerability reminded her of her belief that "sex in the office" or in this case "sex in the workshop" was largely a mythical problem, but one she now felt was potentially a problem for her. She rebuked herself angrily when she caught her thoughts wandering over the possibilities.

Now, on the last day, Dr. Howe, impatiently awaited the beginning of the morning's session and hoped that the chairman would put her report at the top of the schedule. Seated across from Jack Hammond, a bit long-winded but relatively friendly, and next to Mark Thane, she recalled her serious discussion with Mark about the problems of rearing his daughters so they could avoid becoming, in Mark's words, "soft as all the professional women he had ever met." It disturbed her then to think he might see her in the same light, but she didn't pursue the matter with him. She wondered now whether she could be taken seriously as a professional colleague in this group.

## Part B

Looking at his watch and glancing around the table, Dr. Martin Muehl opened the meeting, "Well, it's time we got started and there remain a number of case reports to review before our day ends. Let's let the young lady go first this morning."

Without thinking, Howe retorted, "How about the 'old woman'—that's more accurate."

Muehl looked at her over his reading glasses and blithely amended, "Fine . . . the little lady then."

Now, standing outside herself, Howe wryly predicted that her comments would fall on deaf ears. She composed herself to begin with a description of the case's objectives and an overview of the concepts students would apply to its analysis. However, before she could begin, Jack Hammond launched into a story about how fortunate he had been to ride to work each day with a female colleague and had learned all about the "woman's issue." He had been sensitized through this experience, he assured the group.

"How can he so thoroughly delude himself?" Howe thought to herself. "Before I've had a chance to say a word, he has side-tracked the discussion to center on himself. It's hardly relevant even if he were sensitized! I've got to get my presentation going before my time runs out."

Referring to her notes, Dr. Howe began her presentation the moment Jack indicated the end of his story. "I think it is important to comment on the ways my case report differ from those you have been seeing," she began. "I have written this case to illustrate the application of behavioral principles that affect people's performances in formal . . ."

"Say, Erica," George Kennedy intruded, "where's my page three? I'm missing page three. Does anyone have an extra page?"

"I don't have one, but I have two page sevens in my report, George," Bill VerHove added.

Dr. Howe inwardly groaned, "God, what next! Will I ever get this report going? This scene, important men interrupting trivial women is a classic. I wish I could film this for my class. Is Mark catching the meaning of this diversion? Does he see how this fits with our discussion about the absence of real competition and criticism for women as part of the experience they need to develop fully as professionals?" She glanced covertly in his direction but couldn't read his expression.

"O.K.," Howe replied. "It looks like some of your reports were poorly assembled. I'll fill you in on the substance of the missing page because it is central to the purpose of my case. First, as I was indicating before George discovered the missing page, the case illustrates the way certain behavioral principles affect the actions of people in formal organizations. My work has been directed toward training undergraduates, more specifically, women undergraduates, in conflict resolution by sharpening their skills in assertiveness training."

"Erica, excuse me for interrupting," the normally silent Joseph Grange began, "but I'm troubled by the implicit value judgment you seem to make in your use of assertive training techniques for women."

"Hold on, Joe," Larry Raines blurted, "that's not the purpose of our review. It's really immaterial to the use of the case and will likely lead to a discussion that won't be too profitable."

Turning to Howe, Larry continued, "You know, I had a hard time getting the sense of what motivated your Cynthia Sherrill, Professor Sherrill in the case. I couldn't quite figure her out, and I wondered if you could help me see her more clearly?"

Howe was simultaneously troubled and relieved. Troubled that her main character wasn't clearly portrayed, but relieved that Larry had raised the first serious concern, she replied warmly, "Larry, that's helpful to me. I might be able to clear her up if you could pick out a sentence or something that you find particularly confusing, and I could then tell you what I meant."

"Larry, I didn't have any trouble understanding what the character Sherrill is intended to accomplish." The speaker, George Kennedy, looked with open amazement at Larry.

Immediately several people began to speak at once, and Dr. Howe watched the discussion break down. Seemingly out of the blue, she heard Jack Hammond across from her say with a fatuous grin, "Well, it's nice to have something to look at in here after all. Usually we just have each other to look at."

Stunned, Howe replied with an edge in her voice, "I don't know. I would rather look at Gerry over there—he's a lot more handsome . . ." Her voice trailed off as she knew it served no purpose to continue the discussion.

Feeling a growing sense of helplessness, she said to no one in particular, "Could we go on? I think maybe you, Martin, as the chair of the reviewers, could give me your comments."

Martin, who up to then had said nothing, began, "Yes, I do have several points to make. First, on the cover page, I would suggest that. . . ." To herself, Howe thought, "At last, something concrete, straightforward and substantive. I don't know you, Martin, but you have my everlasting thanks! I feel you have invited me to join this group, even if it means having to hear some critical things about my case. After all, that's what I came for. Now, I must be careful not to act defensive or in any way discourage this sort of direct help."

Following Martin's list of questions and comments, several reviewers vied for the floor, but Jack, as usual prevailed. Undaunted by colleagues' subtle and not-so-subtle suggestions that he stop, he began a tangential story. At the end, he turned to Howe and said, "Here are the names and addresses of two girls in my department who would like to have copies of this case."

Dr. Howe looked at the addresses she had been handed and shook her head in disbelief that the two "girls" referred to were Ph.D. faculty members.

## Part C

"Jack," Howe began in measured tones, "I want to make clear that you are in fact referring to two grown women who are your faculty colleagues?"

"Yes, that's right. One's an associate, the other one's an assistant professor," he answered blandly.

"And do you refer to your male colleagues in the department as 'boy?' " she countered.

"What do you mean? . . . I, uh, these females are girls. Well, one is getting past that now, I guess, since she's actually not so young. But women want to be called girls—that's what they are, really," he blustered and squirmed.

Howe recognized the usual incredulity, defensiveness, disbelief, and finally rejection so common when such a discussion of labels takes place. Unable to let go, she persisted as calmly as she could, "I am sure that you believe what you said, and no doubt there are many women who accept or even prefer to be called 'girls,' but I can only assure you that it is offensive to many adult females to be referred to by a term defined in Webster's as a 'female child, barmaid, or maidservant.' "

There was a heavy silence. All eyes were downcast or averted, and Jack, the target of Howe's lecture, shuffled his papers. George noted that it was close to 10:00 and probably time to wind up the review of Dr. Howe's report. However, the chairman, Martin Muehl reviewed quickly the day's schedule and assured the team that ample time remained for Dr. Howe's report. Dr. Howe hastily assured George and the chairman that she had no wish to belabor the discussion of her work and would try to avoid future off-task exchanges.

Dr. Howe tried to put on a cheerful face and asked the review team for additional reactions. She felt as though she were pleading, and was angry at herself for engaging in the exchange with Jack that so muted the group.

Mark Thayne, essentially silent throughout the session, observed that he knew a woman activist "reformer" working in a different county in Howe's home state who would be a good subject for another case. She thanked him and said she would get the name from him after the session.

Howe looked around the review team with a growing feeling of despair. "Oh damn, now they are really afraid to deal with me except in this 'sweet' fashion. Maybe they think I need handling with kid gloves. O.K., one more try for feedback, and, if that fails, I'll not waste any more time," she thought.

"I thought you might be about to say something, Larry," Howe tried. "Do you have any further questions about what I've written here?"

"No, not really, I guess," Larry replied not looking directly at her. "I think Martin pretty much covered the other questions I had. I am not sure I will ever understand the application of the so-called behavioral principles, but that's my problem."

"Part of your reaction could be due to the way in which I have presented the material in the case. Others might be having difficulty with the same things that trouble you," Howe ventured, hoping Larry would explore more completely his reaction to her report.

"No, not really. I really don't have anything helpful that I can give you." "Hey," he turned to the others, "take me off the hook!"

Howe wilted inside. "Now I've done it! He's cornered, threatened, and I'm the pushy bitch who can't leave well enough alone. I give up. It's a lost cause now."

"Thank you for your help. Your recommendations and observations will help me in the rewrite. I think we should turn to Mark's report now so we can finish at least part of it before the break," Howe concluded.

# EXPERIENTIAL EXERCISE 10

## One-Way versus Two-Way Communications

The process of interpersonal communications is sometimes complicated by our failure to secure feedback. The verbal and nonverbal form of feedback available to the sender also is an important factor in communication. The purpose of this exercise is to demonstrate the impact of various types of feedback on goal attainment. It also may be used to illustrate the importance of organization structure on communications effectiveness.

### Instructions

1. A sender must be selected from the group. She or he will be given some time in which to examine a diagram provided to her by the instructor. (The diagram consists of well-known geometric forms that have been linked to one another.)
2. The sender will demonstrate a "one-way" communications format by describing the diagram to other members of the group without receiving *any form* of feedback. (This can be accomplished by placing the sender behind a screen or by turning his or her back to the group.) Members of the group are not permitted to ask questions or provide any feedback (statements, laughing, etc.) to the sender.
3. After Step 2 is completed, the sender faces the group and describes a second diagram. Group members still may not ask questions about their instructions. In this case, however, the sender is in a position to pick up nonverbal feedback from the group.
4. A third diagram is provided to the sender. This time he or she may observe the group and receive verbal feedback (questions, comments, etc.) directly from group members.
5. Step 4 may be repeated more than once.
6. Measure (count percent of errors) the accuracy for each variation in format.

### Variations

Rules may be established that govern the type of feedback given, the number of times a step is repeated, and who may communicate with the sender. In the last case, the group may be structured in a manner that requires information to flow through or around certain individuals. There are many other variations to the exercise that may be added.

### Questions

1. What differences exist for the sender in one-way versus two-way communications? The sender may want to describe his or her experiences or feelings in each situation.

2. How did different types of feedback affect the efficiency and the effectiveness of the total communications process?
3. What were your experiences as a receiver under different communications arrangements (frustrations, confusion, sense of competence, accuracy, etc.)?
4. What were the advantages and disadvantages of each communications format? Is two-way communications better than one-way communications? Is unstructured feedback better than structured feedback? Discuss.

# EXPERIENTIAL EXERCISE 11

## A Communications Audit

Do you understand the important elements of a communications system and the types of communication that take place within an organization? The purpose of this exercise is to increase your awareness of organizational communications through the process of developing and implementing a limited communication systems audit.

### Preparations

Reread the section entitled "Auditing the Organizational Communications System" in the text of Chapter Seven. Refer to the "audit framework" in Figure 2, noting in particular the different categories of organizational communications (intraorganizational set, output/organizational set, and so forth) and their respective roles. You may also wish to read Harold Greenbaum's article, "The Audit of Organizational Communication," or other relevant selections recommended by your professor.

### Instructions

1. Either alone or with a small group select one communications category to examine.
2. Determine the goal of that category of communication in an organizational setting.
3. Design for that category a series of pertinent questions that can be used to provide information about the nature, effectiveness, and efficiency of the goals, functional networks, communication policies, and specific activities.
4. Administer a questionnaire based upon the items developed in Step 3 within an organization (or unit, e.g., department) of your choosing and analyze the results.
5. Discuss your finding with fellow students. You may also want to present your findings to the manager (head, director, etc.) of the organization or organizational unit in which the audit was conducted.

### Questions

1. What is the purpose of any communication systems audit?
2. In retrospect, do you believe the questions you asked in your audit were adequate? How might they (or the audit process, itself) be improved upon?

Prepared by Donald D. White, University of Arkansas.

# CHAPTER EIGHT

# Group Behavior
# and Impact

Management researchers have shown increasing interest in the role of small groups in organizations since the Hawthorne studies focused attention on the dynamics and impact of group behavior. Since then, many others have studied the influence of groups on individual and organizational effectiveness. Some authors have pointed out that small groups establish restrictive output norms and thus are inconsistent with the attainment of organizational goals. Other writers, however, have suggested that small groups can positively influence productivity.

As was suggested in the socio-technical systems model discussed in Part I of this book, small groups are important components of organizational systems. As such, they represent more than the aggregate behaviors of their members. They are important systems of variables in and of themselves. Groups represent complex social systems that are capable of developing their own identities and, in turn, affecting the behavior of an organizational system. They influence—sometimes positively, sometimes negatively—both productivity and interpersonal relations.

Ronald Levy[1] has concluded, as a result of his research, that a small group actually forms a group self-concept or socio-concept. This socio-concept is not with the group from its inception. Rather, it evolves as the group solidifies itself around some central theme. The socio-concept represents a conscious self-awareness on the part of group members of the purpose, structure, and process of the group and of its relationship with its environment. The sharing of this common image by group members is an indication of the entity's potential impact on the organizational system.

Sociologically, groups have been studied as entities in themselves. More recently, research has examined various types of groups in organizational settings. Chapter Eight looks at task groups, project groups, and informal groups. Other specialized topics, such as boundary spanning, problem solving groups, and decision-making groups, are also discussed.

## Types of Groups

Whenever people get together, they can be considered a small group. However, the circumstances under which they gather make a difference in the way the group is managed and, in some cases, the concepts used in the analysis of the group. Groups may be classified as task, project, or informal groups.

*Task groups* (or functional groups) are determined by their formal role requirements. They "are brought together for the purpose of transforming some inputs (raw materials, ideas, concepts, or objects) into an identifiable group product (an objective, a decision, a report, or some detectable environmental change)." [2] Task group members typically interact with one another on a day-to-day basis. Such groups often take the form of departments or ongoing work teams.

*Project groups* include the many formal assignments to temporary groups, committees, and projects that occur in organizations. All organizations have some activities that require grouping across functional lines. In addition, there are many "high technology" organizations that are characterized by groups made up of specialists who have been brought together for the life of the project. They will return to their normal work activities or go on to another temporary project group after that project has been completed. Examples of project groups include research and development teams, internal consultant groups, and medical teams.

*Informal groups* are perhaps most common to our experience. These groups evolve because people are in a common location and share some common interest or activity (internal influence) or fear (external influence). Social groups result from activities like bowling, lunch, and card-playing. Minor coalitions may result from the need to solve a community problem or an organizational problem of a temporary nature outside the usual channels. Informal groups often arise when people get together to achieve formal ends. As such, similarities and differences among group members may lead to informal activities in organizations.

## The Group Process

Groups are dynamic. They are in a continual state of activity and change. Figure 1 illustrates the complexity of group behavior. Its major variables include leadership, climate, conforming factors, cohesiveness, and norms.[3] Their interaction yields the output of the group. Functional or task groups might yield productivity, while the output of an informal group might be entertainment or some disruptive activity.

Group leaders may be assigned by some higher authority in an organization. On the other hand, informal leaders sometimes emerge as a result of

**Figure 1. The group process.**

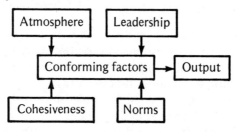

a determination by group members that the leader would be particularly helpful in reaching group objectives. Three characteristics aid emergent leaders. First, leaders generally are socially compatible with group members. Second, the person may be prominent in the eyes of group members. Third, the leader is perceived to be able to help the group attain its objectives. The first characteristic helps satisfy the group's socio-emotional needs. The second and third characteristics help satisfy the group's need for structure and goal attainment.

Successful leaders are generally those whose styles satisfy the needs of group members and appropriately match other situational conditions.[4] Directive leadership generates an autocratic atmosphere and is effective in response to critical and emergency situations, highly automated technologies. A democratic leadership style yields a participative atmosphere and is appropriate in complex and ambiguous situations and people-intensive technologies.

People generally assemble in groups as a result of some factors they hold in common. They may be assigned to certain groups or units because of organizational needs (functional or task groups), or they may come together for informal reasons. Some conforming factors that can cause an informal group to emerge are personality characteristics, common interests, education, sex, and status. Any of these factors can cause informal subgroups to form within larger task or functional groups. In addition, they may have a major impact on the leadership style that will be most effective in that group. For example, a group might consist of a large number of persons who have a distinct need to work in a well-defined environment (authoritarian personalities). Group members looking to someone (a manager or informal leaders) to generate such an atmosphere would function most effectively under a directive leadership style.[5] Groups consisting primarily of nonauthoritarian personality types, on the other hand, would prefer a democratic leader.[6]

*Cohesiveness* refers to the strength of the members' desires to remain in the group and their commitment to the group. Groups whose members have a strong desire to belong to the group or to accept its goals would be considered highly cohesive. If, on the other hand, people belong to a group only because they have to belong, and they find no value otherwise, the group would have low cohesiveness. According to Herold,[7] reasons underlying cohesiveness significantly affect patterns of group behavior and the likelihood of goal attainment. For example, cohesiveness arising from the attractiveness of the group's goals or tasks influences task accomplishment. On the other hand, cohesiveness that is a consequence of the personal attractiveness or friendliness of group members may encourage behaviors that maintain group memberships rather than those that attain group goals. Cohesiveness is a force affecting the intensity of group performance. However, the direction of performance (positive or negative) is a function of the perceived leadership influences in the situation.[8]

When conforming factors and leaders' style are consistent in formal settings, it is likely that cohesiveness will be a positive force.[9] In an informal setting it is possible that the same conditions will yield antimanagement activity. Suppose that employees unite their efforts to get rid of an overbearing supervisor. The commonly held interest in having the supervisor dismissed may temporarily result in a high level of cohesiveness among group members. This may occur even though the same persons might not value their common membership in the group to attain either membership or other goals.

*Group norms* are standards against which the behaviors of individual members are compared. The group's socio-concept, referred to earlier in this section, encompasses these standards. Over time, group member ideas, sentiments, and views melt into shared ways of looking at their world. Individual beliefs and patterns influence norms and vice versa. However, norms technically are a group phenomenon. Therefore, our interest lies primarily in the conformance of individual behaviors to the group's standards. Restrictions in output, attendance, wash-up time, cooperation with superiors, job habits, and commitment to organizational goals often are a product of group norms.

Hackman[10] suggests that norms have five major characteristics. First, norms summarize group influence processes. They state the rules for joining and maintaining membership in the group. Second, norms apply to behavior, not to private thoughts and feelings. Concurrence in the group is required, but private acceptance is unnecessary. Third, norms only apply to behaviors important to most group members. Norms are established to govern behavior patterns that must be continuously, socially influenced. Fourth, norms generally develop slowly, but, if necessary, groups establish norms more quickly by making explicit statements about behavior that is expected "from now on." Fifth, not all norms apply to everyone. High status members have more privileges and leeway than low status members of the same group.

Groups have various methods for bringing about conformance to their norms whether the norms are positive or negative. A slap on the back (friendly or otherwise), caustic comments, looks, meetings, denial of privileges, and the like are ways the group openly or subtly enforces the behavior standards upon which it has agreed. Moreover, group members, due to their immediate presence, are a continuous source of pressure toward conformance to standards that have been established.

## Groups and Organizations

Group processes occur within larger organizational settings. Norms, cohesiveness, and leader emergence all influence group impact. In some instances, a group will select or evolve its own leadership. However, in most formal organizations, an appointed leader (manager) is responsible to see that group processes lead to the attainment of organization goals. The leader's style may conform to his or her own personality or to the needs of the organization unit (e.g., task structure). The degree to which the manager's style conforms to the group's needs is called "leader fit."

In the same way, norms develop in response to the group's own needs. Therefore, they may be significantly different than organization goals, policies, or standards. The degree to which the standards of the organization and the norms of the small group correspond to one another is called "style fit." Reasonable style and leader fit are necessary for organizations to function successfully. Moreover, the higher the conformance of group cohesiveness and norms with organizational standards, the greater the likelihood that high productivity and group satisfaction will exist.

### Problem Solving Groups

A major direction for small group research has been group problem solving. Maier[11] has identified certain critical dimensions in problem solving. The first is the requirement for a technically correct decision, or the "quality" dimension. A second dimension is the degree to which the support of those carrying out the decision is needed. Most literature on decision making emphasizes the quality dimension and ignores the acceptance dimension.[12] The quality dimension is important in a purely cognitive context relative to the *potential* impact of the decision. However, decisions have often been made to increase quality by closely supervising the problem solving process, only to find out later that the decision was not implemented properly because of group resentment. Acceptance, then, is important when the decision must be operationalized by organization members and/or if the decision affects member behaviors or feelings.

Maier's work suggests the need to develop decision-making techniques that will lead to acceptance. A clear implication of this research is how to gain acceptance from the group without sacrificing quality. Decision-making techniques that have evolved to satisfy both criteria include brainstorming,[13] Delphi technique, and nominal group technique.[14]

*Brainstorming.* Brainstorming is the name given to an unstructured meeting that is conducted according to the following guidelines. Participants are asked to generate a large number of ideas or problem solutions. All criticism or other comments regarding ideas must be withheld until after the item-generation phase of the meeting has been completed. Participants are encouraged to be freewheeling and not to be restricted to conventional ideas—the wilder the idea, the better. Items are recorded on flip charts for later reference. After all ideas have been shared, participants are asked to combine and improve on the items that have been generated. The purpose of this final stage is to gain synergistic benefit from the integration of ideas.

*Delphi technique.*   The purpose of the Delphi technique is to arrive at a group consensus by narrowing the range of member responses. This is accomplished through the completion of a series of questionnaires and the feedback of aggregate response patterns to participants. Each succeeding tabulation should result in a tighter grouping of responses. The Delphi technique does not actually require group members to be present. Instead, a questionnaire is developed to provide inputs necessary for decision making. The questionnaire is distributed to group members, then is completed and returned to the leader. The leader (and supporting staff) then summarize the information from the questionnaire and design a second instrument, the purpose of which is to generate additional information that will add to and clarify that gathered from the original instrument.

In addition to receiving the second questionnaire, group members are provided with results of the first questionnaire. In this manner, they are given the opportunity to view the responses of other group members and to take those responses into consideration before completing the second questionnaire. The second set of questionnaires are returned to the group leader and tabulated.

A third and final questionnaire is developed in an attempt to arrive at some final consensus among group members concerning the issues being addressed. Information such as ranges of responses, response rankings, and individual comments may be provided to group members at this time. Results of the third questionnaire are then tabulated, and a final report reflecting the group's consensus is prepared.

*Nominal group technique.*   Nominal group technique (NGT) is a structured group meeting in which participants are presented with a problem in the form of a nominal group question. Each person present is asked to generate a number of responses, in writing, to the question. Verbalization between group members is prohibited. Next, participants are asked to feed back their ideas to the group using a round-robin format. (Each person reads one response from his or her list until all group members have had a chance to contribute; the process is repeated until all ideas have been verbalized). Responses are written on flip charts in front of the group. As with brainstorming, no discussion of individual responses is permitted during the feedback phase.

Once all ideas have been generated, a brief discussion is held to clarify individual items and to eliminate duplication. Finally, group members are asked to vote (or prioritize) items on the flip charts according to the "group's perception" of their relative importance. NGT is designed to encourage group creativity, to balance participation among group members, and to incorporate mathematical voting techniques in order to arrive at a group judgment.

### Groupthink

Earlier, we looked at the impact of group cohesiveness. Cohesiveness can be a positive force in organizations, or, as Janis[15] points out, it can develop into a pattern of behavior labeled "groupthink." As members become more cohesive, the group can develop a "clubby" atmosphere that emphasizes exclusiveness and superiority. New information brought to the group may be seen as inappropriate or even threatening and therefore may be ignored. This unwillingness to examine new inputs effectively closes the system (group) and results in its degeneration (entropy). Group members tend to be no longer open to new ideas.

There are several recognizable behaviors in groups exhibiting groupthink. Members ordinarily have a high *esprit de corps* and may characterize others as "quacks" or "cranks." They feel so secure in their decisions that they nurture an "illusion of invulnerability." These groups are quick to rationalize their bad decisions and to cloak that rationalization in an "illusion of morality" (i.e., they have only the highest goals in mind; therefore, why should they be criticized). Self-censorship minimizes the likelihood that members having contrary views will manifest them, ensuring yet another "illusion of unanimity." Comments like, "We've heard that argument before," and other barriers to outsiders, constitute the last characteristic, "mind-guarding." In other words, groupthink significantly reduces the effectiveness of a group by isolating it from its environment and lessening its sensitivity to the true nature of its internal processes.

### Group Conflict

Group conflict can be separated into intragroup conflict and intergroup conflict. Intragroup conflict occurs between individuals in the group and can be analyzed using the concepts discussed in Chapter Five.

Intergroup conflict is defined as disagreement that occurs between work groups. Intergroup conflict may take different forms. However, researchers agree that necessary preconditions usually include goal incompatibility.[17] Goal incompatibility occurs because units vie with one another to accomplish their own goals at the expense of the goals of others. Conflict may result from this behavior if one unit has the leverage to interfere with another's output.

Boundary-role conflict occurs because some people have membership in two or more units in the organization. An individual occupying such a position owes allegiance to two or more sub-units or to the overall organization as well as to one's own unit (e.g., department). In such a case, the support of unit members is needed to accomplish the task, but evaluation, rewards, or punishments may be handed out by the parent organization.

Another condition for intergroup conflict is hierarchical conflict. This occurs as groups vie for organizational resources, prestige, and status. This type of conflict increases when resources are limited. The last condition arises from the similarity in functions of different units. Initially, this conflict may take the form of friendly rivalry. However, depending on the norms developed in the group toward outsiders, the conflict can become highly disruptive to the attainment of overall organization goals.

## Activities–Interactions–Sentiments

A conceptual scheme that has value in the study of situations involving group behavior is the Activities–Interactions–Sentiments (AIS) model.[18] AIS is a social system model that treats the group as an open system consisting of three primary variables: activities, interactions, and sentiments.

*Activities* refers to the things people do, for example, duties contained in a formal job description. *Interactions* are the interpersonal exchanges people have with one another. *Sentiments* are the ways people feel about one another or some object. Sentiments can be positive or negative or threatening; for example, workers may have an attachment to an old desk or they may fear a new machine.

In the work organization, people in the same organizational unit must interact in order to produce or generate a designated output. These individuals find out a great deal about one another as they work together to accomplish their job goals. Both task and nontask-related sentiments may emerge as a consequence of formal interaction, such as what type of entertainment each one enjoys or common problems with children, wives, or husbands.

Change may be introduced into a group through activities, interactions, or sentiments. Once a change has been introduced through a particular element of the model, the two remaining elements will in turn be affected (see Figure 2). For example, a work group member may be told by the foreman (interaction) that the company is considering automating some job in the plant. This knowledge may cause the subordinate to be fearful (sentiment) of losing his job as a result of the introduction of a new machine. In turn, he may work harder (activity) on his present job.

The sentiment structure is a particularly important aspect of the AIS model. It is a vast, complex arrangement of attitudes toward people or things that may or may not be relevant to the broader group. Norms, discussed earlier in this chapter, represent sentiments that are strongly held in common by members of a group. The AIS model is valuable in its own right as a tool for better understanding the activities of small groups and other so-

**Figure 2.**

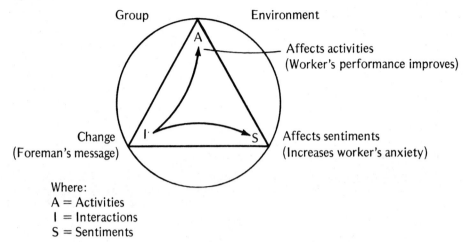

Where:
A = Activities
I = Interactions
S = Sentiments

cial systems. Seiler has chosen to include activities, interactions, and sentiments as major subsystems of the "organizational behavior" component of the sociotechnical systems model discussed in Part I of this book.

## Summary

As many researchers and practicing managers have pointed out, groups have important influences on individual behavior and on organizational effectiveness. Groups significantly affect individual satisfaction and productivity. Group processes focus on variables such as leadership, atmosphere, conforming factors, cohesiveness, and norms. Integrating the small group into the larger organization is important to the practicing manager. The degree to which the leader fits into the group and the larger organization is known as the "leader fit," while the consonance between group norms and standards of the organization is known as "style fit."

Recently, organizational research on groups has centered on problem solving, decision making, and intergroup conflict. Interest has focused on the dimensions of quality and acceptance and the trade-offs which often take place. Several group techniques were suggested for meeting the demands of both dimensions. They included brainstorming, Delphi technique and nominal group technique. A group phenomenon that limits the effectiveness of highly cohesive, decision-making groups by putting up barriers to feedback and careful decision making is known as groupthink. Finally, intergroup conflict is based upon three stimulus conditions. They are goal incompatibility, hierarchical conflict, and functional similarity within task units. Each condition is always present and is a subtle challenge to management under the best of conditions.

The AIS model provides a means by which the dynamics of social systems such as groups can be understood. The three variables—interactions, activities, and sentiments—and their interactions from the major forces within small groups that are reflected in group behaviors and outputs.

## References

1. Ronald B. Levy, *You and Your Behavior* (Boston: Holbrook Press, 1975), p. 341.
2. David M. Herold and Steven Kerr, "The Effectiveness of Work Groups," *Organizational Behavior* (Columbus: Grid Publishing, 1979), p. 96.
3. Robert T. Golembiewski, "Small Groups and Large Organizations," in *Handbook of Organizations*, edited by James G. March (Chicago: Rand McNally, 1965), pp. 87–141.
4. Fred Fiedler et al., *Improving Leadership Effectiveness: The Leader Match Concept* (New York: John Wiley and Sons, 1977), pp. 134–135.
5. T. W. Adorno et al., *The Authoritarian Personality* (New York: Harper and Company, 1958).
6. M. Rokeach, *The Open and Closed Mind* (New York: Basic Books, 1960).
7. Herold and Kerr, op. cit., p. 111.
8. Stanley Schachter et al., "An Experimental Study of Cohesiveness and Productivity," *Human Relations*, vol. 4, 1951, pp. 229–239.
9. M. E. Shaw, *Organizational Dynamics* (New York: McGraw-Hill, 1971).
10. J. R. Hackman, "Group Influences on Individuals," in *Handbook of Industrial and Organizational Psychology*, edited by M. P. Dunnette (Chicago: Rand McNally, 1976).
11. N. R. F. Maier, *Principles of Human Relations* (New York: John Wiley and Sons, 1952).
12. Frederick C. Miner, Jr., "A Comparative Analysis of Three Diverse Group Decision Making Approaches," *Academy of Management Journal*, vol. 22, no. 1, pp. 88–93.
13. Alex F. Osborn, *Applied Imagination* (New York: Charles Scribner's Sons, 1953), pp. 300–301.
14. Andre L. Delbecq et al., *Group Techniques for Program Planning* (Glenview: Scott, Foresman, 1975), pp. 4–35, 40–106.
15. Irving Janis, *Victims of Groupthink* (Boston: Houghton Mifflin, 1972).
16. S. M. Schmidt and T. A. Kochan, "Conflict: Toward Conceptual Clarity," *Administrative Science Quarterly*, vol. 17, 1972, pp. 359–370.
17. R. L. Kahn et al., *Organizational Stress: Studies in Role Conflict and Ambiguity* (New York: John Wiley and Sons, 1964).
18. George C. Homans, *The Human Group* (New York: Harcourt, Brace, 1950); also, William F. Whyte, *Organizational Behavior: Theory and Application* (Homewood: Richard D. Irwin, 1969), pp. 91–146.

## Recommended Readings

Readings marked with an asterisk are included in *Contemporary Perspectives in Organizational Behavior*, edited by Donald D. White (Boston: Allyn and Bacon, 1982).

*P. C. Andre de la Porte, "Group Norms: Key to Building a Winning Team," *Personnel*, vol. 51, September–October 1974, pp. 60–67.
J. Stephen Heinen and Eugene Jacobson, "A Model of Task Group Development in Complex Organizations and a Strategy of Implementation." *The Academy of Management Review*, vol. 1, no. 4, October 1976, pp. 98–112.

*Ronald B. Levy, "The Group Self-Concept, or Socio-Concept," in *Human Relations: A Conceptual Approach* (Scranton: International Textbook, 1969), pp. 7–11.

Norman R. F. Maier, "Assets and Liabilities in Group Problem Solving: The Need for an Integrative Function," *Psychological Review,* vol. 74, no. 4, July 1967, pp. 239–249.

*Edgar H. Schein, "Intergroup Problems in Organization," in *Organizational Psychology,* 2nd ed. (Englewood Cliffs: Prentice-Hall, 1970), pp. 96–103.

Robert Sommer, "Small Group Ecology," *Psychological Bulletin,* vol. 67, 1967, pp. 145–152.

# CASE 28
# Division E

O'Hara Aeronautics was a highly integrated aircraft maintenance organization. Division E was a special engineering branch at O'Hara. It was staffed by four electrical engineers, five engineering technicians, a project leader, two clerks, a quality control specialist, and a chief engineer. The office was involved with the engineering and production of software for automatic computerized testing equipment. Division E was responsible for staff engineering support, which meant they were not involved directly in production. The division was two years old.

O'Hara had contracted for software development with outside firms prior to Division E's formation two years ago. A number of factors caused O'Hara to decide that they could develop in-house capability. Under the pressure of the imminent undertaking of some new contracts, O'Hara set about staffing Division E.

All technicians' positions were filled by transferring men from other divisions (see Exhibits 1, 2, 3). Therefore, none of the technicians had less than fourteen years experience in either his field or some closely related electronics specialty. On the other hand, only one of the four engineers who were needed (Lenny Stokes) was available from within the present organization, and he had only been with O'Hara for about one year. The other engineers eventually hired had varied backgrounds. One had worked for O'Hara for about six months before leaving for military service; he was given an engineering position in Division E upon his return. Two other engineers and one clerk were newly hired when Division E was established.

The remainder of the division was composed of Lester Smithers, a project engineer; Harry Yates, a senior technician and quality control specialist; Sally Ventures, a secretary; and Luke Iler, the Division Chief. Les Smithers and Luke Iler were engineers who had supervised and worked in conjunction with the original contractors and Harry Yates had been a technician involved in automatic testing since its inception. All of these people were associated in some way with the firm's previous contract work. It was not unusual to hear comments around the office about these four persons such as, "They seem to know all the right people," and "Those people were really made for this place." Some of the comments were aimed more directly at Sally. For example, "If you need something done, ask Sally for help. She knows all the people and all the methods of getting things done."

When announcing the establishment of Division E, Michael O'Hara, president of O'Hara Aeronautics, Inc., described its purpose as, "to get projects and develop their test programs and associated test equipment interfaces as

Prepared by H. William Vroman, Towson State University.

## Exhibit 1. Organizational chart.

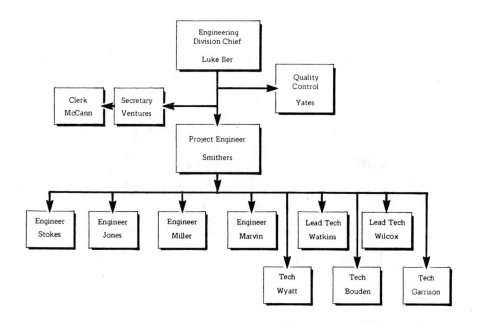

| NAME | POSITION | AGE | YEARS OF SERVICE |
|------|----------|-----|------------------|
| Luke Iler | Supervisor | 35 | 12 |
| Harry Yates | Quality Control | 48 | 23 |
| Sally Ventures | Secretary | 32 | 10 |
| Jane McCann | Clerk | 21 | 2 |
| Lester Smithers | Project Engineer | 38 | 13 |
| Lenny Stokes | Engineer | 28 | 4 |
| Art Jones | Engineer | 30 | 3 |
| John Miller | Engineer | 34 | 2 |
| Clete Marvin | Engineer | 41 | 2 |
| Troy Watkins | Lead Technician | 43 | 17 |
| Jeff Wilcox | Lead Technician | 53 | 26 |
| Greg Wyatt | Technician | 37 | 16 |
| Chuck Bouden | Technician | 34 | 14 |
| Bill Garrison | Technician | 41 | 17 |

## Exhibit 2. Organizational list of employees.

**Exhibit 3.  Seating chart.**

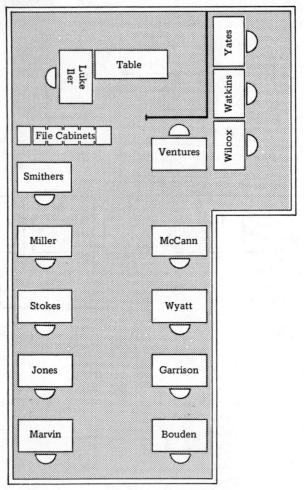

thoroughly and as quickly as possible so that the shop and production facilities will have that knowledge." Mr. O'Hara also expressed hope that Division E would provide assistance to the men in the shop when they encountered technical difficulties. All of the members of Division E seemed to take pride in delivering a complete, neat, and error-free product at all times as indicated in the following exchange.

*Harry:* Les, I think our division is probably the most conscientious at O'Hara.
In general, I'd say we put out some darn good products.
*Les:* I think you're right. Everybody here seems to be trying to set an example for the guys down in production.

The four older technicians were good friends away from the office, and they often socialized at one another's homes. Harry Yates, a former technician, often joined in this socializing. One night, the four technicians and Harry were at Troy Watkins' house (the most frequent meeting place). The conversation turned to the office.

*Troy:* Those engineers sure are cocky, aren't they?

*Jeff:* Yeah, and they average about two years' experience between 'em.

*Troy:* —That compares with our minimum fourteen years' experience. 'Course, they have that degree and that gives you all the know-how you need.

*Jeff:* Yeah, well I've had them come five-six times a week looking for short-cuts and help in programming problems. They know where to come on problems even if they don't acknowledge it.

*Harry:* I'm glad I'm out of the way in the office, that way half the problems miss me. I must confess that I'm confused by their approaches to problems. They just seem to miss the point. Where you guys and the engineers present proposals to the same problem, I'll bet I approve yours most of the time.

*Troy:* Boy, Sally is feeling out-of-it. Maybe we should have invited her over tonight. She was telling me that she doesn't work well with the engineers. Seems they are more compatible with Jane McCann.

*Jeff:* She came in with them—maybe that's why.

*Harry:* One thing though, Troy. Luke Iler has a lot of confidence in you. You're about the first person he talks to when he has a problem.

## A Different View

The engineers usually did not socialize outside the office, even though they got along well at work. Most of their conversations about the office took place over lunch. The following conversation took place at one of their favorite lunch spots.

*Lenny:* Clete, I had what I thought was a beautiful plan for that new project we have been working on. I asked Bill Garrison what he thought of it, and he showed me his plan. Clete, I swear that thing was really ragged. We ended up taking them both to Harry Yates, and guess which plan he approved. Bill's, of course.

*Clete:* I know, Lenny. I would be the first to admit that those technicians have a lot of years of experience, but experience doesn't mean a thing when it comes to new work like you have been doing. That requires free thinking. In some cases their fifteen years' experience is like one year's experience fifteen times.

*Lenny:* The thing that kills me is the way Luke Iler always asks Troy Watkins for his opinion. He never asks any of us.

*John:* Well, you know how it is, Lenny. We can't win for losing. Sometimes it seems that no matter what we do our work won't be accepted.

*Art:* Well, I'm not sure I'd go that far, but it sure is frustrating when we get our work rejected so frequently. By and large, the technicians are pretty good guys.

*Lenny:* I guess you're right, Art. I can see where they could be a lot harder to work with than they are. Say, we've got to get back to the office.

# CASE 29
# The Shipping Department

The men crowded around Chuck Wilcox to welcome him back to the shipping department. Chuck was returning to his old position as department supervisor after a brief period in another location in the plant. Lloyd Roland spoke up, "Damn it, it's good to have you back, Chuck. I still think someone tried to pull a fast one on us. But they should know better than to try to put one over on the boys in the shipping department. We didn't mind it when that efficiency fellow came in here and made a few changes. But Gaylord was just a little too much. We just stuck together and let the plant manager know we wanted you back."

Lloyd Roland had been referring to a series of incidents that had taken place in the shipping department during the last few months. Chuck Wilcox was well liked by the men in his department. Many of them were intensely loyal to him. He was respected as a supervisor and liked as a friend. Chuck was liberal with his men as long as they got their work done. He recognized that most of the workers in the department were close friends. Many of them lived around one another and traveled to and from work together. As a result, he permitted them to talk freely with one another while on the job as long as their conversations did not interfere with accomplishing a day's work. Turnover in the department was low and morale and output were high in spite of low pay and obsolete equipment. Chuck had been supervisor of the department for six years and over that time he, and the men who worked for him, had come to understand and accept one another.

## The Reorganization

Approximately six months earlier, the shipping department was reorganized. Many new men were hired, and much of the obsolete equipment was replaced with new and better equipment. The reorganization itself was supervised by a "trouble-shooter" from the home office. Matthew Johnson was given the authority to make certain decisions regarding new methods, procedures, and the reassignment of jobs. Although he reorganized many of the working stations, he left the work groups themselves intact. At first, there was much concern about the reorganization. However, the workers showed confidence in Johnson and believed that his actions were in their best interest.

When he first arrived in the department, Johnson approached the men in a friendly manner and sought their advice. He worked with Chuck Wilcox and often credited the success of various stages of the changeover to Wilcox and his men. Most workers liked the new ways of doing things and attempted

Prepared by H. William Vroman, Towson State University; and Donald D. White, University of Arkansas.

to make the new system work. Within two weeks after the changeover had been completed, production surged from 4,000 units to 6,000 units a day. After five weeks, production leveled off at 7,000 units per day. Morale in the department seemed to be at an all-time high especially since the men had all received small pay increases.

The new workers who had been hired, with few exceptions, were accepted by the original work group. Satisfaction with the increased output was high, and it was generally conceded that the men had more pride in their work after the reorganization than before the changes had been instituted. This situation was to change dramatically within the next few weeks.

## The "Administrative" Assistant

R. D. Gaylord rambled through the plant without being noticed by most of the workers. Since the reorganization a few months ago, a new face on the work floor was not much of a surprise to anyone. He stopped and talked to a few of the workers and at one point was drawn into a discussion that took place during the morning break. Everyone in the group talked freely never imagining that Gaylord was not "one of them." Later in the day, when Chuck Wilcox returned from a staff meeting, he was approached by one of the workers and questioned about Gaylord. Chuck was somewhat taken aback by the question since he was not familiar with the man in question. After the worker left his office, Chuck phoned the plant manager's office to ask about the new man. The manager was out and his secretary explained that he would not be back until later that afternoon, "He's having lunch with his new administrative assistant, R. D. Gaylord."

The following day, Chuck received a memo from the plant manager's office. The memo directed that a notice be placed on the department bulletin board informing the men that there would be no more talking while on the job. In justification for the decision, it was explained that "the elimination of extraneous conversation was necessary to maintain and ultimately further increase the new production levels." The memo was signed, R.D. Gaylord, Administrative Assistant. Again, Chuck picked up the phone and called the plant manager's office. This time he was able to get through to the manager and ask for an explanation concerning the memo and the newly hired administrative assistant. At once, the plant manager apologized for the fact that Chuck did not know of the new appointment. He explained that Gaylord had been sent by the home office in a surprise move in order to follow up on the reorganization changes that had taken place during the previous few months. The plant manager told Chuck that he had been sent a memo regarding Gaylord two days before but that evidently it had gone astray in the company mailing system. Chuck accepted the explanation of the plant manager and decided to wait and see what further actions, if any, Gaylord might take.

Neither Chuck nor the workers had to wait long. By the end of the week another note had been received by Chuck and signs had been posted throughout his department prohibiting smoking while on the job. The men resented the "No Smoking" signs, and one of the signs was mutilated. Shortly thereafter, Gaylord approached Chuck Wilcox on the parking lot and told him he wanted the man responsible for destroying the sign in his office by Monday morning. He added that he had already talked to a couple of the workers and had told them that they had better comply with the directive if they wished to keep their jobs in the company.

When Chuck arrived at work on Monday morning, he interrupted what sounded like a dull roar coming from the dressing rooms. He stepped inside to see what was going on, and the men immediately began to complain about Gaylord personally telling them what to do. One man stated, "I might not mind hearing things like that from you (referring to Chuck Wilcox), but what the hell is he doing down here in the plant, anyway?" The situation was aggravated further when Gaylord and the plant manager showed up in the department just after lunch. Nothing was said about the incident with the "No Smoking" sign. However, the plant manager informed Chuck that Gaylord would be remaining in the shipping department on a more permanent basis for some time to come. In addition, he told Chuck that Gaylord represented him (the plant manager) and that Chuck and his men "should do whatever Gaylord says."

Gaylord lived up to the men's expectations of him. He began to personally direct the operations of the department. He told the men that the production figures for the department looked good, but that he knew "they could be much better." Since the workers were not used to such close supervision, they began resisting his instructions. Individual workloads mysteriously increased, production records were not complete or were inaccurate and certain "nonsense work" began to complicate the controlling efforts of Chuck Wilcox. Soon Chuck himself was siding with the workers and complaining about Gaylord.

He claimed that Gaylord was inconsistent with his decisions and would sometimes deny even having had the conversation at a later date. Chuck had little recourse against Gaylord and felt that any complaints that he had lodged with the plant manager had fallen on a deaf ear. On one occasion, Chuck even "sabotaged" Gaylord although he felt badly about it, afterward. A call had come in from the plant manager for Gaylord. Chuck answered the phone and told the plant manager that Gaylord "was not around" and that "if this day was like most others, I probably will have tough time finding him around the plant." Actually, Chuck was not lying to the plant manager, since Gaylord sometimes observed the working of the loading dock and other areas in the department by inconspicuously standing away from the activity that he was watching. On the other hand, Chuck knew that Gaylord was never far from the men on the job.

Ironically, Gaylord himself was not aware of the level of animosity that had built up against him. Only in one instance had a subordinate openly confronted him in the shop. At that time, Chuck stepped in and told the man to go back to work. Chuck later stated that he believed the man would have struck Gaylord had he not stepped in.

The straw that broke the camel's back occurred during the week before Christmas. Gaylord advised Chuck that production for the week was far below the department's average output figures. Chuck explained that most of the men probably were thinking about Christmas and that the holiday atmosphere sometimes had a way of disrupting normal activities in the plant. Gaylord was unswayed by Chuck's appeal. He told Chuck that he had decided that the men would have to work the full day on Christmas Eve and would not be permitted to take off early as had originally been planned. He concluded, "If they wanted to get a few hours off on Christmas Eve, they should have thought about it during the week. We simply have to have this production out."

Word of the decision spread rapidly throughout the department. Without warning the men suddenly encircled Gaylord as he was walking through the department. Some of them yelled loudly and shook their fists. Although cooler heads eventually prevailed and there was no violence, a great deal had been said and there could be no mistake in Gaylord's mind about the attitude of the workers toward him. He finally agreed to let them off early on Christmas Eve day as had originally been planned. However, some of the men failed to show up at all when the day arrived. Gaylord was convinced that it was unhealthy to have both him and Chuck in the same department. He explained to the plant manager that he was not sure whether or not Chuck Wilcox had influenced the men against him; but he did believe that it would be better for all concerned if Chuck were transferred out of the department. Chuck was transferred to another department within the plant. A replacement could not be recruited immediately. Therefore, two of the men were given joint supervision of the department. Gaylord hoped that an internal promotion in the department would encourage the workers to improve their output. However, many of the men regarded the move as a ploy. As far as they were concerned, Gaylord was "still calling the shots!"

The two new supervisors were inept at handling their new situation since they had had no previous supervisory training. In addition, some of the workers regarded them as "traitors." Production dropped from the high level of earlier months to a level lower than that which had been achieved before the original reorganization took place a few months earlier.

Eventually, a vice-president from the home office personally intervened and reinstated Chuck into his old position. Gaylord seemed to realize that he had been wrong in the way he had handled many of the situations in the department. He began to spend more time in the office and less time in the shop, and the notes and the speeches to the men soon disappeared. Unfortunately, much of the uneasiness and bitterness that surrounded the events of the past few months remained in the department. The most prominent sign of these ill feelings revolved around the issue of pay. In Chuck's absence, Gaylord had hired a totally inexperienced man and offered him a wage higher than that being payed to some of the more experienced workers in the department. Word about the new employee's wage spread quickly through the department. To date, a number of the workers in the department had filed a grievance demanding wage adjustments.

# CASE 30
# Markham Instrument Company

In the spring of 1959, the management of the Markham Instrument Company was confronted with an impasse in pricing the latest addition to its line of scientific measuring instruments. Markham had two basic product groups, instruments for use in scientific laboratories (Laboratory Products) and industrial instruments for use in manufacturing processes (Industrial Products). The present problem centered around the Dual Sensitivity Level instrument (DSL) which was intended for the more specialized scientific laboratory market.

The line of scientific measuring devices, which the Markham Company introduced in 1924, was adversely affected by the business decline of the 1930s. In 1935, however, the potential for reversing this trend appeared in the form of a major product innovation. A company salesman discovered a young inventor who had developed an electronically controlled measuring device. Markham officials found from comparative tests with their own instrument that the "shoe box" (a name derived from the new instrument's dramatically reduced size) was superior in performance, and they purchased the rights to develop it.

No one at Markham understood the new machine sufficiently to complete its development. Just at this time, however, Alfred Reece (Markham's director of research in 1959) approached the company seeking part-time employment to support his doctoral studies. When he demonstrated a thorough understanding of vacuum-tube technology, he was immediately hired. Working with Roger Finlay (representing sales and engineering) and Caleb Webster (mechanical engineering) he redesigned the "shoe box" until it met scientific and commercial standards.

Several competitors had already introduced comparable electronic devices to the scientific market, but they met considerable customer resistance. Dr. Markham pointed out in retrospect:

The change from electrical controls to a vacuum-tube amplifier was a big one for Markham. Scientists and technicians were against it. We had advertised the electrically controlled version as the only reliable standard regulator, and this had become the general consensus among our customers. Radio types on the market had been widely criticized and we needed strong evidence to justify our change in attitude.

While Markham management believed their "shoe box" to be superior to competitors' electronic machines, they did not rely on this to overcome customer resistance. Instead they appealed to the customers' conservatism, which had been the major factor in blocking acceptance of competitors' machines. The new machine was designed to look and operate as much like the old machine as possible, even to the extent of compromising a few of the advantages of the electronic design. As Finlay said later, "Our customers distrusted the electronic devices which were already on the market, so there was nothing else to do but make ours look and act like the electrical one they were familiar with."

This strategy was successful. Dollar sales volume in 1936 doubled that of 1935, while the number of units actually tripled. Consistent with its past success, however, Markham continued to rely heavily on conscientious customer service to enhance its position in the scientific measurement field. Field sales offices and branch service agencies were set up throughout the country. Company salesmen, continuing their traditional practices, carried customer service to the extremes of repairing competitors' equipment, extending liberal credit and trade-in terms, and offering rapid emergency replacement service.

The next major change in these products occurred in 1946 when the company developed a chemical-sensitive paper, which, among other improvements, eliminated the inconvenient use of recording inks. This development gave Markham a competitive advantage and simultaneously, due to sole control of the paper supply, provided an increase in profit margins. During this period a portable measuring device long sought by scientific field workers was also developed. Although these innovations gave Markham a technical lead, the company still depended on customer service for the basic maintenance of its market position.

During the early 1950s competitors began work on a machine that gave the scientist the option of measuring either of two sensitivity levels simply by throwing a switch. In 1957, the competitors' development work reached fruition and these dual sensitivity level (DSL) machines were introduced commercially. Markham was not disturbed by this new feature on competitive instruments, since potential applications for the additional sensitivity level were extremely limited. Furthermore, management's attention was diverted from this development by the addition to its own line of a transistorized portable, 40 percent lighter than any then available. This machine's compactness was expected to attract scientists engaged in field experiments, while its price, flexibility, and reliability were expected to make it also a machine of the limited applications the customers had for the DSL feature.

During 1958, requests from the field for a DSL became more frequent, and Herb Olson (sales vice-president) began pressing for a reversal of the decision not to produce such a device. He pointed out that salesmen were becoming increasingly embarrassed by customer insistence on DSL features. In view of these increasing requests, Roger Finlay (president) became convinced in the fall of 1958 that Markham should add a DSL to its line, if only to satisfy the gadget appeal of such an innovation. Since the older standard machines were continuing to sell, and since the development of a transistorized

DSL was still problematical, it was decided to proceed with a DSL redesign of the older machine.

Shortly after making the decision to go ahead with a DSL, Roger Finlay met with Herb Olson, Alfred "Doc" Reece (director of research and design, R&D), Caleb Webster (in charge of mechanical design of the DSL), and Bill Reynolds (responsible for electronic design). Finlay told the three R&D men that while he was anxious to get the new machine into production as quickly as possible, the company's reputation was also involved, so that it would be necessary to do the usual careful job. Reece asked if all the same features that were in the standard would be included in the DSL. Finlay replied that while the DSL was to be patterned after the standard model, he wanted all the latest features included. Herb Olson explained that although the DSL was to be offered at approximately the same price as the standard model, they would still have to maintain the traditional external appearance and features of the DSL. In response to a question from Doc Reece, Olson pointed out that they were not too concerned with the weight of the DSL, since it was not to be a portable. As the meeting ended, Reece indicated that they would have to do some careful planning to keep costs down, but he was sure it could be done. Webster and Reynolds agreed, stating that they thought the design could be completed by the end of the year.

In spite of this optimistic appraisal, the members of the research and development department did not greet the decision to redesign the older machine with unrestrained enthusiasm. In the first place, they felt that completing the redesign of the transistorized machine would be ultimately feasible and would be more technically stimulating. Second, they had several other challenging ideas which they believed would place the company in the growing space and missile field. The redesign of the standard machine would cause them to put aside these more exciting projects for several months.

In spite of these reservations, design work went ahead on the DSL. Meanwhile, inquiries and complaints from the field about the delay in offering a DSL continued to come into the home office. While many sales personnel blamed R&D for the delay, Herb Olson explained the problem differently.

All these problems that the laboratory salesmen are having aren't just the fault of engineering. Top management simply didn't think the DSL was important. Well, this was a mistake. Of course, when this happens the people out in the field get to feeling sore and they come ask us why we don't have the equipment.

Ed Greene expressed a similar view.

Sollie (a formerly influential but now deceased member of R&D) was screaming four years ago for a DSL, but top management could see no need for it. Now all the machines on the market have this feature and we are breaking our neck trying to catch up.

The development work on the DSL machine was completed by the end of 1958, and late in January 1959, production received the information it needed to establish production methods and estimate costs. By early March, cost estimates had been completed by the production department, and a meeting was arranged for the morning of March 6 to discuss the DSL selling price. The ten executives named in the seating chart (Exhibit 1) were all present when the meeting started, except Mr. Webster, who arrived later.

Willard Tierney, acting as chairman, opened the meeting by asking Ed Greene to present his cost estimates. Greene's initial position (which he maintained throughout the meeting) was that the DSL was more expensive than had been expected. He concluded his presentation by saying, "You are going to have to sell this machine for a lot more than you thought. I think these figures are sound. If anything, we have been too loose in our estimates and the figures are too low. We can't lower them any more."

Herb Olson took a different position, maintaining that something had to be done to lower costs so the new machine could be sold at a realistic price. Representative of his remarks is the following statement: "The fact that the figures are sound isn't going to help us meet competition. The way you (others at the meeting) are talking we would have to sell this machine for $1,000. If we did that our volume would go to hell in a hand basket."

Olson was not alone in finding the costs higher than expected. Caleb Webster remarked, "I am really surprised at these estimates. I didn't think they would be that high." Doc Reece also felt the estimates were higher than he had thought they would be. Bill Reynolds, on the other hand, found the estimates realistic as far as the electronic parts were concerned. "I'm not at all surprised at Ed's figures, because I knew what they would be from my design work."

Confronted with this impasse, Tierney summarized the situation at the

**Exhibit 1.  Seating arrangement, pricing meeting, March 6, 1959.**

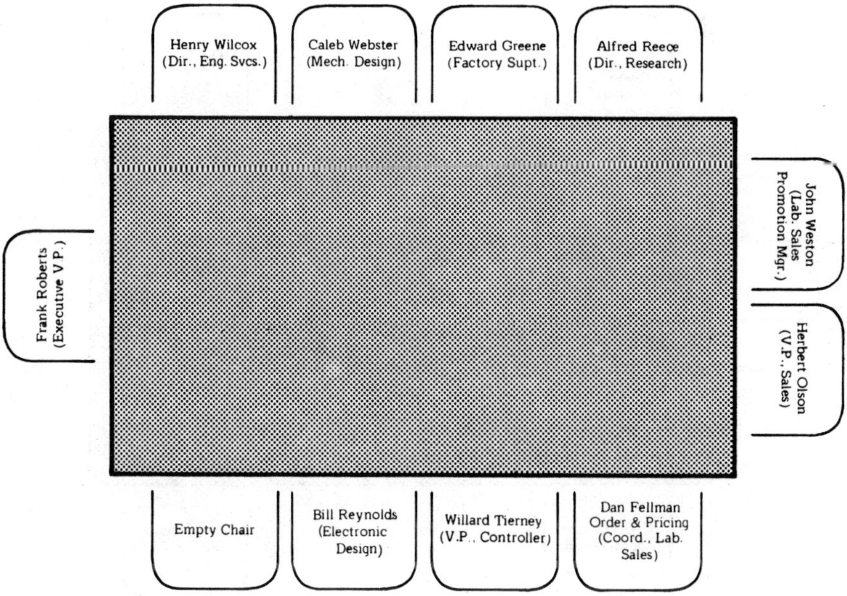

end of the meeting: "I didn't think we could arrive at a decision today, and it doesn't look like we will, so why don't we adjourn and meet again next week? Meanwhile, Ed [Greene], Dan [Fellman], and Doc [Reece] can check over these costs to see if we can reduce them."

As the meeting broke up, Olson remarked, "If we can't do something about these costs, you guys can take it [the DSL] out in the field and give it to the salesmen yourselves. I won't do it."

During the next week Reece, Greene, and Fellman reviewed the cost estimates, and on March 13 a second meeting was held. The participants arranged themselves around the conference table as shown in Exhibit 2. Willard Tierney again served as chairman and opened the meeting by explaining that Doc Reece, Ed Greene, and Dan Fellman had agreed to certain minor changes in the DSL and that they now felt that it could be produced at $110 more than the standard. (This figure represented a decrease of $35 from the highest figure quoted at the previous meeting.) On this basis, Tierney proposed that the DSL be priced at $875, $90 more than the standard. After he completed his remarks there was a full minute of silence, which Caleb Webster interrupted:

*Webster:* "I still don't understand. I'd like to know where the big differences lie because I didn't think it would be that much."
*Tierney:* "Doc, can you itemize these so we will all know what they are in detail?"

Reece and Greene then spent several minutes explaining the costs of various components, as well as the basis for their estimate of assembly costs.

**Exhibit 2. Seating arrangement, pricing meeting, March 13, 1959.**

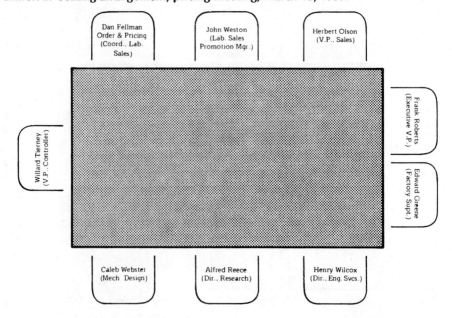

Webster, however, remained unconvinced. Tierney suggested that he and Greene work together to discover if further cost savings were possible.

*Greene:* I don't think there are many big changes we can make. It has been cut to the bone already.

*Olson:* Well, for example, look at that little trap door. It costs a lot of money.

Several minutes were devoted to the costs of the door which Roger Finlay had suggested to improve appearance and operating access. No one suggested changing the door, and the discussion then centered on the differences between the two models. Doc Reece concluded his explanation of the major causes for the difference:

*Reece:* Look, there is twice as much shop time for parts on the DSL as there is on the old one. That is a big part of the difference. (*Pauses.*) Sitting around the table here we aren't going to remove Caleb's [Webster] doubts about the reasons for this big difference. We thought it would be less than $25 and it turns out to be between $90 and $120.

The meeting then divided into several conversations. Herb Olson and Frank Roberts talked together with John Weston listening; Doc Reece and Ed Greene carried on a conversation with Henry Wilcox listening. The others waited. After several minutes Roberts addressed the entire group.

*Roberts:* It appears to me that you aren't going to change the spots on the leopard. We have to fix a realistic price. You have all the estimates you can get.

In spite of this statement, discussion about cost differences continued with Reece and Greene furnishing more details to Webster about the costs of subassemblies. Roberts interrupted this discussion.

*Roberts:* We haven't heard from Herb [Olson]. He's probably got a lot to say.

Olson joked with the group, and then began to discuss the competitive aspects of the situation.

*Olson:* We have to consider the selling price of this machine in comparison to competition. Competitors are selling their machines at between $440 and $460 to the dealers, which means they are about $800 at retail. Measuretech (a competitor) retails at $785, and their machine does everything our does. Of course, like everyone else, they offer discounts. Whatever we do, we have to be in the ball park on the initial list price. Perhaps controlling trade-ins will help some.

*Roberts:* What do you think this price should be?

*Olson:* Oh, I suppose about $795, that's only $10 above the standard model.

Roberts, Wilcox, and Tierney then discussed the minimum DSL selling price. They agreed that using estimated costs, it would be necessary to price it at $875 to obtain the normal margin. Wilcox proposed that they set a target for cutting costs through redesigning the machine, because he thought cabinet and purchase part costs could then be reduced in this manner. Olson supported this proposal, but Tierney disagreed.

*Tierney:* I don't know what we can find. Ed [Greene] has made a careful estimate and there is still a $110 difference.

*Roberts:* Well, maybe it is just being hopeful, but I think we should do what Henry [Wilcox] suggests.

*Reece:* All Ed can control is the shop costs, shop time, and assembly time. I don't think there is much fat in any of these figures.

*Webster:* I still can't see why the machine should be that high. The mechanical costs should be much less.

*Greene:* Let him [Webster] go somewhere to figure and add them up. Then he'll see. Damned if I'll give him any of my figures.

*Tierney:* You know, I still would feel more comfortable pricing it at $875. Otherwise I think we might be cutting it too close.

*Olson:* Competition is rough in this line, Will. $850 sounds much better than $875. Even at $850 we will have to work like hell to beat Asprey and some of the others.

*Greene:* I'll tell you this, I'd still rather build that Asprey machine than ours.

The relative merits of competitors' machines were then discussed. The consensus was that competition was making the same machine, selling it at about $75 less than the $875 figure which had been suggested for the DSL. Olson suggested that Webster be allowed to restudy the design to see if he could reduce the cost so that the DSL could be priced at $850. Tierney replied.

*Tierney:* All right, maybe we should call this meeting off, and give Caleb [Webster] a chance to satisfy himself.

*Roberts:* That's just a waste of time. Let's get this settled.

Greene and Wilcox also objected to further study and Tierney withdrew his proposal.

*Tierney:* You're right. After all, we have never priced any instrument with as much information as we have on this one.

*Olson:* That really doesn't make any difference. We still have to get the price down where we can sell it.

Tierney then continued the discussion of competitors' machines and prices. There was general agreement that the Simpson Company had, at $785, the best DSL on the market. Olson expressed particular concern about the advantage competitors had because of the light weight of their machines.

*Olson:* Look at these competitors' weights. Simpson's only weighs 20 pounds, while ours will be 34 pounds. Even Asprey's is 10 pounds less than ours. This is an important selling point and we can't ignore it.

*Reece:* Damn it, don't start talking weights at this point. We were told from the start that they weren't important.

*Tierney:* Herb [Olson], what do you think the end user pays for an Asprey?

*Olson:* Anywhere from $650 up. It depends entirely upon the deal and the trade-in. I was just wondering, though, if maybe we haven't got too many features on this machine. After all, it is supposed to be sold as a general purpose machine.

*Reece:* We designed it according to what sales wanted. We have to go by what you fellows need. The trouble is that around here everybody wants everything with a frosting on it.

*Olson:* Right, and then we price ourselves out of the market.

*Tierney:* It seems to me that we had better change our whole official attitude if this is the way our market and our competition are acting.

*Greene:* O.K. Then we ought to start with an estimate of the market and the price and then design within that.

*Olson:* That's exactly what got us into this mess. The district managers are really going to be unhappy about this one. Finlay told them the DSL would be available at $800, and now you are talking about a minimum of $50 or $75 more than this. They aren't going to be happy about pushing this one. I still would like to see Caleb [Webster] take another crack at cutting the cost.

*Roberts:* Doc, can you and the mechanic [Webster] take another shot at redesign after we get it into production? Maybe we can reduce costs then.

*Tierney:* I think that is wishful thinking. We have to resolve this on the basis of the information we have.

# CASE 31
## The Case of the Changing Cage

### Part I

The voucher-check filing unit was a work unit in the home office of the Atlantic Insurance Company. The assigned task of the unit was to file checks and vouchers written by the company as they were cashed and returned. This filing was the necessary foundation for the main function of the unit, locating any particular check for examination upon demand. There were usually eight to ten requests for specific checks from as many different departments during the day. One of the most frequent reasons checks were requested from the unit was to determine whether checks in payment of claims against the company had been cashed. Thus efficiency in the unit directly affected customer satisfaction with the company. Complaints or inquiries about payments could not be answered with the accuracy and speed conducive to client satisfaction unless the unit could supply the necessary document immediately.

Toward the end of 1952, nine workers manned this unit. There was an assistant (a position equivalent to a foreman in a factory) named Miss Dunn, five other full-time employees, and three part-time workers.

The work area of the unit was well defined. Walls bounded the unit on three sides. The one exterior wall was pierced by light-admitting, north windows. The west interior partition was blank. A door opening into a corridor pierced the south interior partition. The east side of the work area was enclosed by a steel mesh reaching from wall to wall and floor to ceiling. This open metal barrier gave rise to the customary name of the unit, "The Voucher Cage." A sliding door through this mesh gave access from the unit's territory to the work area of the rest of the company's agency audit division, of which it was a part, located on the same floor.

The unit's territory was kept inviolate by locks on both doors, fastened at all times. No one not working within the cage was permitted inside unless his name appeared on a special list in the custody of Miss Dunn. The door through the steel mesh was used generally for departmental business. Messengers and runners from other departments usually came to the corridor door and pressed a buzzer for service.

The steel mesh font was reinforced by a rank of metal filing cases where checks were filed. Lined up just inside the barrier, they hid the unit's workers from the view of workers outside their territory, including the section head responsible for over-all supervision of this unit according to the company's plan for operation.

Reproduced by permission of the Society for Applied Anthropology, from *Human Organization*, vol. 16, no. 1, 1957.

## Part II

On top of the cabinets which were backed against the steel mesh, one of the male employees in the unit neatly stacked pasteboard boxes in which checks were transported to the cage. They were later reused to hold older checks sent into storage. His intention was less getting these boxes out of the way than increasing the effective height of the sight barrier so the section head could not see into the cage "even when he stood up."

The girls stood at the door of the cage which led into the corridor and talked to the messenger boys. Out this door also the workers slipped unnoticed to bring in their customary afternoon snack. Inside the cage, the workers sometimes engaged in a good-natured game of rubber band "sniping."

Workers in the cage possessed good capacity to work together consistently and workers outside the cage often expressed envy of those in it because of the "nice people" and friendly atmosphere there. The unit had no apparent difficulty keeping up with its work load.

## Part III

For some time prior to 1952 the controller's department of the company had not been able to meet its own standards of efficient service to clients. Company officials felt the primary cause to be spatial. Various divisions of the controller's department were scattered over the entire 22-story company building. Communication between them required phone calls, messengers, or personal visits, all costing time. The spatial separation had not seemed very important when the company's business volume was smaller prior to World War II. But business had grown tremendously since then and spatial separation appeared increasingly inefficient.

Finally in November of 1952 company officials began to consolidate the controller's department by relocating two divisions together on one floor. One was the agency audit division, which included the voucher-check filing unit. As soon as the decision to move was made, lower level supervisors were called in to help with planning. Line workers were not consulted, but were kept informed by the assistants of planning progress. Company officials were concerned about the problem of transporting many tons of equipment and some 200 workers from two locations to another single location without disrupting work flow. So the move was planned to occur over a single weekend, using the most efficient resources available. Assistants were kept busy planning positions for files and desks in the new location.

Desks, files, chairs, and even wastebaskets were numbered prior to the move, and relocated according to a master chart checked on the spot by the assistant. Employees were briefed as to where the new location was and which elevators they should take to reach it. The company successfully transported the paraphernalia of the voucher-check filing unit from one floor to another over the weekend. Workers in the cage quit Friday afternoon at the old stand, reported back Monday at the new.

The exterior boundaries of the new cage were still three building walls and the steel mesh, but the new cage possessed only one door—the sliding door through the steel mesh into the work area of the rest of the agency audit division. The territory of the cage had also been reduced in size. An entire bank of filing cabinets had to be left behind in the old location to be taken over by the unit moving there. The new cage was arranged so that there was no longer a row of metal filing cabinets lined up inside the steel mesh obstructing the view into the cage.

## Part IV

When the workers in the cage inquired about the removal of the filing cabinets from along the steel mesh fencing, they found that Mr. Burke had insisted that these cabinets be rearranged so his view into the cage would not be obstructed by them. Miss Dunn had tried to retain the cabinets in their prior position, but her efforts had been overridden.

Mr. Burke disapproved of conversation. Since he could see workers conversing in the new cage, he "requested" Miss Dunn to put a stop to all unnecessary talk. Attempts by female clerks to talk to messenger boys brought the wrath of her superior down on Miss Dunn, who was then forced to reprimand the girls.

Mr. Burke also disapproved of an untidy working area, and any boxes or papers which were in sight were a source of annoyance to him. He did not exert supervision directly, but would "request" Miss Dunn to "do something about those boxes." In the new cage, desks had to be completely cleared at the end of the day, in contrast to the work-in-progress piles left out in the old cage. Boxes could not accumulate on top of filing cases.

The custom of afternoon snacking also ran into trouble. Lacking a corridor door, the food bringers had to venture forth and pack back their snack tray through the work area of the rest of their section, bringing this hitherto unique custom to the attention of workers outside the cage. The latter promptly recognized the desirability of afternoon snacks and began agitation for the same privilege. This annoyed the section head, who forbade workers in the cage from continuing this custom.

## Part V

Mr. Burke later made a rule which permitted one worker to leave the new cage at a set time every afternoon to bring up food for the rest. This rigidity irked cage personnel, accustomed to a snack when the mood struck, or none at all. Having made his concession to the cage force, Mr. Burke was unable to prevent workers outside the cage from doing the same thing. What had once been unique to the workers in the cage was now common practice in the section.

Although Miss Dunn never outwardly expressed anything but compliance and approval of superior directives, she exhibited definite signs of anxiety. All the cage workers reacted against Burke's increased domination. When he imposed his decisions upon the voucher-check filing unit, he became "Old Grandma" to its personnel. The cage workers sneered at him and ridiculed him behind his back. Workers who formerly had obeyed company policy as a matter of course began to find reasons for loafing and obstructing work in the new cage. One of the changes that took place in the behavior of the workers had to do with their game of rubber band sniping. All knew Mr. Burke would disapprove of this game. It became highly clandestine and fraught with dangers. Yet shooting rubber bands increased.

Newly arrived checks were put out of sight as soon as possible, filed or not. Workers hid unfiled checks, generally stuffing them into desk drawers or unused file drawers. Since boxes were forbidden, there were fewer unused file drawers than there had been in the old cage. So the day's work was sometimes undone when several clerks hastily shoved vouchers and checks indiscriminately into the same file drawer at the end of the day.

Before a worker in the cage filed incoming checks, she measured with her ruler the thickness in inches of each bundle she filed. At the end of each day she totaled her input and reported it to Miss Dunn. All incoming checks were measured upon arrival. Thus Miss Dunn had a rough estimate of unit intake compared with file input. Theoretically she was able to tell at any time how much unfiled material she had on hand and how well the unit was keeping up with its task. Despite this running check, when the annual inventory of unfiled checks on hand in the cage was taken at the beginning of the calendar year 1953, a seriously large backlog of unfiled checks was found. To the surprise and dismay of Miss Dunn, the inventory showed the unit to be far behind schedule, filing much more slowly than before relocation of the cage.

# EXPERIENTIAL EXERCISE 12

## NASA Exercise

As you approach the moon for a rendezvous with the mother ship, the lateral dissimilator malfunctions, forcing your ship and crew to land some 17 craters, or 145 earth miles, from the mother ship. The touchdown results in a great deal of damage to the ship but, luckily, none to the crew. Survival is dependent upon reaching the mother ship. The most critical items must be chosen for the trip.

*Instructions*

Below are the only fifteen items left intact after the landing. Rank order the items in the importance they hold to you and your crew in reaching the rendezvous point. Place *1* by the most important item, *2* by the next most important, and so on, through all fifteen items. You should complete this section in ten minutes.

| Your Decision | Articles | Group Decision |
|---|---|---|
| _____ | box of matches | _____ |
| _____ | food concentrate | _____ |
| _____ | 50 feet of nylon rope | _____ |
| _____ | parachute silk | _____ |
| _____ | portable heating unit | _____ |
| _____ | two .45 caliber pistols | _____ |
| _____ | one case dehydrated pet milk | _____ |
| _____ | two 100-pound tanks of oxygen | _____ |
| _____ | stellar map (of the moon's constellation) | _____ |
| _____ | self-inflating life raft | _____ |
| _____ | magnetic compass | _____ |
| _____ | 5 gallons water | _____ |
| _____ | signal flares | _____ |
| _____ | first aid kit containing injection needles | _____ |
| _____ | solar powered FM receiver-transmitter | _____ |

*Group Instructions*

Because you have to survive as a group, the most appropriate decision making is group consensus. The rank order has to be agreed upon by each member of the group. Because the consequences of wrong decision are so severe—death—you want to be as logical as you can and avoid arguments. In addition, you want to be sure only to agree with that ranking that somewhat meets your solution. Be sure not to employ any voting, averaging, or trading techniques that might stifle and embitter one of your companions on this survival journey.

## Scoring

1. Subtract the group score on each item from your individual score on each item. Write down the difference. For example, you put down an item as 3 on your list, and the group ended up ranking it 6. There is net difference of 3.
2. Add all the net differences together to get your pair score.
3. Collect all the scores in the group, add them, then divide by the number of people in the group.

YOUR NET DIFFERENCE SCORE _____

AVERAGE INDIVIDUAL SCORE _____

    0–20   Excellent
  20–30   Good
  30–40   Average
  40–50   Fair
over 50   Poor

Now take the correct NASA computed rankings and compare the group ranking with it, computing the net difference between the group and the correct ranking.

NET DIFFERENCE SCORE—GROUP AND CORRECT _____

What do these differences mean?

# EXPERIENTIAL EXERCISE 13
## The Bomb Shelter

### The Situation

Your group is the Area Civil Defense Council located in an underground head-quarters in charge of several bomb shelters. The area has just withstood a nuclear attack with a very high incidence of Strontium 89. There are now people in the fallout shelters. You have radio communication with most of the shelters under your jurisdiction.

In one shelter, which has oxygen, supplies, and equipment for a maximum of seven people, there are twelve people. The supplies and equipment, however, will sustain life for the anticipated shelter stay of four to five months.

The only information you have about the occupants of the shelter in question are contained in sketchy personnel files on each of the persons.

### The Task

Your task as a group is to reach a consensus decision on which seven people may remain in the shelter: five persons must be ejected from the shelter. (You do have means of ejecting them.) You must decide who may stay and who must leave. In addition, be prepared to explain your reasons for choosing the persons who must leave and the persons who may stay.

### Biographic Information

1. Dr. Irving Bernstein, M.D., is 36 years old and a renowned surgeon. His wife and child are reported to be safe in another shelter.
2. Fr. James Miller is the pastor of a Catholic Church. He is 64 years old. Previously, he taught theology at a Catholic university.
3. Collins Green, a computer technician, was honorably discharged from the army six years ago. He has a thorough understanding and knowledge of electronic components and equipment. During Mr. Green's attendance at a vocational high school, he was considered a "militant black activist." He is 34 years of age and is not married.
4. Cathy Brian is 21 years old and seven months pregnant. No one knows whether her husband survived the attack. Cathy seems very upset and somewhat emotionally unstable. She has become hysterical on two occasions. Dr. Bernstein had to sedate her. She continually screams that she must "save her baby."
5. George Stuart is a black businessman; he is very prominent in the black business community and an influential member of the state legislature. Last year, he reportedly gave $20,000 to Boy Scouting activities. He is also noted for his contributions to the poor.

Prepared by Eugene C. McCann.

6. Shelly Johnson is a 14-year-old student. Evidently, she had slight brain damage in an automobile accident which has put her in a "slow learner" category. For the past two to two and a half years she has caused a lot of problems for her parents—she has become a "problem child." Her parents and two younger sisters are in another shelter.

7. Colonel Thomas Kelley, age 45, is one of the top military advisers in the Department of Defense. He has assumed command of shelter activities and seems to have activities and duties organized and assigned. In our last communication with the people in the shelter, Col. Kelley said people were somewhat upset by his rationing of food and water, but he felt they should conserve it "just in case."

8. Alex Saslov was the military adviser to the Russian ambassador in Washington. About five years ago, however, he defected to the West. At 39, he is an outstanding authority on radioactive materials.

9. Jim Tyler, who supposedly has cancer, is the only person who has experience in operating and maintaining a radio transmitter. Mr. Tyler has one son who lives in California.

10. Herbert Wigner, a Jew, is a graduate of a West German university whose academic background is in physics. Several years ago he was nominated for a Nobel Prize in science.

11. Raymond Dexter is a very husky 29-year-old man who was convicted of rape. He was recently released on parole after having served eight years of a life sentence, with time off as a result of being considered a "model prisoner." He has been attending a local junior college where he is learning fish hatchery operations and management.

12. George Arnet is a healthy, robust 66-year-old widower. Even at his age, he is very much concerned with physical fitness. He exercises daily and maintains his job as an auto mechanic. Mr. Arnet is also a health food advocate and eats mostly organic foods. It is noted that he has four children and seven grandchildren.

# CHAPTER NINE

# Organizational Conflict and Stress

Organizations are rational, goal-directed groups of persons attempting to accomplish complex tasks. Rational or instrumental behavior normally characterizes the activities of people in organizations. However, incidents such as people arguing with one another, "getting called on the carpet," power struggles, labor walkouts, and even physiological and psychological breakdowns are commonplace. The job of organizing people into a goal-directed unit can be difficult.

Herbert Simon[1] suggests that the difficulties experienced by humans in organizations result from two sources. First, humans have limited rationality. The cumulative intelligence of the managers in an organization is not enough to solve all problems perfectly. Second, organizational phenomena occur in a complex fashion, but humans prefer to deal with their problems one at a time, or sequentially. Naturally many problems do not get handled in a timely way, creating additional pressures and conflicts.

Conflict does not have to be thought of as undesirable or counterproductive. Not all differences of opinion must be resolved on a win-lose basis. A view of conflict that is gaining popularity holds that a controlled or optimal level of dissatisfaction with a situation, a system, or another individual may actually benefit an organization. Consistent with this interpretation is the belief that progress can be achieved and creativity stimulated only if the proper level of conflict exists within an enterprise. Even so, determining and arriving at the desired level of conflict is a major problem facing those who attempt to put the theory into practice.

Chapter Nine is concerned with the existence of conflict in organizations and the stress that the enterprise and other influences create for the individual. Conflict, planned or otherwise, results from the way an organization is managed. Stress is the personal reaction of humans to their environment and its impact on them.

## Conflict Cycles

Conflict is a dynamic occurrence that can be found in all organizations to a greater or lesser extent. Its nature is cyclical,[2] with one conflict setting the stage for the next encounter. The more sensitive people become to repeated conflicts, the more subsequent conflict is likely to occur. Conflict may affect an individual before becoming open by creating feelings of stress or tension.

Managers play an important role in conflict episodes because they react to the conflict when it becomes open. If they react properly, the resolution may lead to future cooperation instead of future conflict. However, inappropriate responses result in unresolved conflicts and may precede yet another conflict cycle.

Figure 1 illustrates the cycle from latent conflict to open conflict. Latent conflict underlies all conflicts and influences all interactions and activities in an organization. Sometimes we sense conflict but don't know exactly what the problem is. The tension may create a search process to bring the source of the difficulty to the perceived level. However, the course of conflict to the open level is unpredictable. In healthy organizations the cycle may stop at the aware level, as people openly discuss and resolve issues. On the other hand, if the search process is inadequate, the cycle may progress to open and disruptive organizational conflict.

### Latent Conflict

Certain conditions which precede or accompany open conflict exist in all organizational settings. These conditions are formal differences in authority and power, scarcity of necessary resources, and a lack of clarity or agreement on goals. They are referred to as types of latent conflict. Differences in authority occur because of the way organizations structure to face their environments. Jealousy and competition between superiors and subordinates sometimes create the conditions for potential conflict. Scarcity of money, people, and materials also may create intrigue and competition for existing resources.

Clarifying goals is difficult in complex organizations. Although a goal

**Figure 1. Dynamics of conflict. Adapted from Lonis Pandy, "Organization Conflict: Concepts and Models," ADMINISTRATIVE SCIENCE QUARTERLY, vol. 12, pp. 296–320.**

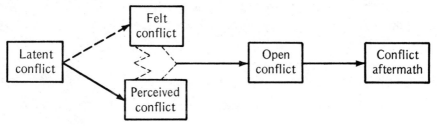

may have been written properly in the first place, transmitting its spirit and its letter to subordinates may still be difficult. The situation is made more complicated when subordinates do not agree with the goal. Latent conflict exists within all organizations. Healthy organizations recognize and attempt to deal with latent conflict conditions before their impact becomes disruptive. Other enterprises do not handle latent conflict effectively. In these cases, conflict evolves to either a felt or perceived level.

### Felt Conflict

An uneasy feeling that something is wrong, with an inability to put a finger on the problem, is felt conflict. Anger or distrust of peers is one feeling that often indicates a felt conflict. Sometimes a search for the cause of discomfort brings awareness. However, formal rules or informal norms that create severe anxiety for a person may prevent the search from taking place. People live with the discomfort because they fear the consequences of pursuing the source of their difficulty. At some point, even these suppressed felt conflicts are manifested by blowing up, quitting, or possibly becoming ill.

A low level of anxiety (feeling of inner tension) may be experienced when the situation is not seen as being too important. Under these circumstances, the individual may not even be motivated to search for the source of discomfort. In other instances, feelings of discomfort might be lost in a flurry of other types of activity. The individual may suffer minor consequences from the conflict. However, those consequences often take place at the unconscious level.

### Perceived Conflict

An individual may be consciously aware that he or she is involved in competition for resources or for symbols of status, but may not be bothered significantly by the situation. Perceived conflict differs from felt conflict in that an individual may be aware of a conflict situation without experiencing discomfort from it. As the model indicates, perceived conflict may lead to discomfort (felt conflict). Likewise, experiencing anxiety over a situation may lead to an awareness of the conflict conditions (perceived conflict). A very rational and cool manager might even plan an open conflict to achieve some other personal or unit objective. However, the competition could begin to affect one's behavior adversely if it continued over a long period of time. Conflict, then, may proceed from the perceived and/or felt stages, to open conflict.

### Open Conflict

Not all conflict becomes open conflict. Conflict may be kept at the personal level. Bad situations disappear, the reasons for conflict are understood and ignored, meetings are held, resources are reallocated, or people simply leave the conflict environment. Thus, conflict cycles can be softened or stopped.

Conflict at the personal level can be a cause for concern by managers. However, open conflict within an organization *is* the concern of all managers. Open conflict might take the form of a verbal altercation, blatant violation of a company rule or policy, or merely a gathering of sympathetic individuals. In any of these situations, the usual managerial response is to deal directly with the conflict itself. Unfortunately, this is often an incorrect response. A cycle that reaches the open stage generally has a long history. If the conflict is relevant to organizational matters, a manager should look back beyond the actual (open) conflict to the conditions (latent) or stages (felt, perceived) that have led to the present situation.

*Aftermath.* Every conflict in an organization becomes part of its history. This history is remembered by the participants in the organization and by those who deal with the organization. Stories of conflict are documented and passed on from older to newer employees. General distrust or suspicion of the actions of others enhances the possibility of conflict and is the residue left after an unsatisfactorily resolved open conflict. On the other hand, open conflict that causes the organization to solve a major problem can leave as its aftermath a problem solving means for positively and effectively resolving future conflicts.

## Role Conflict

Organizational members play roles[3] designed by their places in the organization hierarchy and defined by certain activities and interaction patterns. These factors define roles that limit behaviors a person exhibits while on the job. Other enduring factors—like organization factors (rules, regulations, standards, policies), group norms, and personality factors—form the backdrop for formal interactions and activities. Role participants have many people in daily interaction with them. This interaction creates instances of personal conflict for the participant. The question is: how does the person resolve conflicts that occur during the natural course of being in an organizational role?

Figure 2 illustrates the dynamics of role conflict and the way enduring factors affect the interactions between role occupants. Sender A communicates an expectation to B. At several points the expectation can result in something less than that intended by sender A. First, the communication must be sent in a clear manner. A has to articulate or write the expectation clearly so that B can understand it. After the expectation is sent to B, B must perceive the message expectation as A sent it. However, perception is imperfect. B may have preferences that cause him or her to see things with a certain bias, thus resulting in a distortion of the expectation. In addition, enduring factors can interfere with the expectation. For example, B will listen more closely if A is a respected superior than if A is a peer or subordinate.

**Figure 2. Role conflict model.**

Group norms can affect the message B receives. If group norms are "work slowly," then A's message to speed up will not be heeded. Personality conflicts, also, often interfere with B's understanding. On the other hand, the organization, group, and personality factors may be supportive of expectations in healthy organizations.

After receiving the expectation and perceiving it in light of enduring factors, B responds (or fails to respond), providing feedback to A. The feedback is interpreted by A in relation to the original expectation and influences A's future communications. A may choose to send another expectation if the behavior isn't what was expected.

There are different types of role conflict:[4] intra-sender conflicts, person-value conflicts, inter-sender conflicts, and inter-role conflicts. Briefly, they take the following forms. *Intra-sender conflict* may take place when Superior A tells subordinate B, "Fill the order for Harris in an hour." Subordinate B knows, however, that the task requires a minimum of two hours. In intra-sender conflict, the sender's communication (message) contains an inherent contradiction, thereby creating a conflict for the receiver.

*Person-value conflict* may take place if A tells B, "Go to the Accounting Department and bribe someone to allocate more expenses to Fred's department than mine." Here, values and expected actions are inconsistent with one another.

*Inter-sender conflict* takes place when an individual receives opposing expectations from two senders. For example, a project manager tells an engineer to complete the project as quickly as possible in order to go on to something else. At the same time, this same engineer receives a memo from the chief engineer instructing him, "Stay with that project until you get it right." Such was the situation in "The Case of Two Masters" (Case 15) in Chapter Four of this book.

Finally, an individual may experience *inter-role conflict*. People have more than one role in life. A single parent may be the merchandising manager for a large department store. If her child becomes ill, the manager may be in conflict over which role to assume: "Do I stay home with my sick child, or do I go to work and meet with an important out-of-town supplier?"

The situations illustrated here place individuals in a position where they must weigh conflicting instructions, values, or behaviors that may be related to specific roles and determine what pattern of activities is most effective and most appropriate in a given instance. Individuals may recognize the quandary they are placed in and may avoid conflict by pretending to be ignoring a request. On the other hand, openly discussing the problem with a superior or some other person involved in the situation may help alleviate the conflict. Unfortunately, chains of events sometimes take place too rapidly for discussions and consultations to take place. In addition, personality or general climate factors may cause an individual to fear approaching other parties who are involved.

## Stress in Organizations

Organizational situations place considerable demands on their members. At times, these demands may seem to have no limits. However, we as human beings have only a certain amount of energy to expend. This imbalance between the resources that we can commit to an organization and the resources that are sometimes demanded of us can have a variety of impacts on our personal and organizational lives. The impact may be positive. We may respond by rising to the occasion. However, too often the impact is negative, resulting in poor decision making, inhibited communication, or generally diminished job performance. Even more far-reaching are physical and psychological disorders that may stem from such pressures.

### The Dynamics of Stress

A relatively new term for dealing with the impact of life situations on the individual is *stress*. Stress is a global term which includes stressors outside the body, the interpretation of those stressors, and the reaction of the body to them. Individuals react differently to stress-creating situations. One's specific response is a function of the nature of the stressor, one's vulnerability to it, and the context (social, physical, or psychological environment) in which events take place.[5] Our vulnerability is a function of genetic and developmental influences,[6] as well as diet, general health, and selective conditioning to particular stressors.[7] On the other hand, the form of an individual's symptomatic response to stressors in general is relatively stable. (Variations in degree of response occur relative to changes in stressor intensity, vulnerability, and context.)

The impact of stress is not imagined. Research has indicated that "psychological stressors produce altered measurements of various bodily chemicals, hormones, and organic functions as well as altered levels of anxiety."[8] Considerable evidence indicates a relationship between stress and coronary heart disease, hypertension, ulcers, cancer, and mental illness.[9]

The wheel of stress[10] (see Figure 3) indicates the four basic aspects of stress. *Hyperstress* is the high point of body stress and is generally beyond the manageable limit of that particular body. *Hypostress,* on the other hand, is the point at which the body does not have enough stress to operate

**Figure 3. Wheel of stress.**

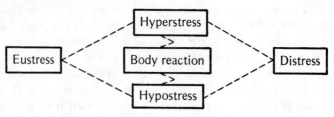

at an optimal level. The optimal level of stress lies somewhere between hypo and hyperstress. In fact, stress-related medical problems seem to occur most frequently among those that are "understressed" and those that are "overstressed."[11] On the left in Figure 3 is *eustress,* which occurs in essentially happy or successful situations. On the right is *distress,* an expression of the body's reaction to threatening stressor agents. The physiological response is the same irrespective of whether a stressor is perceived as favorable or unfavorable. However, eustress (favorable stressors) dissipates tension created by body reactions, whereas distress lingers and seldom results in healthy expression.

Extensive regions of the body deviate from their normal resting state in stressful situations. The physiological basis[12] for reactions to a stressor lies in the hypothalamus gland near the brain, which receives the initial stimulus. In turn, the anterior pituitary gland secretes a chemical, ACTH, which acts on the adrenal cortex, causing secretion of corticoids to the scene of the stress. If the stress is caused by a hostile environment, the adrenals react, alerting all bodily functions for potential problems. If the stressor agents are perceived to be dangerous, the hypothalamus stimulates another part of the adrenals, the medullary, to secrete adrenaline into the blood and generally alert the body for "fight or flight" (meeting the situation head-on or avoiding it).

When our bodies respond to stressors, the activity of the adrenals increases to withstand the stress. The noise of the boiler room, the pressure of a major decision, worry about family difficulties, or other personal conflicts can create strain requiring bodily responses. Stress also has been traced to psychological factors. Situations that result in failure or fear[13] or that present a threat to fundamental personal needs may be stress-producing. Each new venture into the unknown, though enjoyable and beneficial, creates a certain degree of apprehension and anxiety, leading to stress. In fact, any given stimulus that changes the behavior of an organism in a significant way (for better or worse) can be regarded as stressful. Thus, we may conclude that stress is a part of every person's life, and we are more likely to function efficiently if that stress is maintained at a "proper" level. As Selye concludes, "stress is the essence of life; without it, there is no life."[14]

Figure 4 depicts the three-stage response (alarm reaction, resistance, and exhaustion) of a person confronted by a stressor. In the *alarm reaction,* the level of response first decreases in a condition designated as shock.

**Figure 4. The impact of stressors.**

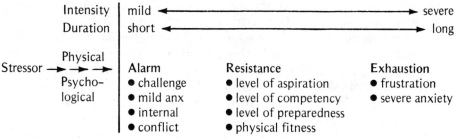

| | | | |
|---|---|---|---|
| Intensity | mild ←————————————————————————————→ severe | | |
| Duration | short ←————————————————————————————→ long | | |
| | | | |
| | **Alarm** | **Resistance** | **Exhaustion** |
| Physical | • challenge | • level of aspiration | • frustration |
| Stressor → → → | • mild anx | • level of competency | • severe anxiety |
| Psycho- logical | • internal | • level of preparedness | |
| | • conflict | • physical fitness | |

The body then responds (countershock) to cope with the stressor stimuli. Following the shock and countershock of the alarm reaction, the system maintains an elevated level of response that is capable of coping with the stressor stimuli. This is referred to as the stage of *resistance*. If the elevated level of response has to be maintained for a considerable period of time, the individual may enter the stage of *exhaustion*. During exhaustion, the response begins to taper off until the stressor stimuli eventually wears the individual down.

As our bodies become physically exhausted, our minds also tend to become confused. Conversely, stimuli resulting from feared psychological failure produce concurrent stress on the physical dimension. Thus, there is an interplay between the physical and psychological dimensions. These two factors interact forming a cycle that potentially can destroy an organism. The confusion of the mind causes the body to deteriorate, causing the mind to become more confused, and so on. Four factors mediate the rate at which a person progresses from alarm to exhaustion. They include the individual's level of aspiration, the level of competency, the level of preparedness, and the physical fitness of the organism.

Relevant situational characteristics in Figure 4 include (1) the duration and (2) the intensity of the stressors associated with a particular situation. It is obvious that, at any given period of time, an individual may be involved in several situations—all of which contain stressors of specific durations and intensities. For example, a person may have a very intense and long-lasting marital problem, a highly stressful executive position, and short-term but intense monetary problems. These conflicts may drive weak individuals to physical or mental breakdown as exhaustion sets in. Those who are physically stronger and have a strong sense of self worth are able to contend with such stressors for a longer period of time. Hopefully, the difficulties or conflicts causing the stress can be settled before an individual is forced to the state of exhaustion.

## Managing Stress

Stressors cause bodily adaptations. In some cases these adaptations are beneficial. At other times they are harmful. The first step in relieving the impact of stressful situations is to recognize one's typical response to stressor stimuli and to adopt appropriate coping mechanisms. Some coping techniques have been found to be particularly effective.

One study found five techniques that were associated with the fewest number of stress symptoms.[15] They included: building resistance through regular sleep; good health habits; separating work and non-work life; engaging in physical exercise; talking problems through with peers on the job; and withdrawing physically from the situation. Eating well, taking good care of one's body, and separating work activities from play or relaxation time characterized low stress in people of all ages. However, some techniques seemed to be more commonly associated with certain age brackets. Older low-stress subjects reported talking with their spouse and withdrawing from the situation to be most effective. Younger subjects seemed to find that changing the strategy of attack in their work helped them successfully deal with stress. Differences in responses appeared related to position on the career ladder, security, and energy level. More active coping strategies include various types of meditation, progressive relaxation, and biofeedback.

While numerous reactions to stress exist, some symptomatic responses have more enduring effects in organizations than do others. In particular, alcohol and drug abuse, migraine headaches, mass psychogenic illness (such as dizziness, lightheadedness, skin rashes, abdominal pain, etc.), sick absences, and lower back pain result in millions of lost hours each year. Managers, by the nature of their jobs, subject themselves to intense if not unique stressors. For example, the need to acquire and maintain power, the responsibility for organizational risk, their influence over interpersonal relationships and conflict resolution, and managing change all create a highly stress-producing work context.[16]

Organizations, then, have a responsibility to their members as well as to their constituents (stockholders, electorate, etc.) to focus attention on the impact of stress in organizational life and to take preventive measures in order to lessen the impact on participants. Steps that can be taken include adopting programs designed to assess current stress levels among organizational members, monitoring the incidence of stress and its cost impact on the organization, focusing on ways organizational stressors can be minimized or eliminated, and placing individuals in positions that are compatible with their stress tolerance levels.[17]

## Summary

Conflict may exist in a latent form without an individual actually being able to identify intrapersonal conflict that exists. If the intensity of the conflict is great enough, or if the conflict exists for a prolonged period of time, it may be felt and recognized. Conflict may be dealt with and controlled on a personal level. However, in some instances it may become open. At this point, its resolution becomes the responsibility of a manager. A primary form of conflict in organizational settings is role conflict. Role conflict is common in everyday organizational life and takes the form of intra-sender, inter-role, inter-sender, and person-value conflict.

Stress occurs in favorable (eustress) as well as unfavorable (distress) situations. People can have too much (hyperstress) or too little stress (hypostress). However, they function best when stress is maintained at an optimal level.

Stressors occur constantly in both negative and positive ways, forcing the body to physiologically adapt. The adaptation occurs through three stages: alarm, resistance, and exhaustion. Each stage is identified by certain physiological and psychological processes. The rapidity with which a person goes from alarm to exhaustion is determined by health, competence, preparedness, and level of aspiration.

Certain coping mechanisms have been found to be related to low stress groups. Building resistance, exercising regularly, and separating work and non-work activity are among techniques commonly used. Millions of hours are lost each year to stress-related body responses. Therefore, programs directed at identifying sources of stress, monitoring stress impacts on organizational behavior, and developing programs to counter stress in the workplace represent sound management practice.

Not all behavior in organizations results in positive feelings or achievements. Organizational behavior may take place in conflict situations. You will notice as you read and analyze the cases that these conflicts may result in negative accomplishments in some situations and positive accomplishments in others. In other words, while more traditionally held values may cause us to avoid conflict, benefits actually may be derived from conflict situations.

*References*

1. J. G. March and H. A. Simon, *Organizations* (New York: John Wiley and Sons, 1958).

2. The discussion following is based on an article by L. R. Pondy, "Organization Conflict: Concepts and Models," *Administrative Science Quarterly*, vol. 12, September 1967, pp. 296–320.

3. M. E. Shaw and P. R. Costanzo, *Theories of Social Psychology* (New York: McGraw-Hill, 1970), pp. 328–344.

4. R. L. Kahn, "Role Conflict and Ambiguity in Organizations," *Personnel Administrator*, vol. 9, March–April 1964, pp. 8–13.

5. Alan A. McLean, *Work Stress* (Reading: Addison-Wesley, 1979), pp. 37–40.

6. Ibid., p. 38.

7. James W. Greenwood, III, and James W. Greenwood, Jr., *Managing Executive Stress: A Systems Approach* (New York: John Wiley and Sons, 1979), pp. 53–64.

8. McLean, op. cit., p. 3.

9. Greenwood and Greenwood, op. cit., pp. 120–121.

10. Hans Selye, "Self-Regulation: The Response to Stress," in *Inner Balance*, edited by E. M. Goldwag (Englewood Cliffs: Prentice-Hall, 1979).

11. Clinton Weiman, "A Study of Occupational Stressors and the Incidence of Disease/Risk," *Journal of Occupational Medicine*, vol. 19, no. 2, February 1977, pp. 119–122.

12. Hans Selye, *Stress of Life* (New York: McGraw-Hill, 1956).

13. Hans Selye, "On the Real Benefits of Eustress," *Psychology Today*, vol. 16, no. 10, March 1978, pp. 60–64.

14. Hans Selye, *Stress Without Distress* (Philadelphia: Lippincott, 1974), p. 32.

15. J. H. Howard et al., "Coping with Job Tension—Effective and Ineffective Methods," *Public Personnel Management*, September–October 1975, pp. 317–326.

16. Greenwood and Greenwood, op. cit., pp. 44–46.

17. Leon J. Warshaw, *Managing Stress* (Reading: Addison-Wesley, 1979), pp. 35–37.

## Recommended Readings

Readings marked with an asterisk are included in *Contemporary Perspectives in Organizational Behavior,* edited by Donald D. White (Boston: Allyn and Bacon, 1982).

Cary L. Cooper and Judi Marshall, "An Audit of Managerial Distress," *Journal of Enterprise Management*, vol. 1 (Manchester, U.K.: Institute of Science and Technology), 1978, pp. 185–196.

*John H. Howard, P. A. Rechnitzer, and D. A. Cunningham, "Coping with Job Tension—Effective and Ineffective Methods," *Public Personnel Management*, September–October 1975, pp. 317–326.

*Manfred F. R. Kets de Vries, "Organizational Stress: A Call for Management Action," *Sloan Management Review*, vol. 21, Fall 1979, pp. 3–14.

Ralph H. Kilman and Kenneth W. Thomas, "Four Perspectives on Conflict Management: An Attributional Framework for Organizing Descriptive and Normative Theory," *Academy of Management Review*, January 1978, pp. 59–69.

Alan A. McLean, "Context, Vulnerability, and Specific Stressors," *Work Stress*, (Reading: Addison-Wesley, 1979), pp. 37–46.

*Stephen P. Robins, "Conflict Management and Conflict Resolution Are Not Synonymous Terms," *California Management Review*, vol. 21, no. 2, Winter 1978, pp. 67–75.

# CASE 32
# The Reluctant Loan Officer

Betty Hampton graduated from State College with a B.A. in English. For three years she worked for a local bank during the day and attended classes at night. At this bank, Betty held various jobs, such as teller, loan clerk, secretary, new accounts clerk, and loan processor.

Although her major area was English, she had taken enough courses to have a second, unofficial major in business administration. Upon graduation, Betty had difficulty finding a challenging job. Finally, in desperation, she accepted a secretarial position with Third National Bank of Brookfield, Betty's home town. A very personable and attractive woman, as well as intelligent, she was easily able to master the routine secretarial chores as well as handle some other areas of responsibility such as new accounts, loan documentation, statement analysis, and computer input.

## Promotion to Management

Betty's work was soon noticed by Ralph Wheelen, the senior commercial loan officer, who remarked to others that since Betty seemed to be doing such a good job processing loan applications, she might make a good loan officer. There was some fear that Betty might be taken advantage of by some customers. It was feared by Mr. Louis, the bank president, that a young attractive woman might not project the stable and conservative image he felt was necessary in a good loan officer. At this point in time, only three women in the bank had supervisory responsibilities. Two women were in operations—one supervising the bookkeeping department, and the other overseeing tellers. There was also one female branch manager, with whom Mr. Louis quite openly had more than a simple business relationship. Mr. Louis believed these women to be appropriately placed, since they primarily supervised other women and had nothing to do with what he considered to be the key profit area in the bank—commercial loans. Nevertheless, on the basis of Wheelen's recommendation and EEO (Equal Employment Opportunity) considerations, Betty was given the chance to move up to loan officer.

Betty realized that the bank was using her as a test case and that the president was concerned she project a "proper" image. Consequently, Betty dressed in longsleeve blouses with high collars. She wore mainly dark colors and attempted to maintain a serious "Marian the librarian" appearance and demeanor at all times both on the job and in the community. Of eight banks in the city, only Third National had a female lender.

The first few months on the job were very challenging ones for Betty. She enjoyed her job and seemed to be progressing well. She was having no

Prepared by J. David Hunger.

real problems getting commercial customers to accept her as a lender or in conducting her "officer calls" during which she visited local business people to encourage them to do business with Third National.

## The Officers' Meeting

One morning, Betty joined eleven other bank officers (loan officers and branch managers) in the conference room for the weekly business development meeting. The meeting was conducted as usual by the senior vice president, Bill Weber. After discussing the week's officer call reports, Bill Weber asked the group how the bank could increase its holdings of mortgage loans. John Sullivan, a loan officer of many years, suggested that someone talk with Amos McLaren, a successful realtor in the community. "If someone could just talk Amos into mentioning Third National to his customers," suggested John, "we could really pick up the business!" "That's an excellent idea," responded Weber. "But, we have to be careful in how we approach him." Turning to Betty, Weber said, "Betty, I think you ought to take Amos out tomorrow night and do whatever is necessary to get his business."

Betty was astounded at the implications of Weber's statement. "Who does he think I am?" she wondered to herself as she looked at the eleven other people in the conference room. Susan Spriggs, a branch manager and the only other female in the room, was looking at the floor and nervously adjusting her watch. No one else seemed to be reacting except for Joe Bibbins, a young but experienced loan officer, who seemed to have a slight smirk on his face. Betty had heard the rumors circulating around the bank of various people sleeping together, but she never realized how far things seemed to be going!

After a moment's hesitation, Betty looked the senior vice president in the face and said, "You have other women on the staff whom you've hired for that purpose. Let them do it."

# CASE 33
# Old Friends / No Friends

## Part A

Al Johnson was a college sophomore at Southeast State College. He had earned the reputation among his peers as being outgoing and a hard worker. In high school, Al had participated in varsity sports and was named captain of the football team in his senior year. He was active in his church and various other young people's organizations in his home town.

Both in high school and his first two years at Southeast State, Al was a "B" student. Toward the end of his sophomore year, he decided that he wanted to major in a field that would prepare him to deal with people both on and off the job. He considered fields in sociology and psychology, but decided instead to take most of his course work in the management field. Al explained:

> I guess you learn about people when you take courses like psychology and sociology, but I want to learn about working with them. It seems to me that that's what they do in management. I suppose that I was influenced by a friend of mine. He was working on his master's degree and assisted in teaching a course in human relations. I took it just to see what it would be like. I learned a lot in that class that I could really put to use when I got out of school.

During the summers, Al had always managed to find work. He once worked for a general contractor and spent a couple of summers as a head lifeguard at an area swimming pool. However, he realized that these types of jobs did not provide him with the income necessary to cover all expenses during the full year at school. He was getting financial assistance from his parents, but he preferred to "pay my own way as much as possible."

### "Jackrabbit"

On June 2, Al began work at National Brickworks. The plant was located two miles from Al's home. It was one of thirteen production facilities operated by National Brickworks. The local plant employed 112 laborers who worked on two shifts. Clerical and administrative employees were officed in a building that was separated from the plant facilities by a railroad spur line. The company employed machinists and laboratory technicians as well as semiskilled and unskilled laborers. All but 6 of the plant laborers were black. The 6 white workers all had seniority of at least twenty-five years at the plant. Seniority

Prepared by Donald D. White, University of Arkansas.

for the black employees ranged from four years to forty-six years. Jobs were assigned on the basis of seniority and qualifications. However, the white employees tended to hold an inordinately high percentage of the "lamb jobs."

Al's first day on the job awakened him to a world that he had not known before. Although he had been friends with a few black students who attended his high school and knew others during his two years of college, he had never been in a position in which he was a member of the racial minority.

There was no official policy of segregation in the plant. However, Al noticed immediately that white employees tended to keep to themselves. In addition, dressing rooms and lockers provided for the employees were segregated. Black employees dressed on the first floor and white employees dressed on the second floor of a small building adjacent to the main plant. There was never any formal indication that the locker rooms were intended to be segregated. However, in a discussion with a white employee he was told, "You eat upstairs." Al never detected any animosity between the black and the white workers at National. The plant had never known open hostility between the two groups, and they talked amiably when working side by side.

During the first week, Al spent most of his time sweeping floors and cleaning up around machines. The plant was always dirty due to the materials that were handled (i.e., various types of clays, bauxite, and other dry mix materials). His first jobs were not difficult, but he quickly tired of the boring work. On Monday of the second week, Al was placed on a work team in which all workers except himself were paid on a piece-rate basis. The other employees worked on an assembly line. Al's job was to throw damaged bricks onto a conveyer belt that carried them to a reprocessing grinder. When he arrived in the morning, approximately 1500 bricks were on the floor in front of the belt. These bricks, it was explained, were wasted materials left by the previous shifts from the day before.

Al began his work at a hectic pace. Although additional wasted materials continually were thrown on the pile, he applied himself so vigorously to the new job that the pile had almost disappeared by the ten o'clock break. During the first two hours at work, some of the men on the line had made jokes about the speed with which Al was working. Al welcomed the opportunity to be part of the work team even if at the moment he were the goat. However, during the break, two of the men approached him. One of the men, who Al later found out was the shop steward, said to him, "Don't work so hard, man. You're going to kill yourself." The second man, Jack Stewart, also commented, "Man, we don't want you to work yourself out of a job. I was on that job last week, and it took me the better part of the day just to get caught up. You know, they don't care if you leave a few bricks at the end of the day." Al thanked each of the men for their concern. He told them that he had always been "the kind of guy who likes to get my work done and relax later." Al continued to work hard for the remainder of the day. He stayed on the job most of the week and never did leave any waste for the night shift.

During the next two weeks, Al was assigned to various jobs in the plant.

He worked hard on each job and helped others around him when time permitted. In not too long, he had earned the name "Jackrabbit."

## Part B: The Night of the Sacker

At the end of his fourth week, Al was approached by the plant foreman, Bob York. "Al, you've shown me that you're a hard worker. You're going to have some overtime on Friday night and I wondered if you and Ted Wilson would like to run the sacking machine." Al was excited and immediately agreed. Ted Wilson was another college student who had been hired about two weeks after Al. Both boys had wanted the chance to "make some real money." The sacker provided them this opportunity. The jobs were considered to be among the choicer piece rate jobs in the plant. Neither Al nor Ted had yet had an opportunity to do piecework. Al and Ted spent all day Friday talking about the job and telling each other how much money they would be able to make that night.

The excitement for the two boys had not worn off by the time the evening shift began. Al had assisted on the sacking job once before, but that had only been to fill in for one of the regular men who had to leave suddenly toward the end of the day. Al and Ted were to load materials into a larger mixer. Materials were blown into cement-type bags weighing approximately 96 pounds each. The bags, in turn, had to be removed from the sacker and placed on pallets. The work was strenuous. But the continual joking and goading of one another took their minds off the hot and dirty work. At one point, Ted pulled out a slip of paper and tacked it to the wall over the mixer. On the paper was a schedule showing various times and the number of bags that Ted believed he and Al could fill. A third column showed what the boys would be paid if they were able to meet Ted's schedule. Al's only reply was, "We'll beat it!"

By the end of the shift Ted and Al had, in fact, beaten their schedule. Their output had more than doubled the standard output of employees who worked on the machine on the day shift. Up until now, their daily take-home pay had been just over $20.00 a day. When the foreman checked their production records, he informed the two boys that their wage for the night shift was $43.75 apiece.

By the following Monday afternoon, word of their feat had spread throughout the plant. A couple of the younger laboratory workers stopped Al as he was preparing to return to work after lunch. They told him that it was about time that someone in the plant showed the men what they were really capable of doing. Later in the day, Bob York called Al over too. He told him he was pleased with Al's work and that he hoped Al enjoyed making a little extra money.

Few comments were heard by either Al or Ted from the other workers in the plant. No one seemed to say much about what had been done. Both boys expressed an interest in working on the sacker again. However, although they continued to press Bob York for the opportunity, they were not able to get back on the job for the remainder of the summer.

Al did receive a raise after two months and occasionally was permitted to work on a piece-rate basis with members of a larger work team. His relationships with the men continually improved and by the end of the summer he felt that he knew many of them quite well.

## Part C: Jim Medwick's Grievance

In the spring of 1976, Al again applied at National for a summer job. His application was accepted and he began work shortly after the end of school. He had visited the plant twice during the school year "just to say hello to some of the guys." Within his first few days back on the job, a number of the men stopped by to welcome him back. Some of the older workers seemed especially pleased to see Al and asked him about his experiences in school during the past year. Al had decided when he first took the job at National not to mention that he was a student at Southeast State unless he was first asked. Few of the men in the plant had completed high school and none of them, including the foreman, had ever had an opportunity to attend college. However, the topic of Southeast State came up more and more frequently in the men's conversations when Al was around. Occasionally, someone would refer to one of the school's athletic squads as "our" team. Another man, Howard Hayes, asked Al if he could get a couple of Southeast T-shirts for his nephews. Al was glad to know that the men in the plant were interested in his personal life away from the job. Ironically, he felt more like a member of the group now than ever before.

Al's work assignments had improved during his second summer at National. Additional college students had been hired, and although his seniority did not carry from summer to summer, he was given preference for jobs on the basis of his early application. No job assignment problems arose for Al until a second shift employee, Jim Medwick, was placed on the day schedule. Jim Medwick had taken a job at National about one week after Al began. He was twenty-four years old, had completed high school and served for four years in the United States Navy.

Shortly after Jim's assignment to the day shift, he began to complain that he was being discriminated against with regard to job assignment. He complained that Al was always given "the better job" and that he had not had a chance to work with a piece-rate team since his transfer. He took his grievance directly to the shop steward. In turn, the shop steward went to Bob York and complained that Jim was a permanent employee while Al was only hired for summer employment. Al heard from others in the plant about what had transpired. He immediately went to Bob York and the following discussion transpired.

*Al:* Listen, Bob, as long as I get to work on piece-rate jobs from time to time, I'm not going to complain. I know that according to the union contract I have

seniority over Jim. On the other hand, I don't see any reason to get everyone
teed off just because of a technicality.

*Bob:* I appreciate you coming in, Al, but this is my plant and I'll run it any damn
way I please. This kid, Medwick, is a hothead black militant type, and he's
not going to throw his weight around here.

*Al:* I know what you mean, Bob, but I work pretty well with these guys and I
don't want something like this to ruin the rest of the summer.

*Bob:* I don't want you to have problems either, but this is my plant and as long
as you have seniority, you'll get first choice of jobs.

Later that week Howard Hayes, one of the older men, came over to Al
during the morning break. He told Al that he had heard about his conversation with Bob and that most of the workers on the shift were behind Al all
the way. Nothing more was made of the incident. Eventually, one of the piece-
rate teams was enlarged and Jim Medwick was added to it.

## Part D: The Incident of the Knife

Al felt that he had become one of the crew. He walked to and from work every
day and on numerous occasions had been offered a ride by a carload of fellow
workers who happened to be passing by. He received favors from the men at
the plant and returned them whenever possible. Of particular significance to
Al was a knife that had been given him by the members of one of the plant
workteams.

It was the job of certain members of the team to rip open heavy drymix
bags and pour the contents into the mixing chutes. Each of the men on the
team had his own personal "ripping knife." The knife was fashioned from a
piece of hard steel and was ground by one of the machinists in the shop. One
day while Al was working in the area, three of the crew members suddenly
confronted him. The younger man drew a knife from his pocket and waved
it at Al. Al was surprised and shocked since he could think of nothing that
might have caused the outburst. Suddenly the men broke into laughter and
the young man handed the knife over to Al. On the handle were scratched Al's
initials. Al knew the meaning of the gesture and prized the knife highly. He
kept it on a shelf close to the work area and ritually checked the shelf to see
that it was there each morning when he arrived at work.

As the summer drew to a close, Al began to discuss with men at the plant
his plans for the coming year. He told them that he would be finishing his
college degree and planned to take a job with a large chemical firm in Chicago.
Some of the men wished him well. Generally, however, little was said about
his plans. During his last week on the job, Al spent a good deal of time daydreaming about the coming year. He chose not to participate in the softball
games that were played during the lunch break, although he did go to the
games and watch the other men. On his final afternoon at the plant, he began
to gather his various belongings and acquisitions. Among these were his safety
helmet, dust mask, and ripping knife. As he reached for his ripping knife, he
was confronted by Jack Stewart. Jack was a member of the work team and one

of the three men who had presented the knife to Al. Jack asked Al what he was "up to" and Al explained. Jack stated that the knife was no longer there and that it must have been picked up by one of the members of the night shift. Al was disappointed that the knife had disappeared just before he was about to leave. He had wanted to take it home as a souvenir.

Jack had been rather abrupt in telling Al about the knife and as he turned away Al heard the sound of metal hit the floor. He looked to Jack's feet to see a knife with the initials "A.J." on the handle. Jack immediately picked up the knife and began to walk away. Al called to him saying that he thought that the knife was his own and that he would very much like to have it back. Jack turned angrily and said the knife belonged to another worker who recently had been laid off. A brief argument ensued. Finally, Al left.

Little was said by anyone in the area. Just before Al left the plant that evening one of the workers handed him his knife, but said nothing more. A few of the men wished Al good luck and told him to pay them a visit sometime. That night, Al reflected on his experiences at the National Brickworks. He was disappointed that he'd left his coworkers on such a sour note.

## Postscript

A few months later, during his Christmas vacation, Al returned once again to the plant to say hello to the men. As word spread that Al was back, many of the men walked over to see him. To his surprise, Jack Stewart was among them. Jack showed no signs of holding a grudge about their argument over the knife. On the contrary, he asked Al about how he was doing in school and about his plans for the following year. Al was glad to come back to friendly faces, but he later puzzled over the warm reception that he had received.

# CASE 34
## The Token Woman

The Mainstream Life Insurance Company, to forestall possible affirmative pressure because of the lack of women in the insurance industry's managerial ranks, decided to actively recruit a woman to fill a recent opening in the research division of the company's trust department. The vacant research analyst position was one of several middle management jobs at Mainstream that traditionally have been the steppingstone for promotion to the executive rank.

The required credentials for this particular opening in the research division of the trust department are an M.B.A. degree (or a comparable graduate degree with a major emphasis in finance, at least two years of academic or business experience, and proven research capability in the investment field. An exhaustive search and meticulous screening resulted in the company hiring Claire Meredith. Claire was an attractive, twenty-seven-year-old single woman whose M.S. degree in finance was awarded "With Distinction" and whose master's thesis was published by a prestigious university press. Ms. Meredith was previously employed as a broker in a highly respected Wall Street investment banking firm. In addition, she had written numerous publications resulting from theoretical and applied research projects. Mainstream was able to hire Ms. Meredith only after John Forbes, her potential immediate "boss" assured her of equal opportunity on all organizational levels. An additional inducement to Ms. Meredith was a starting salary that was $2,000 higher than the other employment offers she had recently received.

At the end of her third month on the job, Ms. Meredith privately acknowledged a pervasive feeling of frustration in connection with her new position. She began reviewing the activities of the past three months in an attempt to determine the basis of her negative reaction.

During the first day on the job, each of Ms. Meredith's colleagues had expressed enthusiastic delight at having her "on board." One colleague observed that "it's high time the company hired a woman for our section we've needed some beautification of the office for a long time now." Another chimed in with the remark that "we better tell our wives that Claire is married so they won't think we're researching *monkey* business!" When Claire, in reply, suggested that they all have lunch together, Roy James, a division programmer, told her that "each of the guys brings a brown bag for lunch and we eat and talk shop in one or the other's office." Accordingly, Claire decided to join her colleagues and announced that she was joining the brown-bag league. She was surprised, therefore, when at noon the following day, Roy James opened his office door and urged, "Come on, you guys let's research our brown bags—Frank, you and Jim get the coffee while David and I get the ice

Prepared by Linda P. Fletcher, Louisiana State University; and Susan M. Phillips, University of Iowa.

cream, and don't forget Don wants double cream in his coffee." Since Claire's name was not mentioned specifically, she decided—after some hesitation—to eat alone in her office. Claire did not feel she should join the secretaries and clerks for lunch although she knew she would be welcome. This routine, with minor variations, subsequently became the established pattern.

Breaks for coffee in the company cafeteria were no exception to the seemingly established separation principle. Only once during the three-month interval had Claire been invited to join her colleagues for coffee. And at that particular coffee break, Claire felt particularly uncomfortable. Although she felt she had an excellent working relationship with her associates, she had little in common with them outside of the work environment. In addition, it was quite obvious that the men in the division seemed to plan social gatherings for both after work and the week-ends. Although her colleagues were very friendly in the office, they never seemed to think to include her in their plans.

Having reviewed the informal social structure of her employment, Claire recognized similar frustrations with respect to various functional aspects of her position. She recalled John Forbes, the head of the research division, explaining the operational features of the section: "We meet once a week in committee to determine the status of current projects, discuss proposals for the future, and make individual assignments of new research projects to be initiated. Any ideas you have—write them up in memo form for distribution to everyone prior to the next meeting and we'll all go over your suggestion at the earliest possible meeting to determine the feasibility of your idea."

Because she was the most recent addition to the staff, Claire deliberately maintained a low profile during the first few weekly committee meetings of the research division. The other members of the committee appeared to endorse her strategy by seeking her opinions only infrequently and by failing to draw her into their policy deliberations. During the fourth weekly gathering, John Forbes, who acted as chairman, noted that his secretary was unable to be present as usual to record the minutes of the meeting. Frank Howard suggested sending for a replacement from the secretarial pool, but Mr. Forbes shook his head and casually replied that "a replacement is unnecessary since the logical substitute is Ms. Meredith—besides, brushing up on her shorthand will give her something to do during the meeting." Claire hastened to reply, "Since I do not know shorthand, I must decline the honor of this additional responsibility."

Shortly after the meeting, Claire decided to abandon her sideline role in the committee. She decided that the next time the group gathered formally, she would present a research proposal that she had been developing in the area of commission reduction through use of regional exchanges.

Claire's specific assignments included responsibility for several on-going projects that required only infrequent attention. The major portion of her time was spent on a "cost allocation" project. Cost allocation was a computer system which, when completed, would provide complete investment information for each of Mainstream's trust customers. All trust funds were pooled for investment purposes. The pooling was necessary since some of the trust accounts were so small that investment income would be difficult to generate for these accounts. Any income would virtually be wiped out by the commission expenses of such small transactions.

The current method of determining investment income for each trust account was to apply the average new investment rate to the pro rata portion of each account's share of the total investment funds. Consequently, several of Mainstream's larger trust accounts had complained that their investment income was "supporting" the smaller accounts. Threatened with the loss of these large trust accounts, the financial vice-president of Mainstream, Bill Newbit, instructed John Forbes to develop some type of allocation system within his department so that each account could be properly charged with expenses while simultaneously enjoying the investment income of the pooled fund investment mechanism.

John Forbes had developed the specifications for the cost allocation system and turned over the system design and programming to a research analyst who had resigned several months before Claire joined the division. Claire later found out through the grapevine that he quit because he felt he was getting nowhere with cost allocation. When Claire was hired, she was told she would have full responsibility for the completion of the system including supervision of the programming by Roy James, developing comprehensive test data, and ultimately getting the system on line. Since investment income for each account was currently calculated by hand under the supervision of Frank Howard, Claire anticipated the usual problems of employee resistance to a new computer system. Therefore, she had begun system orientation classes for the personnel involved. Claire had determined that the existing personnel, with training, would be adequate to effectively use and run the new system. No personnel displacement would be necessary.

Claire was in the final stages of testing the system with Roy James and decided that it was time to show John Forbes some of its output. When she took the first test run into John, he expressed complete surprise. He admitted, "I can't believe that the cost allocation project got off the ground. This system had been knocking around for three years—we never had any usable output, and I really never expected to get any. Frankly, we had just about decided to write off the $800,000 development costs as 'sunk.' I guess we'll have to start thinking about moving on this thing—manpower, planning, and so on."

When Claire left John Forbes' office, she was disappointed at his reaction. As she reviewed his comments, she really began to wonder just what she was supposed to be doing at Mainstream and how she could go about doing it.

# CASE 35
# Affirmative Action!?

Belville Hospital is a large, fully integrated hospital in Memphis, Tennessee. The hospital has 450 beds and is presently planning an expansion to 650 beds. The hospital has never experienced many personnel problems. However, recent actions taken by certain state and federal agencies have caused uneasiness among many of the employees.

Many organizations over the last few years have been approached by the equal employment opportunity commission regarding alleged discrimination in their hiring and promotion practices. In 1970, EEOC charged that certain hiring and promotion practices in the Belville Hospital were discriminatory. After nearly two years of hearings and periodic negotiations, and agreement to resolve most EEOC issues was signed and judicially endorsed in a consent decree by a United States District Court. As a result, the EEOC moved to dismiss its charges against the hospital.

In a memorandum issued by the EEOC, the commission stated that the progress of Belville Hospital in fulfilling commitments that the consent decree set forth would be closely monitored for the next six years. Violations of the consent decree would make Belville liable to citation for contempt of court, and inadequate progress toward fulfillment of the objectives would result in mandatory hiring of blacks, women and other minorities for management level positions.

The effect of the memorandum was quickly evident in hospital communications. For example, the following directive was issued to all persons responsible for acquiring personnel for nonentry level jobs:

In filling vacancies for nonentry level jobs (both inside and outside), Belville Hospital will continue to fill vacancies on the basis of best qualified and seniority. But if the hospital is unable to meet intermediate targets on this basis, a woman or minority member with less seniority and basic qualifications may be selected to permit a department to make satisfactory progress in meeting an intermediate target. Should there be no employees with appropriate basic skills who are available for selection, the company will hire, if necessary, in order to make satisfactory progress in meeting an intermediate target.

The impact of this new program was felt throughout the organization. Such an example took place in the business office.

## A Case in Point

The function of the assignment office was to assign new patients to appropriate rooms and floors, to maintain the patient records, and to communicate by

Prepared by Donald D. White, University of Arkansas; and H. William Vroman, Tennessee Technological University.

phone with nursing stations when problems were encountered or specific information was necessary. The office was part of the Business Office (see Exhibit 1), and consisted of five records clerks (classified as semiskilled), three patient-contact assignors (classified as skilled), and an office manager. The procedures of this office were relatively complicated. Therefore, it was generally conceded that a period of approximately twelve months was required to learn all of the various procedures thoroughly.

The office had been managed by Ellen Nash for the last five years. Mrs. Nash had been with Belville for seventeen years. She worked in the processing department for five years and as an assignment clerk in the assignment office for seven years. She had spent the last five years as the assignment office manager. Mrs. Nash was a high school graduate. She was competent and well liked. Most of the employees recognized her as the "old pro" in the office. When difficult problems in the office arose, they usually found their way to her desk because of her experience.

The processing office was located in the room adjacent to the assignment office and had many interrelated activities with assignment. There was a sequential interdependence between the two offices. Processing handled all patients upon termination of their stay at Belville and maintained continuous records on all out-patients required to take multiple treatments over a period of time. Therefore, the processing office depended upon records forwarded to them by the assignment office. The manager of the processing office was Mr. David Randle. Mr. Randle was a business college graduate and had been manager of the processing department for about nine months. As a result of his inexperience, he too depended upon Mrs. Nash to help him with difficult problems.

Ed Crosby, the hospital administrator, was aware of Ellen Nash's ability and competence. He also was under pressure to meet his assigned targets for placing a certain percentage of women and minorities in various levels of management within his department. Crosby saw in the assignment and processing organizations an opportunity to give Ellen the responsibility for both offices. For all practical purposes, she already was informally administering both of-

**Exhibit 1. Original hospital organization plan.**

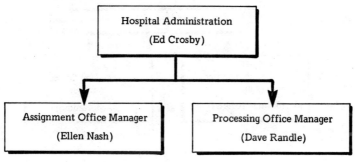

fices, anyway. In addition, he thought that the change would open up another position which in turn could be filled by another woman or a black person. Ed was convinced that the reorganization would be in the best interest of Ellen and the company. Shortly thereafter, he met with Ellen and discussed his proposed action. Ellen's new role was explained to her:

This is a completely new position, Ellen. Your job will be to provide general supervision to the two offices and to help the two office managers maintain current efficiency levels. You really will be serving as an advisor, since I still want the day-to-day decisions to be made by the office managers. By the way, Dave Randle will remain in his present position and we should have a new assignment manager on the job in a week or so. Does everything sound OK to you?

Ellen was pleased with Mr. Crosby's decision. She said that she would do her best to help maintain the good work that currently was being done in the offices. She said that she really had no questions other than who would replace her as assignment manager. Mr. Crosby indicated that no decision had been made yet.

## The Replacement

As Mr. Crosby had suggested, it was not long before someone was hired to replace Ellen as assignment office manager. His name was John Matthews. John was a graduate of Grambling University, a predominantly black school, where he majored in business administration.

He had taken a special course in hospital administration while in school and had worked for about three months in a business office of a large urban

**Exhibit 2. Reorganized hospital.**

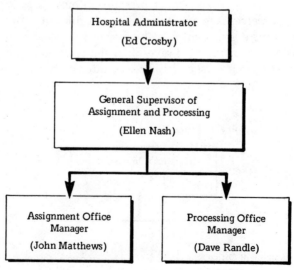

hospital. There, he had worked with customer billing and assisted the business manager more or less as a trouble shooter.

John also received limited training for an assignment office management position. Upon joining the Belville organization, John was given the position that Ellen previously held.

John had been in his new position for four weeks, during which several problems had arisen in the assignment office. The problems had caused some dissension among the employees and had markedly decreased the office's efficiency. Errors in assignments had caused numerous complaints from patients. Ed Crosby informed Ellen of one such incident and asked her to look into it. Ellen examined the records of John's office and determined that a mistake in posting had been made by a newly hired girl. Ellen asked the girl responsible for the error about what she had done. The girl told Ellen that she had asked Mr. Matthews what to do regarding the assignment and that he had told her he simply did not know. Since Ellen was not available to the girl at the time, she used her own judgment on the matter and her decision turned out to be wrong.

After hearing the girl's explanation, Ellen decided to confront John about the problem. She did so the same afternoon as he was preparing to leave the office. She told him he should know better "than to leave the girls in a situation like this," and that he should call her if any other cases similar to this one arose. John was obviously upset by the nature and openness of the discussion. He thought for a moment and then replied, "This is my office, and I can take care of it. Anyway, you weren't here when the girl needed the help." After his remark, he turned and left the room. The next day he told one of the women in the office (the only black assignment clerk), I'm not about to ask a woman who only has a high school diploma how to run my job." A few minor complaints continued to be registered against the assignment office. However, no further altercations took place between Ellen and John for some time.

## New Problems

Approximately one month later, an incident arose that was related to an employee practice formerly condoned by Ellen when she held the position of assignment manager. Several of the women in the office had received permission from Ellen to take off work on occasion for appointments with their beauticians. Ellen and the women had come to an agreement that anyone taking off work for such an appointment would make up the time by either coming in early, working through lunch, or working late. John had noticed the practice during the first few weeks he was on the job but had said nothing. Finally, he issued a memo to the women which stated that they would have to make their appointments on their own time, and that they would no longer be allowed to do so during working hours.

One evening one of the older clerks asked John if she could leave an hour early so that she could be on time for an appointment with her beautician.

John responded by pulling out and waving the memo. He reaffirmed his position on the request, and the woman walked away. When the time came for the appointment, the woman got up and walked toward the door. John stepped before her and told her "you can go if you want to, but if you do, don't come back tomorrow." The woman left and came back the next day. John did not mention the incident to her. None of the other women left work for similar appointments after the incident. However, John overheard them threatening to do so.

Eventually, this incident and others were passed on to Ellen. She confided in one of the girls, "sometimes I think this job is just a lot of headaches." She decided that she must have a meeting about these problems and her own future with the hospital with Ed Crosby. As she was about to enter Mr. Crosby's office, Dave Randle walked out. He looked sheepishly at Ellen and then quickly walked away.

Ed Crosby looked up and addressed Ellen.

*Crosby:* Good morning, Ellen; I was just about to give you a call. You look disturbed. What's the matter?

*Ellen:* I guess I am not sure about this job anymore, Mr. Crosby. I've told you about some of the problems that have been occurring in the assignment office, and they don't seem to be getting any better. Frankly, I don't think John Matthews cares enough about the women that we have working in the office. I have been hearing more complaints about the way he treats them. Also, some of the women think that he is giving special treatment to the new black woman that we just hired. I just don't know what I am going to do.

*Crosby:* Ellen, perhaps you are getting too involved with the personal problems of the women in the offices. You know, that's Randle's and Matthews' jobs.

*Ellen:* Too close to them! Why, in my new position, I don't even have a chance to get involved with the day-to-day operations of the offices anymore. I have so much paperwork to do and so many meetings to go to that I can't see to it that the offices are being run properly.

*Crosby:* You're right, Ellen, we do have a problem. The efficiency rating of the assignment office and the processing office are both lower than before all of these changes were made. I have talked to John Matthews about this matter, and he feels that you have not given him enough help. He also thinks that the women who work around him favor you. Dave Randle also is having some problems. Since he now reports to you rather than directly to me, he has the feeling that he has been demoted.

*Ellen:* I get that feeling, myself. He seems to resent it whenever I offer him a suggestion. In fact, he hardly comes to me anymore for advice.

To tell you the truth, Mr. Crosby, I am not as sure about this job now as I was before. If these problems aren't straightened out pretty soon, I think I'd rather have my old job back.

Mr. Crosby assured Ellen that he would do what he could to help her restore the harmonious and productive atmosphere that had existed before the personnel changes. When Ellen left the room, Ed Crosby called in his secretary. "Get me the personnel folders on Matthews, Randle, and Nash."

# CASE 36
# Decision at Sea

## Part A: The New Assignment

A new assignment in any organization generally brings with it pleasures as well as problems. These costs and benefits may be amplified when the organizational members are confined to definite unyielding physical boundaries. Such was the case when a young Navy ensign just out of training school was assigned aboard the USS *Duarte*. His experiences are recorded in this case.

### First Impressions

It seemed like only yesterday that I had graduated from college and entered the navy's Officer Candidate School. Upon completing my officers training, I was sent to Navy Supply Corps School (NSCS) where I was subjected to a six-month barrage of navy business administration indoctrination. The program had been designed to provide future supply officers with the tools necessary to perform a management job afloat. The training itself was excellent. However, once afloat, I realized that I would have to constantly practice what I had learned or be doomed to failure no matter how bright a politician I might be.

I was met at the processing office by LTJG Collins. It was Lieutenant Collins whom I would be replacing aboard the USS *Duarte*. Collins told me that he would take me directly to the ship and let me "look her over." When we arrived at the dock, I was overwhelmed by the *Duarte*'s size. Although I had seen a picture of the ship, I had no idea that it was so large (almost the length of two football fields). The USS *Duarte* was a new attack cargo ship with 30 officers, a 320-man crew, and 300 Marine Corps troops. By civilian standards she easily could have provided enough electricity for 2,000 homes, enough food to feed 650 men for 90 days, and enough items in stock (26,000) to fill a large department store. The ship had fully air conditioned living spaces, a recreation room, library, bakery, soda fountain, laundry, dry cleaning plant, hospital, barber shop, post office, and a ship's store with sales of $40,000 a quarter. In short, the *Duarte* was a floating small town. The supply officer's responsibilities aboard a ship like this would be very time consuming.

Officers aboard the *Duarte* were not rank conscious as a general rule, but, rather, were job conscious. All officers, except the skipper, ate and socialized in the same wardroom and were generally close and open in communications about day-to-day management. On the other hand, the formally structured chain of command was noticeably present when the ship was loading cargo/

Prepared by H. William Vroman, Towson State University; and Kent Mitchell.

troops or was at General Quarters (war-time cruising, all battle stations manned).

I learned that the supply department had two officer billets (assignments): the Supply Officer, Lieutenant Roberts, and the Assistant Supply/Disbursing Officer, who would be I. The department consisted of sixty men. As their division officer, I had by far the largest division on the ship, with the average division size being twenty men per officer. This responsibility alone would later command me respect from my peers.

After a cup of coffee and some small talk, LTJG Collins said it was time to go meet the executive officer (XO). We knocked on his cabin and heard the customary reply to come in. The office we entered was impressive. It had two couches, a large executive desk, and dark blue wall-to-wall carpeting. LTJG Collins entered the office first. As he greeted the XO, he suddenly appeared to become very nervous. I then noticed, much to my shock, that as I was being introduced, Collins' hands were shaking like dry leaves in a breeze. I spoke to the XO a few minutes describing my background, the trip over, and so on. He seemed easygoing enough, though he obviously demanded a fair day's work. During the whole conversation, I worried about Collins' "shakes." The same thing happened later in the captain's cabin when we went to meet him. I was worried about Collins, but decided to keep the observation to myself. After all, he was leaving the ship in a few days and surely recognized his own problem.

Lieutenant Roberts, the supply officer, had been off the ship when I arrived. However, he came out of his office just as we were completing our rounds. He seemed to be an easygoing person. I was relieved to see that my immediate superior for the next year would not be too hard-nosed. We talked briefly. However, I again noticed Collins' nervousness, so I suggested I get settled in. Lieutenant Roberts agreed, and Collins and I proceeded to my quarters. I did not see Lieutenant Roberts again until we sailed.

No one ever bothered to tell me exactly what my job would or would not entail. Most NSCS graduates had a pretty good idea of their responsibilities before leaving the school. On the other hand, I did expect Lieutenant Roberts to take the initiative at some time and discuss his procedures, problems, and philosophy with me. I approached him about these matters a number of times while I served under him, but he never did provide me with much information.

My functional replacement of LTJG Collins went about as well as could be expected. I reviewed all of the accounts, took possession of about $200,000, and assumed the title of Disbursing Officer. The records of many of the accounts were in poor condition although no gross negligence necessarily could be proved. The enlisted disbursing clerk who was to work under me was a "short-timer" (would soon be leaving the navy), and I would be without help for about six weeks. All of my training at NSCS was based on the fact that I would have two disbursing clerks maintaining the accounts at all times. However, it appeared that this would not be the case.

The training programs at OCS and NSCS were excellent, but the curricula basically were technical. The managerial training we received was more extensive than that which I had encountered in college, but it still seemed overly cut and dried. I soon learned that management decision making was a completely different game. My most important managerial attributes it seemed would be flexibility and common sense.

After I was aboard ship a few days, I was approached by Chief Resor, the senior chief petty officer aboard the ship. Chief Resor quietly asked if we could have a few words alone. We went out on deck and leaned against the starboard rail and began talking. The chief was well educated and alert. He was small in stature but very impressive in know-how. He had served as an aide to two admirals and was serving out his final cruise before retirement. Chief Resor was thought of highly by enlisted men and officers alike. I listened carefully as the chief spoke:

I hope that I don't sound out of place, Lieutenant, but I think it would be best for both of us if you understood some of the facts aboard this ship. You probably already found Lt. Roberts to be a pleasant person. But a pleasant person isn't necessarily going to do the best job aboard ship. I've served under many supply officers in my day, and he certainly is among the worst. The supply department here on the *Duarte* is inefficient. The men's morale is probably lower than in any other department aboard. Frankly, no one from the CO down to the enlisted men has much respect for Lt. Roberts. One of the most serious problems we have is that Roberts doesn't carry his weight well in department head meetings. As a result, Roberts always seems to bend the rules to try to do something just the way another officer wants it done. On more than one occasion, I have had to sit him down and explain why we couldn't do a job the way he had told us to. Then, he spends the better part of the day trying to backtrack to everyone involved and get out of his commitment.

I could hardly believe what the chief had just said. Perhaps, I just didn't want to believe it! I told the chief that I appreciated his concern and would do what I could to hold up my end of the department. I did suggest, however, that nothing more be said about Lieutenant Roberts.

It wasn't long before I noticed certain symptoms of what Resor had described to me. It seems that Lieutenant Roberts lack of functional ability often resulted in a power vacuum that was automatically filled by other officers from outside the supply department. Thus, the leadership was there; but decisions were seldom made in the interest of the supply department and its men.

That evening I went to my quarters and sat down to think about the things that the chief had said. I recognized that Roberts was not in good standing with the other officers on the ship. This, together with his failure to take on the responsibilities of his billet, undoubtedly were responsible—at least in part—for LTJG Collins' poor job as disbursing officer. I thought about my own future on the ship as well as what my performance might mean in terms of subsequent assignments. I was troubled by the implications of my thoughts. Having completed the book *Caine Mutiny* only a few months before, my imagination began to run wild. I began to question what actions I might be forced to take in the months ahead.

The next morning, I awoke with a clearer head. I wondered if the chief had exaggerated his story. Had he had a run-in with Lt. Roberts? Was he trying to use me to shake up the department or was he seriously concerned about what had been taking place? I decided to keep a cool head about the matter and wait until I saw everyone in action while the USS *Duarte* was at sea.

## Part B: A Time for Action

The training I received was thorough in most respects although I soon found that there is no substitute for experience. Performing duties aboard ship is different than performing them in a classroom. Even the physical aspects of the job were different. It was easy to become slightly nauseated and get a headache from it. These symptoms were a mild form of sea sickness. Under such conditions, it was hard to sit still at a desk and run a calculator, and the conditions had to be overcome in order to function. Other adversities presented more formidable problems, however.

We arrived in the Philippines, and we bid farewell to Lieutenant j.g. Collins. I admired Collins in that he openly admitted he had not done a good job, and that perhaps it was partially his fault morale was low in the department. As he left the ship, I couldn't help but wonder what was in store for me.

As I learned my billet and observed those around me, I began to see just what could and could not be taught in the navy schools. In particular, I quickly realized that the functions I was called upon to perform were broader in scope than I had been led to believe. More often than not, it seemed that Lieutenant Roberts could not be found when requests for information came down from the executive officer. I attempted to provide the necessary reports but found myself thinking, "this isn't my job." After a while, it seemed to me that neither the XO nor the department heads even sought out Roberts. Instead, they came directly to me. I made it a point to always inform him when a request was made of me, but he didn't show any concern. Usually, he politely thanked me for helping out and nothing else was said.

Lieutenant Roberts' behavior seemed strange to me. He was not at all what I had expected in a superior. If he asked me to do something, he was very polite about it; in fact, he was too polite. He was kind to everybody and anybody. In my opinion, this trait was a fine personal attribute, but his gentleness coupled with his lack of confidence and lack of professional know-how caused many problems. It seemed as though the junior enlisted men, who knew better, would take advantage of him and use him to get around the orders of their chiefs. It was not too long before the chiefs began to look my way for support and policy decisions. The department heads began to look my way also. I wasn't prepared for this kind of attention, and it often made me feel uncomfortable.

Lieutenant Roberts and I had received the same training, and I knew that things weren't supposed to work this way. It finally started getting to me, and I decided to ask Lieutenant Roberts what the deal was. After being aboard the ship only a short time, I possessed more power—if that's the term—at least informally, than he did. When we talked about it, he told me that he knew he had "screwed-up" a lot of things. He said that the skipper XO, and department heads were stacked against him. The supply corps had a great deal of *esprit de corps*, and I didn't want to scuddle my boss. My conscience really bothered me on that subject. I personally hoped that carrying him would keep us both out of hot water. We each knew the situation, and perhaps it would work itself out. Nevertheless, I felt as though I were sitting on a time bomb.

After a while, I started putting together a mental dossier on Lieutenant Roberts. He was held back a month at OCS. He was at the bottom of his class at NSCS. He had completed two back-to-back disbursing officer assignments (both were shore duty) before coming to the *Duarte* as Supply Officer. He had been "passed over" twice for promotion to LCDR. (If passed over a third time, he would be released from the navy.) He constantly said, "the Captain wants us to . . ." He never once audited my work. He constantly referred to the chief for help. He disappeared often. He often did work that should have been performed by his subordinates. He associated too closely with the junior enlisted men. He was not respected by the chiefs aboard ship. As an individual, he was easygoing and hard to dislike.

I felt sorry for him when I realized that Lieutenant Roberts was weak in his billet. He wanted to stay in the navy badly, but he failed to recognize his over-all responsibilities. It was a fact that many chiefs and first class petty officers "carried" their bosses professionally when it came to running the shop. A superior does not have to know all of the intricacies and technical details of jobs performed below him. However, any superior should have a good idea of the functions, relationships, job responsibilities, and the capabilities of his men. Chief Edwards was perfectly willing to go beyond his call to assist Lieutenant Roberts. I was too. Evidently Lieutenant j.g. Collins had not been able to do so. I wondered how long I would be this willing.

After being at sea about six weeks, things began to get on my nerves. Lieutenant Roberts' actions were hurting the men (although he didn't seem to realize it). The supply department was not well represented topside in the skipper's cabin. The skipper was a tough man, and he was under a lot of fire. The *Duarte* was a "deep draft vessel," an assignment that all navy captains had to fill before promotion to "Admiral." Naturally, the name of the game was to make the skipper look good in the eyes of other commands. It was rumored that the navy supply systems command did not think well of USS *Duarte*. Too many mistakes had cost her more than one efficiency rating. Supply decisions simply weren't being made by the supply department. For all practical purposes, the department had become a pawn of other officers on the ship.

Finally, I decided that some action would have to be taken if I were to salvage the department and my own rating. No one made decisions concerning the supply division or disbursing unless I okayed them. I often consulted my senior petty officers on matters which I felt unsure of. My goal was to provide strength at the top where it belonged. Lieutenant Roberts had been harassed by his fellow officers in the past and I had sometimes felt the impact of their criticism. Now, I had decided that much destructive criticism must be stopped. On two occasions I told officers, flatly, that I disagreed with their assessment of our operations or procedures. Where necessary, I pointed out our SOP's and their justifications and respectfully submitted that they should and must be followed. At the same time, I recognized the need for greater co-operation with other departments but on an even basis. Although I, on occasion, was asked for my opinion of Lieutenant Roberts, I declined comment. However, pressure on me to give my observations on the lieutenant increased as I dealt more directly with officers of his rank or higher.

One morning I was called to the XO's office to explain some budgetary calculations. As usual, I was being asked to explain work that was not mine. Normally, I explained what I could and researched the rest—quickly. The XO had never before discussed with me his feelings about Lieutenant Roberts. As a matter of fact, I was being asked to perform so much, and so often, that I actually started wondering whether people realized that the shoes I was having to fill were not my own. When asked one question that I was having difficulty answering, I jokingly remarked, "You do know this isn't my responsibility!?" The XO stood up and walked across the room. Never looking directly at me, he proceeded, "Alas, Mr. Disbursing Officer, the chips are on the table!"

# EXPERIENTIAL EXERCISE 14

## Group Exclusion

Groups develop certain ways of looking at things. As members show they disagree, the group attempts to bring them into conformity and, if unsuccessful, may
exclude the disagreeing members. The process is a common group activity. This
exercise is designed to give the participant the feeling of going through such an
exclusion process and of being excluded from the group.

### Instructions

1. Assemble into groups of five or six members. One member is designated by
   the professor as a process observer for each group. She or he will observe
   the group activities but not participate in them. Allow enough room between
   groups so they can act independently.
2. Each group selects any case in this book previously prepared for class for a
   ten-minute discussion. (Times can be adjusted for class length.)
3. Spend the next fifteen minutes with the members of your group consensu-
   ally arriving at a criterion for excluding a member of the group. The group
   can choose any reason for excluding one member, but all the other members
   have to agree.
4. Excluded members go to a predesignated place to sit down.
5. For ten minutes the rest of the group takes an "in-class" break. They may
   talk with others about such topics as the case they were discussing, the
   criterion they used to exclude the member, or other class topics. There is to
   be no interaction with the excluded members.
6. When the groups reassemble, the excluded members place their chairs outside the chairs of the members of their old group. They have ten minutes to
   get back into the group by any means they care to exercise. (This step is
   optional.)
7. At the end of this time, the group selects a spokesperson.
8. The excluded person speaks first about why he or she was excluded from the
   group, how justified the action was, and what his or her feelings are toward
   the other excluded members. The spokesman for the excluding group follows and tells what criterion was used and why that member met the criterion.
9. One or more process observers might have been assigned to observe the
   exclusion process without participating. The process observers then tell what
   happened in the group.
10. The entire class then discusses the process in light of the chapter material
    on group dynamics.

Prepared by H. William Vroman.

# EXPERIENTIAL EXERCISE 15
## Standing on Principle

The purpose of this exercise is to illustrate your reaction to stress.

### Instructions

1. Assemble groups of four or five members.
2. A controversial topic is introduced to the class, and each member publicly states his or her stand on the issue.
3. The members of the group then intensely discuss the issues within the group. Each member is to argue the same side of the issue as their public stance.
4. Prior to class, one member of each group has been asked to change his or her actual view on the subject.
5. The group is to argue the issue for fifteen minutes, then spend ten minutes arriving at a consensus on who the individual is that changed his or her actual view on the issue.
6. For twenty minutes the class discusses the event. The feelings of the members and the person accused of changing his or her view are explored.

### Questions for Discussion

1. What feelings did you have during the discussion? How do you believe your stress was reflected in your actions?
2. How did you identify the individual in the group whose position was contrary to his or her normal position on the subject?
3. Did you find your stress to be exhilarating or trying (a) emotionally, (b) intellectually, (c) physically?
4. What factors affected your level of stress during the discussion?
5. In what ways can personal stress be reduced?

Prepared by Donald D. White and H. William Vroman.

# PART V

# MANAGEMENT AND ORGANIZATIONAL DEVELOPMENT

Throughout this book we have addressed the complex relationships between the environment and the organizational system. We have focused on system inputs such as technology, organizational structure, group activities, and of course human beings themselves. Although these many forces operate independently inside the system, the organization and its individual members must co-align their activities in order to accomplish the organization's goals.

A term often used to describe this co-alignment is *development*. Development is the attempt to contend with changes in the environment by planning, anticipating, adapting, and learning. In other words, development implies planned change. Many aspects of an organization require development. For example, marketing spends a good deal of time developing a product to fit the needs of a client group. Production develops ways to meet changes in raw material inputs and new technologies. Finally, people and organizations must also undergo continuous development. Development processes that are of particular importance in organizational behavior are management and career development and organizational development.

Management development refers to the dual process of preparing present managers to meet tomorrow's demands and filling the organization's need for new skilled people. Selecting, training, and establishing career paths are primary objectives of management development. Assessing the interests, capacity, and potential of managers early in their employment allows an organization to plan managerial growth. Through such planning, the enterprise can ensure itself of adequately prepared managerial talent, and individual managers can benefit from personalized training programs.

A variety of strategies and techniques are available for preparing today's managers to meet tomorrow's organizational needs. Strategies and techniques selected are a function of the managers to be developed and the goals of the development program. Factors such as company size, managerial level (executive, middle management, or supervisory), and the abilities and traits of management trainees all influence the program content.

Closely related to management development is the concept of career development. Career development is oriented to the individual more so than to the organization. Career development involves identifying the work roles in which an individual desires to become involved. Career stages often correlate with patterns of adult personality development. Therefore, effective career planning must be coupled with an awareness and understanding of an individual's social and psychological growth.

Just as individuals may develop through a combination of personal and organizational planning, so, too, may organizations experience planned change and development. Organizational development represents an attempt to apply knowledge learned through the behavioral sciences to dynamic, evolving organizational systems. A primary goal of organizational development is to continuously re-orient the system to cope with internal realignment of system inputs and to maintain a healthy and profitable exchange with the environment.

Organizational development is accomplished through a careful diagnosis of the system, identification of areas that require change, and developing and implementing intervention strategies that will successfully bring about the needed change. As with management development, a variety of approaches may be adopted in organizational development. However, those approaches vary in terms of cost, risk to organizational members, and the relevant social or personal system affected.

Organizational development requires the careful guidance of a trained specialist (change agent) to ensure both the attainment of organizational renewal goals and the integrity of organizational members.

# CHAPTER TEN

# Management and Career Development

The organization has an important interest in developing managers to take charge of new departments as it expands or to replace existing managers as they leave. A company is no stronger than the talent of its middle managers. A major organizational effort is required to take young, inexperienced managers and, over a period of years, make them competent decision makers who are available when the organization needs them. This process is called management development.

As organizations develop goals and strategies, so, too, must successful managers plan their own futures. Attention must be given to career goals which satisfy personal objectives, such as material gain or the satisfaction of psychological needs. The sequence of events and associated attitudes toward work-related growth is referred to as a career path. Hall has defined a career as, "the individually perceived sequence of attitudes and behaviors associated with work-related experiences and activities over the span of the person's life." [1]

Organizational management development and individual career development obviously have reciprocal impact on one another. Successful management development depends upon a young manager's willingness to sacrifice to meet the organization's needs. Many managers learn the "rules" of the organization's career ladder and accomplish their goals accordingly. However, the attitudes of young managers toward career, power, and mobility have a constraining effect on what techniques the organization can use to develop them. In addition, increasing numbers of competent, career-oriented women are having an impact on traditional ways of developing managers.

Michael Maccoby in *The Gamesman* pointed out an additional difficulty in the philosophy behind the management development of individuals. [2] Such development is biased toward skills that are needed by the organization and have little bearing on other life skills needed by the individual. Some qualities a company encourages are ambition, self-confidence, intellectual abilities, and cooperative (reliable) attitudes. Maccoby's "heart" qualities like compassion, generosity, and idealism are discouraged by corporate development. The lack of these latter qualities creates the increased risk of mortality and morbidity among the males Maccoby studied. The health and personal difficulties experienced as males pass 40 years and the early average age of death are attributed by Maccoby to the lack of attention to "heart" qualities in management development programs. In addition, overdevelopment of the company-encouraged qualities can be devastating if failure is experienced.[3]

All organizations require managerial competence in order to accomplish their goals and to be ready to meet their needs for expansion and replacement of personnel. Such is the role of management development. Career development, on the other hand, addresses the individual's goals and plans for personal accomplishment in the work world. There are additional skills that are not developed by institutions and not necessarily part of an individual's career plans. These skills are often developed to support activities and aspirations outside the organization.

## Strategies for Developing Managers

Edgar Schein suggests six strategies[4] utilized by organizations to develop their new employees. The intent of each strategy is to gradually increase the learning of the employee to meet the future needs of the organization. Each strategy is designed to test the individual's potential so that only the most competent men and women achieve upper management positions.

1. *Sink or swim.* This strategy involves deliberately building ambiguity into a job position, giving very little guidance or support to the young manager. The intent is to see how the potential manager clarifies the situation, formulates objectives, and accomplishes them. Naturally, the higher you go in management, the more ambiguous the situation. Thus, early experience with ambiguous job situations enhances the probability of later success. A critical factor in the effectiveness of this strategy is the organization's response to failure. Minimizing punishment, providing positive feedback for successful performance, and supporting developing strengths enhance the development effort.
2. *Upending experience.* Using knowledge of individual change, the organization gives the manager jobs at which she or he is almost sure to fail. The failure leaves the manager "shaken" and ready to accept guidance by upper managers.
3. *On-the-job-training.* A more traditional approach, this strategy entails giving the young manager an increasingly challenging job with commensurate support. The success of this approach is dependent upon the quality of the job and expertise of superiors who act as counselors.
4. *Working while training.* An organization may assign an individual to a full-time training program for a period from three to twelve months. However, his or her time alternates between training and short-term job assignments. The effectiveness of this program depends on the intensity of the short-term job assignment and may be limited by the short time spent on each job. The technique also is known as *job rotation.*

5. *Full-time training.* In this case a new manager is scheduled for periods of several weeks to several months in a department. While there, the person is allowed to do all the jobs for a while, generally "helping" a permanent employee of that department. After the time period, the manager goes to another department for the same experience. After traveling to a number of departments, the new manager will have been introduced to the entire organization, and departmental managers will have been given an opportunity to see where they work in best. This approach gives new managers a broad view of the organization. Because the training involves "looking and trying," with no responsibility, it is sometimes perceived as non-work, causing the program to be discounted.

6. *Integrative strategies.* After an on-the-job evaluation, a person is given training based on his or her needs and abilities. This may entail one or more of the first five strategies.

In addition to Schein's six strategies, three more strategies can be identified.[5] The first is a cooperative program between universities and organizations. Students spend alternative years in an organization. Although plans differ in detail, the intent is to give promising students a glimpse of work-life to make academic work more pertinent. The approach has the added advantage to the company of getting a look at potential employees without a long-term commitment to employment.

The second strategy involves outside training. Universities and private training or consulting organizations provide training in skill and management areas for supervisors, managers, and executives. Many organizations rely on outside trainers, while others do most of their training through their own training departments. In-house trainers have the advantage of being more familiar with the personnel and needs of the organization. On the other hand, outside trainers are often more innovative, because they have varied experience and can bring the best of that broad experience to the organization.

The third strategy, a relatively new approach, is the use of assessment centers. Assessment centers are used to determine the potential of young managers for hiring or promotion purposes. Experiential exercises, simulations, tests of skill, in-baskets, and personality tests are used in an off-site setting. The individual results of each person going through the exercises are assessed or judged by experts (psychologists and other behavioral scientists) and by line and staff managers who have an in-depth knowledge of the positions for which the new managers are candidates. Results of the assessments are then used to design a personal development program for the manager. The approach has been widely acclaimed due to both the scope and depth of the evaluation process.

### Training Techniques

Trainers use several teaching techniques to train managers: lecture, case method, experiential exercises, in-basket exercises, role playing, and management games. Trainers develop objectives for each session. They then adopt the techniques that are most likely to accomplish those objectives.

Lecture is a way of transmitting large quantities of information in a short period of time. However, it lacks the involvement that enhances change. The case method, used properly, has the advantage of student involvement in real situations, but it does not transmit large quantities of information as efficiently as the lecture method. Experiential exercises focus on real-life human experiences and attempt to create similar situations in a classroom setting. The student experiences the feeling and sees the behavior of people in that setting.

In-basket exercises put the trainee under time pressure to respond to problems in a manager's "in-basket." The problems are in the form of memos, letters, phone messages, and notes. A variety of problems can be posed in a short period of time. The outcome is an analysis of the trainee's business knowledge and decision-making skills.

Role playing is a technique that increases one's awareness of the dynamics of different situations and roles. Trainees act out roles in which they have only limited experience. Role playing is often used in combination with the case method, experiential exercises, and in-basket activities.

Management games are generally computer simulations of large, complex organizational situations. Normally, teams of trainees make decisions having long-range impacts on larger situations. The computer program simulates what might happen, and results that may take months or years to see in real life are fed back immediately.

### Administering Management Development Programs

In a study of firms noted for the quality of their management development programs, certain key decision points were developed concerning program

**Figure 1. Training strategies by level and size.**

| 1. *Inside or outside trainers?* | | | 2. *Technical or human relations program content?* | |
|---|---|---|---|---|
| *Level of Training* | *Small organization* | *Large organization* | *Small organization* | *Large organization* |
| Executive | Inside | Outside | — | — |
| Middle | Both | Inside | Human relations | Human relations |
| Supervisory | Inside | Inside | Technical | Human relations |

| 3. *Training done on- or off-site?* | | | 4. *Training emphasizes strategy or environmental/philosophical concerns?* | |
|---|---|---|---|---|
| *Level of Training* | *Small organization* | *Large organization* | *Small organization* | *Large organization* |
| Executive | On-site | Off-site | Strategy | Environmental |
| Middle | Both | On-site | — | — |
| Supervisory | On-site | On-site | — | — |

administration.[6] Some of the companies sampled included IBM, Xerox, Citibank, Textron, AT&T, and General Motors. Figure 1 shows some of the findings.

The goals of management development programs were essentially the same, but the methods used to accomplish the goals differed according to organization size. Both the needs of organizations and the resources available (training facilities and trainers) increased with organizational size. Figure 1 illustrates the corresponding changes in strategies between small (fewer than 2,000 employees) and large organizations.

Programs were divided into techniques corresponding to the three levels of organization. Skills associated with the supervisory, middle management, and executive levels were distinct and required separate training. The columns in Figure 1 refer to the major decisions firms have to make about the programs: (1) Should the company use its own or outside trainers? (2) Is the supervisory training to be "hands-on" skill training or more conceptual managerial/human relations training? (3) Are the programs held on company premises (on-site) or at hotels or universities (off-site)? (4) Is the executive-level training curriculum oriented toward traditional topics like business policy and internal processes or toward topics like environmental understanding and philosophy?

Larger companies tended to do more in-house training than small companies. The quality of trainers and their preferences for certain subjects and types of pedagogy make the extensive in-house training a logical step for larger organizations with necessary resources. At the supervisory level, most organizations trained in-house (on company premises), whereas only larger companies trained with company trainers on company premises at the middle-management level.

The results in smaller organizations were mixed. At the executive level, larger organizations sent top-level managers outside for infusion of new ideas, whereas smaller organizations tended to do the training in-house. Large organizations differed in two other respects. First, the nature of the curriculum was different at the supervisory and the executive levels. Second, supervisors in larger organizations received a sizable portion of human relations/conceptual type training. Small organizations, on the other hand, tended to emphasize immediately usable, highly pragmatic skill sessions. The emphasis in larger organizations was to train executives in environmental understanding and general education subjects, while executives of smaller firms concentrated on policy and strategy subjects.

## Career Development

Earlier we suggested that an individual's *career* referred to attitudes and behaviors associated with work-related experiences over the span of one's life. *Career development,* then, refers to a conscious effort on the part of the organization to contribute to the selection of a career area and to help the individual grow and become more involved in that role. Ultimately, the goal of career development is to promote a healthy adjustment to the career choice and thereby contribute to feelings of self-esteem and competence.[7]

*Career Stages*

Chapter One discussed the intermittent periods of transition and stability that characterize adult development. Levinson's model of adult development outlined these changes and identified critical transition points to subsequent life stages.[8] An important determinant of the successful transition from one life stage to another is the successful completion of corresponding career stages. Figure 2 illustrates the relationship of career stages (and related career decisions) to corresponding life stages. Career stages pictured here combine the work of a number of different writers,[9, 10, 11] while the life stages are similar to those depicted by Levinson. Some outstanding characteristics of each stage are listed in Figure 2.

**Figure 2.  Relating life stages to career stages.**

| Age | Life stages | Career stages | Characteristics |
| --- | --- | --- | --- |
| 17 | Childhood & adolescence | Exploration | Part-time jobs; education |
| 17–22 | Adult transition | Exploration | Education for some |
| 22–28 | GIAW | Trial & establishment | Long hours; job change; learning the rules; family starting |
| 28–32 | Transition | Establishment & tenure | Promotions; financial outlay; long hours & take-home work; (women) childbearing decision |
| 33–41 | Settling down | Advancement | Community work; mothers coming back part- or full-time; increasing financial burden; divorces increase; continuing education |
| 40–45 | Mid-life transition | Advancement-maintenance (stable) | Children leaving for school/work; (women) flexibility for work/avocation; declining health for some; increasing need for personal development/reassessment |
| 45–55 | Middle adulthood | Maintenance | Financial demands easing; most likely career plateau; a few advance to executive levels |
| 55–65 | Anticipation of retirement | Decline | Increased leisure activities; plan for retirement |

The early years of seeking and establishing a career are referred to as stages of *exploration*. They are characterized by identifying career possibilities through education and/or part-time work. The next stage, known as *trial and establishment,* results in an initial selection and commitment to a single career area. *Establishment and tenure* refers to the period during which a significant investment of oneself in the job is experienced. Often, establishment and tenure leads to long hours and other extensive personal commitments to the work role. *Advancement* may lead to an extension of the individual beyond the immediate work environment into political, social, and other community activities. Decisions related to social activities play an increasingly important role during the advancement stage. *Advancement-maintenance* begins a period of stabilization in career development. Individual reassessment and recognition of the need for personal development take on particular importance during the period. *Maintenance* reflects a leveling-off in career developments, with further career advancement limited to a select few individuals. Finally, *decline* involves a period of planning for retirement and during which outside leisure activities occupy additional time. Although the timing of these stages is relatively accurate, dissimilarities may occur due to differences in career areas, personal experiences, and sex.

*Women and career development.*   Life stages and career stages have been established with data from male experiences and are consequently biased. An increasing number of women are competing on an equal basis for promotions in organizations. A number of these women follow career stages similar to the outline in Figure 2, but many others do not. According to Sheehy, the pattern women follow is related to childbearing functions.[12] The result of an early decision to have a child is that those mothers start their careers later, get their experiences at later ages, and consequently do not get the same consideration for promotion as similar-aged males.

Figure 2 compares career stages and life stages, with some comments under "characteristics" pointing out sex differences resulting from childbearing decisions. Figure 3 focuses on some of the major decisions a woman must make that complicate her career path. Three major decisions/events are pictured: First the early childbearing decision; second the 7- to 13-year decision to have another child or to have the first. (This decision is related to the belief that the probabilities of having healthy children or any children at all decrease after ages 35 to 40.) The third major event with an impact on women's employment history is divorce. This event can occur any time in a married life and forces an immediate employment decision in most cases. As women occupy a greater number of upper-level positions in organizations, the ages accepted for successful change from stage to stage will no doubt change to take childbearing and divorce into account.

## Summary

Management and career development are two important processes in organizational life. Organizations must develop a strong and competent group

**Figure 3. Women's work participation differences.**[a]

| Decision to bear children | Type of employment | First decade decision[b] | Divorce decision | Employment |
|---|---|---|---|---|
| CHILDREN → YES | Part-time | continue or quit (child) | yes | full-time |
| | | | no | continue |
| | | full | yes | full |
| | | | no | continue |
| | No work | full-part employment (child) | yes | continue |
| | | | no | continue |
| | | continue | yes | full time |
| | | | no | continue |
| CHILDREN → NO | Full-time | continue | yes/no | stay at work |
| | | quit or leave of absence | yes | back to work |
| | | | no | back to work |
| | Part-time | full or part time | yes | continue |
| | | | no | continue |
| | | quit (child) | yes | back to work |
| | | | no | continue |

[a] The highlighted pathways show significant changes in the employment of the women involved on that pathway.
[b] Many women just take a leave to have a baby and go back to work full-time immediately. This option depends, in part, on the availability of suitable nursery services or family close by.

of managers in order to meet the demands for managerial talent in their futures. Individuals have their own work-related aspirations. These take the form of a plan for career development. The organization's program and the individual's career aspirations are intimately related to the life stages that humans go through.

Schein described six strategies organizations use to develop managers: sink or swim, upending experiences, on-the-job training, working while training, full-time training, and integrative component. Other strategies include cooperative programs, outside trainers, and assessment centers. Trainers use different pedagogies to accomplish their objectives. Standard approaches include lecture, case method, experiential exercises, in-basket exercises, role playing, and management games. Consistencies appear to exist in well-managed organizations' management development programs.

However, differences such as location of training and program context are related to organization size and management level, respectively.

Career development stages progress from those of exploration of career roles on through periods of trial, tenure, advancement, maintenance, and decline. Each stage is identified by an approximate age range and corresponds to life stages that are determined by a number of biological and cultural forces. Since most of the data supporting career and life stage development are based on males, the information may have limited application in understanding women in the work force.

## References

1. D. T. Hall, *Careers in Organizations* (Pacific Palisades: Goodyear Publishing, 1976), p. 4.
2. Michael Maccoby, *The Gamesman* (New York: Bantam Books, 1976), p. 226.
3. Ibid., p. 111.
4. Edgar Schein, "How To Break the College Graduate," *Harvard Business Review*, 42, 1964, pp. 68–76.
5. William F. Glueck, *Personnel: A Diagnostic Approach* (Dallas: Business Publications, 1978), *passim* chapters 7, 10, and 12.
6. L. T. Digman, "How Well-Managed Organizations Develop Their Executives," *Organizational Dynamics,* vol. 7, no. 2, Autumn 1978, pp. 63–80.
7. Hall, op. cit., pp. 29–32.
8. Daniel J. Levinson et al., *The Seasons of a Man's Life* (New York: Alfred A. Knopf, 1978).
9. D. C. Miller and William A. Form, *Industrial Sociology* (New York: Harper, 1951).
10. D. T. Hall and Khalil Nougaim, "Correlates of Organizational Identification as a Function of Career Pattern and Organization Type," *Administrative Science Quarterly*, 15, 1970, pp. 176–190.
11. Allen R. Cohen and Hermon Gadon, *Alternative Work Schedules: Integrating Individual and Organizational Needs* (Reading: Addison-Wesley, 1978), chapter 2.
12. Gale Sheehy, *Passages* (New York: Dutton, 1974).

## Recommended Readings

Readings marked with an asterisk are included in *Contemporary Perspectives in Organizational Behavior,* edited by Donald D. White (Boston: Allyn and Bacon, 1982).

Charles P. Bowen, "Let's Put Realism into Management Development," *Harvard Business Review,* July/August 1973, pp. 80–87.

*J. D. Brian, "A Contingency Approach to Management Development: Some Perspectives and a Diagnostic Model," *Management International Review,* vol. 19, no. 1, 1979, pp. 123–128.

Daniel C. Feldman, "A Practical Program for Employee Socialization," *Organizational Dynamics,* vol. 5, no. 2, Autumn 1976, pp. 64–80.

*Marlys C. Hanson, "Career Development Responsibilities of Managers," *Personnel Journal,* vol. 56, September 1977, pp. 443–445.

*Christine D. Hay, "Women in Management: The Obstacles and Opportunities They Face," *Personnel Administrator,* vol. 25, April 1980, pp. 31–39.

*George A. Steiner, "Invent Your Own Future," *California Management Review,* vol. 19, Fall 1976, pp. 29–33.

# CASE 37
# A Woman Co-Oping

Doris Barrette was 19 and a student at Illinois Tech. She came through a troubling academic year in 1978–79. First, her studies in civil engineering were barely satisfactory. Second, she called off an impending marriage. Late in the spring semester 1979, Doris changed her major to industrial technology, a more practical major.

Almost immediately she was offered the opportunity to "co-op," an option often given to students in professional schools. Co-op programs allow a student to gain on-the-job experience by alternating years between school and industry. The year in industry brings the financial rewards of a salary and scholarship and is intellectually rewarding, as well. The company, in turn, has the opportunity to get capable help at reasonable salaries. In addition, the company can get information on the most capable students for permanent employment after graduation.

Doris had her first interviews for the co-op program in early summer 1978. She was a little frightened of the new experience. After interviews with several companies, she was offered a position with National Fidelity Company (NFC). Her role was to help the company's clients comply with national, state, and local laws. She was assigned to the Fort Wayne, Indiana, office.

Doris checked into a moderately priced hotel because she had trouble locating a suitable apartment. Linus Ford, Doris' supervisor, came to pick Doris up on the morning of January 3, 1979, and take her to work.

"I was terrified. I had never met any of these people and I did not know the exact scope of the work that I was expected to do. Arriving at the office, I was introduced to my co-workers and shown to my desk."

The safety representatives were Sam Allyson, Mike Miller, and Jerry Barnaby. Also in the office were three auditors, Kirk Kilter, Carl Clark, and Bruce Lynn, and two secretaries named Sandra White and Wilamena Band (see Exhibit 1 for biographical data). Doris was located at an isolated desk facing the wall right outside the supervisor's office. The supervisor's office was completely enclosed, while the other employees had cubicles.

Doris immediately poured into the work. NFC insured companies against a variety of risks. Doris had to take courses on fire protection, OSHA, defensive driving, and training. The focus of the training was to gain substantive knowledge about safety as well as techniques designed to effectively transmit that knowledge to clients. Besides the training and coursework, Doris started to make inspection calls with the men in the office during this time period.

While at a plant, the NFC team would inspect the facilities and make safety recommendations to the manager, who usually accompany the team on

Prepared by H. William Vroman, Towson State University.

**Exhibit 1. Biographical data.**

---

Linus Ford: 50 years old, Supervisor of Safety Representatives in Kentucky, married, two children, both married.
Sam Allyson: 56 years old, Senior Safety Representative, cattle farmer, married, two children.
Mike Miller: 52 years old, Safety Representative, married, one daughter.
Jerry Barnaby: 27 years old, Safety Representative, married, two children.
Carl Clark: 25 years old, Auditor, single.
Kirk Kilter: 32 years old, Auditor, married, three children
Bruce Lynn: 35 years old, Auditor, married, two children.
Sandra White: 45 years old, Secretary, married, one married daughter.
Wilamena Band: 19 years old, Secretary, married.
Dick Fredericks: 50 years old, Indianapolis Safety Representative, married, two children.
Jim Eastern: 52 years old, Bowling Green Safety Representative, married, two children.
Doris: 19 years old, co-op student, single.
Bill Fleming: 49 years old, Vice President in charge of the Midwest, located in Baltimore, married, one son.
Fred Inglope: 42 years old, South End Safety Representative, two married sons.

---

the tour. The recommendations were to improve the company's safety record and to meet the requirements of the Occupational Safety and Health Act (OSHA). Back at the office, the recommendations would be written out for NFC's files and a copy given to the manager.

The job involved a lot of traveling and overnight trips. Doris would average at least a week of traveling per month. "I was very satisfied with my work and enjoyed it." Along with the substantive aspects of the work, Doris was told about the informal rules of the organization. For example, she was advised to fill out expense accounts to include a little extra money because "if you don't use it this week, you'll need more next week." In addition, Mr. Ford attempted to persuade Doris to go to his church, even though she was going to another one during her time in Fort Wayne. He constantly brought her books about various aspects of religion. As Doris said, "I felt that he was trying to take on the father image and I didn't need that from him."

On March 28, 1979, Doris was to go to Bowling Green, Kentucky, to work with another safety engineer named Dick Fredericks. As it happened, Mr. Ford had to go down to inspect a company there, so he suggested that Doris go down with him and his wife. "This seemed strange. I had been on the road quite a bit already with others and nothing had occurred. The only thing I picked up was in his original conversation with me, he said that his wife was going so nothing would be said about our going together. Overall, the ride was very strained."

Dick Fredericks and Doris worked for three days, and according to Doris, she learned a great deal. Dick was an experienced engineer who had special insights into safety problem and was effective when he dealt with managers. Dick stayed at a motel a few miles away.

Early in May I had to work in Indianapolis with Jim Eastern. He stayed at his home, while I stayed at a motel. When I went to his home one night for dinner, I got the first hint that my presence was creating some difficulties for the male employees. I felt I had been invited because his wife wanted to "look me over." Many thoughts crossed my mind, including resignation, but, cooler thoughts prevailed and I decided to treat the matter lightly.

A week or so after working in Indianapolis, Doris attended a meeting of all the region's safety representatives. The meeting was a gathering to discuss the changes in safety laws, problems that the representatives had been having, and also to have a good time. The second morning, during the break, everyone had gathered around the coffee urn. They sat on the sofa and leaned against the wall. In the course of the rambling conversation, they got to Doris and her work during the co-op.

*Jim:* Well, Doris, you've only got three more months with us here. Have you learned anything?
*Doris:* Certainly have, thanks to you all. And I've worked with nearly everyone —well, let's see. I worked with Dick, Jim, Sam, Mike, and Jerry—that leaves only Fred . . . (looking around playfully Doris added), Well, when's it goin' to be, Fred?

At this point, there was an awkward silence. A couple of throats were cleared, and then Sam responded.

*Sam:* (looking at Doris) Fred's wife has been giving him trouble.
*Doris:* Not because of me!
*Sam:* Yes—you.
*Doris:* (looking at Fred) Is that right?
*Fred:* Yes.
*Doris:* How about the rest of you?

A number of them nodded and murmured. There was an awkward silence, then Sam went for another cup of coffee. With the movement, the others took their leave.

*Carl:* Well, I guess it's time to get to the meeting.

Doris was left standing there. Her head was spinning. Bruce seemed to hang back, but she motioned him to go on. She thought to herself, "Wow, what will I do? I'll resign, that's for sure. Should I go back to the meeting? I don't know . . . the trip to Dick's house for dinner . . . the trip with Linus' wife to Bowling Green. . . ." At that point someone came for a last cup of coffee and said, "Hey, it's time to go." Doris went back to the meeting.

The meeting went as planned. The next morning Doris tendered her resignation to Ford with an explanation of why she was doing so. Ford acknowledged that difficulties had been building for some time but denied that it was getting out of hand. Doris wanted the resignation to be effective immediately, but, after checking with the home office, she found it would take time to process the resignation. A scholarship for schooling the following year accompanied the co-op program; thus, the resignation would have to follow channels.

While it was being processed, Doris was transferred to another office where she mostly did filing and other tasks. About three weeks before her resignation was to take effect, she saw a memo to her present supervisor and to Linus Ford saying that this assignment of duties was not according to the agreement with the university.

The NFC vice president in charge of the Midwest, Bill Fleming, came to Fort Wayne for the annual dinner with the families of the safety representatives and staff. The dinner came at the end of a series of meetings that Bill had with the staff to discuss organization and objectives. He made a special point to see Doris because relationships with the university were important. After telling her that the resignation would be final in three weeks, he made it clear that Doris would be included in the family dinner to be held at the country club.

"It was to be held on a Friday evening, but I had already written it off and accepted a date to go to a concert. However, I went back that evening and cancelled the date. The next morning I was in the coffee room when Linus came in. He casually asked me if I was coming to the dinner. I said that Mr. Fleming had told me that I was invited. Without looking up from stirring his coffee, he said he knew, but, as long as I was resigning anyway, it would be best if I didn't come to the dinner.

"I was hurt. I left the office and went back to my apartment to decide what to do. It was clear that I wouldn't go to the dinner. Instead I would pack and leave—to hell with the resignation, scholarship, and university relations."

Doris ate by herself that evening, then packed her things into suitcases and boxes. It was 2:00 a.m. when the telephone rang. Bill Fleming called to ask why Doris hadn't been at the dinner. Doris recounted the series of incidents that had resulted in her invitation being recalled. She also told him about her decision to have her resignation go into effect immediately.

Bill persuaded Doris to have a drink with him to talk it out. "I wanted to get everything straightened out, so I went. After explaining the situation to him, he reluctantly agreed that I should leave immediately to avoid further hard feelings. I felt much better after the discussion."

Bill called the next morning to see if Doris would be in town that evening to come to dinner with him. Doris refused and left town that afternoon.

# CASE 38
# Belwood Lumber Company

The Belwood Lumber Company was organized in 1932 by two brothers, John and Peter Adams. Initially, the two brothers installed a small sawmill and began buying timber, cutting lumber, and selling it green and air-dried in the southeastern region of the United States from their base of operations in Georgia. The company experienced gradual growth over a thirty-year period and by the mid-1960s was employing 235 persons and producing 30,000,000 feet of lumber per year. To provide a source of raw material supply, Belwood amassed 160,000 acres of excellent pine timberland in South Georgia.

Peter, who had been of valuable assistance to John, left the company in 1958 due to ill health. The following year, a need for capital caused John Adams to broaden the company's ownership base. The Adams brothers retained 62 percent of the common stock. The remaining shares were sold primarily to a few key employees and some personal friends.

In 1973, Mr. Adams, who was then sixty-seven, came to realize that an estate distribution problem was imminent. He made a difficult decision to sell the business. Georgia-Foresters, a large integrated wood products firm, was successful in negotiating the acquisition of the Belwood Lumber Company. The chief asset of Belwood was the 160,000 acres of well-stocked timberland. The timberland would, on a sustained yield basis, support production considerably in excess of that produced by Belwood. Upon selling the company, Mr. Adams told Georgia-Foresters officials that he had no interest in remaining with Belwood in a managerial capacity.

## Fred McNary's Decision

In July 1974, Mr. Fred McNary, Division Vice-President for Georgia-Foresters Company, sat in his office in Atlanta viewing the minutes of a meeting he conducted the previous day with the management group of the Belwood Lumber Company. Georgia-Foresters had just acquired the Belwood firm, and it had become McNary's responsibility to integrate the new acquisition into his eastern division.

McNary recalled that John Adams spent a considerable amount of time in the previous day's meeting defining the way Belwood had been managed. The other managers at the meeting were given little time or opportunity to express themselves. McNary was concerned that this lack of participation by most of the managers at the meeting was representative of the company operation as a whole. His best guess was that the company was characterized by a centralized style of leadership resulting in a minimum of delegation.

Prepared by Richard C. Johanson and Donald D. White, University of Arkansas.

McNary's next step was to gather what information he could on the key management personnel of the company. The profiles (see Forms 1–5) yielded some interesting information.

After carefully studying the profiles, McNary jotted down the following memo for his records:

1. We must immediately replace two retiring managers—Adams and Martin.
2. Ted Barnes must be replaced because of limited managerial and industrial experience.
3. None of the managers rated above "good" on our scale for overall managerial ability. They are all technically competent but appear to lack necessary management skills.
4. All of the managers believe that they are doing a good job. Adams recently reinforced this belief by giving each man a substantial salary increase.
5. Lower-level managers also appear to lack management skills. This is due, in part, to Adams' long-standing domination of company affairs.
6. Internal conflicts between engineering and production and between Adams and the sales division have contributed to recent substandard performance.

Fred McNary realized that he was responsible for the future growth and success or failure of the Belwood operation. He also knew that he had the authority to take whatever action was necessary to insure the survival and growth of this newly acquired operation. Now, he contemplated what he had written and considered how he might conclude the memo before him.

**Form 1.**

---

Georgia–Foresters, Inc.
Appraisal Form

Name: J. D. Adams                              Title: President

General: Joined Belwood in 1932 as one of the two founders and
has served as the chief executive for the past 42 years. His
main objectives have been to acquire for Belwood a strong raw
material base and maintain up-to-date manufacturing facilities.
Adams took the job on himself since his chief interest lay in
mechanical efficiency. He believed that if you had a technical
edge on competition, it would not be necessary to spend so much
time on "managing the company." While Adams has a lot of management talent working for him, it is evident that he desires to
continually tell each person what to do and how to do it. Adams
makes all the major decisions with respect to the purchase of raw
materials, methods of manufacture, products to be manufactured,
plus numerous, minor, daily decisions. On a typical day you can
find Adams in the plant assisting each department head in the
performance of his duties. Adams' philosophy of how to run a
lumber company is to "place most of the emphasis on efficiency of
operation to allow for low-cost production."

    In last year's annual report, John Adams noted that Belwood's
formula for success was for the woodlands department to keep the
mill supplied with logs at the lowest possible cost; the mill
was to produce lumber from these logs at the lowest possible cost;
and the sales department was to sell the production of the mill
at the highest possible price.

Strengths: Experience, technically competent, knows the business
from the ground up, knowledge of the company's operations, knows
the employees.

Weaknesses: Has more technical knowledge and experience than
administrative ability; fails to delegate work, authority, and
responsibility; due to his age, he is not very energetic and
wants to retire.

Evaluation as a manager:  No comment.

---

Georgia–Foresters, Inc.
Appraisal Form

Name: Sam Martin                              Title: Plant Superintendent

General: First became interested in the lumber industry upon
graduation from high school, and he has spent his entire career in
the industry. He has been associated with Belwood for the last 35
years.

Strengths: Loyal to the company, knows the workers very well, also
has a good understanding of Belwood's equipment and facilities.

Weaknesses: Inability to learn new things, doesn't have the drive
and energy necessary for a line production job, had a heart attack
five years ago.

Evaluation as a manger: Poor.

---

**Form 2.**

**Form 3.**

Georgia-Foresters, Inc.
Appraisal Form

Name: Ted Barnes                                    Title: Controller

General: Joined the firm last year.  Has held earlier positions
as accountant and assistant treasurer in a small wholesale
operation. Holds a degree in accounting from Eastern College.
Ted has not shown leadership in his position (possibly due to
Adams' control of financial affairs).

Strengths: Understands financial matters, loyal to Adams.

Weaknesses:  Somewhat introverted and hard to talk to.  Has not
been able to group the intricacies and jargon of lumber business.
No managerial experience.

Evaluation as a manager: Unsatisfactory.

Georgia-Foresters, Inc.
Appraisal Form

Name: John Fry                                    Title: Chief Forester

General: Joined Belwood in June, 1956, after completion of the
requirements for a master's degree in forestry.  John was hired
as a forester by Adams, he was promoted to "Chief Forester" some
15 years ago.

Strengths: Technically competent in forestry and highly motivated,
is well liked by his associates, and has been active in the local
chapter of his professional organization, plus his church.

Weaknesses:  Prefers special research projects over administrative
management duties; he hasn't acquired a broad insight into the total
of Belwood's operations.

Evaluation as a manager: Satisfactory to fair.

**Form 4.**

**Form 5.**

---

Georgia-Foresters, Inc.
Appraisal Form

**Name:** Mike Fleming                    **Title:** Chief Engineer

**General:** Hired in June, 1966, after graduation from Georgia Tech where he earned a degree in mechanical engineering.  His father had been associated with the lumber industry for many years. Therefore, Mike became interested in having an opportunity to con- tribute to the greater mechanization of the various facets of the lumber business.  On various occasions, Mike has experienced difficulty in selling new ideas and innovations for Belwood to Adams.

**Strengths:** Very productive, graduate engineer and technically competent, personally ambitious, good follow-through when given a job to do, very personable and cultured.

**Weaknesses:**  May be overly ambitious, limited experience in management, youngest member of the management staff.

**Evaluation as a manager:** Satisfactory to good.

# CASE 39
## Latino Glass, S.A. (Latino, South America)

Production superintendent, Angel Ramos, obviously was upset. Angel had been with Latino since the company began its operations in his country twelve years ago. He had worked hard during these years and had been recognized for his efforts with numerous promotions. However, he had counted heavily on replacing Roy Webster as plant manager at Latino Glass when he heard that Webster was being promoted to president. Now, he waited outside Webster's office having just learned that an "outsider" was being brought in as the new plant manager of the company. He was unaware that Webster, himself, was concerned about Angel's predicament and that he was discussing it with the company controller at that very moment.

## Background

Latino Glass was founded as a joint venture in Latino, South America. The parent United States company, Stateside Glass Company, produced a wide variety of glass products for both domestic and foreign markets. Latino Glass, unlike most glass plants, produced two products rather than specializing in a single product. Therefore, managers could acquire experience in two product areas simultaneously. The Latino operation was considered by ambitious middle-level managers in Stateside Glass as a good opportunity to gain valuable managerial experience. In addition to the two product experience, the Latino operation was thought to provide decision-making opportunities that comparable level managers in Stateside did not have. On the other hand, it was generally believed that many of the decisions made by Latino managers were reviewed by corporate level managers at the home office of Stateside Glass.

Latino's primary product was black and white television picture tubes. Competition in the area had been limited for some time as a result of a government decree prohibiting the importation of picture tubes into the country. However, one Japanese firm did build and operate a similar plant in Latino. The Japanese firm gained about 20 percent of the total market. In addition, recent trade agreements among several Latin American countries allowed a Mexican producer of picture tubes to market its product in Latino. To date, Latino has not been hurt seriously by the Mexican competition, and sales outside the country are on the increase.

Approximately one year ago, the company decided to expand its present production and add a line of picture tubes for color television. However, a government declaration made shortly after the decision caused the parent company to hold up any action of the addition of the new line. The original plan had called for Stateside Glass to form a second joint venture company in Latino for the express purpose of producing the color television picture tubes.

However, the government declaration stated that all new enterprises begun in Latino must have at least 51 percent Latino ownership. A final decision as to whether or not the company's plans will be nullified by the declaration has not yet been made by the Latino government.

## Roy Webster's Observations

When Angel Ramos found out, by way of the grapevine, that we were bringing in Joe Kent to be plant manager he was quite upset, even somewhat emotional. Indirectly, he threatened to quit. Ramos is a good man and has performed well as production superintendent for three years. He's only thirty-two years old.

When I was plant manager, I never had any trouble with him—we always got along pretty well though he tends to be a little impulsive. I guess when I moved up to president from plant manager, he assumed he would replace me as plant manager. While I was never free to tell him, he was my choice for the job even though I knew he would have had some problems because of his lack of experience in the areas reporting to him—plant accounting and industrial relations, especially. I guess Paul Moore (vice-president of Latin American operations for Stateside) felt Ramos' lack of experience would create too many problems. That's on our agenda of topics to be discussed on my next trip to the states. It is the policy of Stateside Glass to promote nationals as rapidly as they are capable of assuming greater responsibility—and we follow it. Of the 250 people employed by Latino Glass, there are only 3 Americans—the project manager who is coordinating the introduction of the lab products line in terms of production and sales, the plant manager, and myself, the president. Besides, we can't do much without government permission and the industry department likes to see Latinos in high company positions—it improves our image with the government. But, Joe Kent was assigned the job by Mr. Moore and that's the way it will have to stay.

There is another aspect of the Ramos problem that must be considered. The heads of the department reporting to the plant manager are used to having an American over them. When the time comes to move a Latino person into the job of plant manager, we might have problems with the Latino people who report to him. It's all right if an American is the plant manager, but as soon as a Latino native is in that job each of the other Latino people will feel that he should have had the job. I'm not sure they're ready to accept another Latino guy as their boss. When Joe Kent's time is up here and he returns to Stateside Glass, in about three years, I think Angel Ramos will be ready for the plant manager's job. I can't promise him anything because I'll be leaving Latino Glass about that time myself. But I wouldn't be surprised if he were the next plant manager.

Latino Glass has progressed nicely in the past five years. We've had some problems, but I think we're really sailing now. Joe Kent worries me a little. His confidential file indicates he has a short temper, lets everybody know it when things don't go right—or so his file indicates. He spent the first four weeks after being assigned here in an intensive Spanish course—he's actually been on the job less than two weeks. I've noticed that he never uses his Spanish. I guess he's afraid or embarrassed to make mistakes. Our home office personnel committee reviewed the records of the top production superintendents in the Stateside plants, and Joe, evidently, came out as the strongest prospect. Before coming to Latino, he was production superintendent in a color television tube plant. He has been with Stateside Glass for fifteen years—almost all of them in line positions in production. Two years ago he was offered a promotion to plant manager in an overseas operation, in Asia to be exact, but he turned it down. Some people feel that if he had turned down a second promotion, namely plant manager here in Latino, he'd never be offered another chance. I don't think Stateside really operates like that—but Joe might think so. I just hope that he and Angel Ramos get the job done and don't crash head on. If those two don't work together, they will make us all look bad.

I've suggested to Joe, subtly of course, that he use the work objectives program that I started when I was plant manager. It worked for me, it should work for him if I can just get him to try it. I don't know when I'll get around to starting it with the people who report to me. The work objective program, some call it "management by results," consisted of my sitting down with each of my subordinates, individually, and discussing what goals they should strive to reach in the forthcoming six-week period. Then we get together as a group, my subordinates and I, and each subordinate would tell the others what he was going to achieve in the coming period. We discussed each person's objectives as a group because, sometimes, they can help each other achieve their objectives. I like to see them set objectives that are a little higher than what is likely they can achieve —something to shoot at, so to speak. As I said, though, I haven't had time since I've been president to start it with my immediate subordinates. I wish Joe Kent would continue the work objectives program in his area. It could help him do a better job; but if he and Ramos don't get along and don't support each other, we're all going to look bad.

# CASE 40
# Predicting the Future

Jed Barket and Bill Thomas, both members of the board of directors of ABC Manufacturing, were discussing a major dilemma—that of deciding which of three men under consideration should be offered the company's presidency. The former president, Will Ziebuld, had been doing an excellent job when he suddenly collapsed at his desk. Suffering an apparent heart attack, Ziebuld was rushed to a nearby hospital. After extensive tests, Ziebuld was told he would have to go easy from then on. Following this advice, he tendered his resignation as president.

This turn of events left the company's top management stunned. However, the board decided to fill the vacancy as quickly as possible. After screening all possible candidates, the board narrowed its list to three men, two outsiders and one insider. The first two individuals were both presidents of competitive firms, but each indicated that he would be willing to change jobs if given the offer. The third man was the company's executive vice president and the individual Will Ziebuld had been grooming for his job for the past two years.

The board of directors was charged with choosing the new president. However, Jed and Bill were the most senior members and the five other members generally agreed with their recommendations. As a result, the two men were asked to evaluate the three candidates, arrive at a consensus, and present their findings to the board.

The best method of choosing the new president was not clear to either Jed or Bill. Nevertheless, Jed believed strongly that human behavior was predictable from past history.

"You know," he told Bill, "a systematic analysis of an individual can give you a behavioral profile of that person. On the basis of this information, you can predict quite a bit about their behavior. All we really have to do is obtain such a profile of the three men under consideration." Bill, however, was not so sure. "I just don't think you can do it that easily. Give me an illustration."

"I'll do better than that. Let me get you a clipping from a past issue of *Time* and I'll show you how this idea of a behavioral profile is used." Jed left the office and returned a few minutes later. He opened the magazine to the "law" section and handed it to Bill. The story to which he was referring related to some of the latest techniques used by defense attorneys in choosing jurors. In recent years a system has arisen for screening these jurors. It essentially entails bringing in a special team of individuals skilled in psychology

Prepared by Richard M. Hodgetts, Florida International University.

and sociology to work with the defense attorneys. The team identifies those most likely to vote for 'acquittal' or 'not guilty.' "

"In arriving at a decision of whether or not to oppose the sitting of a particular juror, the group divides its operation into three parts: a) making a sociological profile of the community in which the trial will be held; b) a scrutiny in court of potential jurors; and c) a field investigation of their backgrounds. To indicate how successful this approach has been, *Time* reported that the team helped pick thirty-four of thirty-six jurors who voted for acquittal."

*Bill:* Are you suggesting that we merely obtain this type of profile of each candidate?

*Jed:* No, that would be too simple; it would only provide us with a brief sketch of the individual. We might be able to determine how he would vote on a given issue. However, that is too limited in scope. We need to obtain behavioral information that will give us an over-all profile of the person.

*Bill:* How would you suggest we get such information?

*Jed:* Well, I think we ought to hire some qualified people to gather data on the early, formative years of each candidate.

*Bill:* Why?

*Jed:* Because by the time a person is eighteen years old, his options are limited. He's either capable of being a company president or he isn't. The basic behaviors have already been developed.

*Bill:* That sounds like a way-out idea to me.

*Jed:* Look, I'll give you an illustration. Is there anyone you went through grade school with whom you can remember?

*Bill:* Sure, there was a boy named Larry McCracken. He was the smartest kid in the class. Of course, we moved away after seventh grade so I don't know what ever happened to Larry. However, his father was the mayor, so my guess is that the family had roots there and may still be living in the same city.

*Jed:* What do you think Larry is doing today?

*Bill:* Well, if he's not the mayor there, I'd say he's either a successful businessman or a college professor—maybe in mathematics or accounting.

*Jed:* Why do you say that?

*Bill:* Because he was both analytical and good at math.

*Jed:* Okay, let's take a wild shot and call your old home city and find out what he's doing today.

*Bill:* Heck, nobody will remember him. Besides, whom do I call?

*Jed:* Is there any school teacher you had who, if she were still alive, would be living there?

*Bill:* Probably Miss Anna Dunworthy. She was unmarried in those days and the school was her whole life.

*Jed:* Okay, call the information operator, see if Miss Dunworthy still lives there. If she does, ask her about Larry; maybe she remembers.

Bill placed the call and, to his surprise learned that there was indeed an Anna Dunworthy living in the city. Furthermore, upon talking to her he learned that Miss Dunworthy not only remembered him but was able to tell him about Larry—he was the president of the largest bank in the metropolitan area. In fact, at the last annual high school get-together, she and Larry had spent over an hour talking about old times. They wondered what had ever happened to Bill. By the time Bill hung up the telephone, he was amazed.

*Bill:* I can't believe it. He not only still lives in the town but he's in a profession similar to the one I guessed.

*Jed:* Sure, it's like I told you. Tell me something about the person's early years and I'll project his future.

*Bill:* Okay, but you've got to admit that we had awful skimpy data to go on.

*Jed:* Oh, sure, but we could get a lot more information on the candidates for the presidency of the firm. We could have a complete check made on each one.

Bill agreed that the suggestion was a good one and upon hearing of it, the board of directors also agreed. An investigative agency was then hired to obtain the requisite background information. Ten days later the data was in the hands of the two men.

The report revealed that one of the outside candidates, Roger Kenan, was a star pupil in grammar and high school. In addition, he was active in baseball and basketball and was elected president of his high school class. Neighbors and friends remembered him as an easygoing boy who never seemed to get in any trouble. He was fairly well liked although he did not seem to have any close friends. Meanwhile, his grammar school teachers remembered him as industrious and likable. The second outside candidate, William Rheem, was apparently something of a cut-up in both grammar and high school. School reports indicated that he was twice reprimanded for fighting during recess. Nevertheless, he was well remembered by his teachers because of his success in midget, junior varsity, and varsity football. Bill was apparently a superb quarterback. Neither his grammar school nor his high school ever lost a game while he was there. In fact, he was still affectionately known by his old English teacher as "Touchdown" Bill Rheem, because of a ninety-one-yard winning touchdown he ran from scrimmage in the last minute of the state finals. Old neighbors and friends called him a "likable roughneck." One of his friends said, "We figured he'd either do very well for himself or wind up in jail. There's no in-between with Bill."

The third candidate, Martin McChorder, was the inside man Will Ziebuld had been grooming for the presidency. The investigators learned that Martin's parents had been killed when he was a child and Martin had been raised by an elder aunt. Around his neighborhood, Martin was regarded as shy and introverted, a marked changed from his behavior in the firm where he was outgoing and gregarious. Martin had also been quite sickly as a child and missed quite a few days of school. In the sixth grade he was almost left back because he had been absent so often. While he engaged in no contact sports, he was active in the band, glee club, chess club, and was president of the high school's debating team. One of his old school friends said he was "outstanding in intellectual or noncompetitive endeavors."

Jed was still a bit skeptical. However, he knew he and Bill must sit down and make their decision.

# EXPERIENTIAL EXERCISE 16
## Life and Career Planning

This exercise will help you look at your personal life as well as your career plans. In a sense, you are already in motion along a career path. Your past and present have contributed to your future choices, although they will not necessarily govern them. As you complete your life and career planning exercise, keep in mind your goals and the opportunities that lie ahead.

*Instructions*

1. Form groups of three persons each.
2. Think carefully about the issues raised by each item and chart. Then complete that part of the exercise.
3. (a) Outside of class, write a brief statement concerning the goals you had when you graduated from high school. Then list ten adjectives that describe your present progress toward those goals. In class, state your goals to group members and discuss along with them the meaning and significance of your list of adjectives.

   (b) What career goals would you like to achieve five years after you graduate or leave school? Ten years? Twenty years? List ten adjectives that best reflect your career goals. Discuss with group members why the list of adjectives are significant.

   (c) Complete the graph by drawing a line that depicts your past, present, and future career path. Share your graph with the other members of the group. Explain the meaning of the slopes and levels of your career line.

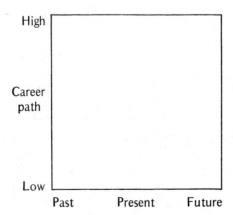

Prepared by Donald D. White, University of Arkansas.

(d) Develop a written "contract" with yourself describing what you expect to receive (career goals) and what you are willing to give (education, training, work experience, time commitment, and the like) in order to achieve those goals. This document represents your personal commitment to your career plan.

# EXPERIENTIAL EXERCISE 17

## In-Basket Exercise: The Tampa Pump & Valve Company

You are about to undertake an in-basket exercise. On each manager's desk is a basket into which papers and notes go that must be considered each day. Generally, an out-basket is stacked on top of the first. When a manager decides what to do with his or her in-basket items, s/he places them in the out-basket so that the secretary can file or process the items.

The objectives of an in-basket exercise are twofold: first, to undertake an examination of your personal managerial style, and, second, to further your understanding of general management concepts through involvement in a reasonably complex administrative situation.

## The Tampa Pump & Valve Company

The Tampa Pump & Valve Company, whose plant manager had been John Manners, is a subsidiary of Florida Chemical & Equipment Corporation. Its operations have been quite successful. Beginning with a capital investment of slightly less than $750,000 shortly after the end of World War II, its capital investment today is in excess of $65,000,000. The Tampa Pump & Valve Company possesses a newly constructed office building and a manufacturing and assembly plant. There are two sales outlets—one in Tampa and one in Jacksonville.

The company, excluding top management, is currently staffed with sixty engineers and thirty-two technicians. Approximately 1,000 persons are employed in the production department, working two forty-hour shifts a week.

Joe O'Malley is the general superintendent in charge of production. All valves and pump assemblies and components that are not purchased are manufactured and assembled in the production department according to job and design specifications. These are shipped to various sites and locations according to orders, or they are stored in the company's two warehouses in Jacksonville and Tampa. Centralized product and planning enables the company to maintain rigid production and quality controls over all units that become a part of completed products. In addition, carefully planned production and shipping schedules reduce the amount of time that completed units must be stored at receiving stations. Thus, shipping costs are reduced, and the company is better able to insure that contracted completion dates are met.

The research and development division, currently under the direction of Tom Everts, has grown from two engineers to its present size of thirty engineers and twelve technicians and draftsmen. Partly because of the plant manager's intense interest, 10 percent of the company's profits are allocated to research and development. The research division recently developed a less expensive and a longer

Prepared by Richard E. Dutton, University of South Florida; and Edwin Mumma.
* Used with permission of the authors, Richard E. Dutton and Rodney C. Sherman, University of South Florida.

lasting rust inhibitor than that previously manufactured. New rotary arc-welding units for the plant have also been developed as well as a new method for testing the strength and quality of welded unions. Also, the division was responsible for the design of expansion joints which are formed and assembled in the company's plant, ready for immediate installation at construction sites.

In addition to being the controller, Bill Marshall is general counsel for the plant. A staff of two attorneys and three legal assistants report directly to him as does the chief accountant and his staff. The accounting department employs approximately fifteen people.

The industrial and employee relations department, under A. C. Cushwell, has a staff of approximately fifteen people. A total of eighty-two employees are employed in the marketing department, which is headed by James Barber.

The accompanying organization charts show the structure of the corporate organization and the relationship between the various functions and departments within the plant.

John Manners suffered a severe heart attack on April 12 and died. It had been noticed that he appeared tired and overworked recently. At this time, Richard West was transferred from the Orlando Pump and Valve Plant, which is a slightly smaller subsidiary of Florida Chemical & Equipment Corporation, to fill the position.

## Instructions

Today is Sunday, April 14, 1975. Richard West has just come into the office, for the first time, at 6:45 p.m. He must leave in time to catch the 10:00 p.m. plane for Caracas, Venezuela, for an important meeting. He will not be back until next Monday, April 23. His secretary is Pearl Powell who was secretary to John Manners before he died.

The materials in this packet were left in the in-basket on his desk by his secretary (Pearl Powell).

You are to assume the role of Richard West and go through the entire packet of materials, taking whatever action you deem appropriate for each item. Every action the group wishes to take should be written down including memos to the secretary, memos to yourself (Richard West), etc. Draft letters where appropriate, write out any plans or agenda for meetings or conferences that you plan. These letters, memos, notes, etc. may be in "rough draft" form.

REMEMBER!  The day is Sunday, April 14, time: 6:45 p.m. Write down every action you take on any item. You cannot call on anyone for assistance. The telephone switchboard is not operating. You must work with the materials at hand. You will be out of the office from 9:45 tonight until Monday, April 22. Be sure to record every action, whether memo, letter, meeting plan, etc.

The solution of your group will be compared with that of other groups and a winner will be determined. This is a test of your group's ability to work together effectively and organize to meet a production goal.

**Item 1A.**

April 13, 1975

<u>OFFICE MEMORANDUM</u>

TO: Richard West

FROM: Pearl Powell

SUBJECT: SAM Presentation (see attached)

Mr. West:

    Just a note to let you know that Mr. Manners did nothing toward developing the program scheduled April 25, except to send the title to Mr. Johnson via phone. The title was announced to the members some time ago. I don't think Mr. Manners discussed the matter with any of the department heads.

Pearl

**Item 1B.**

THE SOCIETY FOR THE ADVANCEMENT OF MANAGEMENT
Dallas Chapter
P. O. Box 9105
Dallas, Texas

April 4, 1975

Mr. John Manners
Plant Manager
Tampa Pump & Valve Company
Tampa, Florida  33601

Dear John:

This is a reminder that we are counting on you and on the
Tampa Pump & Valve Company to provide us with the three-hour
evening program for our meeting April 25.

I know you and your boys will provide a stimulating and
worthwhile program.  The title of the program you are to present,
"The Image of Today's Executive," sounds very interesting and
already the dinner and program is a "sell-out."  Therefore, you
can look forward to a full house on the night of your presentation.

Could you prepare a brief outline of the program and text of
any speeches that will be presented indicating who will present
them so we can go ahead with the programs and press releases?

We are all looking forward to seeing you then.

Best regards,

Paul Johnson,
Secretary Dallas
Chapter, Society
for the Advancement
of Management

PJ:sm

**Item 2.**

P E R S O N A L

April 10, 1975

**OFFICE MEMORANDUM**

TO: John Manners

FROM: A. C. Cushwell, Industrial and Employee Relations

SUBJECT: Frank Batt

I have heard through the grapevine and "unimpeachable" sources that Frank Batt has been looking around and has had an outside job offer on which he is going to give a firm answer next week. I don't think anyone else knows this yet. I just happened to run on to it. I understand that he has been offered more money than we can offer him now based on present wage and salary policy. As you know, Batt has only been with the company a short time and is already making somewhat more than others at his rank. This presents a problem which needs to be ironed out. I am afraid I mentioned the possibility of just such a situation as this when you instituted the plan last November. Perhaps we need to reconsider some of the aspects of your plan before we make offers to June graduates.

I know that you and Everts feel that Frank is one of the most valuable men in research and development, and I thought I would let you know about this for whatever action you want to take.

A. C. Cushwell

**OFFICE MEMORANDUM**

April 7, 1975

TO: John Manners

FROM: A. C. Cushwell, Industrial and Employee Relations

SUBJECT: Testing Program

You recently suggested that we institute a testing program for hiring secretarial and clerical personnel. The following are some suggested tests and other criteria that we might want to consider. Do you have any further suggestions of types of tests or other hiring procedures which we might want to look into before we finalize a program?

    (1) Clerical Personnel:

        (a) Whitney General Clerical Survey (includes measures on spelling, arithmetic, alphabetizing, and general aptitude).

        (b) Mann-Watson Typing Test

        (c) Age to 40

    (2) Secretarial Personnel:

        (a) Whitney General Clerical Survey

        (b) Mann-Watson Typing Test

        (c) Collins Shorthand Skill Inventory (via recording)

        (d) High School Diploma

        (e) Age to 40

A. C. Cushwell

**Item 3.**

**Item 4.**

April 10, 1975

<u>OFFICE MEMORANDUM</u>

TO: John Manners

FROM: Bill Marshall

SUBJECT: Termination of Robert Roberts, Employee #6897

    This is a summary of my reasons for terminating Robert Roberts.
As you know, Mr. Roberts was employed as a legal assistant on
March 4, 19xx.  For almost two years he has been working for us on
a full-time basis while attending law school at night.  He has
continually been a source of irritation to those who have been
working closely with him.  The problem in general has been one of
overstepping his authority.  He has frequently been involved in
controversies with the legal staff over problems with which we felt
he was not adequately prepared to deal nor were any of his concern
since they did not involve his own work assignments.  In general,
he did an adequate job on the work he was assigned, but many of the
staff felt that he was not putting forth a full effort because he
seemed to have a lot of free time which he spent in the coffee bar
or in conversations with others in the department.  The incident
that caused his termination took place about three days before his
termination.  He was told to contact a party concerning a pending
contract.  All he was to do was to secure the necessary signatures
from the other party.  The attorney handling the contract for our
company in the particular case was George Slavin.  Mr. Roberts,
instead of simply securing signatures, evidently discussed the
contract with the outside party, recommending changes, and in
general, so disrupted proceedings that now the whole contract is
in question.  After the customer contacted George, George
immediately discussed the occurrence with me, and we felt that the
incident was serious enough to warrant dismissal.

Bill

April 6, 1975

<u>OFFICE MEMORANDUM</u>

TO: John Manners

FROM: James Barber

SUBJECT: Sales Promotion of Rust Inhibitor

    As you know, we are moving into our campaign to push the new
rust inhibitor.  I would like to have your permission to set up a
contest among our sales representatives with a trip to Hawaii for
the sales representative who sells the highest dollar volume in
the next six-month period.  I want to make the prize good enough
to tempt the sales force.

Jim

**Item 5.**

**Item 6.**

April 11, 1975

<u>OFFICE MEMORANDUM</u>

TO: John Manners

FROM: A. C. Cushwell

SUBJECT: Employment of John Jones, Engineer

    I would like to bring you up to date on my feelings concerning the engineer, John Jones, whom Everts wishes to employ. Everts is from Chicago, and I don't think that he fully understands the morale problems we would have if we hired a black engineer who would have supervision over several white assistants. I realize that we are going to have to protect our interests in government contracts, but I think we can find a better way to do so than starting at this level. I would suggest that you talk with Everts about this problem and the possible complications that could arise.

A. C. Cushwell

---

April 9, 1975

<u>OFFICE MEMORANDUM</u>

TO: John Manners

FROM: Bill Marshall

SUBJECT: Annual Budget Requests

    We are late in turning in our budget proposal to Florida Chemical and Equipment Company for the next fiscal year since the report from R & D is still not in. All other department heads have turned in sound budgets which, if approved, should greatly facilitate the cutting of costs next year. Can you do something to speed up action?

Bill Marshall

**Item 7.**

## Item 8.

April 6, 1975

OFFICE MEMORANDUM

TO: John Manners

FROM: Bill Marshall

SUBJECT: Coffee Breaks

This morning I timed a number of people who took 40 minutes standing in line and drinking their coffee. These people were mainly from the production and research departments. I am able to control this in my department, and I feel you should see that this matter is taken care of by the heads of the other departments. I estimate that the waste amounts to 125,000 man hours (approximately $500.00) a year.

Bill

April 9, 1975

OFFICE MEMORANDUM

TO: John Manners

FROM: Tom Everts

SUBJECT: Allocations for Research

This department has been successful in developing an efficient method for extracting certain basic compounds from slag and other similar by-products that are currently classified as waste by a large number of chemical plants within this area.

It is my recommendation that this company take every step necessary to commercially develop this extraction method. I have brought this matter to Bill Marshall's attention on two separate occasions, requesting that the necessary funds be allocated to fully develop this program. I have been advised by him both times that the funds could not possibly be made available within the next fiscal year. He has also indicated that we should de-emphasize research in the chemical area, since this is unnecessary duplication of functions with the Orlando and Lake City plants.

It is my opinion that this company should capitalize on its advantageous position now, before our competitors are able to perfect a similar method.

The above is for your consideration and recommendations.

Tom Everts

cc:  Mr. O. J. Thompson, Vice-President
     Research & Development

## Item 9.

**Item 10.**

AMERICAN FEDERATION OF FOUNDRY WORKERS
Local 801
Tampa, Florida

April 6, 1975

Mr. John Manners, Manager
Tampa Pump & Valve Company
Tampa, Florida  33601

Dear Sir:

On several recent occasions, I have noticed that you and your staff have employed your company newspaper as a vehicle for undermining the present union administration.

In addition, a series of supervisory bulletins have been circulated that were designed to cause supervisory personnel to influence the thinking of union members in the forthcoming union election. I am also well aware of your "support" for Jessie Sims and others, who have been more than sympathetic towards company management.

As you know, such behavior as I have described is in direct violation of Section 101, Subsection 9 (a) of the Labor-Management Relations Act, as well as being a violation of Article 21 of our contract with your company. I am sure that you are also aware of the negative impact the filing of a charge of unfair management practices could have on future elections and negotiations.

I trust such action will not become necessary and that you will take steps to prevent any further discrimination against this administration.

Sincerely yours,

R. L. Loper, President
A. F. F. W., Local 801

RLL:jg

cc: Mr. A. C. Cushwell

**Item 11.**

April 10, 1975

OFFICE MEMORANDUM

TO: John Manners

FROM: Joe O'Malley

SUBJECT: Quality Control

    The marketing department has put pressure on us to increase production for the next two months so that promised deliveries can be made. At the present time we cannot increase production without some risk in terms of quality. The problem is that marketing does not check with us before committing us to specific delivery dates. This problem has come up before, but nothing has been done. Could I meet with you in the near future to discuss the situation?

                      Joe

---

OFFICE MEMORANDUM

TO: John Manners

FROM: Joe O'Malley

SUBJECT: Pay rate for maintenance men who worked on the U.S. National Day of Mourning.

    It was necessary for me to bring in seven maintenance men last Monday in spite of your order that we would observe the National Day of Mourning due to the sudden death of President Harris.

    The question has arisen as to whether these men should be paid straight time for the work or double time which is customary for work during holidays. I also had 40 people on vacation during this period. Ordinarily, when a legal holiday falls during their vacation they are given an extra day. Since this was an unusual situation I am not sure how to handle it and would like your recommendation.

                      Joe

**Item 12.**

# CHAPTER ELEVEN

# Organization Development and Change

In the preceding chapter we discussed the co-alignment of individual needs and organizational goals through management development. Organization development (OD) attempts the larger task of preparing the entire organization to operate effectively and to meet constant demands for change.

It is through OD that the sociotechnical systems (STS) model of analysis has perhaps its greatest potential for application. This is due primarily to the thoroughness of investigation and the completeness of change strategies that are required of a successful OD intervention. Thus, the STS model discussed in Part I of this book provides an excellent framework for analysis and decision making in organizational development.

## OD Defined

Richard Beckhard[1] defines OD as "an effort (1) planned, (2) organization-wide, and (3) managed from the top, to (4) increase organization effectiveness and health through (5) planned interventions in the organization's processes using behavioral-science knowledge." OD, then, is an attempt to use the theories and technologies of applied behavioral science to aid organizations in developing and maintaining their "system health." Robert Tannenbaum[2] further states that OD is characterized by its focus on (1) humanistic values; (2) personal, interpersonal, organizational, and inter-organizational processes deeply rooted in such values; and (3) the potential for growth (development) in each of these individual and organizational entities. Where management development focuses largely on individual patterns of growth, OD, as the name implies, is concerned with organizational development.

Some authors describe the OD process as one of organization renewal. John Gardner[3] points out that in order for such a revitalization of the enterprise to take place, the organization's internal environment must be hospitable to the individual. Organizations must have built-in processes for self-criticism, flexible internal structures, and some means for preventing organizational policies and procedures from becoming ends in themselves rather than the dynamic means to ends for which they are intended.

Changing human and technological forces in the environment dictate that organizations constantly reassess where they are going and how they are going to get there. This change from the present to the future requires a special management of its own. Managing such transitions requires management consciously to address the need for change, to provide explicit processes and procedures for setting priorities for improvement, to facilitate systematic and constant feedback, and to see to it that participants are rewarded for their involvement in the change process.

## Change Agent

An important figure in the organization development scheme is the OD consultant, or change agent. The change agent observes organizational behavior and sets the scene for managers to solve their own problems. His or her role is to help an enterprise to achieve greater organizational effectiveness by using the latent resources of the organization's own people and its material resources.

Whether a permanent member of the organization (internal change agent) or a temporary contractor from a university or some other organization (external change agent), the role of the OD consultant remains basically the same. She or he must work through organizational participants, enabling them to diagnose the problems at hand and helping them to learn processes and techniques for actually bringing about planned change.

The consultant's role is not to make changes or suggest answers. Instead, the consultant attempts to make people within an organization aware of the myriad of processes evolving from the technological and environmental subsystems. This awareness, together with certain techniques for improving interpersonal understanding, leads to the identification and integration of processes needed to accomplish the organization goal.

## System Diagnosis

Employing techniques based on the behavioral sciences, the change agent must first facilitate a diagnosis of the organization system. Members learn how to explore the effectiveness of human processes and procedures within the enterprise. Inquiry and feedback are among the means used by change agents during this diagnostic stage. Members are guided by the agent as they find answers to questions such as: (1) Where do we want to go? (2) What are our goals? (3) Where are we now? (4) What is the present state of our human and organizational processes? (5) What factors keep the organization from achieving its goal? and (6) What can be done to change these limiting factors? [4] As the change agent probes more deeply into the existing organization, data are generated that enhance member understanding of the system and its problems. This understanding and subsequent analysis lays the groundwork for a specific "intervention" designed to change the situation.

Importantly, a change agent does not personally perform the diagnosis. Instead, he or she guides the diagnostic process leading the client (department, division, enterprise) toward self-renewal.

### Intervention Strategies

An intervention strategy is a planned effort usually involving a specific procedure or technique to bring about individual, group, or organizational change. Intervention strategies typically are developed along the lines of Kurt Lewin's[5] change model. Within the context of this model, the change agent applies one or more of his "technologies." Lewin's approach involves three steps: unfreeze, learn, and refreeze.

*Unfreezing* involves the consultant's use of various techniques to increase awareness and stimulate analysis of present behaviors and processes. The purpose of this stage is to call attention to important behaviors and processes which often are overlooked due to the rapid pace of a manager's life. The result is a greater realization of the gap between what is actually happening within the organization and what participants have assumed was happening. For example, group members may be asked to verbalize their feelings as well as their positions during discussions about a given problem. Another approach might call for the consultant to feed back previously collected attitudinal information to those who supplied it for further analysis.

An even more far-reaching technique for bringing about awareness is the sensitivity or T-group session. Emphasizing the here and now, individuals are urged to share their feelings toward one another openly. Analysis of behavior during the session causes the participants to learn and become aware of the problem solving process and their role in it.

Many of the situations created during the unfreezing stage take place in a "laboratory" environment rather than in the field (on the job). The laboratory environment is more conducive to self-analysis. Often a retreat setting, at a resort or a special room away from the office, is used. Change agents favor a setting which is as close to a laboratory setting as possible. The field, on the other hand, is important in the refreezing stage.

*Learning* takes place after people unfreeze or become aware of what is going on in the organization. Sometimes unfreezing is traumatic because a hidden part of a person's personality is pointed out as undermining effectiveness in the group, unit, or organization. Personal defenses acquired over years may be raised to protect an individual's vulnerability. Therefore, care must be taken during this second stage to permit adequate learning of new values and behaviors to replace the existing ineffective ones. A technique such as role playing or simulation might be used at this point to help personnel learn new behaviors and processes for organizational effectiveness.

*Refreezing* encourages the actual adoption of newly learned processes or behaviors. Carefully structured situations that enhance the likelihood of successfully employing new learning in the workplace, together with positive reinforcement given for desired changes, will increase the likelihood that new behaviors become permanent. *Only* by successfully refreezing a change can the full impact of organizational development be realized.

The time involved in a change program varies with the depth and scope of the intervention. The greater the distrust and ineffectiveness in a system, the greater the depth and scope of the intervention and the longer the time spent by the change agent in the organization. Organizations may continuously monitor their structures and processes in order to determine whether their effectiveness is in any way eroding. Moreover, as was suggested earlier, in-house change agents may be employed on a full-time basis.

### Selecting the Appropriate Technology

An intervention represents a planned effort for change. Specific technologies for change vary in terms of both their approach and the depth of the resulting intervention. Classifying various technologies according to depth helps "promote greater flexibility and rationality in choosing appropriate depths of intervention." [6] The intervention technique adopted not only must be appropriate for the problem at hand, but must be carefully gauged in terms of the degree of emotional impact it will have upon individuals.

Figure 1 describes the relative cost, personal risks, and relevant systems affected by different intervention techniques. The shallowest penetration takes place in an intervention involving an analysis of the operations and related managerial activities within the technological core. Such an intervention would result in machine-type changes aimed at increasing efficiency. A more deeply felt intervention might involve changes in the administrative system (for example, the introduction of management by objectives), struc-

**Figure 1. Depth of intervention.**

| Techniques | Depth | Cost | Risk | Relevant system |
|---|---|---|---|---|
| Operations analysis | Shallow | Low | Low | Formal or required |
| Structural changes | | | | |
| Management by objectives | | | | |
| Survey feedback | | | | |
| Job enrichment | | | | Group or emergent |
| Team building | | | | |
| Process consultation | | | | |
| Grid | | | | |
| Sensitivity training | | | | |
| Transactional analysis | Deep | High | High | Individual or |
| Intrapersonal analysis | | | | personal |

tural changes, or team building. The deepest emotional penetration would be achieved through the use of techniques like sensitivity training and intrapersonal analysis.

The monetary and emotional costs of an intervention increase with the depth of the intervention level. Roger Harrison concluded that two criteria should be used for choosing the appropriate depth of the intervention. "First ... intervene at a level no deeper than that required to produce enduring solutions to the problem at hand; and second ... intervene at a level no deeper than that at which the energy and resources of the client can be committed to problem solving and change." [7]

OD is concerned with the application of the appropriate intervention technique to an organizational problem. This requires the proper diagnosis of the organizational situation. In addition, the system has to be ready for and capable of change. Questions about the scope of the change (single task unit or organization-wide) and the depth of the change (operations analysis to intrapersonal analysis) have to be resolved. The specific intervention technique selected depends upon the nature of the organization situation.

The following section briefly outlines several OD intervention techniques. Keep in mind that each technique is much more complex than can be presented in this section. Moreover, the skill of the change agent is a major determinant of the success of the intervention.

*Management by objectives.*[8] The goal of management by objectives (MBO) is to increase the precision of the planning process at the organizational level and to decrease the discrepancy between employee goals and organizational objectives. MBO also encourages systematic performance improvement and provides a basis for employee appraisal.

Initially, upper-level management establishes long-range organizational goals. These goals are transmitted down the hierarchy in a cascading manner through superior-subordinate meetings. The meetings are designed to integrate superior-subordinate perceptions of goals and to pinpoint subordinate contributions to organizational goals at each level of the enterprise. Objectives for each manager are negotiated and written down so that future performance may be measured against them. Goals should be quantified, linked to a specific time frame, and related to the existing budget. An appraisal of employees and organization units based upon goal-related performance takes place at the end of the designated period. This evaluation serves as the basis for employee rewards, and it provides information for goal-setting in the upcoming operational cycle.

*Survey feedback.*[9] Survey feedback is a technique that involves obtaining data from organizational members concerning individual attitudes, organizational climate, and the general health of the enterprise. Standardized questionnaires are provided to all organization or unit members. The questionnaires are completed and returned to the consultant for tallying an evaluation. The data are then fed back to top management and other participating groups. Organizational leaders, under the guidance of the consultant, hold group meetings in which questionnaire results are discussed and corrective strategies are developed.

*Job enrichment.*[10]    The purpose of job enrichment is to increase job satisfaction by redesigning jobs to provide workers with greater autonomy and responsibility for planning, directing, and controlling their own performance. Supervisors involved in the change effort are asked to identify "unhealthy" jobs and to generate ideas about how the job may be enriched—how to increase opportunities for achievement, responsibility, and growth in the work. Job-content changes are then implemented on either a selective or across-the-board basis. Job enrichment, based on the earlier work of Herzberg (see Chapter Three), focuses on altering the nature of the work itself, rather than on the environment within which a job is performed.

*Team building.*[11]    Team building is an OD intervention designed to improve the performance of and relationships between work group members or others who together seek to achieve the same goal. Initially, questionnaires identify work group or team phenomena such as goal clarity, role ambiguity, participation, individual commitment, group conflict, and cohesiveness.

After analyzing the questionnaires and discussing the results with team members, a series of workshops is held. The change agent focuses on the processes necessary to enhance group communication, conflict resolution, and problem solving. Team building is usually confined to individual units or task groups; however, the approach may be applied throughout an organization

*Process consultation.*[12]    Process consultation is designed to help the client become aware of and become able to "operate on" process events that occur within the organization. Process consultants do not function as experts. Their role is to observe activities within the organization and to feed back information to the client. The process consultant attempts to help the client understand how organizational processes operate so that the client (rather than the consultant) can solve problems and improve those processes.

Four approaches are used most frequently by the consultant. *Agenda-setting interviews* are low-key question-and-answer periods in which the consultant attempts to heighten the management team's sensitivity to their own internal processes. Relevant theoretical articles or comments may be provided to team members by the consultant at these meetings. *Data feedback* is another approach sometimes used by the consultant. Data on operating processes are provided to managers for interpretation and use in improving those processes. *Coaching or counseling* sometimes follows data feedback. The receptiveness of the client to coaching is critical to the approach, as is the consultant's determination of the level of progress that is being made toward process solutions. Occasionally, a *structural approach* is required. Suggesting specific solutions to problems is inconsistent with the "self-awareness/self-change" philosophy of process consultation. However, this more direct intervention approach is sometimes necessary and may be used sparingly by the consultant.

A process consultation intervention is considered successful when managers are able to solve human problems and process issues through diagnostic and problem solving skills. The disengagement of the consultant from the enterprise takes place when both client and consultant agree that a problem solving level has been attained.

*Grid organizational development.*[13]   The managerial grid, a concept developed by Robert Blake and Jane Mouton, permits a manager to identify his or her style and approach to problem solving. Individual styles are compared to "ideal grid style," and team meetings are held to develop "grid" philosophies and strategies. Discussions are held to reduce win-loss norms between groups and to reduce barriers that separate the organization from its ideal state. Grid organizational development is normally carried out on a system-wide basis and is tailored to the managerial grid theory itself.

*Sensitivity training (encounter groups).*[14]   The purpose of sensitivity training is to increase individuals' awareness of their interpersonal behaviors and defense mechanisms. The approach provides an opportunity to clarify goals and personal values and to be reflective about the way in which one interacts with others.

Although a variety of agendas may be adopted in sensitivity training, sessions usually involve five to ten individuals and a group facilitator. No formal agenda is provided; instead, individual personalities and group relationships emerge out of the lack of structure. From time to time, individuals are encouraged to examine these evolutionary processes and their results. The facilitator is not a teacher. Rather, he or she provides a supportive atmosphere encouraging growth through openness and genuineness. At the same time, the facilitator observes the rate of disclosure and self awareness to help ease participants through "high risk" experiences that might result in psychological damage if not handled properly.

In addition to discovering the nature of one's personality through sensitivity training, encounter group members are encouraged to develop interpersonal skills emphasizing openness and trust in relationships with others. The intervention is of sufficient depth and risk (see Figure 1) to require careful use under the direction of a skilled facilitator.

*Transactional analysis.*[15]   Transactional analysis (TA) was discussed at some length in the first chapter of this book. As an organizational development technique, TA is used to create greater awareness of oneself and of those with whom we experience transactions. The approach calls for managers to recognize the Parent, Adult, and Child modes that control communications and behaviors. TA provides a way to understand interpersonal relationships and to affect communications between organizational members. Role playing and problem solving using TA concepts along with script analysis and game analysis are the principal techniques.

## Summary

Organizational development represents an effort to improve organization effectiveness through the use of planned diagnosis and intervention. Rather than addressing itself to individual growth, as in management development, OD focuses on the resources, processes, and goals of the total organization or unit. The purpose of OD is to "renew" the organization by enabling managers to draw on the behavioral sciences as they affect the organization's transition from present to future.

The change agent (consultant) plays an important role in creating an atmosphere conducive to data gathering and feedback within the organization and bringing about necessary change in the system. The change agent should approach each organization as though it were a unique system. No single intervention strategy (or OD technique) is best for all organizational situations. A careful diagnosis of the system is conducted with the help of the client organization. The depth of the intervention depends upon the consultant's assessment of the organization and the client's readiness to respond. Interventions may range from shallow ones—such as structural changes or management by objectives—to much deeper penetrations—like sensitivity training or intrapersonal analysis. Between these extremes lie a variety of approaches for bringing about a revitalized organization.

The approach adopted by the consultant normally is implemented along the lines of Lewin's change model. As such, any intervention must go through stages involving the *unfreezing* of present attitudes and behaviors, *learning* new patterns of organizational thought, and *refreezing* those newly acquired patterns in the organization. Only through the cooperation of the change agent and key members of the organizational management team can a successful OD intervention and organizational renewal take place.

*References*

1. Richard Beckhard, *Organization Development: Strategies and Models* (Reading: Addison-Wesley, 1969), p. 9.
2. Robert Tannenbaum, in "Academy of Management Newsletter," edited by D. D. Warrick, Winter 1978, p. 3.
3. John W. Gardner, "How to Prevent Organizational Dry Rot," *Harper's*, October 1965.
4. Richard Beckhard and R. Harris, *Organizational Transitions: Managing Complex Change* (Reading: Addison-Wesley, 1977).
5. Kurt Lewin, *Field Theory in Social Science* (New York: Harper and Bros., 1951).
6. Roger Harrison, "Choosing the Depth of Organizational Intervention," *Journal of Applied Behavioral Sciences*, vol. 6, no. 2, 1970, p. 183.
7. Ibid., p. 201.

8. Wendell L. French and Robert W. Hollmann, "Management by Objectives: The Team Approach," *California Management Review*, vol. 17, no. 3, Spring 1973, pp. 13–22.

9. David R. Nadler, *Feedback and Organization Development* (Reading: Addison-Wesley, 1977).

10. Robert Ford, *Motivation through the Work Itself* (New York: American Management Assoc., 1969).

11. William G. Dyer, *Team Building: Issues and Alternatives* (Reading: Addison-Wesley, 1977).

12. Edgar Schein, *Process Consultation: Its Role in Organization Development*, (Reading: Addison-Wesley, 1969).

13. Robert Blake and J. Mouton, *Building a Dynamic Corporation through Grid Organizational Development* (Reading: Addison-Wesley, 1969).

14. R. Golembiewski and A. Blumber, eds., *Sensitivity Training and the Laboratory Approach* (Itasca: F. E. Peacock, 1970).

15. Harold F. Rush and P. S. McGrath, "Transactional Analysis Moves into Corporate Training: A New Theory of Interpersonal Relations Becomes a Tool for Personnel Development," *Conference Board Record*, vol. 10, no. 7, July 1973, pp. 38–44.

## Recommended Readings

Readings marked with an asterisk are included in *Contemporary Perspectives in Organizational Behavior*, edited by Donald D. White (Boston: Allyn and Bacon, 1982).

Bruce D. Jamieson, "Behavioral Problems with Management by Objectives," *Academy of Management Journal*, vol. 16, no. 3, September 1973, pp. 496–505.

*Robert Kahn, "Organizational Development: Some Problems and Proposals," *Journal of Applied Behavioral Sciences*, vol. 10, no. 4, 1974, pp. 485–502.

*John M. Nichols, "A Systems Analysis Approach for Planning Evaluations of OD Interventions," *Academy of Management Proceedings*, August 1977, pp. 358–362.

*Virginia E. Schein and Larry E. Greiner, "Can Organization Development Be Fine Tuned to Bureaucracies," *Organizational Dynamics*, vol. 5, no. 3, Winter 1977, pp. 48–62.

John P. Wasson, "Who Wants Job Enrichment?" *S.A.M. Advanced Management Journal*, vol. 41, Summer 1976, pp. 15–22.

Gerald Zaltman and Robert Duncan, *Strategies for Planned Change* (New York: John Wiley and Sons, 1977).

# CASE 41
## A.T.&T.'s Human Resource Center

In January 1970, American Telephone and Telegraph Company's department of environmental affairs established a manpower laboratory for the purpose of finding innovative means to solve existing manpower problems. Recognizing that the same old methods of dealing with manpower problems were no longer as effective as they once were, A.T.&T.'s management charged the manpower lab with increasing the Bell System's competence in recruiting, in training, in utilizing, and in maintaining the human resources necessary to provide a continued improvement in communication services. Of particular concern were the ever-present problems of absenteeism, tardiness, and turnover. Thus, the manpower lab saw its role in treating the human and organizational needs as a four-step approach: 1) the identification of work force problems; 2) the development of new methods for minimizing these problems; 3) the evaluation of the methods used; and 4) assisting in the carrying out of the more successful approaches throughout the Bell System.

As it was obvious to the leadership of the manpower lab that their initial effort could not be used on a system-wide basis, it was necessary to work within a company that was located in an urban area that represented a microcosm of the Bell System. The district that was selected for the pilot was within Pacific Telephone and Telegraph. Besides meeting all the criteria as a typical urban district, the experimental demonstration area (EDA) received the approval and support of local, district, area, and regional management.

## Staffing and Organizational Relationships

By June of 1970 the manpower lab was ready to staff the pilot operation which was to be known as the human resource center (HRC). The HRC staff was selected from the EDA and consisted of four program designers (one each from the plant, commercial, traffic and switching departments), four designer/trainers (one from each department), two program analysts, a technical writer, three clerk typists, an employment interviewer, and a coordinator. For the most part, staffing requirements were met internally, drawing heavily from the lower levels of P.T.&T.'s line management. As the HRC was meant to change organizational behavior, the decision to hire people who were knowledgeable about the company's problems and procedures was deemed necessary to actually help facilitate change. Although none of the HRC staff had experience of the kind required, familiarity with the company was thought to be more important than expertise. Besides, the HRC would have an abundance

Prepared by G. James Francis, Colorado State University.

of highly qualified consultants available from the manpower lab to provide training and assistance whenever needed.

The organizational relationship of the HRC and P.T.&T. was made formal by having the HRC coordinator report to the general personnel manager of the area. In addition P.T.&T. organized an advisory committee to make a monthly review of the activities of the HRC. This three-man group was comprised of the assistant vice-president, the general personnel manager, and a senior person to be selected from the manpower lab. An interdepartmental coordinating committee consisting of division and district managers of the four operating departments and the industrial relations manager further guaranteed the compatibility of the HRC efforts and Company goals.

## Purpose of the HRC

The major concern of the HRC was the identification and treatment of manpower problems. Changes that occur within the work environment that have an impact upon the interface between human needs and organizational needs received special attention. Although the manpower lab originally defined the problem as the "need to more effectively utilize human resources," the HRC chose to view the problem to be dealt with as a combination of tardiness, absenteeism, and turnover. Since the HRC staff was drawn from the lower levels of P.T.&T. management, they tended to be influenced by the needs of line management. Consequently, the HRC's definition of the problem was closely aligned with the views of P.T.&T.

Stemming from the HRC problem definition was the assumption that job satisfaction is closely related (inversely) to absenteeism, tardiness, labor turnover, and work performance. Thus, the HRC experiment would attack the problem as defined by concentrating its efforts on improving the quality of work life for entry level employees. It was hoped that any success that was experienced in this pilot project would be carried over to all levels of employees throughout the Bell System.

## Programs

The programs designed to accomplish HRC objectives were divided into 1) information projects and 2) action projects.

### Information Projects

The information projects were designed to generate data for the action projects while providing training for the HRC staff. By causing the staff to think more creatively about the functioning of P.T.&T. while they were working on the information projects, they would be better prepared to assure the successful operation of the action projects. In addition, the various analyses would be used to identify organizational problems.

The first information project to be used in the summer of 1970 was the functional analysis. Important to this project was the analysis of how P.T.&T. business was handled. Attention was focused upon the functions that comprise each operation. Complementing the functional analysis was the job task analysis. This involved a detailed breakdown of six different entry level jobs (frequency of task, length of time to perform each task, etc.).

A job training content analysis was conducted as a supplement to job task analysis. Its major purpose was to determine the processes involved in learning the tasks comprising a job and how the worker was prepared for his job.

### Action Projects

There were four action projects that were designed to attack some of the more pressing manpower problems within P.T.&T. The attendance award program (AAP) was an attempt to reward those who had good attendance records. Positive reinforcement was provided in the form of a half day off or a half day's pay for every every twenty-five consecutive work days of perfect attendance. It was recognized that patterns of absenteeism would probably go unchanged, but it was hoped that the overall absenteeism rate would be minimized.

Another action project was the employee supportive services program (ESSP) which was to complement the attendance award program. The ESSP was essentially a counseling program that was to give vocational guidance, employee orientation, interpretation of work rules, and referrals to company and community resources when they were needed. During the brief six-month duration of the ESSP (January, 1971 through June, 1971) the counseling services were used very little by the employees and, consequently, there were few positive results.

An employee job information program (EJIP) was to have been set up but never really got off the ground. As an internal job mobility program, the EJIP was intended to be used for making transfers easier for entry level employees and to keep them informed of openings within the company.

In an attempt to use a more objective appraisal system the nonmanagement appraisal program (NMAP) was installed as a pilot project. Although the NMAP was tried within only one department, it appears to have a great deal of potential and could be one of the most successful of the four action projects. Task performance measures were used and assignment of points based upon performance was reviewed by the appraisor, appraisee, and a peer of the appraisee known as an advocate. Videotape was also used in the review session and was available for viewing to all three people involved in the review session.

## The Relationship of Consultants and Line Managers

Because of the background of the HRC staff and to insure the success of the HRC, it was necessary to use consultants to assist in the activities of the program. Among the consultants to the HRC were those from the manpower lab and those coming from consulting firms external to A.T.&T. There was seemingly no coordination of effort by the consultants as each tried to become "involved" in the work environment in his own way. The most usual approach used by the consultants was to ask someone "What is your job? May I help you with the program?" However, even this somewhat disjointed attempt at assisting line management soon gave way to a still more "passive role."

This passivity, as viewed by line managers, was perhaps due more to a misunderstanding of what the consultants were actually intended to do. It was the opinion of line management that the consultants were to assist in structuring the HRC and become actively involved in the process of solving manpower problems by applying their technical expertise to problem areas. Line managers thus viewed themselves as resource personnel who would be available to give the consultants information concerning the company, personnel, jobs, etc.

The team of consultants, on the other hand, believed their job to be one of training the line management and the HRC staff. As such, the consultants attempted to treat the HRC as a vehicle to train P.T.&T. personnel as diagnosticians and organizational behavioralists. Once the HRC staff was trained in the necessary techniques, the consultants could withdraw and allow the HRC to function on its own. Although the time span for learning some fairly sophisticated approaches to solving manpower problems was short, the consultants insisted on putting the HRC staff on their own from the very beginning. Learning by doing was the key to the consultants' ideas of carrying out the HRC.

The following quotes by P.T.&T. line managers serve to accentuate the differences that existed (both real and imagined) between line management and consultants:

They (consultants) would tell you where to look in the library for information or something useless like that. But there were many cases when you had to get something done fast. You couldn't afford to research the entire topic. . . . They'd want you to research it thoroughly and then generate your own ideas.

I didn't like the way the whole consultant thing was set up. It seemed to me their responsibilities were sufficiently diffused that they could, in fact, talk very glibly in generalities and never really be of any concrete help when it came to operational things.

You had one person this week and somebody else next week . . . I was sick to death of telling consultants—I don't know where they all came from—sick to death of telling them what I was doing all the time and having them say "that's very interesting" and then wander off, never to be seen again.

A summation of the consultants' views can best be presented by a statement made by one of the consultants:

I suppose that if I can be metaphoric—the people (the line management and HRC staff) didn't seem to have . . . that fetal momentum. I mean that the fetus may look like it's unstructured, but it really knows what's happening to it. . . .

From an external point of view, maybe I would have looked just as unstructured as they looked, but there's some underlying cohesiveness that existed in me that didn't exist in them. Or at least it appears like that.

Despite the foresightedness of A.T.&T. and an expensive and time consuming effort expanded by the manpower lab and P.T.&T., the HRC lasted only about one year. Although there were many beneficial results stemming from the HRC, the "payoff" did not appear to be of enough immediacy or quality to warrant further experimentation.

# CASE 42
# A Time for Change

The maintenance sector of a United States Air Force wing has the responsibility for keeping the wing's aircraft in a state of operational readiness. Maintenance is an autonomous organizational unit under the direction of the Deputy Commander of Maintenance. The appropriate specialists were dispatched from the central maintenance shop at Harley Air Force Base whenever it was determined that maintenance was required on a squadron's aircraft. Upon completion of the job, the men returned to the shop.

Flying squadrons at Harley sometimes were required to deploy their aircraft to overseas bases. In these instances, certain key maintenance specialists and crew chiefs were temporarily assigned to the squadron. These men accompanied the squadron on its mission and were responsible for providing normal service to the aircraft. Typically, then, Maintenance had to bring together various specialists and decide who would accompany a squadron each time an overseas deployment occurred. The procedure was time consuming and often created friction among the various specialists in the maintenance department. In some cases the specialists would vie with one another for "plush" assignments or try to use their seniority to stay away from certain squadrons.

## An Informal Reorganization

Both the flying crews and maintenance specialists were aware of the personnel problems that often accompanied overseas deployments. The subject was the major topic of conversation in the squadrons and maintenance shop as well. Finally, a decision was made jointly by the squadron commanders and ranking officers in the maintenance shop to request that a change be made in assignment procedures. A meeting was scheduled with the deputy commander of maintenance to discuss their ideas.

At the meeting, Major Henry Owens, a squadron commander, presented the group's thoughts on the assignment of maintenance specialists:

The aircraft at Harley are permanently assigned to each squadron. Therefore, it seems logical that a complete team of maintenance specialists and crew chiefs also be assigned or attached to each squadron. A squadron could automatically take along its own maintenance personnel if it was deployed. While the aircraft are at Harley, this same maintenance unit can be responsible for repairs and servicing.

The deputy commander was in agreement with the position taken by the

Prepared by Donald D. White, University of Arkansas; H. William Vroman, Towson State University; and Wayne T. Meeks, University of Georgia.

officers. He liked the idea of the reorganization but believed that a formal reorganization would be rejected further up the chain of command. He suggested, instead, that an informal reorganization similar to the proposed take place. The officers agreed. In addition, they decided that the effects of the experimental change should be evaluated approximately six months after the new assignments were made.

Within thirty days of the meeting, most maintenance personnel at Harley were assigned to individual aircraft on this informal basis. The new reorganization worked smoothly. Besides simplifying the assignment of personnel, the relationship between maintenance specialists and the air crews themselves improved. There was pride and competition between the maintenance sections of each squadron and records were kept to see which squadron had the least number of late take-offs or cancelled missions because of maintenance problems. Aircraft commanders reported that their equipment was cleaner and in better shape than before the reorganization. In addition, mission effectiveness ratings improved and complaints pertaining to deployments practically were eliminated.

## A Personnel Shortage

However, before a formal assessment of the change could take place, problems began to plague the squadrons. A demand for qualified maintenance personnel to fill overseas assignments began to take its toll at Harley AFB. The ranks of the maintenance group were depleted as an increasing number of men were sent to other bases to fill vacancies. The personnel losses at Harley were not unexpected. However, replacements were not immediately available. As a result of these personnel shortages, squadrons found themselves having to "borrow" specialists from each other. Conflicts began to arise as to who would be sent, when they would be released, and how soon they must be returned to their informally assigned "home" squadrons. In addition, many of the specialists felt that they were being overworked and that they did not have adequate time to maintain their own squadron's aircraft.

Requests by Maintenance were put in for additional personnel. However, it soon became obvious that replacements could not be expected in the near future. After some discussion of the problem in the maintenance group, the decision was made to return all maintenance personnel to a central dispatching area. Thus, maintenance specialists were placed back under the direct control of the maintenance group. The informal reorganization was terminated, and once again the group resembled its original formal structure.

## The Late Take-Off

Captain Phil Rogers arrived at the base and immediately drove to Base Operations. There, he began preparing the flight plan for his day's mission. Captain Rogers was scheduled to fly an aero-medical evacuation flight with three severely burned patients to Brooks Medical Center in Texas. He considered his medi-vac duties to be an important responsibility and took his job quite seriously. Suddenly, he heard his name being paged over the loudspeaker system.

He picked up the phone and recognized the voice of Glenn Kennedy, his flight engineer.

*Msgt. Kennedy:* Captain Rogers, I don't think we will be able to get off when we are supposed to.

*Capt. Rogers:* What's the problem? Is the aircraft out of commission?

*Msgt. Kennedy:* I don't know yet, sir. The crewchief was supposed to be here two hours before me to open the aircraft and perform his "Dash-Six Inspection." He hasn't made it in yet, and I can't perform on my own preflight inspection until he gets here and does his job. I did get the aircraft opened and there are several write-ups that haven't been taken care of. The aircraft isn't very clean either.

*Capt. Rogers:* Have you called Maintenance for assistance?

*Msgt. Kennedy:* Yes, Sir, but they haven't been able to do much so far.

*Capt. Rogers:* O.K. Go back to the aircraft and wait there. I'll try to get some help.

*(Phil Rogers placed a call to Maintenance Control).*

*Capt. Rogers:* Sergeant Vinson, this is Captain Rogers. Are you aware   he fact that I have a critical mission, and the aircraft hasn't shown up ye

*Tsgt. Vinson:* Yes, Sir, we are trying to find Sergeant Andrews now. B.it he either isn't home or isn't answering his phone.

*Capt. Rogers:* Is this the Sergeant Andrews who was the crewchief on Aircraft 7885 in the 40th Squadron?

*Tsgt. Vinson:* Yes, Sir, it is.

*Capt. Rogers:* That's strange. He was my crewchief for six weeks in South America and was one of the best I've ever seen. He took pride in the cleanliness of his airplane and always bragged that he'd never had a late take-off or mission aborted because of maintenance.

*Tsgt. Vinson:* I know, Sir. I've heard some good reports on him, but frankly, his performance here lately has been less than desirable. We've had complaints about the condition of his aircraft several times. He had two late take-offs last week. Once he was late with his preflight, and the other time a write-up wasn't corrected when it should have been. He doesn't seem to care anymore.

*Capt. Rogers:* Andrews isn't alone in this matter. I've noticed that we've been having a helluva problem with morale, supposed sickness, quality of work, and so on around the flight line.

*Tsgt. Vinson:* I know what you mean, Captain. It seems that a lot of these guys just don't give a damn anymore. Frankly, I'm afraid that we might be losing some good men. I've heard Sergeant Andrews and Sergeant Janson talking about getting an early out. Both of those guys are top-notch; it just doesn't figure.

*Capt. Rogers:* No, and it doesn't do much for encouraging re-ups among the troops either. Well, I can't worry about that, now. I've got to have a crewchief out there soon. We have to get off as soon as possible. Try to find one from another aircraft.

*Tsgt. Vinson:* Yes, Sir. We'll try our best, but it's getting more and more difficult to find these guys and get them to preflight someone else's aircraft.

## Deployment

Later that week Captain Rogers was in the hangar checking out his aircraft. The 38th had received orders for deployment to Germany. Captain Rogers had been attempting to determine what, if any, maintenance would be needed to make the long trip. As he was preparing to leave, he was approached by Sergeant John Ryan, a hydraulic specialist who was at one time attached to the 38th squadron of maintenance.

*Capt. Rogers:* Hello Sergeant Ryan, I haven't seen you since you came down to Lima that time to fix the hydraulic leak in that #3 engine. How has life been treating you?

*Sgt. Ryan:* Well, not too bad, Sir, but it could be better. That's what I want to talk to you about. I know you're getting ready for a rotation, and I wondered if you could possibly help get a couple of changes made?

*Capt Rogers:* Well, I don't know. I'll do what I can, but you know that now we don't really have any say-so or control over who goes on rotation with us from Maintenance.

*Sgt. Ryan:* Yes sir, I realize that. But I thought maybe you might talk to them or get your commander to talk to them. They don't seem to hear us, or else they just don't care.

*Capt. Rogers:* What seems to be the problem?

*Sgt Ryan:* Well, we have two hydraulic specialists now—myself and Sergeant Joyce. You guys are my old squadron and the 36th is Sergeants Joyce's old squadron. The 36th is going to Germany in three months to replace you, I suppose. I had counted on going with you guys since I know most of you and also the aircraft. But now they say I can't go, and Joyce is going. Then I'll have to go with the 36th. I don't know any of those guys and Joyce doesn't know any of your guys, but they said that didn't matter. Somebody set it up, and the commander's office said that it would be too much trouble to change it. We talked to our supervisor, but he said to forget it. Joyce and I have to spend two or three months overseas away from our families, and it makes the tour a lot easier to take if you know the people you're with. On top of everything, Sergeant Joyce is having some family problems and really needs to be here to try to straighten them out. We even went in together and explained this. I volunteered to go in his place. They still wouldn't change us. There is no logical reason I can see why it would matter to them which one of us went. You would think they would try to keep us happy with our work since there are only two of us when we're supposed to have four hydraulic specialists.

*Capt. Rogers:* Sergeant, I wish I could give you more encouragement, but you know how these things are handled now. I'll talk to the colonel and explain your problems to him since he has a little more pull than I do. I'll tell him you're a good hydraulics man. He probably remembers how you rescued me in Lima without any spare parts. Maybe he'll call your commander and make a personal request for you to be sent with us. As I said, officially, we have to take whoever Maintenance gives us, but I'll see what we can do.

*Sgt Ryan:* I really appreciate it, Sir. Boy, things have really changed! When I was in the 38th, at least I could count on someone listening to my problems and trying to help out. No one seems to care anymore.

# CASE 43
# A Seminar in "Understanding"

Farmington Stores, Incorporated was a large retail chain with central and branch department stores throughout the northern United States and Canada. The company's organization chart showed at least six separate levels within the organization not including staff departments responsible to managers throughout the Farmington system. In recent months many of the stores in the system had experienced minority-hiring pressure from state and federal agencies. In an effort to comply with the request of the agencies, an active program of minority recruitment and hiring was initiated throughout the system. Subsequently, employees from all parts of the enterprise began to experience tensions accompanying the rapid change within the organization.

## Talking Out the Problems

Managers from throughout the company forwarded to the personnel office complaints and examples of the problems they were encountering in the new hiring policies. Subsequently, the vice-president of personnel recommended to the president of the company that a series of seminars be designed to promote greater understanding between older employees of the organization and those newer minority hirees. He based his recommendations on excessive turnover rates, absenteeisms, and grievances that had been reported in those parts of the company where managers had most often complained about the new hiring policies. In addition, he reported that a substantial number of the grievances that had been filed recently dealt with alleged social and ethnic discrimination. Recognizing the potential seriousness of the problem, the president endorsed the recommendation, and the stage was set for a series of seminars to "promote greater understanding between employees at Farmington Stores."

The first of these seminars was held at a university campus just outside of Cleveland, Ohio. The participants were selected from a number of different stores in the region as well as the Farmington home office. They represented all levels of the organization and some of the staff departments. The group had been structured intentionally so that there was a balance of organizational participants from various levels; however, the proportion of minority group members attending the seminar was notably larger than the proportion of minority employees actually employed by the company. In addition, the group leaders themselves also were minority group members. These conditions were instituted in order to make it easier for the rest of the group to understand the frames of reference of the minority groups who were represented. The program had been planned by the vice-president and two members of his staff. The

Prepared by Donald D. White, University of Arkansas.

group concluded that improving race relations throughout the organization could be achieved through a loosely directed group interaction approach. Group leaders would provide the stimulus while individual group members reacted to the inputs. It was hoped that the results of this interaction process would benefit all participants through their exposure to differing points of view. The planners also believed that the interactions would have a cathartic effect on those participating by allowing them to express both their overt and covert feelings of prejudice.

## The First Day

On the first day of the seminar, the group leader immediately experienced difficulty. He found that it was difficult to break through a veil of skepticism which seemed to exist in the group and to elicit honest responses to the situations he presented. Consequently, he found it difficult to judge what sentiments were present in the group and how to deal with them. It was impossible to form new sentiments with regard to specific problems when group members were reluctant to identify with the problems themselves. This unwillingness to respond was compounded further by the presence in the room of persons who had at one time worked together as supervisor and subordinate. Seminar planners had thought that bringing together individuals from different levels of the organization hierarchy would increase the number of perspectives brought to the meetings. However, lower-level personnel generally were inhibited by the presence of the higher-ranking, corporate managers.

The group leader attempted to generate participation by discussing a variety of topics. For example, he made remarks about interracial marriage, minority living conditions, educational disparities, and welfare. By the end of the day, it was easy to see that participants had fallen into one of three subgroups. Later, the seminar faculty and coordinator identified two of the groups as having either conservative or liberal views on the topics discussed. The third group was made up of the minority representatives themselves. The conservatives tended to be suspicious of many of the topics that were brought forth. The liberals, on the other hand, promoted such ideas as guaranteed income, welfare improvement, and improved education and housing for minorities. This group also tended to be problem oriented. Members of the minority groups represented were in the limelight and were the subject of much of the discussion and verbal jousting. In general, they supported the aims and methods of the liberals and spoke up accordingly.

Comments tended to be made by a few persons who dominated the group. Generally those involved in the discussions were either middle or upper level managers or employees who held no management position at all. Among the latter, it was not unusual to leave the topics at hand and instead discuss issues that were only remotely related. Although topics were specified by the group leaders, discussions often seemed to carry the members far from the initial subject.

Early in the day, it became difficult for the group leader to "work the group" due to the dominance of one of the group members. The member, a divisional vice-president, had been placed at one end of the conference table. Initially, he monopolized the group discussion on the basis of his position in the organization. The executive's attempt to act as an informal group leader seemed to be resented by most of the participants. The group leaders had been told that all top level personnel had been informed of the way in which the meeting was to be conducted. He had been assured that the type of difficulty he was encountering with the executive would not occur.

Just before the group adjourned for lunch, the group leader instructed the participants to remove their name tags from the table. He explained then that the original seating arrangements were merely a matter of administrative convenience, and that they would be free to sit wherever they would like when they returned to the seminar room. He asked them to "simply replace the name tag on the table in front of where you sit down." (Originally, the name tags arbitrarily were set around the table without regard to the participants' titles or the stores or department which they represented.)

During the noon break, the group leader pondered how he might minimize the contribution of the vice-president and encourage others to speak out more freely. However, he noticed early during the afternoon session that the executive's comments were significantly fewer in number and shorter in length than they had been that morning. In addition, following a break later in the afternoon, the vice-president voluntarily took a seat along the side of the table and said little for the remainder of the day.

## Little Change

Events of the second day tended to parallel those of the first, although a few more of the participants spoke out on the issues. The sentiments expressed by various individuals reflected their values and beliefs and roughly were the same ones that they held upon entering the seminar. Even so, the sentiments expressed generally were within the limits anticipated by the seminar planners. Changes in sentiments that did occur resulted from the interactions within the group as participants used their personal frames of reference to evaluate what was being said. Although sentiments expressed during the second day of the seminar were not always positive, they did serve to enlighten other group members.

By the end of the second day, small groups had formed around the table. (Exhibit 1 illustrates seating arrangement at the end of the second day's session along with the pattern of interaction which took place.) The "free choice" seating arrangement had seemed to foster the emergence of spokesmen for each group rather than encouraging all persons in the meeting to speak out. Moreover, it was not unusual for persons who did speak out to conclude their comments by directly addressing those persons sitting immediately around them.

**Exhibit 1. Seating arrangement on second day.**

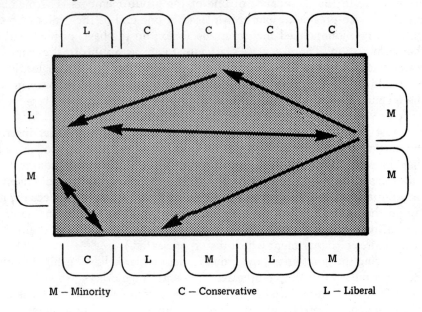

**Exhibit 2. Seating arrangement on third day.**

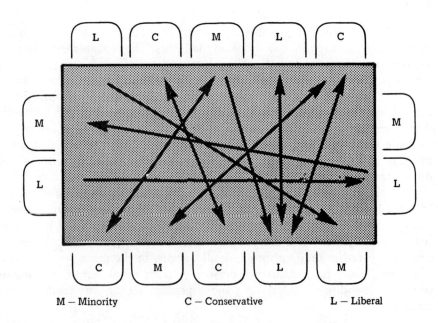

## Reassessment and Change

Upon completion of the second day's session, the group leader met with the program coordinator and university consultants who had been contacted by the coordinator. He explained that the discussions during the second day seemed to be more numerous and more fruitful than those of the first. However, he also expressed concern that any shifts in position were few and not very significant. If anything, he thought that some participants might be becoming more ingrained in their beliefs rather than more open to new ideas. He reported that inevitably those who spoke out concluded their comments by turning and addressing the persons with whom they were sitting or with whom they shared some belief.

The problems were discussed at length. It was agreed that the "common interest groups" had to be broken down if a freer flow of ideas was going to take place on the last day of the seminar.

The next day, the participants entered the room and found their name tags once again moved to different seats around the table. (The new seating arrangement and the interaction which took place between participants during the third day of the seminar is shown in Exhibit 2.)

That evening the group leader reported to the program coordinator that the participants seemed to have become much more involved in the day's discussions than during either of the two other sessions. In addition, he added that a number of the participants had thanked him for his leadership when the final session ended and that he was relatively pleased with their progress He concluded his remarks by saying, "I'm not saying that any ardent bigot left today as a bleeding-heart liberal, but a lot of people may be a little more open to what 'the other guy' has to say in the future. I just wish we had one more day."

# CASE 44
# From Disequilibrium to Disequilibrium

At the close of the Jackson Regional Medical Center's (JRMC) monthly board meeting, Mr. Bibbins, the hospital administrator, brought out what he felt was the most important issue on the meeting's agenda:

> Gentlemen, and of course you, too, Ms. Dixon, recently I have given a great deal of thought to our upcoming facility expansion. As you know, this move into our new facility is going to take a tremendous amount of coordination and cooperation on the part of our entire organization. The staff has mentioned to me on several occasions that the employees and supervisors are becoming increasingly restless and apprehensive as a result of the anticipated move. After some preliminary investigation and considerable thought, we have decided to recommend to the board that JRMC contact a consultant to assist us in adapting to this ongoing expansion program.

The board was aware of the hospital's past instability and the need for outside management assistance was acknowledged. After a brief discussion, the members unanimously recommended to Mr. Bibbins that he contact the local university for assistance. Members of the university management department had previously provided consulting assistance.

## History of JRMC

JRMC was a 160-bed general hospital in northeastern Arkansas. The American Hospital Association classified JRMC as a short-term ambulatory hospital. In 1975 the hospital officially became a regional facility and adopted the name of Jackson Regional Medical Center. The community in which JRMC operated was expanding, primarily due to the influx of retired individuals and a growing university community. Due to this expansion in the immediate area, demand for medical services had increased significantly. A major physical facility expansion program had been adopted in 1972, and a projected completion date of June 1977 was set. Construction began and has been progressing on schedule. The project is scheduled for completion in eighteen months.

JRMC presently employs approximately 500 persons. This employment figure was planned to be increased by approximately 22 percent when the expansion program was completed. The expanded facility will have 240 beds. The structure of JRMC management also has changed. Prior to the initiation of the physical expansion program, there was only one assistant administrator. When the program is completed, there are to be three assistant administra-

Prepared by Daniel S. Cochran, Mississippi State University; Donald R. Latham, University of Mississippi; and Donald D. White, University of Arkansas.

tors. All functional departments anticipate expanding employment rosters, with the need for additional nurses particularly critical.

JRMC has had four administrators in the past eight years. The present administrator, Mr. Bibbins, has been with JRMC for less than one year. The previous three administrators were asked to resign for various reasons. Mr. Bibbins seemed to have established his credibility with department heads and general employees. However, an aura of uncertainty continued to surround the administrator's position. This uncertainty has been a contributing factor to one present departmental dilemma—that of departmental autonomy. Various departments throughout JRMC tended to segregate themselves into autonomous groups rather than to work closely with one another. Many persons familiar with internal conditions at JRMC believed that permanent leadership emanated from department heads, rather than from the Administrator's Office.

## Consultants' Meeting with JRMC

Two weeks after the monthly board meeting Dr. Harold and Dr. Black, from the university's management department, met with Mr. Bibbins, his assistant administrator, Mr. James, and the director of personnel and training, Mr. Arnold. The men discussed their organization's problem of trying to adapt to the facility change. Mr. Bibbins and his staff quickly briefed the two management professors on their facility's expansion situation and stressed the "disequilibrium" which existed within the hosptal as a result of this organizational change.

Dr. Harold and Dr. Black, I feel I must warn you before we go any further that our employees, including our supervisors, are extremely suspicious when it comes to 'outsiders'! They are even suspicious of anyone outside of their particular department, and especially the administration. In fact, I'm confident that by this afternoon, rumor will have it that 'the administration' has just hired two New York psychologists to analyze our organization.

After additional discussion, Dr. Black concluded the meeting by suggesting that after the consultants' intervention, the administrator provide some feedback to the hospital employees about the nature, purpose, and worth of the consultants' assistance. Mr. Bibbins and his staff agreed to this suggestion.

## Intervention Strategy

As a result of the first meeting, it was concluded that obtaining inputs from employees in the form of either ideas or suggestions might clarify those real and imagined problems that the employees believed were related to a major building program. This was thought to have the advantages of enumerating real problems and of obtaining an awareness of the perceived problems at various employee levels. It was hoped that a free flow of uninhibited responses could be generated.

Group meetings rather than the questioning of individuals through opinion surveys was decided upon as the information-gathering approach to be used. It was agreed that "group think" would probably yield better results than isolated individual reactions to printed questions and would save time. Harold and Black informed Bibbins that they were involved in the study of a number of such group decision-making processes. They were convinced that any of the group processes they had been working with would be beneficial to the medical center. However, they saw in the hospital's present situation an opportunity to study the performance of three specific group techniques in a field setting. Consequently, they requested permission to conduct a series of group meetings using these three information-gathering processes.

Harold explained to Mr. Bibbins, "We are agreed that the group approach to gathering this information will no doubt be superior to obtaining employee inputs on an individual basis. I think that Dr. Black and I can safely say that the information we will gather from your employees will be beneficial to JRMC no matter what group technique we use. However, this will afford us an excellent opportunity to determine for future use which technique might be best in this type of setting." After a brief discussion between Bibbins and Harold, the administrator gave his consent to the joint consulting-research effort.

The three group decision-making processes used in the project were nominal group technique (NGT), brainstorming, and interacting group. The employee groups were administered all three technologies, while the supervisors were administered the NGT and brainstorming technologies. Each technique utilized the same beginning question: "What significant personal and/or organizational factors (or changes) must be taken into account in connection with a hospital expansion program?" It was felt this question would generate relevant ideas that would help the hospital better adapt to changes resulting from its present expansion program. The actual ideas generated from these techniques are included in the Appendix.

## Methodology

A separate systematic random sample was drawn from a computer printout of pay records for daytime employees and supervisors. Five groups (three employees and two supervisors) of six individuals each made up the sample; however, additional individuals were selected as alternates. The names selected were examined by departments to ensure that the sample was representative.

A brief orientation meeting for the participants was conducted a week prior to the actual experiment. The purpose of this introductory meeting was to help ensure that employees could participate at the scheduled time and to generate favorable interest in the project.

To minimize interviewer bias one consultant conducted both NGT sessions, and one consultant conducted both brainstorming sessions and the interacting group session. Each group meeting was conducted at approximately the same time of day in the same surroundings (JRMC library).

Anonymity was a prime concern, and each group interviewed was told the importance of keeping the session private until all groups had met.

## Final Report and Follow-up

After all of the group meetings were held, the results were analyzed by the consultants and submitted to Mr. Bibbins. The report was accompanied by a request that a subsequent meeting be held between the three men to discuss its content after the findings were reviewed by him. However, unexpected problems with the building program occurred during the same week in which the report was transmitted. Mr. Bibbins became involved in extensive negotiations with the contractor and failed to get back to Harold and Black. Six months later Mr. Bibbins still had not acted on the consultants' report.

### Appendix A. Group 1 (NGT) supervisor.

1. Need more personnel.
2. Priorities on purchasing equipment.
3. Priorities on equipment requirements prior to even planning.
4. Adequate expansion for meeting public needs.
5. Communication coordination among department.
6. Creation of new status among present personnel.
7. How to perform effectively while in the midst of moving.
8. Communication with employees to make them feel they are a part of the program (expansion).
9. Inadequate preplanning—resulting in inadequate facilities.
10. Versatile and open-minded staff.
11. Satisfying personnel remaining in old building.
12. Different functions as a result of moving.
13. New facilities may not be adequate.
14. Coping with financial increases—all internal cost increases.
15. Only one walkway between old and new building.
16. Concern with physical movement of patients to new facility.
17. Uncertainty of move for some departments.
18. Insufficient number of elevators for quantity of supplies, visitors, patients.
19. Salary increases.
20. Scattered centers of attention due to layout.
21. Mental adjustment of from small to large operation.
22. Through improvement of serious nursing services, the quality of care given will be improved.
23. Dealing with hostilities in departments that have been overlooked during expansion.

### Appendix B. Group 2 (brainstorming) supervisor.

1. Well planned (exceptionally).
2. Temporary confusion.
3. Leadership changes.
4. Decision-making process (changes).
5. Lacking continuity of concepts.
6. Communications.

7. Employee Understanding.
8. How will it be financed.
9. Priorities of financing.
10. Priorities in planning total project.
11. Changes in staff.
12. Informal power structure changes.
13. Coping with the change (people).
14. Quality control changes.
15. Lines (levels) of communications will change.
16. Responsibility will change (institution).
17. Internal responsibilities will change.
18. Employee auto.
19. Need to be more competitive (patients, personnel, services, and wages).
20. Change of community image.
21. Expectations of hospital by community will change.
22. Depersonalization among employees and community.
23. Maple trees cut down!
24. Parking.
25. Security of facility (internal and external).
26. Promoting urbanization!
27. Outpatient facilities.
28. Longer hours for employees.
29. Escort services.
30. No salary increases as result of expansion (money drained away).
31. Physical layout problems (directional).
32. Competition for expansional space (internal—departmental).
33. Handling of disappointment due to poor planning (i.e., not getting what wanted or needed).
34. Work flow problems.
35. Recruitment of personnel.
36. Training and retraining (in-service education).
37. Regulatory standards change.
38. Safety problems.
39. Public orientations of availability of services.
40. Better facilities for specific diseases.
41. Public reactions to health care changes (cost!)
42. Present inconvenience.
43. Need tolerance until more complete.
44. Present fatigue of staff (mental and physical).
45. Disbelief of eventuality of results.
46. Insecurity about jobs, personal space, job description, and loss of familiar surroundings (community included).
47. Increased opportunity for employment (positive).
48. Need of bad debts (patients) to decrease to help finance new building.
49. Inflation problems.
50. More job satisfaction (positive).
51. Prestige of working in a medical center (positive).
52. Disillusionment.
53. Now have a greater teaching capacity (positive).
54. Can now draw more from university due to size (in-service education, etc.).
55. Expansion is a good idea! Necessary.
56. Expansion is a continual process.
57. Lack of consultation with personnel involved prior to decision making.
58. Employee turnover.
59. Cost of high turnover.

60. Hidden cost of education (financial resources not available for needed training).
61. Hidden cost of donation.
62. Administrative continuity.
63. Need for internal socialization and recreation.
64. Lack of support from administration and medical staff.

## Appendix C. Group 1 (interacting) employee.

1. Probably bother nursing more.
2. Major problems with switchboard!
3. Dietary—only one lab.
4. Very little known about expansion program.
5. Purchasing problems (when order, kind of service, maintenance contracts
6. New personnel techniques.
7. Size of departments will increase.
8. Will have to learn more.
9. Training new personnel.
10. Recruiting new personnel.
11. Changed telephone system (but we don't know about the new system Centrex!).
12. Need training on new system (telephone).
13. Apprehensive about new telephone system.
14. Personnel, supply, and new equipment problems.
15. Parking problems.
16. Moving supplies a problem.
17. Reorder points (supply) will change.
18. New dietary facilities will be better (more room).
19. Haven't been told anything about the move!

## Appendix D. Group 2 (NGT) employee.

1. We are here for the good of the patient, and the public and all personnel should work toward that end.
2. Personnel shortages new and in the future more obvious.
3. Re-evaluate what we are doing—jobs.
4. Need for more administrative people.
5. Building safety.
6. Need for additional parking—place for employees.
7. Need for additional personnel after expansion.
8. Need for additional compensation to "live."
9. Financial responsibility to the public.
10. Need for employees to see what is going on.
11. New employees need a job description.
12. Need for more doctors.
13. Employees training—present.
14. Communication between administration and employees.
15. Need for new and better equipment for patients.
16. Need for new and better equipment for employees.
17. Need for more efficient food processing.
18. Need for food that patients would like.
19. Need for larger cafeteria.
20. Need for free parking for employees.
21. Need nursery for visitor (keep them out of lobby).

22  Mandatory insurance needs to be done away with.
23. Present care is good.
24. Priority system for employee duties.
25. Need for isolation floor (only).
26. Need for psychiatric facilities.
27. Need for separation of patients due to illness.
28. Employee safety—diseases in hospital.
29. Need more patient accessory—linen, etc.
30. Need additional day care facilities.
31. Need for better laundry.
32. Need for specialized training for employees.
33. Employees need better understanding with supervisors.
34. Need for employees to know what's being built.
35. Need for more facility to be more efficiently designed than old.
36. Need recreation facilities for patients.
37. Lounge for patients.
38. Need prayer room.
39. Present prayer room is inadequate.
40. Need new administrative system.
41. Need more work clerks.
42. Need employee pool (all departments).
43. Need additional security.

### Appendix E.  Group 3 (brainstorming) employee.

1. Orientation to new facility.
2. Parking problems.
3. Need for more space.
4. Noise!
5. More elevators.
6. Work flow (uniform) from old to new hospital.
7. Traffic flow.
8. Visitor control.
9. Security control.
10. Proper staffing for new facility.
11. Lack of equipment.
12. Dining room space!
13. Education of personnel.
14. Immediate community concern.
15. Automobile traffic control around hospital (narrow streets and congestion).
16. Financing of new facility.
17. Bigger waiting room for visitors.
18. Separate surgical waiting area (with hostess).
19. Bathrooms (more)!
20. Overnight facilities for family of seriously ill.
21. Orientation (tours!) for child patients.
22. Play room facilities for pediatric patients.
23. Separate pediatric patients by age (rooms—teenagers and children).
24. Communications between departments.
25. Telephone system (is it adequate?).
26. How will departments work while moving to new building.
27. Time allotted for moving.
28. Personal relationships during move (tempers!).
29. Are architects familiar with hospital design needs?

30. Never consulted with employees concerning expansion!
31. Concerned about emergency room facilities (enough?).
32. Separate emergency room entrance (*not* lobby).
33. Need *signs* to direct people to hosiptal.
34. Special facilities for prisoner patients.
35. Fire prevention (regulations, etc.).
36. Adequate storage facilities.
37. Need to anticipate future needs (expansion!—buy land).
38. Heating and air conditioning control (separate or master control).
39. Linens (more).
40. All supplies (more).
41. More adequate control supply.
42. Is pharmacy going to be adequate?
43. Security of drugs!
44. Servicing of facility.
45. Need oxygen and suction in new surgical holding area.
46. Lounges for employees (locker space, eat lunch, and secure personal gear, and resting area beds).
47. Attitudes of patients during move.
48. Remodeling of old hospital.
49. Concern for phasing out old jobs and entrance of new
50. Enforcing smoking regulations (positive!).
51. Control of safety regulations.
52. Fire drills (actual).
53. Need a full-time safety director.
54. Necessary emergency power.
55. Disaster drills (actual!).
56. Enforce ID regulations (especially doctors).
57. Is there an alarm system to alert security personnel?

# EXPERIENTIAL EXERCISE 18

## Team Development Exercise

The probability of accomplishing a group task is increased if individuals jointly share the responsibility of goal achievement. As a result, it may be desirable to develop a team spirit where the work team agrees upon the goals of the team and the roles which each member will play in obtaining those goals. The process of disclosure and discussion between individuals may be used to enhance the mutual understanding necessary for effective group action.

### Directions

The list of questions below is designed to stimulate group discussion around work-related topics. The following ground rules should govern this discussion:

1. Take turns asking questions, either to specific individuals or to the group as a whole.
2. You must be willing to answer any question which you ask.
3. Any member may decline to answer any question which someone else asks.
4. Work with the person who is answering to make certain that effective two-way understanding takes place.
5. All answers remain confidential within the group.

### Questions May Be Asked in Any Order.

1. How do you feel about yourself in your present position?
2. What do you see as the next step in your career development?
3. What personal characteristics do you have that get in the way of your work?
4. What are you doing best right now?
5. What are you trying to get accomplished in your work?
6. Where do you see yourself ten years from now?
7. How are you perceiving me?
8. What would you predict to be my assessment of you?
9. What was your first impression of me?
10. How many different "hats" do you wear?
11. How do you typically behave when a deadline is approaching?
12. What kind of relationship do you want with me?
13. What things do you do best?
14. What factors in your job situation impede your goal-accomplishment?
15. Whom are you having the most difficulty with right now? (What is that person doing? What is your reaction?)
16. To whom are you closest in your work situation?
17. Where would you locate yourself on a ten-point scale of commitment to the goals of this group (1 is low, 10 is high)?
18. What part are you playing in this group?

19. How do you want to receive feedback?
20. What do you think I'm up to?
21. What puzzles you about me?
22. How are you feeling right now?
23. What issue do you think we must face together?
24. What do you see going on in the group right now?
25. What personal growth efforts are you making?

# EXPERIENTIAL EXERCISE 19

## Diagnosis, Change, and Implementation

### Introduction

The object of this simulation is to illustrate the phases of diagnosis, development of a change strategy, and implementation of change in an organization setting where absenteeism and turnover is a problem. As you get involved with each of these concepts and wrestle with the critical questions, the complexities and multiple relationships will become evident.

There is no 'right' way to solve the problem. There are many ways to deal with it. Some ways will have more merit than others. Look carefully at the facts of the case and use your empathetic skills to understand some of the unwritten feelings, views and attitudes of the participants.

## Narrow Rivers

Narrows Rivers is a private continuing education center/health spa with 350 apartments, a constant population of 535 people who stay from 3 days to several months, and a staff of nearly 200 full and part-time employees. A part-time staff of 40, 2 full-time supervisors and 2 cooks, run the facility for the manager-trainees who attend. Part-timers work 4 hours daily and range in age from 18 to 60.

The employees work in three shifts during the day. Starting times for the help are 6:00 a.m., 10:00 a.m. and 4:00 p.m. One of the cooks starts at 6 a.m. and the second quits at 8:00 p.m. The supervisors are expected to oversee the entire project and fill in where necessary.

Narrow Rivers draws its part-time employees from the surrounding rural area. Seventy percent of the group are women. Most are housewives. The males are an assortment of old and young people partially supported by other jobs. The initial racial composition of the group was 70% white, 12% black, and 18% hispanic.

### The Problem

Martin Traynor, the director, has hired you to be a change agent with the organization. There are many sources of irritation at Narrow Rivers due, Traynor believes, to its recent opening just a year ago. There seems to be some understanding of the "opening" problems, but none for food service difficulties. The clients have no patience for the slip-ups in the kitchen/dining area. They harrangue, criticize, send food back, and visit the cook and director frequently. The situation has gotten so bad that the attitudes toward other services in the community are being affected. Educational efforts are hampered; maids and gardeners are being hassled. On some days 20% of the part-time help might be missing. There have been five new

Prepared by H. William Vroman.

cooks hired during the year. All who left found other employment without difficulty.

The food service has been subcontracted to TRISTAR. Narrow Rivers had agreed to a two-year contract with a clause for review after one year. Martin presently is in the process of reviewing that subcontract in light of the difficulties. His attitude is that there is obviously some problem and the TRISTAR has been as diligent as he has been in trying to find a solution. Wages and benefits seem to be in line with the surrounding wage rates, and the people hired seem not to be "the" problem. Troubles are now intensifying as Narrow Rivers and TRISTAR have to go further away to acquire their labor force. Over the year, the racial composition of the employees has changed from that stated earlier to 50% white, 30% black, and 20% hispanic.

## Assignment

1. Prior to coming to class, your job is to establish an orderly approach for dealing with the problem. Separate your analysis into three sections· diagnosis, change strategy, and implementation. Detail your analysis and provide the rationale for your choice. Use the intervention of Process Analysis to start with. Develop a notebook just as though you were actually a change agent at Narrow Rivers. In developing the notebook entries, use your imagination about incidents you confronted and how you responded to them.
2. Form groups of three to five students in class and take turns presenting your analysis. This is done without critical comment. Clarifying questions are appropriate. (30 minutes)[1]
3. Develop a common view of the intervention, change strategy and implementation within your group. Analyze the pros and cons of each plan, determining feasibility, and potential resistance. (40 minutes)
4. Prepare a two-part role play. First, assign one member of your group to be Martin Traynor. The remaining two will be on the consultant team. Prepare in reasonable detail, a dialogue between the characters. Martin Traynor *is* dubious about the process and your findings. The remaining member(s) of your group should observe the proceedings and be prepared to discuss the consultants' activities and techniques when the role play is completed.

[1] Times can be reallotted depending on the length of your class.

# Index

# S

Scientific method, 4
Sensitivity training (encounter groups), 391
SOBA model, 8, 11, 14, 21, 26
Sociotechnical systems, 11, 14
Staff authority, 124
Stress
    dynamics of, 317
    in organizations, 317
    managing, 319
    organizational, 312, 321
Subsystems, 10
Suprasystems, 10
Survey feedback, 389
System diagnosis, 386
Systems, sociotechnical, 11, 14
Systems theory, 9

# T

Task groups, 278
Team building, 390
Thorndike's law of effect, 69
Training techniques, 351
Transactional analysis (TA) 7, 14, 387, 391

# W

Women and career development, 355
Work, meaning of, 27
Work, the motivation to, 90